Gang Transitions and Transformations in an International Context

Cheryl L. Maxson • Finn-Aage Esbensen
Editors

Gang Transitions and Transformations in an International Context

Springer

Editors
Cheryl L. Maxson
Department of Criminology, Law and Society
University of California
Irvine, CA, USA

Finn-Aage Esbensen
Department of Criminology and Criminal Justice
University of Missouri-St. Louis
St. Louis, MO, USA

ISBN 978-3-319-29600-5 ISBN 978-3-319-29602-9 (eBook)
DOI 10.1007/978-3-319-29602-9

Library of Congress Control Number: 2016940989

Printed on acid-free paper

This Springer imprint is published by Springer Nature
The registered company is Springer International Publishing AG Switzerland

We dedicate this volume to all of our
colleagues who have contributed
to the Eurogang Program to enhance
our understanding of youth gangs
and of the policies and programs
that might reduce the negative consequences
of these troublesome youth groups
for our communities and families
and other gang members.

Contents

Contributors

Meagan Cahill Rand Corporation, Santa Monica, CA, USA

Dena C. Carson School of Public and Environmental Affairs, Indiana University Purdue University Indianapolis, Indianapolis, IN, USA

Scott H. Decker School of Criminology and Criminal Justice, Arizona State University, Tempe, AZ, USA

James A. Densley School of Law Enforcement and Criminal Justice, Metropolitan State University, St. Paul, MN, USA

Marijke Drogt Department of Applied Psychology, Hogeschool Leiden, University of Applied Sciences, Leiden, The Netherlands

Jillian L. Eidson Department of Criminal Justice, Temple University, Philadelphia, PA, USA

Finn-Aage Esbensen Department of Criminology and Criminal Justice, University of Missouri-St. Louis, St. Louis, MO, USA

Torbjörn Forkby Department of Social Work, University of Gothenburg, Gothenburg, Sweden

Kristina Thompson Garrity Department of Criminology and Criminal Justice, University of Missouri-St. Louis, St. Louis, MO, USA

Frank van Gemert Department of Criminal Law and Criminology, VU University Amsterdam, Amsterdam, The Netherlands

Wim Hardyns Department of Criminology, Criminal Law and Social Law, Institute for International Research on Criminal Policy (IRCP), Ghent University, Ghent, Belgium

Elke Van Hellemont Leuven Institute of Criminology (Linc), KU Leuven (University of Leuven), Leuven, Belgium

Beth M. Huebner Department of Criminology and Criminal Justice, University of Missouri-St. Louis, St. Louis, MO, USA

Stanley J. Huey Jr. Department of Psychology, University of Southern California, Los Angeles, CA, USA

David Squier Jones School of Criminology and Criminal Justice, Northeastern University, Boston, MA, USA

Jan Dirk de Jong Faculty of Social Work and Applied Psychology, University of Applied Sciences Leiden, Leiden, The Netherlands

Gabrielle Lewine Department of Psychology, University of Southern California, Los Angeles, CA, USA

Cheryl L. Maxson Department of Criminology, Law and Society, University of California, Irvine, CA, USA

Chris Melde School of Criminal Justice, Michigan State University, East Lansing, MI, USA

Lieven J.R. Pauwels Department of Criminology, Criminal Law and Social Law, Institute for International Research on Criminal Policy (IRCP), Ghent University, Ghent, Belgium

David C. Pyrooz Department of Sociology, University of Colorado—Boulder, Boulder, CO, USA

Shannon E. Reid Department of Criminal Justice and Criminology, University of North Carolina at Charlotte, Charlotte, NC, USA

Robby Roks Department of Criminology, School of Law, Erasmus University Rotterdam, Rotterdam, The Netherlands

Caterina G. Roman Department of Criminal Justice, Temple University, Philadelphia, PA, USA

Amir Rostami Department of Sociology, Stockholm University, Stockholm, Sweden

Miriam Rubenson Department of Psychology, University of Southern California, Los Angeles, CA, USA

Revital Sela-Shayovitz David Yellin Academic College and Institute of Criminology, The Hebrew University of Jerusalem, Jerusalem, Israel

Russell Turner Department of Social Work, University of Gothenburg, Gothenburg, Sweden

Ellen Vandenbogaerde School of Global Studies, University of Sussex, Brighton, UK

Maarten De Waele VVSG, The Association of Flemish Cities and Municipalities, Brussels, Belgium

About the Editors

Cheryl L. Maxson (Ph.D., University of Southern California) is the Department Chair and Professor of Criminology, Law and Society at the University of California, Irvine. She was one of the coeditors of the first Eurogang volume, has coedited the well-received *Modern Gang Reader* (all four editions) and is coauthor of two other books (both by the Oxford University Press).

Finn-Aage Esbensen (Ph.D., University of Colorado, Boulder) is the E. Desmond Lee Professor of Youth Crime and Violence at the University of Missouri–St. Louis and Chair of the Department of Criminology and Criminal Justice. He coedited *American Youth Gangs at the Millennium*, is a coauthor of a criminology textbook (the ninth edition will be published in 2015), and is a coauthor of a research monograph by Temple University Press.

Together, the editors have extensive publication records and have been affiliated with the Eurogang Network since its inception, have participated in each of the 15 workshops, and serve on the group's Steering Committee. They collaborated on the editing of the fourth Eurogang volume, *Youth Gangs in International Context*, also published by Springer.

Chapter 1
Participation in and Transformation of Gangs (and Gang Research) in an International Context: Reflections on the Eurogang Research Program

Cheryl L. Maxson and Finn-Aage Esbensen

1.1 Introduction

The other chapters in this volume report original research by scholars associated with the Eurogang Research Program. Preliminary findings from a number of these chapters were previously presented at recent workshops sponsored by Eurogang while other chapters are the product of collaborations fostered by the Eurogang network. This is the fifth published volume of Eurogang research, and it seems a timely place to reflect back on the origin of the group, its purposes, and how the work in the current volume embodies those objectives. Accordingly, we first provide a brief history of Eurogang and then move on to an examination of how Eurogang has helped to further gang research—comparative and otherwise—in Europe and elsewhere. We illustrate this with a discussion of the contents of this volume, paying particular attention to the Eurogang objectives of encouraging cross-national collaborations and the incorporation of multiple research sites, common gang and gang member definitional approaches, and the use of diverse methodologies to understand gangs and responses to them. We conclude with our

C.L. Maxson (✉)
Department of Criminology, Law and Society, University of California, Irvine, Irvine, CA, USA
e-mail: cmaxson@uci.edu

F.-A. Esbensen
Department of Criminology and Criminal Justice, University of Missouri-St. Louis, St. Louis, MO, USA
e-mail: esbensen@umsl.edu

C.L. Maxson, F.-A. Esbensen (eds.), *Gang Transitions and Transformations in an International Context*, DOI 10.1007/978-3-319-29602-9_1

reflections on the status of comparative research on gang transitions and transformations.

1.2 A Brief History of the Eurogang Research Program

Eurogang was the brainchild of American gang researcher Mac Klein.[1] Mac traveled extensively in Europe during the 1980s and 1990s to explore whether the types of gangs and gang issues that he had been studying in the United States since the 1960s might be there as well. He concluded that there probably was, but that we needed far more information about European youth groups to make that determination. He used the occasion of a conference in Leuven, Belgium, in 1997 to convene a small group of European youth researchers to pose the question of whether there was sufficient interest in the possibility of European street gangs to hold an academic conference on the matter. He was encouraged by the response, and with support from a variety of governmental agencies and universities, the first Eurogang workshop was held in Schmitten, Germany in 1998. The presentations and discussions at the Eurogang I meeting addressed: the status of gang research in various European places; the challenges of gang scholarship in the United States and their implications for European gang research and policy; other (than gang) forms of delinquent youth groups in Europe; various definitional issues, moral panic, and the application of US stereotypes to the European context, or what Klein dubbed, "the Eurogang Paradox" (Klein 2001). Also in the first Eurogang volume (Klein et al. 2001), Weitekamp (2001) provided an analysis of European gang structures and Maxson (2001) offered a proposal for multi-method comparative gang research that incorporated the three levels (city, neighborhood, group) of analysis proposed at the Schmitten meeting.

The Schmitten meeting concluded with enthusiasm for continued conversation and optimism for fostering multi-method, comparative research on gangs. A second meeting in Oslo, Norway spawned a series of working groups to further discussions of methods, definitions, and potential funding sources. The working group facilitators became members of the steering committee. Over a series of several more workshops, we arrived at a consensus definition,[2] established a listserv and website (http://www.umsl.edu/ccj/Eurogang/euroganghome.html) and developed, pretested, and translated five instruments and protocols to gather information defined

[1] The Eurogang effort has been previously described in a number of publications, including the prefaces of the four previous volumes of Eurogang research (Decker and Weerman 2005; Esbensen and Maxson 2012; Klein et al. 2001; van Gemert et al. 2008), various chapters and articles by Klein (2001, 2007, 2009a, 2011, 2012), and a training manual of Eurogang instruments (Weerman et al. 2009). The coeditors of this volume have attended all 15 workshops held to date and helped to organize, facilitate, and fund a number of them.

[2] Eurogang defines a street gang as any durable, street-oriented youth group whose involvement in illegal activity is part of its group identity. The Eurogang Program Manual (Weerman et al. 2009) provides a detailed description of the development and operationalization of this definition.

by the group as critical to understanding gangs and gang activity in diverse locales. An important development occurred in the Albany workshop (EGVII in 2004) when the group decided that all instruments would be made available to anyone who requested them. The meeting in Los Angeles (EGIX in 2008) addressed the challenges of conducting such research in a comparative framework and spawned a commitment to document the development of the instruments to encourage widespread use (Weerman et al. 2009).[3] Klein authored a quasi-fictional book, *The Gangs of Euroburg* (2009b), to communicate further the purpose, method, and challenges of Eurogang research.

While the first several workshops focused upon methodological developments, presenters also discussed ongoing research efforts and the status of gang activity in European locations. The first workshop exclusively devoted to substantive gang research was in Onati, Spain (EGVIII in 2005), although the preceding meeting at Albany focused papers and discussion on violence. Since then, workshops have highlighted a variety of themes (e.g., group processes, definitional issues, theoretical advancements, gang migration, police, and community programs). While workshop papers are often solicited around given theoretical, methodological, and/or substantive themes, additional topics often emerge from submitted abstracts. We invariably set aside time for location-specific updates and descriptions of current research activity. All five volumes of Eurogang research reflect this eclectic approach to workshop content. In addition to providing networking and collaborative opportunities, the workshops have provided a rich venue for sharing preliminary findings, and the edited volumes have furthered the dissemination of European and North American gang scholarship.

To date, we have held 15 workshops with the 16th scheduled to convene in Gothenburg, Sweden in June 2016. These workshops are usually held in a European location (see Table 1.1 for a listing of dates and locations of EG meetings) over a 3-day period. To facilitate participation in these workshops, organizers seek external funding (see Table 1.2 for a list of past funders) so that, at a bare minimum, lodging and meals are provided to participants. Frequently, funding has also been available to subsidize some or all travel costs as well. We are particularly interested in facilitating participation for young scholars who may not have the resources to travel internationally.

Each workshop has attracted new participants to Eurogang, and thus we begin each meeting with an overview of the history and purposes of the group as well as some of the guiding principles that have emerged over time. Eurogang was founded on the belief that decades of research on American street gangs had failed to produce meaningful and effective gang prevention and intervention strategies because scholars used widely varying definitions and methods to conduct studies primarily in single sites and thereby undermined efforts to uncover participation and activity patterns that could guide strategic responses. Simply put, the primary purpose of the group is to foster multi-method comparative research on street gangs. Of course, the optimal approach to achieving this is to conduct studies designed prospectively to insure comparability. Eurogang members have applied for funding to

[3] The instrument manual and instruments are available on the Eurogang website, noted above.

Table 1.1 Eurogang workshop dates and locations

EG I	Sept 1998—Schmitten, Germany
EG II	Sept 1999—Oslo, Norway
EG III	Oct 1999—Leuven, Belgium
EG IV	Sept 2000—Egmond an Zee, the Netherlands
EG V	July 2002—Straubing, Germany
EG VI	July 2003—Straubing, Germany
EG VII	July 2004—Albany, NY, USA
EG VIII	May 2005—Onati, Spain
EG IX	May 2008—Los Angeles, USA
EG X	June 2010—Neustadt an der Weinstrasse, Germany
EG XI	Sept 2011—Hillerod, Denmark
EG XII	May 2012—Stockholm, Sweden
EG XIII	June 2013—Canterbury, UK
EG XIV	June 2014—Stavern, Norway
EG XV	June 2015—Blaubeuren, Germany
EG XVI	June 2016—Gothenburg, Sweden

do just that on several occasions but have thus far been unable to secure the necessary resources to do so.[4]

The principles which guide our work embrace the value of both qualitative and quantitative methodological techniques, place importance on comparing street gangs to other forms of youth groups, and recognize the need for a dynamic research design as the body of knowledge about gangs in a wide range of places grows. Thus far, the group has maintained allegiance to the consensus Eurogang definition although debates about improvements are a regular fixture in our meetings as well as in written work (see below).

1.3 How the Fifth Eurogang Volume Reflects the Eurogang Context

We have divided the other chapters that comprise this volume into three parts. The latter two parts reflect the book's title themes of gang and gang member transitions and the programs and policies meant to impact these dynamic processes. The first

[4]The International Self-Report Delinquency Study (ISRD) also aims to use standardized instruments and data collection procedures in multiple countries. Mac Klein was also a founding member of this project. This group of researchers has managed to execute three sweeps of student surveys since 1992 without centralized funding. However, the study designs proposed by Eurogang involve executing five methods in multiple country locations at considerable expense. European funding agencies have thus far not prioritized the study of street gangs over other pressing social problems.

Table 1.2 Past funders of Eurogang workshops

Arizona State University
Danish Crime Prevention Council
Dutch Ministry of the Interior
Dutch Ministry of Justice
E. Desmond Lee Collaborative Vision, University of Missouri-St. Louis
Economic and Social Research Council (UK)
German Ministry of Justice
Jerry Lee Foundation
Municipality of Oslo
National Consortium of Violence Research (NCOVR)
Norwegian Association of Local and Regional Authorities (KS)
Norwegian Ministry of Children and Family
Norwegian Ministry of Children, Equal Opportunity and Inclusion
Norwegian Research Council
Norwegian Ministry of Justice
Stockholm Gang Intervention and Prevention Project
University of Illinois-Chicago
University of Missouri—St. Louis
University of Nebraska—Omaha
University of Southern California
US Department of Justice, National Institute of Justice
US Department of Justice, Office of Juvenile Justice and Delinquency Prevention

section illustrates the eclectic nature of Eurogang research interests, with chapters highlighting definitional issues, patterns of gang activity and organization, and theory. It is worth noting how the chapters in this volume (especially in the first section) illustrate the Eurogang principles we discussed above.

1.3.1 Collaboration Among Researchers

Cross-national collaborative gang scholarship was presented at the very first Eurogang workshop. Huizinga and Schumann (2001) reported their comparative analysis of patterns of joining gangs and gang activity from their respective studies in Denver, Colorado and Bremen, Germany. Esbensen and Weerman (2005, see also Weerman and Esbensen 2005) also analyzed differences between gang and nongang youth in Esbensen's sample of students in 11 US cities and Weerman's Dutch students in The Hague. Both studies revealed remarkable similarities and some differences between the United States and European gang members.

Other comparative work has capitalized on the inclusion of Eurogang definitional indicators in the ISRDII studies (see footnote 4). Haymoz and Gatti (2010) note similarities in gang patterns evident in student surveys in Italy and Switzerland even while Gatti et al. (2011) report widely varying gang prevalence rates in the 30 country sample. Drawing from this same dataset, Haymoz et al. (2014) illustrate the challenges of explaining the differences in gang risk factors they detect in analysis of city-based samples in 19 countries. Pyrooz and his colleagues (2012) profit from common gang measurement among student surveys in two Caribbean nations and several US cities to study gang organization and offending patterns, finding more differences than similarities.

The current volume contributes two more cross-national comparisons that grew out of collaborations spawned at Eurogang workshops. Vandenbogaerde first presented her research on Caracas gangs at the EGIV workshop in Stavern, Norway. She discovered a comparative opportunity in Van Hellemont's study of Brussels gangs and the resulting chapter. "Fear and Retaliation: Gang Violence in Brussels and Caracas" reveals the nuances of retaliatory violence processes underlying gang dynamics in these two very disparate gang communities.

Sela-Shayovitz spoke with Pyrooz and Decker about their study of the use of the Internet by gang members at the Eurogang XI workshop in 2011. Their chapter in this volume, "Israeli and US gangs in the Virtual World," further documents cross-national similarities among gangs, in this case regarding Internet use to express collective activity but not in a particularly transformative way. The study finds some intriguing differences in offending patterns that warrant further investigation.

Both of these chapters illustrate the value of cross-national comparisons, yet both suffer limitations from the methodological differences in studies designed for different purposes. Eurogang has been successful at fostering deeper analysis of existing datasets even while these often reveal what is lost by not being able to conduct research that plans for these comparisons prospectively.

It is not unusual for chapters in Eurogang volumes to be co-authored by scholars of different nationalities (see Chaps. 3, 7, 8, 14, and 16 and this introduction). The Eurogang network reflects the global mobility of scholars such as Vandenbogaerde, a Belgium native, trained in the United Kingdom, conducting research in Venezuela. She is emblematic of yet another Eurogang principle. Eurogang has embraced the value of incorporating young scholars into the network and provided support for them to attend workshops. We recently expanded the Eurogang steering committee to include four young scholars, even as many of the long-term members transition out of the group. This is one attempt to inject vitality into the group even as we incorporate new approaches and understandings of gangs in new places and provide for the longevity of the Eurogang Research Program.

1.3.2 Defining Street Gangs

Agreeing on definitions of gangs and gang members is central to advancing comparative gang research. This is an area in which we have made considerable progress. The Eurogang definition has been widely adopted and appears regularly in publications, even those produced by scholars who have not been involved in Eurogang. Thus, it is clear that the definition has been found useful.

Several studies have advanced our understanding of the nuances of this definition as well as the implications of its adoption. In the fourth Eurogang volume, Matsuda et al. (2012) observed that the utilization of the Eurogang definition generated different prevalence rates from that of either self-nomination or identification of a youth friendship group as a gang, but their analysis of risk factors suggests that similar types of youth fall into the different categories. Drawing from their research in an English city, Aldridge et al. (2012) challenge the validity of the Eurogang definition due to its capture of groups of drug using youths whose members engage in little other delinquent activity (see also Medina et al. 2013). Smithson and her colleagues (2012) also question the utility of the Eurogang definition in the United Kingdom.

Several chapters in the current volume help to expand our knowledge in this area. In "Street Gang Definitions Across Two US Cities," Roman, Cahill, and Eidson pay particular attention to the two operationalizations of the group crime identity aspect of the Eurogang definition (i.e., that committing crime is acceptable to the group and that group members commit crime together). Their work reveals that many youth that do not endorse these items report contradictory information elsewhere in the interview, suggesting that measurement might be a problem. Interestingly, they find that belonging to a territorial group is associated with both aspects of the group crime identity. Thus, the application of the Eurogang definition may be influenced by the territorial nature of gangs in a given location. Their work also underscores the importance of gang definitions for identifying clients for programs and resources. Rostami's chapter, "Policing Gangs and Organized Crime," finds that Swedish police waste resources and make the gang problem worse by misidentifying groups, particularly as this is related to the misapplication of "organized crime" definitions.

Melde and colleagues tease out the patterns of criminal offending when youth join or leave gangs, as defined by self-nomination, peer group identification, or the Eurogang approach. In "Gang Membership and Involvement in Violence among US Adolescents," they show similar effects of gang participation on a general measure of offending regardless of definition. However, although the Eurogang-defined youth commit more violence upon joining an EG-defined gang, these youth commit proportionately fewer violent acts—relative to their overall offending—than those falling within the other two gang definitions and even nongang youth. This is a finding that will be important to pursue in different samples as it suggests that the groups captured by the Eurogang definition may have different internal group dynamics that generate different crime profiles.

Carson and Esbensen wonder whether the reasons youth offer for leaving gangs vary according to gang definitional approaches. In "Motivations for Leaving Gangs in the US," they document that youth who meet both the Eurogang and self-nomination definitions of gang membership report similar reasons for gang desistance as those who identify as gang members but do not meet the Eurogang definition. Whether youth meet only the Eurogang definition, only self-nominate as gang members, or fit both gang definitions, the most common reason for leaving the gang was moving. The inconsistency of youth reports revealed in the Roman et al. chapter is echoed by Carson and Esbensen: the reasons for gang desistance offered by youth relatively soon after they leave are rarely the same as those reported several years later.

There is little consensus among these studies regarding the degree to which different definitional approaches really matter. There seems little doubt that different youth are captured by different approaches, but regardless of definition, gang youth consistently differentiate from youth not meeting the definition.

1.3.3 Diverse Methods for Studying Gangs and Responses to Them

The Eurogang network encourages diverse approaches to studying gangs, and this volume illustrates a range of approaches to identifying samples and gathering information. Each section of the book includes chapters employing quantitative and qualitative approaches but only one chapter (Carson and Esbensen) draws from both types of methods. Thus, the vision articulated by Eurogang founders to promote multi-method studies has not been realized. This volume illustrates the diversity of methods that can be used as well as the lack of integration of these methodological strategies.

1.4 Transitions and Transformations

There is a robust literature on gang joining and this work is enhanced by the development and test of theories of gang participation such as that offered by Pauwels and Hardyns in their chapter, "Micro-place Conditions and Social, Personal and Situational Control Mechanisms" as well as the investigation by De Waele and Pauwels on "Why do Flemish Youth Participate in Right-wing Disruptive Groups?" The Huebner and Garrity chapter ("Youth Gang Members' Transitions into and within US Prisons") suggests that motivations to join gangs in prison may have common ground with reasons to participate in street gangs. Reid and

Maxson's chapter ("Gang Youth and Friendship Networks in California Correctional Facilities") reveals that gang members form different types of friendship networks in youth institutions than do those that do not identify as gang members, but they cannot address whether these social networks may differ from those of street gang members.

We have relatively little knowledge about how gangs may evolve over time. Using key informants, Van Gemert describes changes in Crips gangs in the Netherlands ("Dutch Crips Run Dry in Liquid Society"). This work documents the challenges that such groups face in sustaining membership over time particularly in an environment that offers alternatives, especially employment, to young men.

The final section of the volume looks at a myriad of approaches to aiding transitions out of gangs. In "A Brief Review and Meta-analysis of Gang Intervention Trials in North America," Huey, Lewine, and Rubenson provide evidence of the difficulty practitioners face in attempts to encourage gang desistance. Relying on both published and unpublished sources, these researchers located two dozen controlled evaluation studies of gang-focused interventions reporting gang outcomes. Negative or null results are reported in twice as many of the studies as are positive outcomes. None of these studies took place outside North America, despite the researchers' attempts to find evaluated programs elsewhere. As more European sites identify gang problems and launch responses to them, it will be important to conduct randomized experiments to determine whether these programs might be more successful.

The other chapters in this final section each point to the difficulties in providing effective programs to gang youth. De Jong ("The Real Deal") and Forkby and Turner ("Collaboration as Usual") discuss the political dynamics that make delivery of services a challenge. The different law enforcement cultures in St. Paul and London seem to have contributed to the differential implementation of the Group Violence Initiative approach described by Densley and Jones ("Pulling Levers on Gang Violence in London and St. Paul"). This targeted deterrence strategy is quite distinct from the activities that Rostami describes being used in Stockholm in his chapter, "Policing Gangs and Organized Crime."

The Eurogang Research Program has greatly exceeded the expectations of Mac Klein and others who participated in the first EG meeting in Schmitten. Little did we expect to be editing a fifth volume of research or planning the 16th EG workshop. While the Eurogang Program has contributed to enhanced understanding of gangs in international contexts, it has hardly transformed the nature of gang research. The workshops are a forum for researchers trained in different disciplinary, theoretical and methodological traditions to come together and find common ground (or not). In the absence of the prospective, comparative research that was our raison d'etre, we cannot know whether the kinds of similarities and differences described by the research reported in this volume would withstand systematic comparison. Until then, we will continue to accumulate knowledge on gangs in Europe and the United States on an incremental, albeit piecemeal, basis.

References

Aldridge, J., Medina-Ariz, J., & Ralphs, R. (2012). Counting gangs: Conceptual and validity problems with the Eurogang definition. In F.-A. Esbensen & C. L. Maxson (Eds.), *Youth gangs in international perspective: Results from the Eurogang program of research* (pp. 35–51). New York: Springer.

Decker, S. H., & Weerman, F. W. (Eds.). (2005). *European street gangs and troublesome youth groups*. Walnut Creek, CA: Altamira Press.

Esbensen, F.-A., & Maxson, C. (Eds.). (2012). *Youth gangs in international perspective: Results from the Eurogang program of research*. New York: Springer.

Esbensen, F.-A., & Weerman, F. M. (2005). Youth gangs and troublesome youth groups in the United States and the Netherlands: A cross-national comparison. *European Journal of Criminology, 2*(1), 5–37.

Gatti, U., Haymoz, S., & Schadee, H. (2011). Deviant youth groups in 30 countries: Results from the second international self-report delinquency study. *International Criminal Justice Review, 21*(3), 208–224.

Haymoz, S., & Gatti, U. (2010). Girl members of deviant youth groups, offending behavior and victimization: Results from the ISRD 2 in Italy and Switzerland. *European Journal of Criminal Policy Research, 16*, 167–182.

Haymoz, S., Maxson, C., & Killias, M. (2014). Street gang participation in Europe: A comparison of correlates. *European Journal of Criminology, 11*(6), 659–681.

Huizinga, D., & Schumann, K. F. (2001). Gang membership in Bremen and Denver: Comparative longitudinal data. In M. W. Klein, H. J. Kerner, C. L. Maxson, & E. G. M. Weitekamp (Eds.), *The Eurogang paradox: Street gangs and youth groups in the U.S. and Europe* (pp. 231–246). Dordrecht, The Netherlands: Kluwer.

Klein, M. W. (2001). Resolving the Eurogang paradox. In M. W. Klein, H.-J. Kerner, C. L. Maxson, & E. G. M. Weitekamp (Eds.), *The Eurogang paradox: Street gangs and youth groups in the U.S. and Europe* (pp. 7–20). Norwell, MA: Kluwer.

Klein, M. W. (2007). *Chasing after street gangs: A forty year journey*. Upper Saddle River, NJ: Pearson Education.

Klein, M. W. (2009a). Bootlegging: A career caught between fantasy and reality. *Criminology and Public Policy, 8*(1), 1–12.

Klein, M. W. (2009b). *The street gangs of Euroburg: A story of research*. Bloomington, IN: iUniverse.

Klein, M. W. (2011). Who can you believe? Complexities of international street gang research. *International Criminal Justice Review, 21*(3), 197–207.

Klein, M. W. (2012). The next decade of Eurogang program research. In C. L. Maxson & F.-A. Esbensen (Eds.), *Youth gangs in international perspective: Results from the Eurogang program of research* (pp. 291–301). New York: Springer.

Klein, M. W., Kerner, H. J., Maxson, C. L., & Weitekamp, E. G. M. (Eds.). (2001). *The Eurogang paradox: Street gangs and youth groups in the U.S. and Europe*. Amsterdam, The Netherlands: Kluwer Press.

Matsuda, K., Esbensen, F.-A., & Carson, D. C. (2012). Putting the 'gang' in 'Eurogang': Characteristics of delinquent youth groups by different definitional approaches. In F.-A. Esbensen & C. L. Maxson (Eds.), *Youth gangs in international perspective: Results from the Eurogang program of research* (pp. 17–34). New York: Springer.

Maxson, C. L. (2001). A proposal for multi-site study of European gangs and youth groups. In M. Klein, H. J. Kerner, C. Maxson, & E. Weitekamp (Eds.), *The Eurogang paradox: Street gangs and youth groups in the U.S. and Europe* (pp. 299–307). Dordrecht, The Netherlands: Kluwer.

Medina, J., Aldridge, J., Shute, J., & Ross, A. (2013). Measuring gang membership in England and Wales: A latent class analysis with Eurogang survey questions. *European Journal of Criminology, 10*(5), 591–605.

Pyrooz, D., Fox, A., & Katz, C. (2012). Gang organization, offending and victimization: A cross-national analysis. In F.-A. Esbensen & C. L. Maxson (Eds.), *Youth gangs in international perspective: Results from the Eurogang program of research* (pp. 85–106). New York: Springer.

Smithson, H., Monchuk, L., & Armitage, R. (2012). Gang member: Who says? Definitional and structural issues. In F.-A. Esbensen & C. L. Maxson (Eds.), *Youth gangs in international perspective: Results from the Eurogang program of research* (pp. 53–68). New York: Springer.

van Gemert, F., Peterson, D., & Lien, I.-L. (2008). *Street gangs, migration, and ethnicity*. Uffculme, Devon, England: Willan.

Weerman, F. M., & Esbensen, F.-A. (2005). A cross-national comparison of youth gangs: The United States and the Netherlands. In S. H. Decker & F. M. Weerman (Eds.), *European street gangs and troublesome youth groups*. Lanham, MD: Altamira Press.

Weerman, F. M., Maxson, C. L., Esbensen, F.-A, Aldridge, J., Medina, J., & van Gemert, F. (2009). *Eurogang program manual background, development, and use of the Eurogang instruments in multi-site, multi-method comparative research*. Retrieved from the Eurogang Network website: http://www.umsl.edu/~ccj/eurogang/Eurogang_20Manual.pdf

Weitekamp, E. G. M. (2001). Gangs in Europe: Assessments at the millennium. In M. Klein, H. J. Kerner, C. Maxson, & E. Weitekamp (Eds.), *The Eurogang paradox: Street gangs and youth groups in the U.S. and Europe* (pp. 309–322). Dordrecht, The Netherlands: Kluwer.

Part I
Gang Participation and Impacts on Individual Behavior

Chapter 2
Street Gang Definitions Across Two US Cities: Eurogang Criteria, Group Identity Characteristics, and Peer Group Involvement in Crime

Caterina G. Roman, Meagan Cahill, and Jillian L. Eidson

2.1 Introduction

Across academia, defining gangs remains an actively debated issue. The topic of gang definitions became a flashpoint as the body of work on gangs mounted from the 1920s through the 1960s and researchers began to highlight the wide differences in definitions and classification schemes (Hardman 1967). The issue's importance, however, goes beyond academia and mere knowledge accumulation. Settling on a uniform definition of a gang and gang membership has implications not only for researchers, but also for policymakers and practitioners seeking to prevent and reduce gang involvement and the attendant violence. Utilization of a consensus-based definition and the requisite set of validated criteria would provide a solid baseline for measuring trends, making comparisons among counties, cities, and countries, and for creating programs that work—a backdrop from which a program can match appropriate high-risk youth with program elements most likely to have impact (Melde et al. 2011).

To date, there are three main approaches researchers use to identify gang members: (1) self-nomination, (2) asking whether the respondent has friends in a gang, and (3) the consensus-based Eurogang definition that does not use the word "gang." Each has supporters and detractors. Self-nomination is the most commonly employed definition, based somewhat on its extensive use in large, representative

C.G. Roman (✉) • J.L. Eidson
Department of Criminal Justice, Temple University, Philadelphia, PA, USA
e-mail: croman@temple.edu; Jillian.eidson@temple.edu

M. Cahill
Rand Corporation, Santa Monica, CA, USA
e-mail: mcahill@urban.org

C.L. Maxson, F.-A. Esbensen (eds.), *Gang Transitions and Transformations in an International Context*, DOI 10.1007/978-3-319-29602-9_2

surveys of adolescents. Early work has demonstrated its use as a robust measure of gang membership, but it is not without flaws. Some research has shown that self-nomination captures perhaps too-wide a range of individuals—active gang members, past members who are no longer active, and "wannabe" members (Battin et al. 1998; Winfree et al. 1992). Self-nomination also has been shown to undercount gang youth because of the potential stigma of being labeled a gang member, with youth simply unwilling to admit to gang membership (Matsuda et al. 2012). In addition, researchers have begun to find evidence that the connotation of "gang" for many street-oriented youth, even those in street gangs, suggests highly structured and organized gangs. Members of loose street groups may not see themselves as gang members (Bjerregaard 2002), and fail to self-nominate (Matsuda et al. 2012). Defining gang members as youth who indicate they have friends in a gang has its own problems—research has shown that youth identified by this method are more likely to be associates and are less likely to have the characteristics typical of gang members (Curry et al. 2002; Melde and Esbensen 2011).

The Eurogang definition was created to address numerous issues related to the definitional problem, partly in response to the need for cross-national comparison research and the fact that the term "gang" does not translate well in some nations. Instead of asking a youth to self-nominate, the Eurogang definition identifies key common features of gangs or similar groups: "A street gang (or troublesome youth group corresponding to a street gang elsewhere) is any durable, street-oriented youth group whose involvement in illegal activity is part of its group identity" (Weerman et al. 2009: 20). Having a consensus definition can advance the implementation of standardized designs to collect data on gangs and troublesome youth groups in multiple sites around the world—a specific goal put forth by the Eurogang Program. The consensus definition was developed in 2002 by the Eurogang Program and was made available to researchers around the world after 2003. The central elements of the Eurogang definition do not involve using the word "gang," but instead focus on the qualities believed to reflect central gang characteristics—the necessary *definers* of a gang, not descriptive aspects such as organization level, wearing colors or having a name.

Given the relatively recent adoption of the Eurogang approach by many academics, the current study seeks to add to the nascent body of research describing the results of this approach by examining the characteristics of youth who meet the Eurogang criteria and those who do not across a sample of street-oriented delinquent youth in two East Coast cities in the United States. The study used a purposive sampling strategy to recruit street gang members for participation in a longitudinal social network study of gang membership, desistance, and criminal behavior. Recruitment for study inclusion utilized a two-step process across both cities that included direct outreach by street workers familiar with gang youth and a short screening tool used by the research team to validate the selection of youth by the outreach workers.

The study's methodological framework—using a *community*-recruited sample to study the personal networks of street gang members in two cities—provides a unique opportunity to examine aspects of the Eurogang definition. Most often in the

United States, quantitative, multisite studies of gang members rely on school-based samples or arrestee samples, which tend to miss segments of the youth population (Pyrooz et al. 2013). Our objectives in this research are threefold: (a) what is the extent of overlap between our community-based delinquent street youth sample and those who meet the official Eurogang definition? (b) To what extent are empirically supported concepts of gang processes and embeddedness capable of distinguishing the central "illegal group identity" criteria of Eurogang-defined youth? And (c) to what extent do these findings vary by site?

2.2 Background

There are four main elements to the Eurogang consensus definition: (a) *durable*: has been in existence for at least several months, (b) *street-oriented*: spending group time outside of locations that have adult supervision (and does not necessarily have to be on the street, but could be any location highly visible to the public); (c) *youth*: most of the group consists of individuals in their teens and early 20s; and (d) *illegal activity is part of its group identity* in that behavior deemed criminal, and not simply bothersome, is part of the group culture. Implicit in any research definition, is the importance of the associated measures or operationalization of the key elements. Under the Eurogang consensus process, the core elements of the definition were translated into survey items; youth must respond appropriately to six survey items to be considered meeting the consensus definition:

1. *In addition to any formal groups, some people have a certain group of friends that they spend time with, doing things together or just hanging out. Do you have a group of friends like that?* [Must answer "yes"]
2. *Which one of the following best describes the ages of most of the people in your group?* [Must choose age groups between 12 and 25 years old]
3. *Does this group spend a lot of time together in public places like the park, the street, shopping areas, or the neighborhood?* [Must answer "yes"]
4. *How long has this group existed or how long has your group of friends been hanging out together?* [Must be 3 months or more]
5. *Are illegal things accepted by or okay for your group?* [Must answer "yes"]
6. *Do people in your group actually do things together that are against the law?* [Must answer "yes"]

As researchers freely acknowledge, no definition is perfect, without detractors, and indeed, the Eurogang definition has been questioned along a few dimensions. The studies that have begun to assess and validate the Eurogang approach have yielded a mix of findings—some highlighting the validity of the Eurogang definition in identifying youth with typical gang characteristics and levels of violence and others suggesting that there remains work to be done conceptually and cross-culturally in operationalizing key components of the definition. In the following section, we briefly review the research that has been conducted specifically to assess the Eurogang definition, and then place the current study's questions within this context.

In one of the first published studies to comment on definitional issues relative to the Eurogang definition, Sharp et al. (2006) conducted preliminary analysis using data from the 2004 Offending, Crime and Justice Survey in England and Wales to examine the relationship between various Eurogang criteria and the group composition and structure and the extent of involvement in group criminal activity. They found that 17 % of people who responded "no" to the item "is doing illegal things accepted by or okay for your group?" went on to admit, when presented with a list of criminal activities, that their group did illegal things. They suggested that respondents perhaps wanted to demonstrate that they knew right from wrong, or that perceptions of illegality may differ across youth. The final survey analyses did not utilize the full Eurogang criteria; the "accepted as okay" criterion was dropped and a new criterion was added: a group must have at least one structural feature often associated with gangs (e.g., leader/name/place/rules).

A 2012 study by Matsuda, Esbensen, and Carson examined whether depictions of gang members were similar across different gang definitions. Using Wave 4 data from the national evaluation of the Gang Resistance Education and Training (G.R.E.A.T.) program (Esbensen et al. 2012), the authors used their racially and ethnically diverse sample to compare the three main approaches to defining gangs: self-nomination, has friends in a gang, and the Eurogang definition. Of the 384 youth (~12 %) from the Wave 4 sample who were gang involved using at least one of the definitions, they found that the Eurogang definition identified the most gang members, 6.8 % of the total Wave 4 sample. Five percent self-reported gang membership and 5.5 % reported that their friends were in a gang. Importantly, only a third of youth who were identified as a gang member by any definition were defined as gang members by more than one definition. The highest overlap existed between self-nomination and having friends in a gang—21 % met both of those definitions. Although there was not a large overlap among youth by the different criteria, the authors found the three groups were similar to each other—on average, most of the behavioral and attitudinal correlates associated with gang membership were common to all three definitions.

Aldridge et al. (2012) set out to specifically address the conceptual validity of the operationalization of Eurogang criteria related to: "involvement in illegal activity as part of its group identity." They highlighted four related issues: (1) that the definition results in groups that should not be considered gangs, (2) the theoretical and conceptual basis to operationalize "group identity" has not been sufficiently developed, (3) the items on the instrument are not accurately comprehended by respondents, and (4) the Eurogang definition elicits individuals not involved in offending activity. The authors brought together analyses from a qualitative study of six gangs in the United Kingdom and two large youth surveys, one in England and Wales and one from regions in and around Madrid,

Spain. They found several sources of misidentification: a lack of street presence by groups otherwise considered gangs excluded them from the gang definition. In addition, groups involved in minor illegal behaviors—mainly centered on group drug use at dance parties (e.g., ravers, clubbers)—were classified as gangs. They also found that 12 % of youth who answered "yes" to all of the Eurogang items on the surveys subsequently responded in the negative when presented a list of criminal behaviors. The authors suggested that the Eurogang items perhaps should be revised to specify examples of criminal activity within the questionnaire item, but admit that adding complexity might create new, unforeseen issues.

Medina et al. (2013) examined the conceptual and empirical adequacy of the Eurogang definition using a nationally representative survey of young people in England and Wales. While they found that the definition identified a distinct group of youth who had gang characteristics, they also determined that the definition captured a separate group of youth whose only criminal activity was recreational drug use. The analyses assessing measurement variance across age found that the Eurogang definition appeared to better measure younger, as opposed to older, deviant youth groups.

In the current study, we follow in the tradition of the studies described above to contribute to the debate on the elements or definers of gang membership that can help inform survey design, as well as continued descriptive research on the relative importance of group processes and group identity in defining gangs. We followed the direction of Matsuda and colleagues (2012) who suggested that "future research should explore the qualities and conditions that lead youth to fall in different definitional categories" (p. 30), as well as Maxson and Esbensen's (2012) specific call for "the exploration of group processes` that provoke one designation over another" (p. 310). We are particularly interested in aspects of the Eurogang definition that have received the most attention—the conceptualization of *illegal group identity*. We conduct analyses to determine which characteristics of our street-oriented youth sample predict whether a youth responds "yes" to each of the two criteria that operationalize *illegal group identity*—those who say illegal activity is "okay or accepted" by their group and those who respond that people in their group "actually do things together that are against the law."

2.3 Methods

2.3.1 Sample and Design

This study uses data from Wave 1 of a longitudinal study of street group youth and their personal social networks. The U.S. Department of Justice-funded study was designed to examine whether and how one's personal social network is associated with desistance from gangs. Data were collected in Philadelphia, Pennsylvania, and the District of Columbia (DC) over a 2-year period beginning in the summer of

2013 and concluding in the spring of 2015. Participants were interviewed at three time points at least 6 months apart. Although the project consisted of three waves of data collection, this chapter will focus only on the results from Wave 1, which consists of 227 street group youth, both males and females, across the two cities.

Respondents were recruited for Wave 1 by street outreach workers affiliated with gang reduction programs in each city. In DC, the recruitment partner was a community-based organization that had been working in the gang prevention and intervention field for decades. In Philadelphia, the partner was a university-based gun violence reduction program that targets high-risk, predominantly gang youth.[1] Over a number of meetings, outreach workers from both sites (most of whom were ex-gang members) were trained by the research team to recruit gang youth who, conceptually, would meet the Eurogang definition. Because the outreach workers indicated their dislike for the term "gang," during the trainings, the research team relied on the phrase "street group" instead of "gang" to form the basis of the training. Outreach workers were asked to not think about their personal definition of street groups or gangs. Youth identified as street group members and that were between the ages of 14 and 25 were invited by outreach workers to meet the research team to complete a self-guided, computer-based survey. Participation in the survey was voluntary. Parental consent and youth assent were obtained from youth under 18 and individual consent was obtained from those 18 or older. All research protocols were approved by the RAND Corporation's human subjects review board.

Because of the possibility that, during recruitment, youth hanging out with "survey eligible" youth might accompany recruited peers to the survey site given the large incentive payment (US$50), the research team used a screening tool to determine final sample inclusion. In addition to being between the ages of 14 and 25, youth had to answer in the affirmative to having a peer group and, at minimum, one of the following items: ever involved in at least some type of illegal activity (individual or group activity), have friends in a gang, or calls their peer group a "gang" or "crew." The screening also helped identify individuals who may have been eligible, but were unwilling to honestly report their behaviors on a survey—important to a study whose primary focus was examining the process of leaving a gang, thereby necessitating the identification of those in street gangs. Using these criteria and age, a total of 50 youth were excluded from the final data set (20 in Philadelphia and 30 in DC). With the exception of youth being between the ages of 14 and 25 and having a peer group, the post-outreach worker recruitment screening process utilized by the research team did not include the Eurogang criteria.

The survey included questions about the respondent's demographic characteristics, living arrangement and environment, work, school and leisure activities,

[1]Outreach workers at both survey sites were compensated for their efforts. The honoraria process for outreach worker compensation differed by site—in Philadelphia, outreach workers were paid an honorarium for each respondent (completed interview). In DC, outreach workers were assigned by their employer to spend part of their workday recruiting youth for the study. The organization was compensated directly and outreach workers who recruited a large number of eligible youth for the study were given small bonuses to thank them for their help.

delinquency, group characteristics and involvement, and attitudes towards gangs and gang joining. For the social network portion of the instrument, the survey asked respondents to name 20 individuals who are important to them and are at least 10 years old. The social network component yielded information on each network member's ("alter") demographic characteristics, how the respondent met the alter, how often they spent time together, how much the respondent liked the alter, whether the alter was in a gang and whether the alter committed crime with the respondent. Each participant also indicated the extent of the connections between each alter and all of the other individuals the respondent named. Respondents were paid 50 US dollars at each survey wave.

2.3.2 Characteristics of the Sample

Of the 227 street group youth in the sample (131 in Philadelphia and 96 in DC), respondents were predominantly male (66 %). According to the outreach workers, within each site, the youth represented multiple street groups. With regard to the street nature of the sample, 97 % reported their group regularly hangs out in the street or other public places, had a particular neighborhood location outdoors where they congregated outside, or drive around locally most evenings in cars or motorcycles. The average age was 21.6 years and a majority identified as Black (86 %). The DC site, however, included significantly more Hispanic youth (40 %) than the Philadelphia sample (6 %). Seventy percent reported engaging in some type of group-based illegal behavior in the last 6 months and 58 % reported ever being in a gang fight. Over one-third of the total sample reported that, within the last 6 months, they attacked someone with the intention of seriously hurting him or her (37 %). Just over one-third (35 %) reported currently being on probation or parole, and 44 % reported ever carrying a gun. There were no significant differences between the two sites on these criminal behavior characteristics.

2.3.3 Measurement of Variables

In addition to key demographics, the measures employed in this study, for the most part, represent a set of *non*-criminal behavior measures that have been shown to be related to street group culture, status attainment, and group identity—the processes that make gang membership distinctive (see Maxson and Esbensen 2012). By not including individual and group criminal behavior in predictive models, we avoid any tautological issues given that two of the Eurogang criteria relate to illegal activities. For purely descriptive analyses, we include some group delinquency measures.

2.3.3.1 Demographics

The demographic variables include age, sex, ethnicity (Latino = 1), site (DC = 1; Philadelphia = 0), attached to school/work. Because the sample age range was wide (14–25 years of age), to measure attachment to the traditional institutions of school or work, we combined two items to form a dichotomous measure as to whether the respondent was either in school or employed. If either, the variable was coded “1.”

2.3.3.2 Group Processes and Embeddedness

Three dichotomous measures were created for aspects of group involvement in: (a) providing protection; (b) claiming a territory; and (c) defending a territory. Questionnaire items were, respectively: “In the past 6 months, has your group provided protection for each other?” “In the past 6 months has your group defended an area or place against other groups?” “Does the group have a territory it claims as its own?”

Four measures were included to capture an individual’s relationship with the group. First, a core/periphery measure (Esbensen et al. 2001) was derived from a questionnaire item that showed a five-ringed concentric circle (i.e., a target) and respondents were asked to think of the circle as their group and indicate “how far from the center of the group are you?” The values range from a “1” representing the center/core to a “5,” representing the periphery. Second, a measure was created to designate whether the respondent joined his/her group for respect (“Did you join your group or do you hang out with your friends to get respect?”), which research has shown to be a core “pull” in the processes related to gang joining (Decker and Van Winkle 1996). The third measure in this category included a dichotomous measure of whether the respondent had recently left his/her group or was thinking about leaving. Last, because some of the respondents were working with social workers and street outreach workers to reduce their criminal and gang-related behaviors, we included a measure for whether the respondent was currently attached to an outreach or social worker.

For descriptive analyses, we developed two dichotomous measures of violent and group activity. To measure whether the respondents themselves had engaged in recent acts of violence, we included a variable coded “1” if the respondent indicated that in the last 6 months he or she had used a weapon or force to get money or things from people, or attacked someone with a weapon with the idea of seriously hurting or killing them. To measure group involvement in illegal activity, a dichotomous measure for “any group crime” was created from seven survey items asking the respondent in the past 6 months, whether his/her group had done any of the following: been in fights with gangs/crews; damaged or destroyed property; stolen things; stolen cars or motorcycles; robbed other people; sold marijuana; and sold other illegal drugs.

2.3.3.3 Composition of Respondent's Social Network

Characteristics of the respondent's personal social network[2] were operationalized from items which asked about each of the alters he or she named. For the current study, we used three network measures. Based on studies showing that most street gangs are formed around neighborhood networks (Decker and Van Winkle 1996; Klein 1995), we included a measure capturing the proportion of one's network that lived in the respondent's neighborhood. Two items that assessed the criminal nature of the social network included questions about carrying guns (How likely is it that X carries a gun (including in his/her car)?) and gang membership (how likely is it that X is currently in a gang?). The proportion of alters carrying a gun and currently in a gang were created from ordinal response categories: "not at all likely," "somewhat likely," and "very likely." For each variable, the latter two categories were recoded to "1" and alters scoring a "1" were summed and divided by the total number of alters in one's network. "don't knows" were recoded as "not at all likely." The final network measures were proportional values (from 0.00 to 0.100).

2.4 Results

We first examined the frequency distribution, by site, of surveyed youth meeting the overall Eurogang criteria and those respondents who replied "yes" to the two criteria items related to illegal group identity (see Table 2.1). Only 38 % of respondents met all the Eurogang criteria. Roughly half of the sample did not meet the criteria because they reported neither condoning nor actually committing illegal behavior. A small percentage of the study sample (7.5 %) met both illegal group identity criteria but did not meet the full Eurogang criteria definition. Figure 2.1 illustrates how the study sample fares with regard to the Eurogang criteria.

There are notable differences by site—a significantly higher percentage of youth from DC met each of the two illegal group identity criteria, as compared to those from Philadelphia. The table also shows—*for those youth responding in the negative to the two criteria*—the percentage of youth who responded earlier in the survey that their group was involved in, during the last 6 months, some type of group behavior or group-based criminal activity when presented with a different set of questions on group behavior (i.e., not the Eurogang criteria questions). The "A" and "B" rows of Table 2.1 focus, respectively, on youth who indicated for the Eurogang items` that: (A) *doing illegal things is not viewed as okay by group*; and (B) *illegal*

[2] An individual's personal social network is different from a gang network. For the current study, personal networks are defined by the people named using the following question: *Please list 20 people important to you and who are at least 10 years old. Start by thinking of the people you hang out with or might see regularly in a typical day. Then, think of the people you talk to or see the most. For example, you can name family members, friends, neighbors, or even people you don't like.*

Table 2.1 Eurogang definition and criteria frequencies, by site

	Total ($n=227$)	DC ($n=96$)	Philadelphia ($n=131$)
Met all Eurogang criteria	37.89 %	45.83 %	32.06 %
Met criterion: doing illegal things okay by group	55.95	67.71	47.33**
Met criterion: illegal activity committed by group	54.63	61.51	48.09*
Met both "illegal group identity" criteria	45.37	63.54	35.88**
Did not meet all Eurogang criteria but met two illegal group identity criteria	7.50	12.50	3.82
A. Doing illegal things not viewed as okay by group, but…	($n=100$)	($n=31$)	($n=69$)
a1. Illegal activity committed by group (Eurogang item)	21.00	16.13	23.19
a2. Group engages in any crime[a]	48.00	48.39	47.83
a3. Group fights other gangs/crews	35.00	35.48	34.78
a4. Group sold marijuana	23.00	19.35	24.64
a5. Group sold other drugs	21.00	16.13	23.19
a6. Group defends territory	37.00	38.71	36.23
a7. Group protects each other	65.00	61.29	66.67
a8. Group claims a territory	36.00	32.26	37.68
a9. Used weapon in recent violence	34.00	48.39	27.54
a10. Twenty-five percent or more alters in gang	19.00	25.81	15.94
B. Illegal activity not committed by group, but…	($n=103$)	($n=35$)	($n=68$)
b1. Illegal things viewed as okay (Eurogang item)	23.30	25.71	22.06
b2. Group engages in any crime[a]	44.66	48.57	42.65
b3. Group fights other gangs/crews	32.04	40.00	27.94
b4. Group sold marijuana	20.39	14.79	23.53
b5. Group sold other drugs	14.56	14.29	14.71
b6. Group defends territory	33.96	42.86	29.41
b7. Group protects each other	65.05	62.86	66.18
b8. Group claims a territory	35.92	31.43	38.24
b9. Used weapon in violence	31.07	42.86	25.00
b10. Twenty-five percent or more alters in gang	20.39	31.43	14.71

*$p<0.05$, **$p<0.01$

[a]Any crime includes the following crimes committed by the group: been in fights with gangs/crews; damaged or destroyed property; stolen things; stolen cars or motorcycles; robbed other people; sold marijuana; and sold other illegal drugs

activity is not committed by the group. The intent here is to depict the characteristics of respondents who do not meet the illegal group identity criteria.

Roughly 45 % of youth across both sites indicated some group-based criminal activity in the recent 6 months even though responding in the negative to each of the two Eurogang criteria—for those who reported illegal things are not viewed as okay (i.e., don't condone illegal activity), 46 % reported earlier in the survey that their group committed at least one type of crime in a group in the last 6 months; and for those who

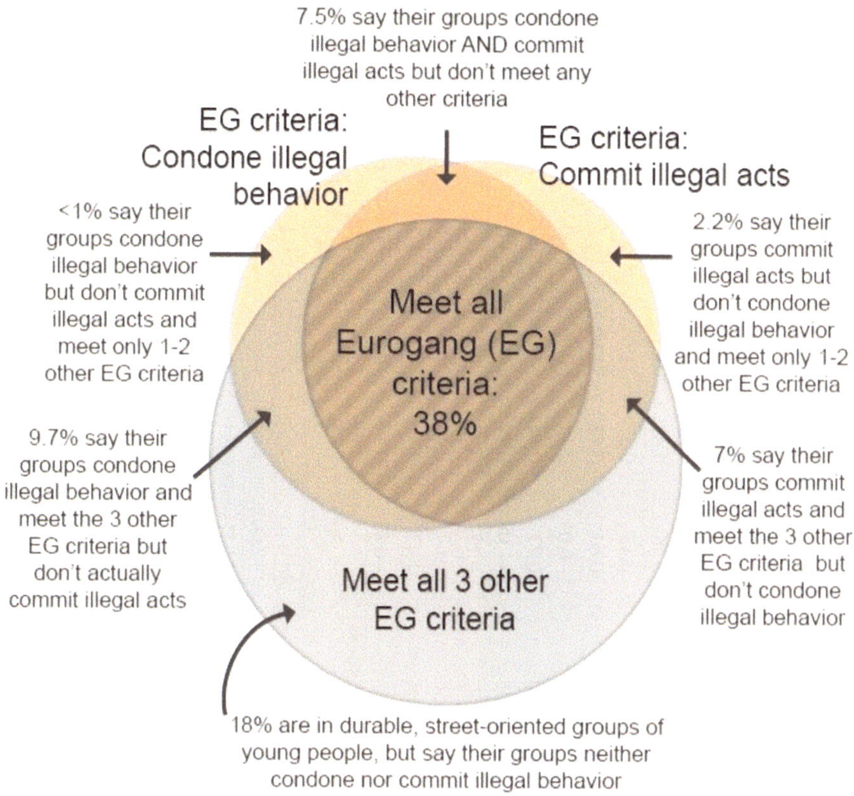

Fig. 2.1 Eurogang criteria overlap for study sample ($n=227$)

reported illegal activity is not committed by group, 44 % reported earlier in the survey that their group was recently involved in at least one type of group crime. Fighting other gangs/crews appears to be a key activity among at least a third of respondents whose groups do not condone illegal activity (35 %) or who say they do not engage in illegal activity (32 %). Sixty-five percent of the youth who said that their group does not condone illegal behavior also responded that their group protects each other. Protecting each other was also common (65 %) among those who said illegal activity is not committed by their group. Roughly one-third of youth who responded in the negative to the criteria (37 % of those who do not view illegal things as okay and 34 % of those who reported illegal activity is not committed by group) indicated their group *defended* their territory in the last 6 months. Similarly, about one-third of respondents who report that their group does not believe illegal activity is okay claims a territory (36 %) and a similar percentage (36 %) of those who reported illegal activity was not committed by their group also reported that their group claims a territory.

Table 2.2 shows the results of the logistic regression analyses to examine the extent to which empirically derived concepts of gang processes (those related to solidarity, status attainment, collective identity, etc.) were capable of distinguishing

Table 2.2 Logistic regression results predicting Eurogang criterion

	Model 1a: doing illegal things accepted by group			Model 1b: doing illegal things accepted by group, with network composition measures			Model 2a: group engages in illegal activity			Model 2b: group engages in illegal activity, with network composition measures		
	B	SE	Odds	*B*	SE	Odds	*B*	SE	Odds	*B*	SE	Odds
Age	–0.09	0.08	0.91	–0.10	0.09	0.90	0.03	0.08	1.03	0.05	0.08	1.05
Latino	–0.05	0.45	0.95	–0.01	0.53	1.01	0.46	0.47	1.58	0.51	0.51	1.67
Site (DC = 1)	0.88	0.37	2.42*	0.73	0.44	2.08	0.48	0.37	1.61	0.31	0.41	1.36
Outreach worker	0.14	0.41	1.15	0.11	0.49	1.11	0.64	0.43	1.90	0.42	0.47	1.52
Core/periphery (core = 1)	–0.13	0.12	0.88	–0.07	0.13	0.94	–0.05	0.12	0.95	0.02	0.13	1.02
Joined for respect	0.61	0.34	1.83	0.09	0.40	1.10	0.77	0.34	2.16*	0.42	0.37	1.53
Thinking of quitting/quit	–0.60	0.37	0.55	–0.43	0.42	0.65	–1.08	0.39	0.34**	–1.00	0.41	0.38*
Defended territory	0.35	0.35	1.41	0.12	0.39	1.12	0.72	0.35	2.06*	0.55	0.37	1.74
Protected group	0.73	0.42	2.08	0.44	0.46	1.56	0.67	0.43	1.94	0.50	0.46	1.65
Claims territory	1.44	0.33	4.22***	1.40	0.37	4.05***	1.42	0.33	4.13***	1.31	0.35	3.72***
In job or school	–0.66	0.35	0.52	–0.46	0.40	0.63	–0.83	0.37	0.44*	–0.60	0.39	0.55
Alters in gang (prop.)				4.91	1.12	135.39***				2.74	0.97	15.50**
Alters live in neigh. (prop.)				1.57	0.79	4.84*				0.53	0.76	1.69
Alters carry gun (prop.)				–1.88	0.84	0.15*				0.13	0.77	1.14
Constant	0.97	1.76		0.24	2.03		–2.00	1.81		–3.14	2.04	
	$X^2(11) = 45.14^{***}$			$X^2(14) = 58.67^{***}$			$X^2(11) = 48.64^{***}$			$X^2(14) = 55.36^{***}$		
	–2LL = 311.47			–2LL = 308.67			–2LL = 239.86			–2LL = 309.95		
	Nagelkerke $R^2 = 0.33$			Nagelkerke $R^2 = 0.49$			Nagelkerke $R^2 = 0.37$			Nagelkerke $R^2 = 0.46$		
	$n = 227$			$n = 225$			$n = 227$			$n = 225$		

$^*p < 0.05$, $^{**}p < 0.01$, $^{***}p < 0.001$

the youth who meet the illegal group identity criteria of the Eurogang definition. In addition to key demographics, the variables included in these models are *non-criminal behavior* measures that the literature has shown to more likely characterize core street gang youth (see, for instance Esbensen et al. 2001; Pyrooz et al. 2013). To assess any possible differences between the cities, we included a dummy variable for site. For each of the two Eurogang criteria, we ran two nested models—one with the measures of embeddedness and gang processes typically found in gang studies and a second model that added in the three new network-based measures. Although the larger study created a wide variety of network compositional measures that may be relevant to gang identity (e.g., proportion of network that sells drugs, proportion of network that are co-offenders), only three were included in the models in the current analyses due to issues with collinearity.

The results of the first model show that there are two variables that significantly predict whether a respondent indicated that doing illegal things is accepted by the group—whether the group claims a territory and if the respondent lives in DC (compared to Philadelphia). When the network variables are added to the model (Model 1b), the effect of site goes away. In addition, belonging to a group that claims territory and all three network variables are significant predictors. Claiming a territory, having a higher proportion of alters in a gang and having alters that live in the respondent's neighborhood all significantly increase the odds of responding that doing illegal things is accepted by one's group. However, and contrary to expectations, having a higher proportion of alters that are likely to carry guns reduces the odds of responding that doing illegal things is accepted by the group.

For the models predicting the Eurogang criterion: *group engages in illegal activity*, additional predictors become important. Specifically, the results of the model without network measures show that joining a group for respect, belonging to a group that recently defended territory and claiming a territory all increase the odds of responding that the group engages in illegal activity. Quitting a group or thinking about quitting and remaining in school/having a job each decrease the odds of responding "yes" to the criterion. In the model with network variables, institutional attachment (job or school) and recently defending your group's territory lose significance. Claiming a territory, the proportion of alters in a gang, and recently quitting a group or thinking about quitting are significant predictors of the criterion. Comparing the results of the full models across the two illegal group identity criterion shows that the predictors are similar to each other and highlight the salience of being in groups that claim territory and are defined by having higher proportions of their social networks that belong to gangs. However, the odds are roughly nine times higher for the measure representing the proportion of network members in a gang when predicting the criterion that illegal things are accepted by the group versus actually engaging in illegal activity. The *r*-squared statistics, representing the improvement of the full model over the intercept model, are roughly the same across the two criteria.

2.5 Discussion

The Eurogang Program has made great strides by achieving a consensus definition supported by gang experts from many nations—and one that has been applied to research in over 30 countries (Klein 2012; see, for example Haymoz et al. 2014). Studies have begun to reflect on the utility of the Eurogang definition for theory and practice. What are the characteristics of youth who meet the criteria for having an illegal group identity? Do they have other typical gang-like characteristics that set them apart from other youth and youth groups? We approached these questions from the standpoint of a study that was designed as a purposive sample of street group youth who had engaged in some type of illegal activity in their lives and were directly recruited by ex-gang member outreach workers. At the outset of the study, we had the expectation that the overwhelming majority of youth surveyed would meet the two illegal group identity criteria of the Eurogang definition because the outreach workers, deeply familiar with the neighborhoods, had recruited the respondents—most of whom were already known to them.

The results of the current analyses showed, that across the two cities, only 45 % of respondents met both the Eurogang criteria related to illegal group identity. This unexpectedly low percentage could be a function of the survey recruitment and the screening process, which included youth who were in the process of leaving a gang. However, it is also clear that many of the surveyed youth who did not meet the two criteria had characteristics of gang youth who met the Eurogang criteria. For instance, although the multivariate analyses showed claiming a territory was a key predictor for the two illegal group identity criteria, 36 % of those who did not meet each item responded that their group claims a territory. It is worthwhile to mention, however, that claiming a territory may be a factor unique to DC and Philadelphia. One-third of the street youth who did not meet the illegal group identity criteria had recently committed a violent crime with a weapon—and more than half of those did so more than once (not shown). These same youth have friends in a gang (see Table 2.1) and co-offenders (not shown).

In light of findings such as ours and other researchers (as described earlier), that the non-Eurogang-defined youth in our sample have many criminal behavior-related characteristics similar to Eurogang-defined youth, it is important to think about how findings from studies using gang terminology and publishing statistics on prevalence rates influence policy and practice. If the non-Eurogang-defined youth in this sample engage in group crime and have recently committed violent crimes, or claim and defend territory, but do not do these things as frequently or appear to be as embedded in gang culture as those meeting the stricter Eurogang definition, do they deserve less attention by policymakers? Should they be overlooked when developing enrollment or recruitment criteria for violence reduction programs or programs to prevent gang joining or encourage desistance? The violence wrought by these individuals is worthy of attention regardless of its frequency or the gang label—these youth are visible on the street to the police. It is highly possible that some of the youth who did not meet the illegal group identity criteria have marginal or fringe gang status (what police agencies might call "associates") and are not current core members of street gangs. But if they are involved in group-related violent activities even a few times in a short time period, should they be considered members?

With the tremendous rise in "focused deterrence" law enforcement strategies in the Unite States and other offender-focused strategies that explicitly target individuals within places, and specific groups as well (Braga and Weisburd 2010, 2012; see also Densley and Jones in this volume), it is likely that any routine group offending, and particularly violent offending, will bring the attention of law enforcement. If gang research wants to be policy relevant, then researchers might benefit by developing studies that start with a delineation of the characteristics of the groups that are most likely to receive law enforcement attention and compare these characteristics to those that have emerged as most salient for gang youth identified through surveys. Understanding this overlap with an eye towards evaluation of these enforcement strategies would simultaneously benefit research and practice.

Furthermore, the findings highlight the need to better understand the particular characteristics that set street gangs apart from other delinquent youth groups. As suggested in the Eurogang Program Manual (Weerman et al. 2009), survey-based research on gangs should always include question items about group-related processes and organizational features (e.g., having colors, leaders, symbols). Continued comparative research could help solidify this distinction and contribute structural dimension data that could be fit into Maxson and Klein's typology of gangs (Maxson and Klein 1995)—a typology which was created to contribute to the definitional need, and one that, according to the developers, can be situated within the Eurogang definition (Klein and Maxson 2006, p. 194). It is possible that our non-Eurogang-defined street youth resemble Maxson and Klein's "collective group" category of gang member, which is more of an unorganized mass of adolescents and young adult members without clear characteristics such as a name, structures, or subgroups. Does this type of gang have a diminished collective group identity? The current study was limited in that it did not include, until Wave 3, survey items asking respondents about organizational features of their group.

Klein (2007) echoes the need for research to help distinguish street gangs from other delinquent youth groups: "There has been too little research (especially in the United States, less so in Europe) on ongoing youth groups to which street gangs might be compared… the uniqueness of the gang would be clearer and better understood in the context of the more numerous and the more 'normal' groups that young people generally form" (pp. xiv–xv). As Klein and Maxson have both stressed (Klein 2007; Klein and Maxson 2006; Maxson 2001), gang studies should consider combining broad survey methods with ethnographic methods that will help inform the distinction between street gangs and other forms of youth groups and enable findings to be understood within the larger context of cities—methods that surely will benefit comparative research when common instruments are employed.

The findings from the current study also imply that context is important in the study of gang processes that facilitate an illegal youth identity. We found significant differences across the two cities—a higher percentage of youth in DC met the illegal group identity criteria. Table 2.1 suggests there are other differences between sites in drug dealing and use of violence, and how youth in each site reflect on these behaviors in relationship to their group identity. These differences were not significant, but this was likely due to very low cell size. The question is: are these differences due to differences in the type of gangs that the youth represented, or are they due to more macro features of the political, economic, and socio-legal environment of the cities and the micro-neighborhoods within? Additional qualitative work that is ongoing with this sample may shed some light on these questions, but the bigger picture for gang research moving forward begs for multi-method studies that use common instruments to carefully document context and its relationship to resultant gang processes, such as gang formation, the dominant aspects of gang culture, and gang desistance. This will help create generalizable knowledge and minimize the conflicting implications that have come before (Klein 2012).

Returning to definitional issues, a review of the research using the Eurogang definition shows that the issues highlighted here, and other issues, have resulted in some academics expanding or modifying the Eurogang definition in their studies. The authors of the UK survey (Sharp et al. 2006), for instance, added a criterion about group structure. A number of studies by Alleyne and Wood (2010, 2014) use cluster analysis to identify an expanded set of youth who did not meet all the Eurogang criteria but have similar characteristics—these "expanded" Eurogang definition youth are then included in their subsequent analyses as street gang youth. As the Eurogang criteria continue to be employed around the world, a focus on the characteristics of youth who appear to resemble Eurogang-defined youth is warranted. This type of examination would help provide more conceptual clarity to support a broadening of relevant survey items to inform the operationalization of illegal group identity, while "remaining 'pure'" (Klein 2012, p. 296) to the consensus Eurogang definition.

Acknowledgments This study was part of a larger project supported by Award No. 2011-JV-FX-0105, from the Office of Juvenile Justice and Delinquency Prevention, Office of Justice Programs, U.S. Department of Justice. Opinions or points of view expressed are those of the authors and do not necessarily reflect the official position or policies of the U.S. Department of Justice.

References

Aldridge, J., Medina-Ariz, J., & Ralphs, R. (2012). Counting gangs: Conceptual and validity problems with the Eurogang definition. In F.-A. Esbensen & C. L. Maxson (Eds.), *Youth gangs in international perspective: Results from the Eurogang program of research* (pp. 35–51). New York: Springer.

Alleyne, E., & Wood, J. L. (2010). Gang involvement: Psychological and behavioral characteristics of gang members, peripheral youth and non-gang youth. *Aggressive Behavior, 36*(6), 423–436.

Alleyne, E., & Wood, J. L. (2014). Gang involvement: Social and environmental factors. *Crime & Delinquency, 60*(4), 547–568.

Battin, S. R., Hill, K. G., Abott, R. D., Catalano, R. F., & Hawkins, J. D. (1998). The contribution of gang membership to delinquency beyond delinquent friends. *Criminology, 3*(6), 93–115.

Bjerregaard, B. (2002). Self-definitions of gang membership and involvement of delinquent activities. *Youth & Society, 34*(1), 31–54.

Braga, A. A., & Weisburd, D. L. (2010). *Policing problem places*. New York: Oxford University Press.

Braga, A. A., & Weisburd, D. L. (2012). The effects of focused deterrence strategies on crime a systematic review and meta-analysis of the empirical evidence. *Journal of Research in Crime and Delinquency, 49*(3), 323–358.

Curry, G. D., Decker, S. H., & Egley, A., Jr. (2002). Gang involvement and delinquency in a middle school population. *Justice Quarterly, 19*(2), 275–292.

Decker, S. H., & Van Winkle, B. (1996). *Life in the gang: Family, friends and violence*. New York: Cambridge University Press.

Esbensen, F.-A., Peterson, D., Taylor, T. J., & Osgood, D. W. (2012). Results from a multi-site evaluation of the G.R.E.A.T. program. *Justice Quarterly, 29*(1), 125–151.

Esbensen, F.-A., Winfree, L. T., Jr., He, N., & Taylor, T. J. (2001). Youth gangs and definitional issues: When is a gang a gang and why does it matter? *Crime & Delinquency, 47*(1), 105–130.

Hardman, D. G. (1967). Historical perspectives of gang research. *Journal of Research in Crime and Delinquency, 4*(1), 5–27.

Haymoz, S., Maxson, C., & Killias, M. (2014). Street gang participation in Europe: A comparison of correlates. *European Journal of Criminology, 11*(6), 659–681.

Klein, M. W. (1995). *The American street gang*. New York: Oxford University Press.

Klein, M. W. (2007). *Chasing after street gangs: A forty year journey*. Upper Saddle River, NJ: Pearson Education.

Klein, M. W. (2012). The next decade of Eurogang program research. In C. L. Maxson & F.-A. Esbensen (Eds.), *Youth gangs in international perspective: Results from the Eurogang program of research* (pp. 291–301). New York: Springer.

Klein, M. W., & Maxson, C. L. (2006). *Street gang patterns and policies*. Oxford, England: Oxford University Press.

Matsuda, K., Esbensen, F.-A., & Carson, D. C. (2012). Putting the ‘gang’ in ‘Eurogang’: Characteristics of delinquent youth groups by different definitional approaches. In F.-A. Esbensen & C. L. Maxson (Eds.), *Youth gangs in international perspective: Results from the Eurogang program of research* (pp. 17–34). New York: Springer.

Maxson, C. L. (2001). A proposal for multi-site study of European gangs and youth groups. In M. Klein, H. J. Kerner, C. Maxson, & E. Weitekamp (Eds.), *The Eurogang paradox: Street gangs and youth groups in the U.S. and Europe* (pp. 299–307). Dordrecht, The Netherlands: Kluwer.

Maxson, C. L., & Esbensen, F.-A. (2012). The intersection of gang definition and group process: Concluding observations. In C. L. Maxson & F.-A. Esbensen (Eds.), *Youth gangs in international perspective: Results from the Eurogang program of research* (pp. 303–315). New York: Springer.

Maxson, C. L., & Klein, M. W. (1995). Investigating gang structures. *Journal of Gang Research, 3*(1), 33–40.

Medina, J., Aldridge, J., Shute, J., & Ross, A. (2013). Measuring gang membership in England and Wales: A latent class analysis with Eurogang survey questions. *European Journal of Criminology, 10*(5), 591–605.

Melde, C., & Esbensen, F.-A. (2011). Gang membership as a turning point in the life course. *Criminology, 49*(2), 513–552.

Melde, C., Gavazzi, S. M., McGarrell, E. F., & Bynum, T. (2011). On the efficacy of targeted gang interventions: Can we identify those most at risk? *Youth Violence and Juvenile Justice, 9*(4), 279–294.

Pyrooz, D. C., Sweeten, G., & Piquero, A. R. (2013). Continuity and change in gang membership and gang embeddedness. *Journal of Research in Crime and Delinquency, 50*(2), 239–271.

Sharp, C., Aldridge, J., & Medina, J. (2006). *Delinquent youth groups and offending behaviour: Findings from the 2004 offending, crime and justice survey*. London: Home Office.

Weerman, F. M., Maxson, C. L., Esbensen, F.-A., Aldridge, J., Medina, J., & van Gemert, F. (2009). *Eurogang program manual: Background, development, and use of the Eurogang instruments in multi-site, multi-method comparative research*. Retrieved from http://www.umsl.edu/ccj/Eurogang/euroganghome.html

Winfree, L. T., Jr., Fuller, K., Vigil, T., & Mays, G. L. (1992). The definition and measurement of 'gang status': Policy implications for juvenile justice. *Juvenile and Family Court Journal, 43*(1), 29–37.

Chapter 3
Gang Membership and Involvement in Violence among US Adolescents: A Test of Construct Validity

Chris Melde, Finn-Aage Esbensen, and Dena C. Carson

3.1 Introduction

Street gangs have been a staple of criminological focus and public attention for over a century, in large part due to their penchant for criminal activity, especially violence, and open displays of affiliation. The scientific study of gangs and their members, however, has long been troubled by a lack of definitional clarity on the subject. The inability to create a definition that can unambiguously identify what is, and what is not a gang has made it difficult to conduct research across space and time in a manner that ensures consistency in the population under study. This reality makes replication and independent assessment of study findings difficult to accomplish with any level of certainty. This has led to concerns that studies of gangs and their members might either overestimate or underestimate the extent of gangs and gang members, and the suggestion that research on gangs and gang members is not in line with the problems these groups pose to communities (Katz and Jackson-Jacobs 2004). Most importantly, inconsistency in identification of gangs and gang members can impact the adequacy of programmatic responses to these groups and their members, leading to inefficient or ineffective interventions.

C. Melde (✉)
School of Criminal Justice, Michigan State University, East Lansing, MI, USA
e-mail: melde@msu.edu

F.-A. Esbensen
Department of Criminology and Criminal Justice, University of Missouri–St. Louis, St. Louis, MO, USA
e-mail: esbensen@umsl.edu

D.C. Carson
School of Public and Environmental Affairs, Indiana University Purdue University Indianapolis, Indianapolis, IN, USA
e-mail: carsond@iupui.edu

C.L. Maxson, F.-A. Esbensen (eds.), *Gang Transitions and Transformations in an International Context*, DOI 10.1007/978-3-319-29602-9_3

One resolution to this definitional problem has been the reliance on self-report data on gang membership, where police and/or researchers simply ask subjects whether or not they are members of a street gang. Those who respond in the affirmative are taken at their word, while others are considered non-gang youth, unless a series of other identifiers suggest otherwise (Barrows and Huff 2009). While this approach has the advantage of not relying on an external criterion of who is and is not a gang member, it remains limited given differences across individuals in their own interpretation of what it means to be a member of a street gang. Studies on the validity of this approach suggest that self-nomination is a robust and efficient way of identifying gang members (e.g., Curry 2000; Esbensen et al. 2001; Decker et al. 2014).

Alternatively, researchers have utilized a slight alteration to the self-nomination method, whereby respondents are asked whether or not their friends are a gang. Specifically, the International Self Report Delinquency Survey, led by Junger-Tas et al. (2010) included a measure that asked youth "Do you consider your group of friends to be a gang?" Those who responded in the affirmative were considered gang affiliated, while those who did not were coded as non-gang youth (see also, Melde and Esbensen 2011; Melde et al. 2009). This strategy is useful in that it is intended to avoid the potential bias that could arise if youth are sensitive to identifying themselves as gang involved, and the resulting undercounting of youth involved in gang activity. By characterizing their group of friends as belonging to a gang, the youth does not have to self-identify, but researchers are still afforded the opportunity to examine the characteristics of youth involved with gang groups to determine whether or not there are unique qualities associated with such a status. Indeed, research has demonstrated that youth who report their friends are a gang have characteristics similar to self-reported gang youth (Matsuda et al. 2012), including changes in attitudes, emotions, and behaviors consistent with a major life transition as youth enter and exit these groups (Melde and Esbensen 2011). There is the possibility, however, that youth are misidentified as gang involved using this method, especially if neither the respondent nor their associates consider them to be part of the gang. Accordingly, research may mischaracterize gang youth based on studies using this method, and thus lead to faulty policy and/or programmatic responses (Curry et al. 2002).

Yet another method to identify individuals as gang involved was developed by The Eurogang Project (Esbensen and Maxson 2012; Klein et al. 2001), a network of researchers, policymakers, and practitioners primarily from across Europe and the United States, who study gangs, gang members, and public responses to these groups. This method relies upon a series of questions on key characteristics of the respondent's peer group, which measure what are considered necessary, though not sufficient, elements of gang involvement, and are consistent with the group's consensus definition of a street gang. Specifically, the Eurogang consensus definition of a street gang states: A street gang (or troublesome youth group corresponding to a street gang elsewhere) "is any durable, street-oriented youth group whose involvement in illegal activity is part of its group identity" (Esbensen and Maxson 2012, p. 5). Key to the operationalization of this definition are the terms durable, street-oriented, youth group, and group—not individual—involvement in illegal activity.

A series of questions were compiled to identify each of these characteristics, with youth who answered each question in a manner consistent with the Eurogang definition identified as gang involved. For the group to be considered **durable**, respondents had to report that their current peer group has existed for 3 months or more when asked "How long has this group existed or how long has your group of friends been hanging out together?" **Street orientation** is measured through a question that asks "Does this group spend a lot of time together in public places like the park, the street, shopping areas, or the neighborhood," with respondents who report yes to this question considered to be in a street-oriented group. To be considered a **youth group**, respondents had to report that the majority of their group was between the ages of 12 and 25 when asked "Which one of the following best describes the ages of most of the people in your group?" Finally, to gauge whether or not **illegal activity** was part of their group's identity, respondents were asked two questions: (1) "Are illegal things accepted by or okay for your group?" and (2) "Do people in your group actually do things together that are against the law?"

Importantly, the strategy utilized to operationalize this definition does not make use of the term "gang" in this series of questions, which has a number of advantages. First, as was discussed above, the term "gang" is potentially charged, and thus can lead to respondents misrepresenting themselves when reporting on their gang status, either to appear gang involved when they are not, or denying gang involvement in order to conceal their identity (e.g., to avoid potential consequences if their answers were shared with an authority figure). Second, the term "gang" may not be well understood in many contexts: there is likely wide variation in what individuals consider to be gangs, and thus persons in similar groups may respond differently to questions about their gang involvement. This is especially the case with respect to international and comparative gang research, where the term "gang" is not easily translated in terminology (i.e., there is no word for gang in the native language) and/or meaning (i.e., the term for gang in the native language does not share the same meaning) across languages and cultures. Thus, while there may be gang-like groups in many countries around the globe, use of the term "gang" in instruments meant to identify these groups may not provide valid or reliable estimates due to differences in the meaning of the term (or the lack of the term "gang" in that language altogether). In order to conduct such research in a meaningful way, therefore, respondents are asked to respond to questions about the characteristics of their peer groups, so that comparisons can be made across persons involved in groups with similar characteristics.

Research using these three methods of measuring gang membership, both in isolation and comparatively, suggests that each method is useful in identifying individuals involved in a disproportionate level of deviant and criminal behaviors, as well as individuals who hold antisocial attitudes and emotional dispositions. For instance, Matsuda et al. (2012) examined a single wave (i.e., wave 4) of data from the second National Evaluation of the Gang Resistance Education and Training (G.R.E.A.T.) program, which included all three measures of gang membership discussed above (i.e., self-report, friends in a gang, and Eurogang), and found striking similarity in the behavioral and attitudinal measures across these gang measures. Each gang category was significantly more antisocial than non-gang youth across a host of indicators. There were interesting differences in the demographic makeup of the groups, however, despite the similarities in indicators of antisocial behaviors. For instance, the Eurogang method of gang identification was more likely to include females than the other two strategies to the extent that females were the majority of those included in this category (54 %). On the other hand, black and Hispanic youth were more likely to report that their friends were a gang than white youth. Interestingly, the degree of overlap in respondents identified by these measures was not overwhelming (33 % in Wave 4), indicating that while these measurement strategies led to the identification of respondents with high criminal propensities, these groups were by and large distinct in absolute composition, and evinced idiosyncrasies in demographic makeup.

Medina et al. (2013) utilized latent class analysis to examine whether or not the Eurogang definition of gang membership produced a class of youth that resembled what is typical of gang involved adolescents. Similar to Matsuda et al. (2012), Medina et al. (2013) found that the Eurogang definition strategy produced a sample of youth with disproportionately high levels of delinquent and criminal involvement, as one might suspect. Dissection of their results, however, revealed that the strategy may have misidentified drug-using youth groups as gangs, where their other associated behaviors did not coincide with traditional gang norms of conduct, such as elevated levels of violence, which is often considered a critical element of gang activities (Decker 1996; Melde and Esbensen 2013). But, some research suggests that there are specialty gangs that concentrate on specific forms of illegal activity and do not conform to the wider finding of "cafeteria-style" delinquency of gangs (e.g., Klein and Maxson 2006).

Together, these studies suggest that the Eurogang strategy for measuring gang involvement appears quite adept at identifying a subset of individuals with heightened criminal propensities, but not a group synonymous with self-identified gang members, nor those who report associating with gangs. Limitations in the above studies, however, suggest further research on the practical application of these various gang identification strategies is necessary. For instance, both Matsuda et al. (2012) and Medina et al. (2013) utilize cross-sectional data sources, which were adequate for their purposes, but fail to address another potential source for clarifying the unique impact of gang membership on youth: change in criminal and violent behaviors as a result of joining and leaving these groups. That is, research on youth gangs has generally been supportive of an enhancement framework (Thornberry et al. 1993), whereby youth who are already involved in delinquent and criminal behavior join a street gang, only to report a substantive increase in involvement in these behaviors (Gordon et al. 2004; Melde and Esbensen 2011, 2014; Pyrooz and Decker 2013). Use of panel data, which can explore within individual changes in behaviors associated with transitions into and out of gangs, can be utilized to determine whether or not involvement in these groups produces comparable rates of change in behavior, consistent with the body of work suggesting an enhancement in offending as a result of gang membership. Further, given both theory (Decker 1996) and research (Melde and Esbensen 2013; Pyrooz and Decker 2013) suggesting gang membership has an especially pronounced impact on involvement in violence, one would expect that involvement in gangs, as indicated by any of the three aforementioned measures, should produce a disproportionate increase in acts of violence if they are capturing gang membership.

The current study makes use of recent advancements in Item Response Theory (IRT) modeling of criminal propensity to conduct a test of construct validity associated with three measurements of gang membership—self-report, friends are a gang, and the Eurogang approach—by determining whether or not each of these measures impacts involvement in offending and violence in a manner consistent with theory and research on gang membership. We also explore whether or not involvement in gang groups, as measured in these three ways, produce comparable changes in offending and violence across these three groups. Specifically, our study seeks to answer the following questions:

1. Do the three measures of gang membership (i.e., self-report, friends are gang, and Eurogang) produce changes in overall offending propensity in a way consistent with theory and research?
2. Do the three measures of gang membership (i.e., self-report, friends are gang, and Eurogang) produce a disproportionate increase in the rate of involvement in violent behavior, over and above what is expected given their overall criminal propensity?
3. Do the three measures of gang membership (i.e., self-report, friends are gang, and Eurogang) lead to comparable changes in criminal propensity and violence involvement?

3.2 Data and Methods

We examine the relationship between multiple measures of gang membership and violence propensity using data collected as part of the second National Evaluation of the Gang Resistance Education and Training (G.R.E.A.T.) program (Esbensen et al. 2013). The survey component of this evaluation began in 2006 and was completed in 2011. Sites were selected based upon four primary criteria, including the existence of an established G.R.E.A.T. program, the desire to include sites from across the United States in order to obtain geographic diversity, the ability to obtain a diverse sample across demographic characteristics, and evidence of gang activity in the local community. Based upon these criteria, the following seven cities were included in the evaluation: Albuquerque, NM; Chicago, IL; a Dallas-Fort Worth area suburb; Greeley, CO; Nashville, TN; Philadelphia, PA; and Portland, OR. After securing agreements with school districts in each city, four to six schools were identified in each location that, together, would represent the district as a whole. A total of 31 schools were selected through this process, wherein a process of random assignment led to the identification of 102 treatment and 93 control classrooms. Active parental consent was obtained from 79 % of eligible students (Esbensen et al. 2008). Following the work of Melde and Esbensen (2013), the current study

Table 3.1 Sample descriptive statistics

	Total sample				
Level 1 (item level)	*n*	mean	s.d.	minimum	maximum
Delinquency frequency	185,348	.48	1.73	0	11
Level 2 (within person)					
Age	13,328	12.68	1.31	9	18
Age (centered at 11)		1.64	1.30	−2	7
Age squared		4.37	5.35	0	49
Eurogang member		.06	.23	0	1
Friends are gang members		.07	.26	0	1
Self-reported gang member		.05	.22	0	1
Level 3 (between person)					
Male	3726	.48	.50	0	1
White		.27	.45	0	1
Black		.18	.38	0	1
Hispanic		.40	.49	0	1
Other		.15	.36	0	1
Level 4 (school level)					
% Free and reduced lunch		.69	.24	.12	1.00

utilizes five waves of data with associated completion rates of 98, 95, 87, 82, and 75 % for the pre-, post- and 1-, 2-, and 3-year surveys, respectively. For a more complete description of the site selection process, consult Esbensen et al. (2013). For a more detailed description of the active consent procedures, see Esbensen et al. (2008).

This selection process resulted in a diverse sample for analysis, with a slight majority of female respondents (52 %) (see Table 3.1). The modal racial/ethnic background in the sample was Hispanic (40 %), followed by white (27 %), black (18 %), and those that reported some "other" category (15 %). Given the G.R.E.A.T. program is regularly taught in the sixth grade, almost two-thirds of the sample (61 %) reported being 11 or younger at the pretest.

3.2.1 Measures

Gang membership was measured in three unique ways in the current study. *Self-reported gang membership* was determined based upon the response to the following question across five waves of data: "Are you currently a gang member?" consistent with the work of Melde and Esbensen (2013). Those who responded "yes" to this question received a score of "1," while those who did not receive a score of "0." *Friends are a gang* was measured using the following question: "Do you consider your group of friends to be a gang?" consistent with Melde et al. (2009) and the International Self Report Delinquency Survey (Junger-Tas et al. 2010).

Table 3.2 Descriptive statistics for gang involved youth

	Gang status		
Years in a gang	Self-report	Friends are a gang	Eurogang
0	3308	3122	3086
1	322	430	464
2	104	171	169
3	46	59	64
4	31	27	27
5	9	11	10
Sex: male	58 %	60 %	54 %
Race/ethnicity			
Non-Hispanic White	16 %	16 %	23 %
Black/African-American	27 %	23 %	15 %
Hispanic/Latino	45 %	49 %	49 %
Other	12 %	12 %	13 %
Age at wave 1 [mean (s.d.)]	11.60 (.79)	11.64 (.77)	11.64 (.77)

Note: Group characteristics are based upon valid data, and represent the characteristics of those who reported belonging to a respective group on at least one occasion during the study

Those responding "yes" were coded "1," and those responding "no" received a "0." Finally, *Eurogang members* were identified using the funneling approach described above, wherein youth who answered a series of questions in a manner consistent with the criteria set forth in the Eurogang definition of a street gang were coded as a "1," and all others coded "0." Specifically, youth who reported having a peer group had to answer all of the following questions in a manner consistent with the Eurogang definition:

- "How long has this group existed or how long has your group of friends been hanging out together?"
- "Does this group spend a lot of time together in public places like the park, the street, shopping areas, or the neighborhood?"
- "Which one of the following best describes the ages of most of the people in your group?"
- "Are illegal things accepted by or okay for your group?"
- "Do people in your group actually do things together that are against the law?"

Unlike popular belief, gang membership does not typically last more than a year or two, meaning that most youth are in and out of gangs in a rather short period of time (Esbensen and Huizinga 1993; Peterson et al. 2004; Thornberry et al. 2003). Table 3.2 demonstrates this phenomenon across all three gang groups included in the current study. As can be seen in the table, the modal number of years involved in a gang is one for self-reported gang members, those who identify their friends are gang members, and Eurogang identified youth, with the number of youth reporting multiple waves of any type of gang involvement diminishing substantially beyond this single year. This suggests there is a lot of movement into and out of gangs during the study period.

Table 3.2 also provides descriptive information on those respondents who reported involvement in gangs at some point during the study. While a slight majority of the study sample was female (52 %; see Table 3.1), a small majority of respondents in each gang group are male. Non-Hispanic white youth are underrepresented in each gang group, relative to their absolute representation in the study sample (i.e., 27 %), although there are slightly more white respondents in the Eurogang category (23 %) than in the self-report (16 %) and friends are a gang (16 %) groups. African-American respondents appear less likely to be in Eurogang designated groups (15 %) than in either self-report (27 %) or friends as gang groups (23 %). Hispanic/Latino respondents were overrepresented in each group relative to their representation in the overall sample (i.e., 40 %), where 45 % of self-reported gang members, 49 % of friends as gang, and 49 % of Eurogang members reported this ethnicity. Finally, the mean age across gang groups was very similar.

Delinquency. Our measure of criminal propensity is identical to that used by Melde and Esbensen (2013), who followed the work of Osgood and Schreck (2007). Twelve delinquency items were used in our outcome measure, including less serious acts of deviance such as having "skipped classes without an excuse," to very serious offenses such as "used a weapon or force to get money or things from people." The full list of items included in this measure are available in Appendix 3.1, including their associated means and standard deviations across all waves included in the study. Available responses represented a count of the number of times the respondent committed the offense in the previous 6 months, with a maximum response of 11, which indicated having participated in the activity "more than ten" times in the preceding 6 months. Altogether, this measure follows a Poisson distribution, whereby the overall mean (.48) is substantially less than the standard deviation (1.73; see Table 3.1), indicating that most youth are not involved in these activities, but a small minority of respondents are involved in a substantial number of such acts.

Demographics. Demographic variables (i.e., sex, race/ethnicity, age) were included as controls to account for potential systematic differences across groups in criminal propensity and involvement in violence. Biological sex was measured as a dichotomy, with male equal to one, and female equal to zero. For race/ethnicity, a series of dummy variables were included in the models, including black/African American, Hispanic/Latino, and a variable for "other" race/ethnicity. Non-Hispanic/white respondents were omitted from all models, and thus served as the reference group. The mean age across study observations was 12.64, with a standard deviation of 1.31, and the range in ages was from 9 to 18 across the study period. Age was group mean centered at 11 in all models to ease in interpretation of study findings.

Percent Free or Reduced Lunch. Because of the nested structure of the data, with students clustered by school, it is possible that school level processes could impact student behavior. We included a measure of the percent of students on free and reduced lunch for each school to account for the influence of community-level socioeconomic status. As shown in Table 3.1, the mean percent of students on free or reduced lunch was 69 % (standard deviation = .24) across all schools, although the range was from 12 to 100 % of students. To ease interpretation, this variable was grand mean centered in multivariate models.

3.3 Analysis Strategy

To measure the potential influence of our measures of gang membership on criminal propensity and the odds of involvement in violent offending, we followed the procedures outlined in Melde and Esbsensen (2013). They combined the IRT methodologies discussed by Raudenbush et al. (2003), Johnson and Raudenbush (2006), and Osgood and Schreck (2007),[1] which are based on Rasch model assumptions. Under these assumptions, the probability of criminal behavior is the product of two factors, criminal propensity and the severity of the offense under question.

[1] In the style of notation used by Raudenbush and Bryk (2002), the Level 1 regression equation is:

$$\ln(\lambda ij) = \psi_{0tij} + \psi_{1tij} Violence + \sum_{i=2}^{I-1} \psi_{xtij} D_{ij} \tag{3.1}$$

The Level 2 regression equations are:

$$\psi_{0tij} = \pi_{00ij} + \pi_{01ij} * (\mathrm{X}_{1tij}) + \pi_{02ij} * (\mathrm{X}_{2tij}) + \ldots + e_{0tij} \tag{3.2}$$

$$\psi_{1tij} = \pi_{10ij} + \pi_{11ij} * (\mathrm{X}_{1tij}) + \pi_{12ij} * (\mathrm{X}_{2tij}) + \ldots + e_{1tij} \tag{3.3}$$

$$\psi_{xtij} = \pi_{x0ij} \tag{3.4}$$

The Level 3 regression equations are:

$$\pi_{00ij} = \beta_{000j} + \beta_{001j} * (X_{1ij}) + \beta_{002j} * (X_{2ij}) + \ldots + r_{00ij} \tag{3.5}$$

$$\pi_{10ij} = \beta_{100j} + \beta_{101j} * (\mathrm{X}_{1ij}) + \beta_{102j} * (\mathrm{X}_{2ij}) + \ldots + r_{10ij} \tag{3.6}$$

$$\pi_{xj} = \beta_j \tag{3.7}$$

The Level 4 Regression Equations are:

$$\beta_{000j} = \gamma_{0000} + \gamma_{0001} * (X_{1j}) + u_{000j} \tag{3.8}$$

$$\beta_{100j} = \gamma_{1000} + \gamma_{1001} * (X_{1j}) + u_{100j} \tag{3.9}$$

$$\beta_{xj} = \gamma_{xj} \tag{3.10}$$

Therefore, by controlling for crime severity in our models, which is assumed to be an inverse function of the frequency with which the crime is reported in the study sample overall (i.e., the more frequently the crime is reported in the sample, the less serious the crime is considered) we can identify criminal propensity. To control for crime severity, item indicator variables for each delinquency item included in the study are included at the first level of a hierarchical linear model as part of a measurement model (Osgood and Schreck 2007). The resulting coefficients related to each item indicator control for relative item severity across time (see Appendix 3.1), and are treated as fixed. The resulting coefficients in multivariate analyses, therefore, equal their correlation with criminal propensity. Given the structure of the data utilized in the current study, where students are nested within schools, the model utilized in the current study had to incorporate four levels of analysis, where individual offense items (i.e., the measurement model; level 1) are nested within time (i.e., observations of people over time; level 2), which are nested within individual respondents (i.e., time stable person characteristics; level 3), who are nested in 31 schools (i.e., school level characteristics; level 4).

Osgood and Schreck (2007) utilized this IRT framework to produce a novel statistical procedure to disentangle overall criminal propensity from an associated measure of the odds of involvement in violence. To do so, they proposed including two latent variables at level 1, the first representing overall offending propensity (ψ_{0j}), as discussed above, and the second, which represents a measure of violence specialization (ψ_{1j}). This measure of violence specialization is identified through the inclusion of a group-mean-centered dummy variable, "Violence," which is set to one for each variable that represents a violent offense, and minus one for each variable that represents a nonviolent act. By including two latent constructs in the level 1 measurement model, separate equations can be utilized to examine the correlates of overall offending propensity and the measure of violence specialization. Coefficients related to the measure of violence specialization are interpreted as the difference in the log of the expected event-rate for violent offense items to the log of the expected event-rate for nonviolent offense items (McGloin et al. 2011). Youth who never report gang membership of any kind serve as the reference category in these analyses, and thus a positive coefficient related to the violence specialization term suggests that the group is involved in a larger proportion of violent to nonviolent crime than those who never reported gang membership, while a negative score is associated with a lower proportion of violent to nonviolent offending. Importantly, a negative score does not indicate the group engages in less violence in absolute terms, rather, it suggests that of the offenses committed a smaller proportion is violent.

Use of five waves of panel data allowed us to incorporate time varying predictors in the model at the second level. We account for within individual change in gang status by including all three dichotomous measures of gang membership from each wave of data collection as predictors of overall criminal propensity (ψ_{0j}) and our measure of violence specialization (ψ_{1j}).[2] To account for potentially systematic

[2] Collinearity diagnostics suggest that this is not a problem in the current data. No variance inflation factor (VIF) scores were 2.00 or above.

Table 3.3 Repeated measures reliability and variance of overall offending and violence specialization

	Overall offending			
	Level 1	Level 2	Level 3	Level 4
Reliability	.946	.725	.791	–
Variance (τ)	1.15*		1.71*	.16*
	Violence specialization			
	Level 1	Level 2	Level 3	Level 4
Reliability	.738	.503	.672	–
Variance (τ)	.22*		.20*	.02*

*$p < .05$ (chi-square)

Note: Results are based on the unit-specific nonlinear model with the log link function and full penalized quasi-likelihood (PQL) estimation using an overdispersed Poisson regression

changes in criminal propensity and involvement in violence as the result of aging, we also included a time varying indicator of respondent age, centered at 11, as well as a measure of age squared. This specification provides information on whether or not there are systematic intra-individual changes associated with gang status transitions and aging. Demographic characteristics that do not change across time were incorporated at level three of our hierarchical model to account for between individual variance in both latent constructs. Lastly, to account for correlated errors among youth surveyed in the same school, as well as the potential influence of school context, we incorporated a measure of the percent of students on free or reduced lunch at each school at level four. For a more detailed description of these modeling procedures, see Melde and Esbensen (2013). As is often the case in studies using a count of delinquent and criminal behaviors as an outcome, an overdispersed poisson regression model with a log link function is utilized. By default with four level models in HLM 7.00 for Windows (Raudenbush et al. 2011), results are based upon penalized quasi-likelihood estimation.

3.4 Results

We begin our results section by determining whether there is enough variation in our latent constructs across levels to support our proposed four-level hierarchical model as well as by discussing overall model fit. Consistent with Melde and Esbensen (2013), there was significant variation in our two latent constructs across levels, which supports our use of a four level model (see Table 3.3). As was the case in other research examining violence specialization consistent with Osgood and Schreck's (2007) model specification, reliability estimates related to overall offending propensity are higher than for violence specialization. Further, we used the Bayesian Information Criterion as a measure of model fit (Snijders and Bosker 1999),[3] and compared these figures across an unconditional model, which includes

[3] Our measure of the BIC was calculated as $BIC = -2LL + [\ln(n)*p]$, where p is the number of parameters in the model, and n was the total number of observations at level 1.

Table 3.4 Repeated measures IRT analysis of the effect of gang status on overall offending and violence propensity

	Overall offending			Violence propensity		
	Coefficient	s.e.	IRR	Coefficient	s.e.	IRR
Intercept	−3.23*	.32	.04	.33	.41	1.39
Percent free and reduced lunch	.83*	.20	2.30	−.15	.09	.86
Male	.34*	.04	1.41	.10*	.02	1.10
Race/ethnicity (White = reference)						
Black	.03	.07	1.03	.02	.04	1.02
Hispanic	−.07	.06	.93	−.04	.03	.96
Other	−.03	.07	.97	−.05	.04	.96
Age (centered at 11)	.34*	.03	1.40	−.06*	.02	.94
Age squared	−.03*	.01	.97	−.00	.00	1.00
Eurogang defined gang member	1.00*	.05	2.72	−.08*	.03	.93
Friends in a gang	.75*	.05	2.11	.06*	.03	1.06
Self-reported gang membership	.99*	.06	2.70	.18*	.03	1.20

*$p < .05$
Note: Results are based on the unit-specific nonlinear model with the log link function and full penalized quasi-likelihood (PQL) estimation using an overdispersed Poisson regression

only our item indicators and violence specialization term (13 parameters), and our fully specified model (33 parameters). Results suggest substantive improvement in model fit for our fully specified model (i.e., unconditional = −278,339.81; full model = −278,183.82; Δ BIC = 155.99) over our unconditional model. Together, this information suggests our hierarchical modeling strategy is supported by the data, and thus we move on to a discussion of our study results.

Given that our research questions are related to our measures of overall criminal propensity and violence specialization, we discuss our results related to these latent constructs separately. First, with respect to overall criminal propensity, results suggest that a one-unit increase in the percent of students receiving free and reduced lunch was associated with a .83 ($p < .05$) unit increase in crime propensity (see Table 3.4). Consistent with prior research, males are significantly more crime prone than female respondents (coefficient = .34; $p < .05$). Overall, as youth aged their criminal propensity increased (coefficient = .34; $p < .05$), although this increase was tempered across time given a significant and negative age squared term (coefficient = −.03; $p < .05$). With respect to our measures of gang membership, an interesting pattern emerged. All three measures of gang membership produced an effect consistent with the enhancement framework, whereby periods of gang membership were associated with a substantive increase in criminal propensity. In fact, relative to observations of non-gang youth, the impact of Eurogang defined gang membership (coefficient = 1.00; $p < .05$) and self-reported gang membership (coefficient = .99; $p < .05$) produced a nearly identical impact on criminal propensity, whereas having friends in a gang produced a slightly smaller impact (coefficient = .75; $p < .05$).

Examination of the impact of these correlates on involvement in violent incidents, which again is interpreted as the difference in the log of the expected event-rate for violent items to the log of the expected event-rate for nonviolent items, suggests the processes associated with changes in criminal propensity are not synonymous with those correlated with changes in violence specialization. Unlike overall criminal propensity, the percent of students on free and reduced lunch is not significantly correlated with violence specialization. Male youth reported a significantly higher ratio of violent-to-nonviolent offending than females (coefficient = .10, $p < .05$). While overall offending propensity increased with age, the likelihood of violent offending actually decreased over time (coefficient = −.06, $p < .05$). Consistent with theory and research, periods of involvement in gangs, as measured through self-reported gang membership (coefficient = .18, $p < .05$) and having friends in a gang (coefficient = .06, $p < .05$) was associated with significant increases in the likelihood of violent over nonviolent offending. With respect to self-reported gang membership, periods of involvement in these groups was associated with a 20 % increase in the odds of violent-to-nonviolent criminal involvement, whereas having friends in a gang led to a 6 % increase. Inconsistent with gang research, when youth were involved with peer groups consistent with the Eurogang definition of gang membership their ratio of violent-to-nonviolent offending was actually lower than that of non-gang involved youth (coefficient = −.08, $p < .05$). That is, the pattern of delinquent and criminal involvement among Eurogang identified youth was systematically nonviolent, relative to non-gang involved youth.

3.5 Discussion

Research on adolescent youth gangs has exploded since 1990 (Pyrooz and Mitchell 2015) with more than 500 articles appearing in academic journals during a recent 2-year period (2012 and 2013). In spite of this volume of coverage, a lingering concern continues to challenge researchers, and, importantly, practitioners and policy makers; that is, are gang-involved youth accurately identified via contemporary methods? In this chapter, we examined the validity of three commonly accepted strategies for assessing gang membership (self-nomination, friends are a gang, and the Eurogang definition) by investigating changes in criminal and violence propensity of youth as they entered and left groups captured by each definitional approach.

Violence plays an important role in the lives of gang youth and a substantial body of research reports that gang membership is associated with elevated levels of not only overall offending, but violent offending in particular (e.g., Decker 1996; Melde and Esbensen 2013; Peterson et al. 2004). An important question is whether the increase in violence is simply a result of committing more crime in general or whether gang joining leads to a greater increase in violence relative to the increase in overall offending. That is, are gang members violent simply because they are frequent offenders who also happen to engage in violence? Or, do they engage in a disproportionate level of violence relative to their rate of offending? We speculated that gang-identified youth, regardless of definitional criteria should report elevated levels of violence relative to their overall offending levels and that both of these offending types would be significantly greater than those of non-gang youth.

In order to examine our hypothesis, we merged two prior avenues of research. First, as presented in the recent collection of Eurogang research, Matsuda et al. (2012) compared the demographic, attitudinal, and behavioral similarities and differences of gang members identified by these three definitions (self-nomination, friends are a gang, and the Eurogang definition). They found some idiosyncratic differences but concluded that each method captured a group of adolescents who were significantly different from non-gang identified youth and that the three gang groups are, overall, quite similar. Second, we drew upon earlier work by Melde and Esbensen (2013), which utilized the self-nomination approach and found that gang youth had a 21 % increase in their violent to nonviolent offending relative to non-gang youth (Melde and Esbensen 2013). The current chapter expands on these two prior studies to further compare the validity of differing gang definitions. That is, are the findings of enhanced violent offending replicated when using different measures of gang affiliation? To guide our analyses, we posed three questions: (1) Do the three measures of gang membership (i.e., self-report, friends are gang, and Eurogang) produce changes in overall offending propensity consistent with prior gang research; (2) do they produce a disproportionate increase in the rate of involvement in violent behavior, over and above what is expected given their overall criminal propensity; and (3) do they lead to comparable changes in criminal propensity and violence involvement?

In regard to the first research question, the results presented here suggest a similarity across these definitional approaches on overall criminal propensity. All three measures of gang membership were associated with elevated levels of overall criminal propensity as youth entered these groups. Importantly, and in response to our third research question, all three definitions produced increases in criminal propensity of relatively similar magnitude. In other words, all three definitions demonstrated high construct validity in that they produced similarly elevated levels of criminal propensity. Turning our attention to our second research question, the results point to a qualified yes. Two of the groups of gang-identified youth (self-identified and friends a gang) reported higher levels of involvement in violent offending relative to their overall criminal propensity. On the other hand, the Eurogang group reported a ratio of violent-to-nonviolent offending that was lower than that of non-gang youth. However, it is important to note that this does not mean that youth included in the Eurogang group are not violent; only that their ratio of involvement in violence relative to their involvement in overall offending is lower than the ratio for non-gang youths. Given they are just as likely to be involved in overall offending as the other two gang-identified groups, controlling for severity, means they are likely involved in violence, but just at a rate below our other measures of gang membership and non-gang youths. With respect to the magnitude of these differences (i.e., our third research question), the changes in violent offending were largest for self-reported gang youth, although those who reported having friends that were gang members demonstrated a significant increase in violent over nonviolent acts.

We know from prior research that the three different approaches to defining gang members produce different groups of youth—recall that Matsuda et al. (2012) found only a 33 % overlap in youth fitting two or three of the definitions. However, as reported by Matsuda et al. (2012), the gang youth, regardless of definition are higher risk than the non-gang youth. They express more antisocial attitudes and report engaging in more criminal activity than non-gang youth. Not only do the gang youth, regardless of definition engage in more offending in general, they also commit more violence. However, the ratio of violent offending to overall offending is greater for only two of the definitional approaches (self-nomination and friends are a gang). The Eurogang group committed more violent offenses than non-gang youth by virtue of their absolute level of involvement in crime and delinquency more broadly, but their proportion of violent to nonviolent behavior was actually less than non-gang youth. Future research on the Eurogang method for identifying gang involved youth should seek to identify the sources of these differences in behavior change as a result of group membership. For instance, perhaps there are group-level differences across these methods of gang identification that may affect group processes that promote violence, as was discussed by Melde and Esbensen (2013). After all, given that the current study was conducted entirely in the US context, where the word gang is well known and carries with it an expectation for violence, belonging to a delinquent peer group that does not call itself a gang may not support such activities to the extent of groups who openly identify as a gang. For instance, it is entirely possible that the groups identified through the Eurogang definition are similar to those identified by Medina et al. (2013) as recreational drug users. Our analyses, however, did not include recreational drug use in the models, and thus our Eurogang defined gang members appear to be involved in a large number of property crimes and nonviolent delinquencies, but their proportion of violent acts is relatively low compared to non-gang youth. Future research should further explore the relative involvement in drug use across these gang definitions.

Overall, the findings reported here lend further support to the conclusions reached by Matsuda et al. (2012) that each definitional approach identifies youth who are significantly more "at risk." This points to an important conclusion for practitioners and policy makers, that if the purpose of identifying gang-involved youth is to provide prevention and intervention services, then any of these unique definitions is likely to identify appropriate youth. If the goal is to address violence reduction, specifically, then youth identified through the self-nomination or friends are gangs would be better options. The overarching conclusion, however, is that regardless of definition or analytic strategies, youth who are identified as gang-involved contribute disproportionately to the crime problem in general and in the form of violence in particular. The enhanced propensity to commit violence suggests that there is indeed some feature of the gang that promotes this particular type of behavior and therefore may warrant special intervention strategies.

Acknowledgements This research was made possible, in part, by the support and participation of seven school districts, including the School District of Philadelphia. This project was supported by the National Institute of Justice, Office of Justice Programs, U.S. Department of Justice, award No. 2006-JV-FX-0011. The opinions, findings, and conclusions or recommendations expressed in this publication are those of the authors and do not necessarily reflect the views of the Department of Justice or of the seven participating school districts.

Note: An earlier version of this chapter was originally presented at the 2013 meeting of the Eurogang Program of Research, on the campus of the University of Kent in Canterbury, UK.

Appendix 3.1: Descriptive Statistics and Estimated Item Severity

	Volume	Frequency					Coefficient	
Item		Wave 1	Wave 2	Wave 3	Wave 4	Wave 5	Estimate	S.E.
Avoided paying for things such as movies, bus, or subway rides	No	.42(1.59)	.79(1.74)	.70(2.02)	.81(2.19)	.88(2.20)	*Reference*	
Skipped classes without an excuse	No	.31(1.27)	.52(1.64)	.82(2.07)	1.08(2.36)	1.59(2.99)	.59*	.01
Lied about your age to get into some place or to buy something	No	.75(1.97)	.87(2.18)	1.09(2.46)	1.03(2.37)	.88(2.25)	.73*	.01
Purposely damaged or destroyed property that did not belong to you	No	.54(1.64)	.66(1.91)	.89(2.23)	.74(2.00)	.63(1.91)	.43*	.01
Carried a hidden weapon for protection	Yes	.47(1.77)	.58(2.06)	.68(2.21)	.73(2.36)	.72(2.36)	−.54	.89
Illegally spray painted a wall or a building	No	.18(1.07)	.26(1.34)	.36(1.53)	.38(1.56)	.39(1.65)	−.42*	.02
Gone into or tried to go into a building to steal something	No	.12(.86)	.17(1.06)	.27(1.32)	.26(1.30)	.24(1.24)	−.82*	.02
Hit someone with the idea of hurting him/her	Yes	.81(2.16)	1.00(2.47)	1.15(2.60)	1.03(2.14)	.92(2.27)	−.06	.89
Attached someone with a weapon	Yes	.15(.99)	.20(1.18)	.22(1.22)	.20(1.21)	.19(1.14)	−1.74	.89
Used a weapon or force to get money or things from people	Yes	.07(.66)	.09(.76)	.13(.99)	.15(1.10)	.12(.95)	−2.38*	.89
Been involved in gang fights	Yes	.33(1.49)	.35(1.57)	.40(1.64)	.45(1.73)	.37(1.62)	−1.05	.89
Sold marijuana or other illegal drugs	No	.05 (.61)	.10(.91)	.19(1.19)	.26(1.44)	.32(1.56)	−.99*	.02

*$p < .05$

Note: Individual wave frequencies represent means and (standard deviations). Coefficient estimates represent estimated item severity

References

Barrows, J., & Huff, C. R. (2009). Gangs and public policy: Constructing and deconstructing gang databases. *Criminology & Public Policy, 8*(4), 675–703.
Curry, G. D. (2000). Self-reported gang involvement and officially recorded delinquency. *Criminology, 38*(4), 1253–1274.
Curry, G. D., Decker, S. H., & Egley, A., Jr. (2002). Gang involvement and delinquency in a middle school population. *Justice Quarterly, 19*(2), 275–292.
Decker, S. H. (1996). Collective and normative features of gang violence. *Justice Quarterly, 13*(2), 245–264.
Decker, S. H., Pyrooz, D. C., Sweeten, G., & Moule, R. K., Jr. (2014). Validating self-nomination in gang research: Assessing differences in gang embeddedness across non-, current, and former gang members. *Journal of Quantitative Criminology, 30*(4), 577–598.
Esbensen, F.-A., & Huizinga, D. (1993). Gangs, drugs, and delinquency in a survey of urban youth. *Criminology, 31*(4), 565–589.
Esbensen, F.-A., & Maxson, C. L. (2012). The Eurogang Program of Research and multimethod comparative gang research: Introduction. In F.-A. Esbensen & C. L. Maxson (Eds.), *Youth gangs in international perspective* (pp. 1–14). New York: Springer.
Esbensen, F.-A., Melde, C., Taylor, T. J., & Peterson, D. (2008). Active parental consent in school-based research: How much is enough and how do we get it? *Evaluation Review, 32*(4), 335–362.
Esbensen, F.-A., Osgood, D. W., Peterson, D., Taylor, T. J., & Carson, D. C. (2013). Short- and long-term outcome results from a multisite evaluation of the G.R.E.A.T. Program. *Criminology & Public Policy, 12*(3), 375–411.
Esbensen, F.-A., Winfree, J., Thomas, L., He, N., & Taylor, T. J. (2001). Youth gangs and definitional issues: When is a gang a gang and why does it matter? *Crime & Delinquency, 47*(1), 105–130.
Gordon, R. A., Lahey, B. B., Kawai, E., Loeber, R., Stouthamer-Loeber, M., & Farrington, D. P. (2004). Antisocial behavior and youth gang membership: Selection and socialization. *Criminology, 42*(1), 55–87.
Johnson, C. S., & Raudenbush, S. W. (2006). A repeated measures, multilevel Rasch model with application to self-reported criminal behavior. In C. S. Bergeman & S. M. Boker (Eds.), *Methodological issues in aging research* (pp. 131–164). Mahwah, NJ: Erlbaum Press.
Junger-Tas, J., Marshall, I. H., Enzmann, D., Killias, M., Steketee, M., & Gruszczynska, B. (2010). *Juvenile delinquency in Europe and beyond: Results of the second international self-report delinquency study*. Dordrecht, NY: Springer.
Katz, J., & Jackson-Jacobs, C. (2004). The criminologists' gang. In C. Summer (Ed.), *The Blackwell companion to criminology* (pp. 91–124). Oxford, England: Blackwell.
Klein, M., Kerner, H.-J., Maxson, C. L., & Weitekamp, E. G. M. (Eds.). (2001). *The Eurogang paradox: Street gangs and youth groups in the U.S. and Europe*. Dordecht, The Netherlands: Kluwer.
Klein, M., & Maxson, C. L. (2006). *Street gang patterns and policies*. New York: Oxford University Press.
Matsuda, K. N., Esbensen, F.-A., & Carson, D. C. (2012). Putting the "gang" in "Eurogang" characteristics of delinquent youth groups by definitional approaches. In F.-A. Esbensen & C. L. Maxson (Eds.), *Youth gangs in international perspective: Results from the Eurogang Program of Research* (pp. 17–34). New York: Springer.
McGloin, J. M., Schreck, C. J., Stewart, E. A., & Ousey, G. C. (2011). Predicting the violent offender: The discriminant validity of the subculture of violence. *Criminology, 49*(3), 767–794.
Medina, J., Aldridge, J., Shute, J., & Ross, A. (2013). Measuring gang membership in England and Whales: A latent class analysis with Eurogang survey questions. *European Journal of Criminology, 10*(5), 597–605.

Melde, C., & Esbensen, F.-A. (2011). Gang membership as a turning point in the life course. *Criminology, 49*(2), 513–552.
Melde, C., & Esbensen, F.-A. (2013). Gangs and violence: Disentangling the impact of gang membership on the level and nature of offending. *Journal of Quantitative Criminology, 29*(2), 143–166.
Melde, C., & Esbensen, F.-A. (2014). The relative impact of gang status transitions: Identifying the mechanisms of change in delinquency. *Journal of Research in Crime and Delinquency, 51*(3), 349–376.
Melde, C., Taylor, T. J., & Esbensen, F.-A. (2009). "I got your back": An examination of the protective function of gang membership in adolescence. *Criminology, 47*(2), 565–594.
Osgood, D. W., & Schreck, C. J. (2007). A new method for studying the extent, stability, and predictors of individual specialization in violence. *Criminology, 45*(2), 273–312.
Peterson, D., Taylor, T. J., & Esbensen, F.-A. (2004). Gang membership and violent victimization. *Justice Quarterly, 21*(4), 794–816.
Pyrooz, D. C., & Decker, S. H. (2013). Delinquent behavior, violence, and gang involvement in China. *Journal of Quantitative Criminology, 29*(2), 251–272.
Pyrooz, D. C., & Mitchell, M. M. (2015). Little gang research, big gang research. In S. H. Decker & D. C. Pyrooz (Eds.), *The handbook of gangs* (pp. 28–58). Malden, MA: Wiley.
Raudenbush, S. W., & Bryk, A. S. (2002). *Hierarchical linear models: Applications and data analysis methods*. Thousand Oaks, CA: Sage.
Raudenbush, S. W., Bryk, A. S., & Congdon, R. (2011). *HLM 7.0 for Windows (Version 7.0)*. Skokie, IL: Scientific Software International.
Raudenbush, S. W., Johnson, C. S., & Sampson, R. J. (2003). A multivariate, multilevel Rasch model with application to self-reported criminal behavior. *Sociological Methodology, 33*(1), 169–211.
Snijders, T. A., & Bosker, R. (1999). *Multilevel analysis: An introduction to basic and advanced multilevel modeling*. London: Sage.
Thornberry, T. P., Krohn, M. D., Lizotte, A. J., Smith, C. A., & Tobin, K. (2003). *Gangs and delinquency in developmental perspective*. New York: Cambridge.
Thornberry, T. P., Krohn, M. D., Lizotte, A. J., & Chad-Wiershem, D. (1993). The role of juvenile gangs in facilitating delinquent behavior. *Journal of Research in Crime and Delinquency, 30*(1), 55–87.

Chapter 4
Fear and Retaliation: Gang Violence in Brussels and Caracas

Ellen Vandenbogaerde and Elke Van Hellemont

4.1 Introduction

This chapter aims to compare qualitative research findings on gang-motivated violence in two very different cities, Brussels and Caracas. This introductory section engages briefly with the existing literature on gang violence, before exploring respective research contexts and methodologies in the next section. Subsequent empirical sections outline some similarities in gang violence that transcend these contexts, underlining the core argument; that the characteristics of gang-motivated violence itself, rather than the gang group or its ostentatious rules, facilitate further violence.

In what follows we use "gang violence" to refer to "gang-motivated violence" (Rosenfeld et al. 1999), that is, violence that is committed by one or more gang member(s) in alleged defense of the gang or one of its members, values, and/or territory. It is a form of "social control," punishment for a past wrong, but also deterrence of future wrongs (Black 1983; Jacobs 2004). This understanding explicitly excludes "gang affiliated" violence, which may be committed by gang members outside of their "gang identities," such as for instance intimate partner violence committed by a gang member (Klein and Maxson 2006).

Several scholars grant the premise that "a gang facilitates violent behavior among members" the status of "a universal given" (Wood and Alleyne 2010, p. 101). Some even state that "to ignore that, is to ignore (or worse, to excuse) the

E. Vandenbogaerde (✉)
School of Global Studies, University of Sussex, Brighton, UK
e-mail: ellen.vdb@sussex.ac.uk

E. Van Hellemont
Leuven Institute of Criminology (Linc), KU Leuven (University of Leuven), Leuven, Belgium
e-mail: Elke.VanHellemont@law.kuleuven.be

C.L. Maxson, F.-A. Esbensen (eds.), *Gang Transitions and Transformations in an International Context*, DOI 10.1007/978-3-319-29602-9_4

violence gang members commit against each other and their communities" (Curry and Decker 1997, p. 514). Many studies find that gang members (1) commit significantly more violence while they are active as a gang member than before or after leaving the gang (Melde and Esbensen 2013; Thornberry et al. 1993) and (2) that gang members commit more violence over and beyond the association with offender peers (Battin-Pearson et al. 1998), other youth groups (Esbensen et al. 2001), or delinquent peer groups (Battin et al. 1998). Thornberry et al. (1993, p. 81) conclude that "Clearly, being in the gang is generative of violent behavior among these boys." Despite these strong claims and the significant amount of research conducted, these studies leave us largely in the dark about how to understand the "gang effect" on the commission of violent behavior. In other words, while a "facilitation" effect is generally accepted, its particulars aren't well understood (Decker et al. 2012; Matsuda et al. 2013).

This chapter argues this facilitation effect remains obscure partly because it is often attributed to some "unique" aspect of the gang or its members rather than the violent behavior itself. Many researchers use cultural value or "street code" (Anderson 2000) explanations for gang violence that classify this type of violence as part of a stand-alone "gang culture." They regularly measure to what extent individual gang members subscribe to this code to explain the violence they use, foregoing the group nature of this violence (Brezina et al. 2004; Matsuda et al. 2013; Stewart and Simons 2006). Other authors have indeed looked at how the process of violence itself generates expectations for further violence and a "normative structure" by which violence becomes an *expected* response to threats (real or perceived), fosters group cohesion, and ultimately legitimates the "gang" itself (Decker 1996; Hennigan and Spanovic 2012). Fagan et al. (2007) talk of an "ecology of danger," in which expectations of future violence generate environments, where violence spreads quickly. These approaches often acknowledge the central role played by retaliation in gang violence (Decker 1996; Klein and Maxson 1989; Papachristos 2009).

This chapter contributes to these process approaches by identifying some characteristics of gang violence that are constant across two distinct empirical contexts that have not received much scholarly attention. It thus contributes to the literature in two ways. First, what is known about gangs is based predominantly on research conducted in North America. This chapter takes advantage of the global diversity of gangs by exploring gang violence in two otherwise unrelated and little researched capital cities: Brussels (Belgium, Europe) and Caracas (Venezuela, Latin America). While these cities are almost polar opposites and experience gang "problems" on different scales, similar processes are found to operate, permitting greater confidence in the validity of the findings (Gerring 2007). Secondly, this chapter builds upon process approaches to gang violence, by disentangling some characteristics of retaliation and drawing on insights from social psychology and sociology to show how this violence ends up reproducing itself, as well as group boundaries. It draws specifically on the social psychological literature on "Groupthink" (Janis 1982) to illustrate how cohesive groups are subject to a number of cognitive distortions, leading to illogical consequences, in this case often incompetent violence. Collins

(2009) used the term "incompetent" violence to illustrate how violence is typically "hard," people need to overcome substantial emotional barriers for violence to be "successful." He argues that much violence is actually unsuccessful and "incompetent"; innocent bystanders are hit, or nobody is hit at all. He describes gang violence in particular as essentially unfair; gang members overcome the emotional barriers to violence by attacking weak victims. This type of violence, and the fear it generates, reinforces the need for carrying weapons, but also belonging to a gang and ultimately strengthens group boundaries.

We argue that these processes are endogenous to gang violence rather than attributable to a gang code, culture, or "milieu." What is "essential" about gangs is not a cultural "code" or "set of values"; it is the nature of the violence they use. Rather than seeing a "code of violence" as a stand-alone driver of gang violence, we identify some characteristics of retaliation that legitimate the violence, as well as the gang in both of the contexts that were studied. The similarities between these disparate research contexts question the existence of a "unique" cultural value system, but draw attention to the dynamics and processes of violence itself. It shows how retaliatory violence generates the conditions that "facilitate" gang group cohesion and further violence.

4.2 Methods

Table 4.1 shows a number of socio-demographic indicators for the cities and respective countries, where the research was conducted. Venezuela ranks 47 places behind Belgium in terms of its Human Development Index (67th vs. 21st), an indicator that combines average incomes, education levels, and life expectancy. Their respective capitals, Caracas and Brussels, are almost 8000 km apart. Both are ethnically and

Table 4.1 Socio-demographic comparison of research locations

	Human development index (HDR 2014)	Income poverty (%) (OGWB, INE 2011)	Population (official country estimates, 2014)	Inhabitants/km^2 (official country estimates, 2014)	Homicide rates/100,000 (UNODC 2014)
Belgium	0.881	15	11,198,638	364	1.6
Brussels	n/a	33	1,138,854	7025	2.6
Venezuela	0.764	33	30,206,307	30	53.7
Caracas	n/a	13	1,943,901	4489	122

Note 1. For Caracas, data refer to the "Capital District," which does not include all of Caracas' municipalities

Note 2. For Belgian poverty data, the poverty line is defined as earnings of at least 60 % of the median national income. In Venezuela, the value of the basic food basket is used as a poverty line. These numbers cannot thus technically be compared; it is probable that Belgium's poverty figures would improve if the basic food basket were used and vice versa

racially diverse cities with high population densities and substantial poverty. Brussels has a population of 1.1 million people of which a third (33 %) live on an income below the poverty line (OGWB 2014). Surprisingly, income poverty in Caracas is lower (13 %) but a different standard[1] is used so these numbers may not reflect the same underlying variable. Caracas has low levels of poverty in relation to the rest of Venezuela, whereas Brussels has relatively high levels of poverty in comparison to the rest of Belgium. Importantly, in Brussels, many of the poor are "captured" by the state, receiving some sort of state benefits (OGWB 2014). The majority of Caracas' almost two million people live in informally constructed "barrios," surrounding more exclusive wealthy centers. The "state" is almost nonexistent; people rely on informal networks for the provision of various services. Venezuela's youth gangs, "malandros" as they are colloquially referred to, have been around in these barrios for decades. They have institutionalized to varying degrees and are sometimes trusted more than a historically arbitrary police force. Black African gangs in Brussels are a more recent phenomenon and are closely related to Belgium's colonial past. These gangs are the result of an influx of refugees of the Democratic Republic of Congo in the beginning of the 90s, spurred by the atrocities that often tend to come along with situations of political instability.

Venezuela currently has the bleak reputation of being the second most violent country in the world with 53.7 homicides per 100,000 inhabitants, whereas Belgium ranks 194th, with 1.6 homicides per 100,000 (UNODC 2014). Both Caracas and Brussels have higher homicide rates than the national average. Nevertheless, Brussels' annual homicide rate of 2.6 per 100,000 is insignificant in comparison to Caracas' 122 per 100,000. Much of Venezuela's deadly violence is perpetrated with guns (up to 90 %, depending on the source) and attributable to "gangs." Police statistics classify up to 70 % of homicides to conflicts between gangs, using the ambiguous category of "settling of scores." Very little empirical research has explored this type of violence in Venezuela or its presumed protagonists (Zubillaga 2007; Rodgers and Baird 2015). In Belgium, a "gang" category is not even available in homicide statistics, and the only place where "gang crime" is registered at the police level is Brussels. Gang violence in Brussels mostly relates to less lethal assaults with knives, for which statistics are much more prone to reporting and recording biases. Nevertheless, even gang homicide statistics have their problems. For instance, none of five "gang homicides" in a 2009 police report[2] are actually attributable to conflicts *between* gangs.

In both cities, research was guided by traditional qualitative principles of detailed understanding and rich insight, rather than quantifiable explanation or generalization. The ethnographic fieldwork in Brussels involved a suite of qualitative data collection methods (30 in-depth tape-recorded ethnographic interviews with gang affiliated men, many informal interviews and 18-month participant observation with an active gang in Brussels). Fieldwork was conducted between January 2010

[1] Belgium's poverty data are calculated using the median income, Venezuela's using the basic food basket, see table notes.

[2] Internal Report, *Bandes Urbaines*, Police Ixelles-Capitale, 2009.

and June 2011. Observation-as-participant research was undertaken with the *1140*, a group with an established gang reputation of about 30–40 first- or second-generation male Congolese migrants between 16 and 25 years old. The fieldwork involved moving to the Brussels' neighborhood perceived as the 1140s home base. Only 3 months after the start of the fieldwork in 2010, a member of their group, Gregorio, with whom the ethnographer was well acquainted, was lethally stabbed in revenge for a stabbing in 2008. As it involved a close-to-home ethnography, the contact with the group has remained for more than 4 years now. The tape-recorded interviews involved (ex-) members of different gangs (e.g., Finest, Black Face, Versailles, and Bagdad) and were conducted after the 18-month ethnographic research. The latter is essential as the ethnographic fieldwork substantially enhances the trust relationship between the researcher and interviewees. Together with the "insider position" acquired during the fieldwork, it augments the quality and even the trustworthiness of interview content.

The fieldwork in Venezuela also involved a varied set of data collection methods, including participant-observation and in-depth interviews with community stakeholders, local residents, and gang members in two different cities, Caracas and Cumana. In Caracas, over a period of 9 months and on top of field notes with observations and details of many more informal chats, 89 individual and 19 group interviews were recorded with a total of 155 unique respondents, of which 19 had at one point or another engaged in gangs. The original research goal in Venezuela was a better understanding of a theoretical relationship between inequality and violence, and it was not anticipated to engage with its "malandros." As fieldwork proceeded, it became clear these "malandros" are indeed responsible for most of the violence, and access was gained to a number of sites of encounter and exchange between them. In Caracas, one was a house; two others were street "spots" where boys convened in variable numbers to chat, laugh, play computer games, and/or sell and consume drugs. Two major drug transaction sites, where large quantities of drugs are transacted and rifles openly carried, were also visited.

In both studies, the position of the researchers is marked by an extreme "otherness." Both researchers were white Belgian females working with Latino or black African male groups and in both cases the language in which the research was performed was not their mother tongue. For more details on respective methodologies and research questions, see Van Hellemont (2015) and Vandenbogaerde (2016). The comparative analysis for this chapter involved a continuous dialogue between the two researchers, comparing and contrasting each other's research findings and field notes to identify similarities and differences between the respective research contexts.

4.3 The Predictable Unpredictability of Retaliation

In these substantially different contexts, surprisingly similar characteristics were found to steer gang violence. As outlined in the introduction, other researchers have referred to a "street code" (Anderson 2000), as a major determinant of gang violence.

Both in Brussels and Caracas, our observations showed that gangs indeed often made reference to an unwritten "code" to justify their use of violence. They claim to use violence only in response to perceived instances of "disrespect," violations of this "code." A closer look at this retaliatory violence shows it is defined more by uncertainties than clear rules. We found that, in Caracas as well as Brussels, the pernicious nature of gang violence lies not so much in a "code" but in six characteristics of retaliation that make its occurrence certain but its particulars vague. These uncertainties generate a pervasive fear, in which violence is often incompetent (Collins 2009) rather than "honorable."

First, there is the aspect of *infinity*. Every act of retaliation triggers in itself an act of counter retaliation, as this act is seen by its "victim(s)" as a new instance of disrespect, inevitably setting up vicious cycles of violence. There is no honorable losing, no final whistle. In Caracas gang members use a fitting metaphor for the conflicts they arouse, "la culebra," meaning snake. One murder generates "a 1000 culebras," as one gang member put it:

> It never stops! It always multiplies. (…) They might kill 500, instantly 1000 [new culebras] get out … like everything here, everyone, in different barrios, everyone is involved in 'culebras.'

In Brussels, the infinity aspect of retaliatory violence is captured with the idea of a never-ending game. Or as this older gang member explains:

> In the beginning, it is just a game. But then it becomes violent and later on it becomes even more violent. But once you realize what is happening, it is already too late. You are in the game and from that point on there is no way back.

Second, the aspect of *superiority* prescribes that every act of revenge should be at least equal, if not superior, to the act that triggered it. This continuous need for more elevated forms of violence often leads to escalation, as weapon behaviors spread and gangs engage in veritable arms races. Or as explained by this older "Black Face" gang member in Brussels:

> It started with knife attacks, and saws. After that it went to revolvers and all of that, you see. They always want to outdo the other […] So it's just to show that: 'Us? We're better than everyone else,' you see. 'Us, when we're there, it really kicks off!' When they come; they may have knives, we'd have revolvers […] It's just to show that the degree of violence is hefty.

Where knives do remain the weapons of choice in Brussels, in Caracas, guns have become the standard, as gangs similarly try to outdo each other. One of Caracas' interviewees, referring to the "code," puts it this way:

> There is respect. I'll treat you how you treat me. If you don't respect my family, I won't respect yours. If you don't respect me, I don't respect you. If you draw a gun on me, I'll draw you two, that's the code of today.

The third aspect is *omnipresence*: the game is always on. The "code" sets few rules that define conditions for retaliation. Thus, even when taking on the role of father, son, employee, or other quotidian characters, this characteristic entraps those who seek or sought revenge in the spiral of violence created by the former two aspects.

Malandros in Caracas say their role is to be continuously "pendiente" or "activo," always on guard for lurking danger. They are often prevented from finding stable employment as their "culebras" could easily establish where to find them. In Brussels, moving around in the city becomes increasingly problematic for gang members. Just crossing each other accidently can be enough to start a fight. To be safe from retaliatory acts, young men limit their movement throughout the city as much as possible. Or as this young *1140* explains:

> When we were in conflict with *Versailles* (*Brussels' gang*) [...] You know, at a certain point, the only walk I would do was from *Rue Germinal* to the school down the road. Every day I did nothing but this walk!

The fourth aspect is *obscurity*. Although the trigger for the desire to retaliate is clear at the start of the process, the spiral of violence obscures the initial event that started the process. Violence becomes but the remedy to wipe out the humiliation of a previous lost fight. Or, as explained by a member of *1140* in relation to the homicide that happened during the fieldwork in Brussels:

> Because of such a stupid thing, we lost Greg [Gregorio]. We don't even know why we started fighting in the first place. It becomes, it becomes so absurd! The fact that you're fighting over such stupid things. You do not even know why you started fighting anymore. It is stupid. It is just stupid.

In Caracas, the original reasons for culebras between sectors are completely obscured, decades of violence over and between have led to mere association with a different gang becoming a perfectly valid reason to shoot and kill. One respondent has this to say about the prospect of encountering people from another sector with which a culebra has existed ever since he started hanging out on the streets:

> I'll get my gun out fast. If I'm here and one of them comes by, I'll shoot him quick! I have to respond and kill him quickly, he can't be passing by here, I'm not going to his area either am I...

That retaliation can be applied to anyone associated with a gang brings us to the fifth aspect of *transitivity*. "Gangness" is metonymic in nature. This means that while a gang is understood as a collective, a group, the gang is represented by every young man who associates with it. As such, an assault on a gang member, or anyone close to them, always has the potential to generalize retaliation to a group level and thus to include many other young men in the process. Caracas' and Brussels' gang members explain it this way:

> (Caracas) Respondent 1: So, this guy wants another guy dead, but he's from another gang. So, it's already [a culebra] with you[r gang]... They got him and killed him and that's where it went off properly. We started killing people left, right and center. Respondent 2: It was like a massive war. So many people with so many other people. Respondent 1: After that they killed the brother of another mate, which just created more suffering ... There were like 2 or 3 deaths a day.
>
> (Brussels) For *1140*, whether you insulted Evere (Homebase of the gang *1140*) or attacked a person of the group, it is like you attacked all of us! That's the thing! This is what holds us together.

The sixth and final aspect is the only definite and most intrusive one, *fatalism*. The only certainty in retaliation, whether on the attacking or receiving end, is that it is coming and one has to face it. Refraining from retaliation labels a group in Brussels as “une bande de gamins”—a group of kids and their members as “bidons”—losers. Failure to retaliate does not result in being ignored or discarded, or escaping the vicious cycle of violence. In a perverse way, these groups become easy targets. Getting out of the spiral of violence seems to be only possible through physical injury or to step out of “the game.” The latter often means that young men have to disappear from the Brussels gang scene altogether. As older members of *Bagdad* and *Black Face* in Brussels put it:

> You always have to react, there is no end. These gangs are really a vicious thing, the gang …, you can’t just leave [the game].
>
> You should not come to Brussels! Make sure we do not spot you here! Your name mustn’t pop up in a story about an event that has in fact nothing to do with you. If you manage that then you might have a chance to live a normal life.

In Caracas, this principle is explained this way:

> When they disrespect you it’s final, you have to (…) till the end. Time is both your friend and your worst enemy. The culebra sticks around. The people you kill have family. It takes a generation and still… these things don’t pass, they may pass [temporarily] but more like clouds above your head, the culebra stays around. (…) you can’t run away from your culebra! Nowhere! You can run from the police, if they’re looking for you, you can go someplace else. From the culebra you can’t hide, you have to stay, it’s an ethic, a professional ethic. (…) If you’re involved in a culebra you have to take responsibility for what you’re doing.

Men in Brussels almost romantically capture the fatality of this code in a throwaway phrase: “tu finiras entre quatre murs ou quatres planches—meaning ‘you’ll end up between four walls (prison) or four planks (a coffin).’” Where prison can be a “way out” in Brussels, in Caracas it pushes people further into “el malandreo,” as gangs control the prisons. Once one is caught up in these spirals of violence it is indeed very hard to get out; leaving the gang means one does not only lose a sense of belonging, friendship, and respect, but also protection.

In all, gang violence is always seen to be retaliatory to a perceived threat to or violation of gang rules, whether in Brussels or Caracas. It is targeted at people (whether or not by association, through transitivity) that “deserve” it, have broken or ridiculed these rules one way or another. A gang member cannot just randomly and without provocation or justification attack someone; “unprovoked” violence is often condemned. Particularly on the deadly streets of Caracas, gang members that endanger the gang and the community by “acting out” against “innocent” people, or community members are often stigmatized (they’re dubbed “cocosecos,” naïve and stupid). They may even be subject to retaliatory violence themselves, as they can be seen to have offended the gang by acting in a dishonorable way. However, even if gang violence is, in principle, always retaliatory to a perceived instance of disrespect, in practice, it is often more defensive than retaliatory, and incompetent rather than well executed. This is because the fear generated by the uncertainties of retaliation distorts the gang’s perceptions and covers up often incompetent violence as necessary and even courageous, as we will explore in the next section.

4.4 Fear, Groupthink, and Incompetent Violence: Distortions in the Retaliation Process

These aspects of retaliatory violence, and particularly its certainty under uncertain circumstances, generate what Fagan et al. (2007) described as an "ecology of danger," where fear, use of deadly weapons and violent identities reinforce each other and spread rapidly. The predictably unpredictable nature of retaliation has generated an oppressive climate of fear among gang members in Brussels and Caracas. In Brussels, members of *1140* explain:

> Everybody is afraid! Everybody is in fact scared of everybody else!' 'That is it! Everybody is afraid of everybody else!
>
> We are afraid all the time. But we are afraid of what will happen to us as much as we are afraid of what we are capable of.

In Caracas, gang members did not often express this fear in so many words, but it was visible in their eyes and actions. On a ride on an informal bus, Ramos kept looking over his shoulder and never felt at ease, always keeping his hands in close proximity to the gun in his belt. Not long after fieldwork, he was shot dead by a gang in an adjoining sector. Gun and knife behaviors are extremely contagious in this atmosphere of ever-present danger, stabbings in Brussels, and gun violence in Caracas. Gang members *know* retaliation is nigh (fatalism), they're just not sure when (infinity), how (reciprocity), where (omnipresence), why (obscurity), or even against whom (transitivity). Many gang members carry weapons primarily in anticipation of violence, over and above a desire for revenge or to command toughness and respect. Expecting others, just like them, to carry weapons, they need to be prepared. An older member of the Brussels' gang *Finest* said:

> When you walk around with a knife? That means that you are scared of something. You are afraid that something will happen to you.

The fear of violence is genuine and serves a self-fulfilling prophecy, whereby carrying these weapons also makes a violent outcome more likely. Carrying a knife or gun thus becomes part of a dire logic. Or as explained by this 23-year-old gang member in Brussels:

> It is not a matter of attacking someone, it is all about defending yourself. It's always to defend yourself! If my opponent is reaching for his knife, I will do the same. Maybe he will feel intimidated and it might push him to drop his weapon. If we have to fight then, we will fight with our bare hands. Because if he gets his knife and I don't have one, he will stab me. He will try to stab me and I will have nothing to defend myself with. But if he gets his knife and I get mine too, he will be afraid. He'll be afraid, like me, but he'll be afraid! So, it is mainly to intimidate our opponents as we know that they're always armed with knives.

Retaliation and the fear thereof do not simply promote carrying deadly weapons. They also encourage gang group cohesion, as these young boys find safety in numbers. Many other authors have described how gang bonds are strengthened through violence (Decker 1996; De Jong 2012). This group cohesion is highly conducive to "Groupthink" (Janis 1982), leading to decision failures and highly incompetent violence (Collins 2009). "Groupthink" is a process by which decisions are made on the basis of unchallenged information in cohesive in-groups. Stories are told which enhance the group's image as morally right and physically superior. This is no different in the gang group, where myths are made and reinforced through storytelling about "other" gangs that do not actually play by the rules; they shoot or stab innocent people for a "bad look" or "a pair of shoes," are morally "wrong," and thus deserving of retaliatory violence. As an interviewee in Caracas put it:

> Interviewer: So you think I'm stupid for going to these sectors.
>
> Respondent: Stupid no, crazy! Not stupid. There are serious people like us who don't get women involved. (…) Others are really bad! (…) There are boys, because of drugs they don't know what they're doing. (…) Suddenly they'll shoot you in the leg or something.

The gang's own incompetent violence is covered up under a blanket of disciplinary necessity and honorable violence. These myths become "true" in the collective memory of the gang as members conform for fear of being ostracized. Or as explained by a member of *Bagdad* in Brussels:

> Today many of our younger brothers are incarcerated. Many of them reacted to legends, some of them also to true stories. Of course they also exist. But, you see, there are many legends too. Many story elements seem to change from one narrator to another. A story can really be transformed in this way.

In Brussels and Caracas, this means that gang members need to be ready, "activo" for other, more "crazy" gangs. Even if one is fearful, these gang myths establish that the other gang is more brutal and will kill for no reason. A boy in Caracas has this to say about the gang that shot and killed his cousin:

> These boys are bad, they're bad. They have the cold blood to shoot at someone and kill them, yes they do, but they're screwed, because they're stupid, they're stupid, they can't handle their guns.

It is expected that the other will attack. In encounters, there is little choice but to attack first. These distortions explain why much gang violence is steered more by expectations of success than by honorable execution. In other words, while many acts of violent gang retaliation may originate out of a codified desire for retaliation, their execution is determined more by considerations of "ease" and "success" than a code's dictates. A gang member in Brussels explains how "ease" is often an important consideration:

> Respondent: Say that you were there with him. He, he assaulted my friend. I can't find him, so I'll take you. I already spotted you two together, you are his friend, so I'll attack you. But in fact you, you don't have a clue of what is happening.
>
> Interviewer: So how should I understand this? Is it a sort of collective culpability?
>
> Respondent: Maybe, maybe. In fact … euh it is more about easiness. We mostly like the ease of it.

While purposive gang raids have happened, in Brussels they only do so rarely. The majority of the lethal assaults there tend to occur when men affiliated with different gangs accidently bump in to each other. This also explains why many of these "gang fights" happen in public transport settings, especially in the Belgian subway (Buy

2007, p. 29). In Caracas, gangs try and find each other's weak spots; they sneak into the other's territory from behind, often on motorcycles for a quick escape or when they know the other gang can be caught off guard, e.g., during a football match. Attacking a weak victim is one way to guarantee a more successful outcome (Collins 2009). Easy targets are preferred, and even facilitated by the vague rules of retaliation. In this way, assaults on young men who are at the wrong place in the wrong time are a frequent occurrence.

Pervasive fear and incompetent violence are partly absorbed and even covered up by the gang, under the much more honorable umbrella of retaliation. Incompetent violence is justified post-fact. Fear drives much of the violence and often distorts the ostentatious rule of plain retaliation. Gang members find this hard to admit, even to themselves, as their "code" is supposedly sacred. The code hides this fear under an iron blanket of respect, toughness, and retribution, but, in fact, it is this fear rather than toughness or strict retaliation that guides much of the violence. As formulated by one of the older gang members in Brussels:

> Because people in those days, they were not afraid to stab someone and they knew how to stab someone. They knew how to stab to hurt someone without getting him killed. These days those who kill someone in a stabbing … they are all kids. I don't know if you really looked into it, hein! But they're all kids who kill each other! And in most cases it was: 'I just wanted to defend myself!' So, most of the boys who end up killing another boy are actually truly terrified deep down. They're deeply afraid of the person in front of them. And when you feel a fear like that? Whoever you are, you are capable of killing someone. Whoever you are! Why? Because the fear of the one in front of you and the stress thereof make that you will stab him somewhere where you'd better not.

Instances of "random" violence feed back into the unpredictability of retaliation and gang myths, making full circle in the ecology of "danger." The preference for "easiness" instead of relevance in victim selection means that the determinism of the unwritten "code" of violence, and its main principle of retaliation is significantly distorted. The actual occurrence of violence is for that reason predictably unpredictable. While one can fairly well predict that something is coming up, the form it is going to take, the timing and even who will become the victim is more dependent of highly unpredictable circumstances and estimated easiness, than the rules set by the code. The same respondent whose cousin had been killed in Caracas puts it this way:

> I'm not going to feel at ease, feel comfortable until I see them all dead. Why? Because Caracas isn't big… Caracas is small… Everyone knows everyone. I'll live with the fear that I'll be selling my gear and run into one or other of them … It has happened before, I ran into these types, and they saluted me out of fear, they don't usually, in the center they salute because if I'm carrying anything at that time, they know…

4.5 Conclusion

While qualitative research was conducted on two different continents with substantially different populations by two different researchers, their findings both suggest that gang violence is predominantly retaliatory in nature. The features of retaliation make gang violence predictably unpredictable. This generates what Fagan et al. (2007) called "an ecology of danger," where use of weapons and "Groupthink" distort the actual process of retaliation and continuously reproduce this climate of fear and often incompetent violence. This chapter thus attributes the "facilitation" effect of gang violence to processes endogenous to this violence itself, rather than a "code" to which gang members supposedly unequivocally subscribe. Even if gang members themselves like to justify their violence by this "code," the characteristics of retaliation and the fear thereof appear to drive many instances of violence in both Brussels and Caracas.

References

Anderson, E. (2000). *Code of the street: Decency, violence, and the moral life of the inner city*. New York: WW Norton.

Battin, S. R., Hill, K. G., Abbott, R. D., Catalano, R. F., & Hawkins, J. D. (1998). Contribution of gang membership to delinquency beyond delinquent friends. *Criminology, 36*(1), 93–115.

Battin-Pearson, S. R., Thornberry, T. P., Hawkins, J. D., & Krohn, M. D. (1998). *Gang membership, delinquent peers, and delinquent behavior*. Washington, DC: US Department of Justice, Office of Justice Programs, Office of Juvenile Justice and Delinquency Prevention.

Black, D. (1983). Crime as social control. *American Sociological Review, 48*(1), 34–45.

Brezina, T., Agnew, R., Cullen, F. T., & Wright, J. P. (2004). The code of the street: A quantitative assessment of Elijah Anderson's subculture of violence thesis and its contribution to youth violence research. *Youth Violence and Juvenile Justice, 2*(4), 303–328.

Buy, S. (2007). *Les Bandes Urbaines-Arrondissement administratif de Bruxelles-Capitale*. Service 'Analyse Stratégique' de la Police Fédérale déconcentrée de Bruxelles.

Collins, R. (2009). *Violence: A micro-sociological theory*. Princeton, NJ: Princeton University Press.

Curry, G. D., & Decker, S. H. (1997). What's in a name? A gang by any other name isn't quite the same. *Valparaiso University Law Review, 31*(2), 501–514.

De Jong, J. D. (2012). Typically Moroccan? A group dynamic explanation of nuisance and criminal behavior. In F.-A. Esbensen & C. L. Maxson (Eds.), *Youth gangs in international perspective* (pp. 225–236). New York: Springer.

Decker, S. H. (1996). Collective and normative features of gang violence. *Justice Quarterly, 13*(2), 243–264.

Decker, S. H., Melde, C., & Pyrooz, D. C. (2012). What do we know about gangs and gang members and where do we go from here? *Justice Quarterly, 30*(3), 1–34.

Esbensen, F.-A., Winfree, L. T., He, N., & Taylor, T. J. (2001). Youth gangs and definitional issues: When is a gang a gang, and why does it matter? *Crime & Delinquency, 47*(1), 105–130.

Fagan, J., Wilkinson, D., & Davies, G. (2007). Social contagion of violence. In D. Flannery (Ed.), *The Cambridge handbook of violent behavior and aggression* (pp. 687–724). New York: Cambridge University Press.

Gerring, J. (2007). *Case study research: Principles and practices*. New York: Cambridge University Press.

HDR (Human Development Report). (2014). *Sustaining human progress: Reducing vulnerabilities and building resilience, Human Development Report*. New York: United Nations Development Programme. Retrieved from http://hdr.undp.org/en/content/human-development-report-2014

Hennigan, K., & Spanovic, M. (2012). Gang dynamics through the lens of social identity theory. In F.-A. Esbensen & C. L. Maxson (Eds.), *Youth gangs in international perspective* (pp. 127–149). New York: Springer.

INE (Instituto Nacional de Estadistica). (2011). *Encuesta de Hogares por Muestreo*, Sintesis Estadistica de Pobreza e Indicadores de Desigualdad 1er semestre 2011. Venezuela. Retrieved from http://www.ine.gov.ve/index.php?option=com_content&view=category&id=104:pobreza&Itemid=45

Jacobs, B. A. (2004). A typology of street criminal retaliation. *Journal of Research in Crime and Delinquency, 41*(3), 295–323.

Janis, I. L. (1982). *Groupthink: Psychological studies of policy decisions and fiascoes* (2nd ed.). Boston: Houghton Mifflin.

Klein, M. W., & Maxson, C. L. (1989). Street gang violence. In N. A. Weiner & M. E. Wolfgang (Eds.), *Violent crime, violent criminals* (pp. 198–234). Thousand Oaks, CA: Sage.

Klein, M. W., & Maxson, C. L. (2006). *Street gang patterns and policies*. New York: Oxford University Press.

Matsuda, K. N., Melde, C., Taylor, T. J., Freng, A., & Esbensen, F.-A. (2013). Gang membership and adherence to the "code of the street". *Justice Quarterly, 30*(3), 440–468.

Melde, C., & Esbensen, F.-A. (2013). Gangs and violence: Disentangling the impact of gang membership on the level and nature of offending. *Journal of Quantitative Criminology, 29*(2), 143–166.

OGWB. (2014). *Welzijnsbarometer 2014*. Observatorium voor Gezondheid en Welzijn van Brussel-Hoofdstad—Gemeenschappelijke Gemeenschapscommissie, Brussel.

Papachristos, A. V. (2009). Murder by structure: Dominance relations and the social structure of gang homicide in Chicago. *American Journal of Sociology, 115*(1), 74–128.

Rodgers, D., & Baird, A. (2015). Understanding gangs in contemporary Latin America. In S. H. Decker & D. C. Pyrooz (Eds.), *Handbook of gangs and gang responses*. New York: Wiley.

Rosenfeld, R., Bray, T. M., & Egley, A. (1999). Facilitating violence: A comparison of gang-motivated, gang-affiliated, and nongang youth homicides. *Journal of Quantitative Criminology, 15*(4), 495–516.

Stewart, E. A., & Simons, R. L. (2006). Structure and culture in African American adolescent violence: A partial test of the "code of the street" thesis. *Justice Quarterly, 23*(1), 1–33.

Thornberry, T. P., Krohn, M. D., Lizotte, A. J., & Chard-Wierschem, D. (1993). The role of juvenile gangs in facilitating delinquent behavior. *Journal of Research in Crime and Delinquency, 30*(1), 55–87.

UNODC (United Nations Office on Drugs and Crime). (2014). *Global study on homicide 2013—Trends, contexts, data*. United Nations Office on Drugs and Crime. Vienna: United Nations. Retrieved from http://www.unodc.org/documents/gsh/pdfs/2014_GLOBAL_HOMICIDE_BOOK_web.pdf

Van Hellemont, E. (2015). *The gang game: The myth and seduction of gangs*. PhD Dissertation, University of Leuven (KU Leuven).

Vandenbogaerde, E. (2016). *Networks, Malandros and social control: exploring the connections between inequality and violence in Venezuela*. Unpublished PhD Dissertation, University of Sussex (forthcoming).

Wood, J., & Alleyne, E. (2010). Street gang theory and research: Where are we now and where do we go from here? *Aggression and Violent Behavior, 15*(2), 100–111.

Zubillaga, V. (2007). Los varones y sus clamores: Los sentidos de la demanda de respeto y las lógicas de la violencia entre jóvenes de vida violenta de barrios en Caracas. *Espacio Abierto: Cuaderno Venezolano de Sociología, 16*(3), 577–608.

Chapter 5
Micro-Place Conditions and Social, Personal, and Situational Control Mechanisms: Testing an Integrated Theory of Gang Membership in Belgium

Lieven J.R. Pauwels and Wim Hardyns

5.1 Introduction and Goals of the Present Study

Youth gangs or gangs have been a classical theme in criminology for a long time. Explications have been proposed from the Chicago School's disorganization perspective (Thrasher 1927; Braga et al. 2010), social learning perspectives (Bandura 1986), anomie and subcultural theories (Cohen 1955; Cloward and Ohlin 1960; Miller 1958), control theories (Kornhauser 1978), modern lifestyle/routine activities theories (Riley 1987; Osgood et al. 1996), and self-control theories (Gottfredson and Hirschi 1990). While all these separate perspectives have their merits, scholars seem to have chosen the way of theoretical integration. One of the first integrated frameworks that emerged was the much-debated integrated delinquency theory of Elliott et al. (1979). More specific and of great importance for gang research was Thornberry's interactional theory (1987), which has served as an example for contemporary integrative theory-testing research. Gangs long have been the subject of studies in the USA; only recently have scholars in Europe shown interest (Bjørgo and Haaland 2001; Decker and Weerman 2005; Haaland 2000; Huizinga and Schumann 2001). In the past 10 years, the scholarly activities of the Eurogang working group have been expanding, resulting in numerous publications from scholars within and outside Europe (e.g., Decker and Weerman 2005; Esbensen and Maxson 2012; Esbensen and Weerman 2005; Sharp et al. 2006). Comparative studies have also been conducted (Haymoz et al. 2014; Huizinga and Schumann 2001). An increasing number of studies has taken a life course perspective with a focus on

L.J.R. Pauwels (✉) • W. Hardyns
Department of Criminology, Criminal Law and Social Law, Institute for International Research on Criminal Policy (IRCP), Ghent University, Ghent, Belgium
e-mail: Lieven.Pauwels@UGent.be; Wim.Hardyns@UGent.be

C.L. Maxson, F.-A. Esbensen (eds.), *Gang Transitions and Transformations in an International Context*, DOI 10.1007/978-3-319-29602-9_5

transitions and changes in crime involvement during periods of gang membership (Melde and Esbensen 2011, 2014; Weerman et al. 2015). Despite observed differences between characteristics of "street gangs" in the USA and in Europe, we cannot deny the existence of juveniles involved in "troublesome youth group" in European cities. This has previously been documented by Maxson and Klein (1995) and Klein et al. (2006).

Research on gang membership, young people's offending, and its causes is a research tradition that is nascent in Belgium. An overview of published Belgian self-report studies was conducted by Pauwels and Pleysier (2009). Belgium participated in the second wave of the International Self-Report Delinquency study (ISRD-2), which included questions on gang membership (Gatti et al. 2011; Haymoz et al. 2014; Pauwels et al. 2011). It seems that the millennium shift has brought about a renewed interest in testing theories of crime causation, victimization, and fear of crime in the Belgian context (Pauwels 2008, 2010). The goal of the present study is threefold: (1) we present an integrated general theoretical framework that may help us understand how youths become involved in gangs; (2) we present an empirical test of the elaborated model based on a large-scale Belgian sample of young adolescents; and (3) we examine the stability of the key findings in multiple groups by gender and immigrant background combined.

(Semi-)general theoretical frameworks are useful and deserve attention as they try to uncover mechanisms that apply in multiple settings. From a mere theoretical point of view, they have a broader scope than middle-range theories. We should, however, avoid situations where we end up with different theories for each and every phenomenon. Criminology is already characterized by the embarrassment of riches. The standpoint taken in this chapter is that we need both general frameworks and middle-range theories. The framework that we use and test is an integrated theory which unites elements of *ecological*, *social*, *personal*, and *situational* mechanisms for a better explanation and understanding of violent youth group involvement (henceforth, gang involvement). *A key ecological setting characteristic* is the micro-place context of residence, in line with contemporary studies on crime and place (see Weisburd et al. 2014). Attachment to parents, parental monitoring, and the school social bond are considered as key mechanisms of *informal social control*. Legal cynicism, external locus of control, and poor ability to self-control refer to the absence of personal control mechanisms. Finally, the theory takes into account the role of absence of *situational controls*, especially lifestyle risk, as a key indicator of exposure to criminogenic moral settings (see Wikström and Butterworth 2006; Wikström et al. 2012), which consists of both peer exposure and exposure to settings conducive to crime (measured by unstructured routines).

The structure of this chapter is as follows: firstly, we discuss the importance of an analytical approach. Secondly, we present an integrated control model. Thirdly, we empirically test the integrated model using generalized structural equation models for count, dichotomous, and continuous variables (Muthén and Muthén 2011). And finally, we discuss the findings of the test of the theoretical model in the general sample and in subgroups based on gender and immigrant background. The rationale for testing the proposed general theoretical framework is precisely to challenge general models that stress mechanisms that should be applicable to explain offending and gang involvement.[1]

5.2 Towards an Analytical Approach Towards the Study of Gang Involvement

Regarding the study of gangs, criminological theories have for a long time failed to lack consensus on:

- What gang membership is (to clearly define what a theory of gang membership aims to explain, e.g., joining, becoming involved, and taking up different roles).
- What it is that moves people to get involved in gangs (i.e., to present an adequate action theory explaining gang membership as "situated choice").
- How personal and environmental factors interact in moving people to get involved in a gang (to properly integrate key insights from personal and environmental explanatory approaches).
- The role of the broader social conditions and individual development/life histories (to analyze their influence not as causes but as causes of the causes).

Earlier, Wikström et al. (2012) made a highly similar statement about the state of affairs in crime causation theories. The point of view that is taken here is that *mechanism-based action theories* are fruitful to the interdisciplinary study of the causes and mechanisms that can account for gang involvement. The key philosophy behind this approach is that social phenomena (such as the amount of gang-related crime occurring in a neighborhood, city, or society) need to be explained from a constellation of social phenomena, actors and their actions, and interactions that are related to gang involvement in such a way that they usually bring about the social phenomenon or collective action that we try to explain (Hedström 2005). Action is behavior that results from processes of deliberation. Involvement in all kinds of troublesome groups can be seen as situated choice, i.e., a consequence of the interplay between individual and setting characteristics. These interplays shape levels of gang involvement in neighborhoods, cities, and societies. The idea is that actions of individuals bring about the emergence of social facts. What studies into the etiology of gangs are lacking, is a strong research program based on a sound philosophy of science that allows for an integrated

[1] Different positions with regard to the effects of gender and immigrant background are taken by scholars (Esbensen and Deschenes 1998; Esbensen and Winfree 1998). Due to limitations we will not go into details, but instead refer to a clear contribution by Miller and Brunson (2000). Our position is a mixed one: we expect that the same mechanisms apply to both males and females, immigrants and non-immigrants but also believe in differential vulnerability of different subgroups.

study of causes and mechanisms (the why's and how's of gang involvement) at multiple levels. We submit that an analytical criminology may provide such a way of theorizing. This way of theorizing is a critical realist approach to gang involvement that is deeply rooted within the tradition of analytical sociology (for a discussion, see Hedström and Swedberg 1998; Hedström 2005). Analytical sociology has as its primary goal to explain complex social processes by carefully dissecting them and then bringing into focus their most important constituent components. Through dissection and analytical abstraction the important cogs and wheels of social processes are made visible and intelligible (Edling and Hedström 2005, p. 1).

Macro-micro questions in criminology are a consequence of long-time observed correlations between social facts, such as structural characteristics of ecological settings, and crime and offense rates of these settings as social outcomes. According to Bunge (2012), the action of individuals (e.g., why they offend, why they join and leave gangs, why they remain in gangs) as social actors cannot be understood without taking contexts, networks, and even broader structures of individuals into account. On the contrary, these contexts should be studied together with the individual desires, beliefs, opportunities, and constraints of actors. The environmental determinists view is wrong, because it does not take individual characteristics into account, whereas the atomist is wrong for ignoring the context, i.e., behavior settings to which one is exposed. Individuals are intertwined in multiple micro-, meso-, and macro-contexts. *Emergent systemism* (the CESM approach or Composition-Environment-Structure-Mechanism approach) is a way of combining both views. We submit that emergent systemism (Bunge 2012) can provide a rich analytical framework for the study of gang involvement and thus fill a gap in studies of gang involvement. The term emergent is important as it provides a framework for explaining how higher-level outcomes emerge out of lower-level outcomes. In an emergent systemic approach to the study of gang involvement one needs to make a distinction between (1) the *composition* of the system, i.e., the collection of parts of the system and their individual characteristics; (2) the *environment* of the system or the collection of entities that are not a part of the system but do have an influence on parts of the system (the micro-place context is one example of the environment); (3) the *structure* of the system, i.e., the whole of structural relationships between the parts of which a system consist,[2] the social ties among the group members and the social ties that group members have outside the group (e.g., social relationships with other primary units such as the family); and (4) the *mechanisms* that function within a system. A mechanism is a process in a definite system that is able to bring about or to prevent an effect in that system. The CESM-model is a valuable guide to study gang involvement: theories should pursue to answer questions that are posed in the CESM-model. Our integrated framework addresses the role of context and intervening mechanisms.

---

[2] Structure cannot be confused with the composition of the system. The term "structure" in Bunge's systemism refers to the relationships between the actors in a system.

5.3 An Integrated Condition-Control-Exposure Model of Gang Involvement

Our integrative model relies heavily on previous work of Esbensen et al. (2010), Wikström et al. (2012), and Sampson and Laub (2003), combined with Bunge's CESM-model as philosophical and meta-theoretical backbone. Since the 1990s, developmental and life course theories stimulated scholars' interest to develop newer theories, such as Thornberry's interactional theory (Thornberry 1987; Thornberry et al. 1998), Sampson and Laub's (2003) age-graded informal control theory, and recently Wood and Alleyne's (2010) unified framework, a promising overarching framework for the study of causes and consequences of gang membership. Contemporary (cross-level) integrated theoretical models that have been proposed from either the classic or contemporary social disorganization tradition or the neighborhood disorder tradition have identified social controls (social bonds, parental monitoring, and the school social bond) and personal controls (moral beliefs, external locus of control, and self-control), as mediators of the effect of neighborhood disorganization (Bernburg and Thorlindsson 2005; Guterman et al. 2009; Jones and Lynam 2009; Oberwittler 2004; Thorlindsson and Bernburg 2004). In 2007, Vowell presented and tested such an integrated control model of adolescent offending. From such a theoretical perspective the neighborhood context was hypothesized to reduce informal social control mechanisms, thus affecting offending primarily through informal social controls. These informal social controls were clearly taken from social bond theory and self-control theory. Vowell (2007) argued that youth, residing in disorganized neighborhoods, having weak social bonds and reporting a lack of self-control, would also be more likely to associate with groups having deviant definitions which ultimately led to an increased likelihood of offending. Vowell also stressed the role of peers. The role of peers has traditionally been explained from both social learning theories and unstructured routines/opportunity theories. In social learning theories peers provide a learning context, while in routine activity/lifestyle theories both peers and unstructured routines are considered to be situational instigators. Sampson and Laub (2003) defended the situational interpretation, mainly due to their criticism of human nature in social learning theories (the blank slate principle) which rendered it less attractive for integrating the role of peers in their age-graded informal control theory. Also Wikström and Sampson (2003) and Wikström and Butterworth (2006) have argued that the social disorganization perspective is more compatible with theories that stress the role of unstructured routine activities (or more general risky lifestyles) like mechanisms in the explanation of offending (Forde and Kennedy 1997; Maxfield 1987; Wikström and Butterworth 2006). The main reason is that the frameworks of social disorganization, social control, self-control, and the routine activity theory of general offending share highly compatible visions of human nature and social order (Lilly et al. 2014). These models leave room for agency. Wikström and Butterworth used the concept of lifestyle risk and argued that lifestyle risk is a more general ("overall") concept that reflects exposure to criminogenic moral settings, either through unstructured routines or the presence of peers. Based on these ideas, some scholars have proposed and tested an end-to-end integrated control model that incorporated the concept of lifestyle risk to explain individual differences in gang involvement (Pauwels and Svensson 2013, 2014; Pauwels 2014). In fact, this study elaborates on these previous studies. Hereafter, we further specify the ecological (*condition*), social and personal (*control*), and situational (*exposure*) mechanisms of gang involvement. The specific characteristic of our theoretical model is that it brings back in locus of control in explanations of delinquency and gang involvement.

5.3.1 Micro-Place Disorder (Condition)

While a multitude of studies of adolescent offending and gang involvement have focused on social disorganization/disorder at the neighborhood or census tract level, there is a growing consensus that it is of primordial interest to open the black box and see what is going on in micro-places, as most of the youths who live in disadvantaged areas do not evolve to be seriously delinquent. It has also been acknowledged that it is important to study the effect of disorganization/disorder at the micro-place level, such as the street-level (Oberwittler and Wikström 2009; Weisburd et al. 2012). In the present study we introduce the theoretical concept micro-place disorder to the study of gang involvement and we have operationalized micro-places at the street-level. We thus focus on micro-place disorder using observational measures of crime and disorder at the street-level.

5.3.2 The Unexplored Role of External Locus of Control (Control)

We find it striking that one of the major concepts on social psychology, locus of control, has predominantly been omitted from control theories. Growing up in disorderly micro-settings may have consequences for the development of the learned belief of fatalism, or *external locus of control*. This was already mentioned by David Matza (1964) in his classic book, and has recently emerged in Colvin's theory (2000). Building on Mirowsky and Ross (2003), we argue that (1) the presence of social disorder in micro-settings may promote the view that people are by nature untrustworthy, and unhelpful, and that life is alienating and beyond personal control and (2) that the presence of counter-narratives (e.g., subcultural values) may promote the view that law-abiding is futile and deterrence is non-existent. Micro-place disorder may also start a negative causal chain by decreasing parental monitoring and installing subjective powerlessness in youths. Consequently these characteristics shape (through learning principles) beliefs that normlessness rules.

We maintain that control theories that take into account personal controls cannot be complete without taking locus of control into account. The development of the fatalistic belief that one is not in charge of one's own life should be considered as an additional mechanism that may have consequences for youth gang involvement in several ways in the integrated theory:

1. External locus of control refers to a belief in fatalism, which may produce feelings of alienation toward the conventional moral standards. This is called *legal cynicism* or the belief that conventional moral standards are no longer legitimate (Sampson and Bartusch 1998). Respecting rules stated in laws makes less sense in a world that is perceived to be driven by fate. Living by conventional moral standards pays off in the long run, but that makes less sense to individuals that have an external locus of control, as such youths are not guided by a belief that they can control the outcome of their action and thus their future.
2. External locus of control is a belief that challenges the establishment and maintenance of the inhibitory executive functions (impulse control and anger management) of *self-control* as it promotes an orientation towards the present instead of towards delayed gratification. Individuals who share the belief that they are not in control of the future instead concentrate on the present, on oneself, and put less effort into controlling immediate gratification and temper, and thus make one less resistant to withstand temptation and provocation.

5.3.3 Lifestyle Risk as Exposure to Criminogenic Moral Settings (Exposure)

Individuals who have a low ability to apply self-control are more likely to become involved in criminal, deviant, and accidental behaviors than those who possess high levels of self-control. Gottfredson and Hirschi (1990) considered the relationship between gang involvement and offending as a spurious relationship, and argued that low self-control would be the ultimate common cause. However, many empirical studies revealed that self-control is not the only necessary condition leading to criminality (Pratt and Cullen 2000).

Routine activity theory (Bernasco et al. 2013; Felson and Boba 2010) argues that delinquency results, in part, from individuals' spending time in situations that offer appealing opportunities for that behavior. This perspective finds support in evidence that many problem behaviors are associated with spending time in unstructured and unsupervised socializing with peers (e.g., Higgins and Jennings 2010; Haynie and Osgood 2005; Osgood et al. 1996). When an individual is frequently exposed to the street-corner lifestyle, the likelihood of his or her becoming affiliated with gangs are further situationally increased. The street-corner lifestyle is characterized by unstructured socializing with delinquent peers that one considers to be similar to oneself. This lifestyle reflects living on the edge, being involved in exciting unstructured routine activities day by day, unhindered by feelings of future responsibilities, which have primarily been neutralized by lowered levels of personal control, weak social bonds, and perceived normlessness. Lifestyles were originally considered of importance as a causal mechanism in the explanation of victimization, while some more recent studies actually suggest that lifestyles are of much more importance in explaining individual differences in offending (Osgood et al. 1996; Wikström and Butterworth 2006).

5.3.4 The Condition-Control-Exposure Model

The above-presented mechanisms have been discussed in the empirical literature on covariates of gang involvement (Alleyne and Wood 2010; Curry and Decker 2003; Katz and Fox 2010; Sharp et al. 2006; Thornberry et al. 2003). The key causal factors involved in the Condition-Control-Exposure (CCE)-model can be distinguished in (1) mechanisms referring to ecological exposure (the condition of micro-place disorder), (2) mechanisms referring to control systems (parental attachment, parental monitoring, school social bond, external locus of control, low self-control, and legal cynicism), and (3) situational exposure (lifestyle risk). Exposure to criminogenic moral settings is a consequence of both delinquent peers and places (and especially the interaction between both) and our measure (index-see measurement issues) combines both delinquent peers and places. The integrated CCE-model is visualized in Fig. 5.1.

In the conceptual framework, a series of direct effects are hypothesized for all endogenous variables in the system of equations. The absence of an arrow thus simply means that we did not hypothesize a direct effect. As can be seen from Fig. 5.1, we hypothesized a series of direct effects based on the logic of the end-to-end theoretical integration: micro-place disorder is hypothesized to have a direct effect on parental attachment, external locus of control, low self-control, and parental monitoring. Parental attachment has a direct effect on parental monitoring, external locus of control, and the school social

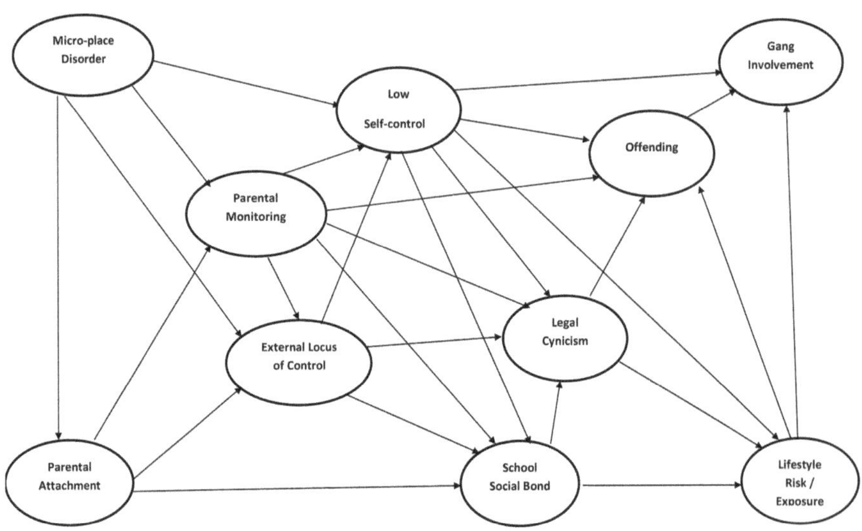

Fig. 5.1 Conceptual model of social, personal, and situational controls and gang involvement

bond. Parental monitoring has a direct effect on external locus of control, legal cynicism, low self-control, and offending. External locus of control has a direct effect on the school social bond, legal cynicism, and low self-control. The school social bond has a direct effect on legal cynicism and lifestyle risk. Low self-control has a direct effect on the school social bond, legal cynicism, offending, lifestyle risk, and gang involvement. Lifestyle risk has a direct effect on offending and gang involvement. Finally, offending has a direct effect on the likelihood of being involved in a gang.

5.4 Data and Methods

5.4.1 Setting and Participants

The Antwerp Youth Survey is a school survey consisting of 2486 young adolescents in 23 schools and 42 neighborhood clusters (all neighborhood clusters of Antwerp) in the first cycle of the Belgian secondary school system. The first cycle of the Belgian secondary school system is compulsory and corresponds to grade 7 and 8 in the US school system. The sample frame consisted of youths in early adolescence that lived and went to school in Antwerp neighborhoods. The average grade 7 student is 13 years old and the average grade 8 student is 14 years old. Data collection took place between January 2005 and June 2005. This sample frame was chosen for several reasons: a disproportionate number of youth studies on adolescent offending focuses on mid-adolescence. The main reason cited in the literature for this historical disproportional overrepresentation of youth in mid-adolescence is the well-documented age crime curve. However, the early adolescent years (11–14 years of age) are a crucial time when youths are exposed to gangs and may consider joining a gang. Some gang researchers clearly show that the average age when adolescents join gangs is 14 years old (Sweeten et al. 2013; Pyrooz 2014) and sometimes even younger ages are found (Esbensen et al. 2010). From a devel opmental life course perspective, it is stressed and well-documented that risk factors of offending and gang involvement vary at different stages of development. The Antwerp Youth Survey was an attempt to fill a gap in crime causation studies in a country where criminology as a discipline has no strong tradition in the etiological research on offending and gang involvement.

The study design was a cross-nested sample of individuals in schools and census-tract clusters. The respondents lived and went to school in Antwerp, the largest municipality in Belgium with approximately 502,000 inhabitants in 2005 (approximately 510,000 inhabitants in 2014). The response rate was 92.5 % of the students in the participating schools. The Antwerp Youth Survey consisted of 49.4 % boys and 50.6 % girls. Almost three-quarters of the respondents were aged 12–14, while 26.2 % of the respondents were 15–16 years old.[3] Fifteen percent of the respondents lived in a single parent/caregiver family, and 85 % of the respondents lived with two parents or caregivers.

[3] From a life-course developmental approach one could argue to omit the 15–16 year old students. The vast majority of these students were 15 years old. The processes that are studied are however

Almost half of the respondents had a fully native background (both parents from Belgian descent), around 10.0 % of the respondents had one parent with an immigrant background, while 45.5 % of the respondents had two parents with an immigrant background. The overrepresentation of immigrants is partially due to a higher participation of schools in inner-city areas. Although all schools that offer teaching for grade seven and eight (US school system) were contacted, only 33.3 % of these schools participated.[4] Of course, this issue may raise concerns regarding the external validity of the results. As the sample was drawn from a non-random selection of schools in Antwerp, it is not a representative sample of Belgian youth, but it is highly varied in terms of ethnic background and education. Demographic background variables like gender and immigrant background were unable to explain individual differences in refusal to cooperate and were unable to explain item non-response on the delinquency items at the individual level.[5] At the school level, the decision to participate by the school principal was significantly higher in inner-city poor areas. Significantly more schools in rich neighborhoods and all schools for religious minorities (e.g., Orthodox Jewish Religious Schools) refused to participate. We were concerned with the potential effect of the decision of school principals to participate: decisions to participate might have led to overrepresentations of sample respondents in some areas. To know whether this was the case, we evaluated the extent to which this sample is representative at least at the neighborhood level.[6] Following a strategy developed by Oberwittler (2004), we compared aggregate survey-based demographics and population data at the census tract level. These ecological analyses revealed quite high correlations between both survey-based and census data-based measures of neighborhood structural characteristics.[7] In the next paragraph we describe all scales. Detailed information on all scales, i.e., the wording of the items and measurement models (factor loadings), is provided in Appendix 1. For the descriptive statistics of all the variables included in the analysis, see Table 5.1. We did not impute missing data in the present study.

---

expected to be found in every age group. In fact, we ran analyses by subgroup and we did not detect any significant difference.

[4] We remind the reader that in Belgium, grade seven and eight form a separate cluster in secondary compulsory education (which consists of three clusters that each take 2 years). These school buildings are separate from the school buildings in which education is provided for other students in higher grades.

[5] Logistic regression models resulted in pseudo-R^2 of zero percent.

[6] This was a very important concern for us, as the original goal of this study was the evaluation of neighborhood effects (effects of administratively defined areas) on juvenile delinquency using multilevel modeling. We found no neighborhood effects and have widely published on that (e.g., Pauwels et al. 2010), and because of the growing interest in studying effects of micro-places we re-analyzed the survey data using street-level information for the occasion of the present article.

[7] The neighborhood-level correlation between the percentage of adolescents with at least one parent with an immigrant background (whose parents were born outside the European Union in 2007) and the percentage of inhabitants from Morocco and Turkey (census data-based indicator) was 0.82 ($p > 0.001$), and the neighborhood-level correlation between the concentration of family disadvantage (survey-based information) and a measure of neighborhood disadvantage (administrative data) was 0.58 ($p < 0.001$). For more details we refer to the original study and additional articles (Pauwels 2012, 2013).

5.4.2 Measures of Scale Constructs

Micro-place disorder is measured using observational measures of street-level disorder: a combined index of ten situations that may be observed very close to ("street" definition) the respondents' residences.[8] The respondents were asked how many times they observed ten disorderly events (e.g., people selling drugs, people being threatened, and adolescents starting a fight) on a four-point scale (never, sometimes, often, very often). High values on this measure indicate high levels of perceived disorder. Alpha is 0.84.

Parental attachment is an additive index that was measured by four items (e.g., I can get along pretty well with my parents) on a five-point scale. Alpha is 0.79.

Parental monitoring was measured by five items (e.g., parents know where I am, when I am not at home) with an Alpha of 0.71. High values on this measure indicate high levels of monitoring. The scale has been used in different studies on different populations (Pauwels and Svensson 2013; Pauwels 2013).

External locus of control or subjective powerlessness was measured using the "external locus of control for adolescents" scale. The scale has been previously used in Belgian studies of educational sociology and school contextual effects (Brutsaert 2001). The scale consists of three items that reflect the belief that personal action does not lead to results (e.g., I believe that planning things does not guarantee success). Our justification for the use of this scale lies in the fact that these items reflect the fatalism that was discussed in Matza's seminal work "Delinquency and Drift." High values on this scale indicate external locus of control. Alpha is 0.58.[9]

Low self-control is an additive index mainly based on the items used and developed by Grasmick et al. (1993). This scale measures whether an individual had difficulties resisting temptation and provocation. High values on this measure indicate low self-control. Seven items were included: Three items measure temper

---

[8] If respondents mentioned they lived in a very large street, we used the alternative "five-minute walk" definition. Although we used observational questions, all observations of the environment go through perception, i.e., our senses. However, these observations do not come out of the blue, but are strongly related to the events happening (Wikström et al. 2012). Wikström and Sampson (2003) have further argued that the study of neighborhood effects such as the effects of disorganization and disorder may benefit from a reconceptualization of neighborhoods as activity fields. The activity field is a small part of the environment that can be perceived by our senses (Wikström et al. 2012). Large geographical areas can therefore not be considered as part of the individual's activity field. Some ecological units of analysis are simply too heterogeneous to be potential candidates for serving as a behavioral setting. Sizes and boundaries are thus key issues in the study of neighborhood effects.

[9] The alpha value was somewhat lower than the alpha values of the other constructs, but factor analysis revealed that all items had sufficiently large factor loadings on a single factor (all loadings >0.50). It is important to stress that there were no cross-loadings of external locus of control items on other personal control measures (e.g., low self-control and legal cynicism). A cross-loading means that an indicator has sufficiently high factor loadings on more than one concept (e.g., an X and Y variable). If that would have been the case, our measure would be biased and a tautology problem could have arisen. Indicators should be unbiased indicators and refer to only one latent concept. There is clearly conceptual differentiation.

(anger management, e.g., I get angry easily) and four items measure impulsiveness (or immediate gratification, e.g., I often do things without thinking). Alpha of the combined scale is 0.78.

The school social bond measures attachment to school (e.g., making efforts to do homework, caring about what teachers say,...) and is an additive index that was measured by three items. Alpha is 0.65.

Legal cynicism or perceived illegitimacy of moral rules is measured using a scale that contains items taken from Sampson and Bartusch's (1998) legal cynicism scale (e.g., rules are made to be broken, it is ok to break rules, as long as you're not caught). Alpha is 0.78.

Lifestyle risk or situational exposure is measured as a combined index of unstructured routines (how often adolescents hang around in the city center and how often adolescents hang around on street corners) and peer delinquency. Alpha of the peer delinquency subscale is 0.81. The overall lifestyle risk measure is a combined risk score summing the risk (+1 standard deviation above mean), balanced (between −1 standard deviation and +1 standard deviation), and protective (−1 standard deviation below mean) ends of the peer delinquency scale and the unstructured routines items. The result is an overall risk summation score that varies between −3 and +3 (Wikström and Butterworth 2006; Svensson and Pauwels 2010; Pauwels and Svensson 2013).

Offending is a summation score (variety scale) that summarizes how many different offense items the respondent has committed: (1) "Vandalism," (2) "Fighting outside school," (3) "Theft>25 euro," (4) "Graffiti," (5) "Threatening persons," (6) "Shoplifting," (7) "Buying stolen goods," (8) "Burglary," (9) "Hit and injure on purpose." As nine offense items were questioned, the variety scale ranges from zero to nine.

Gang involvement is measured using a funnelling technique, i.e., we combined answers to one filter question and five follow-up questions to measure self-reported gang involvement/participation. The leading question was: "Some adolescents have a steady group of friends to do things together, or to hang around outside. Do you have such a group of friends?" (1=yes, 0=no). The five follow-up questions were: (1) "Are the members of this group involved in fights and quarrels with other adolescents?" (2) "Do members of this group act before talking when the group's image is at stake?" (3) "Are there some members of this group prepared to do dangerous and exciting things?" (4) "Are members of this group involved in fights with other cliques?" (5) "Are members of this group involved in law-breaking?" These follow-up items were originally presented on a four-point scale (0=never, 1=sometimes, 2=often, 3=very often) but were dichotomized (1=yes, 0=no). Respondents were categorized as involved in a gang if they answered affirmatively to the leading question as well as the five follow-up questions.[10] Our measure of youth gang

[10]To the introductory question (n=894), 36% of the total sample answered positively, 27.8% answered positively to the first follow-up question; 18.3% answered positively to the second follow-up question; 21.2% answered positively to the third follow-up question; 27.8% answered positively to the fourth follow-up question; and 20.4% answered affirmatively to the fifth follow-

involvement is partially inspired by previous work of Weerman (2005), Esbensen and Weerman (2005) and partially based on the instrument developed by Heitmeyer et al. (1995). Our measure uses the funnel technique, but was crafted before the Eurogang consensus definition. Therefore it is somewhat different, e.g., it did not include questions on duration of group membership, as was done in the ISRD-studies (Haymoz et al. 2014). Table 5.1 presents the descriptives for the key variables that are used in the multivariate analyses, i.e., the scale scores (in their original metric), gang membership and the variables used to split the sample (gender and immigrant background). As one can see, listwise deletion results in a sample of 2173 respondents. Previously, we analyzed item-non-response and the effects of imputation on the correlations between imputed and non-imputed scale scores. That study revealed that the correlations between variables were virtually identical (see Pauwels and Svensson 2008 for a detailed description of the study of item non-response).

5.4.3 *Analysis Plan*

Structural equation modeling (SEM) for continuous and dichotomous variables was used to calculate path coefficients between the exogenous and endogenous variables. All analyses were conducted using Mplus, version 7.12 (Muthén and Muthén 2011). Structural equation models are considered common extensions of the linear path model (Jöreskog and Sörbom 1993; Bollen 1998). Path models, which combine dichotomous outcomes (such as gang involvement) or count data (such as counts of offenses) with exogenous continuous variables, can be handled with Mplus (Byrne 2011). Mplus also allows for adjusting the standard errors. Respondents are clustered in neighborhood clusters (level of analysis somewhere between ZIP-codes and census tracts) and schools. Assumptions regarding the independence of observations between neighborhoods were not violated, but the data were gathered through school surveys (Pauwels et al. 2011). Therefore adjusted standard errors were used to control for the school level clustering. Micro-place disorder refers to the street-level. We did not have a sufficient number of respondents per street to provide reliable street-level aggregate measures of micro-place characteristics (see also Pauwels and Svensson (2014) for a more detailed explanation). All scale scores were standardized before entering the equation. SEM is used for testing direct effects of a series of exogenous variables on a series of endogenous variables. SEM is highly suitable to evaluate our

up question. Only 8.1 % responded positively to the leading and all follow-up questions. In early publications we coined the term violent youth group involvement, to avoid misunderstandings. While our work is highly influenced by the rich studies of the Eurogang network, this study was conducted before the Eurogang consensus definition was used. We especially thank Dr. Frank Weerman who advised us to include a measure of gang membership in our study and who provided us with questionnaire examples.

previously made statements of direct and indirect effects of the ecological, personal, social, and situational mechanisms. Model fit indices such as RMSEA and CFI are used together with the more traditional R^2 to evaluate the hypotheses and explanatory power.[11]

We bear in mind that cross-sectional data are far from ideal to test such relationships and were therefore extremely careful when interpreting the results. Unfortunately no panel study of self-reported offending and gang involvement has ever taken place in Belgium. For reasons of parsimony only the best fitting models are presented. All effects have reached statistical significance ($p<0.01$). A calculation of total effects is not done as the key dependent variable is a dichotomy and offending is a count variable and the test of direct and total effects in combined linear and nonlinear models is still problematic (Byrne 2011). All coefficients are beta-coefficients, except for the direct effects on gang involvement; these are log-odds, as gang involvement is a dichotomous outcome. The direct effects on offending are B-coefficients from a negative binomial regression model. The R^2 measures for the scale variables can be interpreted as OLS R^2 measures. The R^2 measure for gang involvement is a pseudo-determination coefficient (Nagelkerke R^2) and the offending R^2 relates to a corresponding linear model (while a negative binomial model is run). The RMSEA is 0.04 and also corresponds to a maximum-likelihood linear structural equation model, as generalized models do not provide the traditional fit indices.[12]

5.5 Results

In what follows, we restrict the discussion to the direct effects for every endogenous variable in the model (see Fig. 5.2 and Table 5.2). We did not calculate indirect effects as concern exists on how to calculate indirect effects in regression models in which different parts have different coefficients (odds-ratios, linear regression coefficients, and binomial regression coefficients). There is a negative effect of micro-place disorder on parental attachment ($\beta=-0.16$). Parental monitoring is directly related to micro-place disorder ($\beta=-0.19$) and parental attachment ($\beta=0.42$). External locus of control can be explained by micro-place disorder ($\beta=0.20$), parental attachment ($\beta=-0.16$), and parental monitoring ($\beta=-0.10$). Although none of these effects are really strong, these effects operate as expected from the theoretical framework.

[11] The RMSEA fit index should preferably have a value below 0.05 while the CFI index should have a value above 0.96 (Bollen 1996).

[12] Models of complex and multiple mediation with multiple mediators (categorical, count, metric, see Hayes 2013) such as is the case in the present study are very difficult to fit. Therefore the analyses are restricted to the study of the direct effects. Ignoring the complexity of the data, and applying a maximum likelihood estimation (as is done in the simplest linear path models) would make it possible to get insights in each and every indirect effect (Muthén 2011). Therefore we decided to stick to the study of direct effects when discussing the findings.

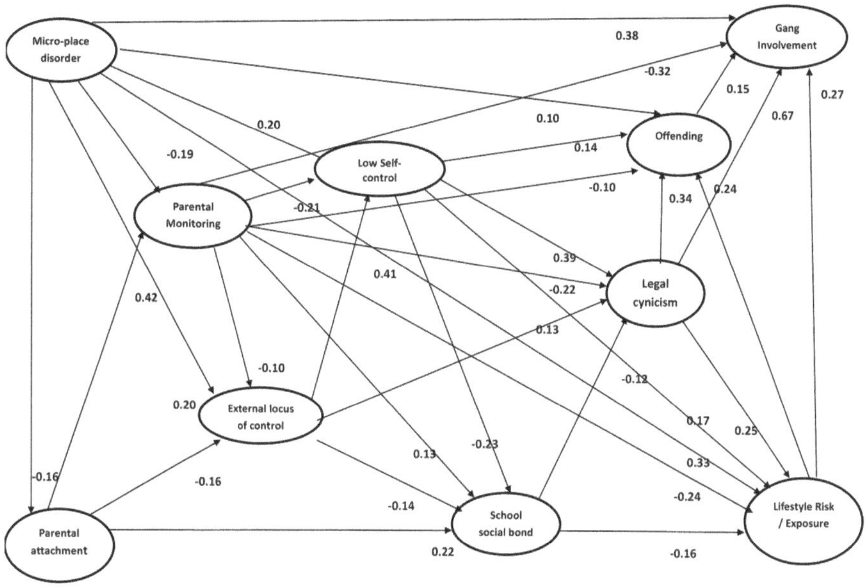

Fig. 5.2 Best fitting model (only significant direct effects are shown)

Next, we take a closer look at low self-control. While direct effects are found from micro-place disorder (β=0.20) and parental monitoring (β=–0.21), it is striking to see that the strongest direct effect is found from external locus of control (β=0.41). An external locus of control inhibits the exercising of self-control. Regarding the school social bond, we found direct effects of low self-control (β=–0.23), parental monitoring (β=0.13), external locus of control (β=–0.14), and parental attachment (β=0.22). Legal cynicism, or the view that moral rules are illegitimate, is directly affected by low self-control (β=0.39), external locus of control (β=0.13), the school social bond (β=–0.12), and parental monitoring (β=–0.22). Lifestyle risk is directly related to legal cynicism (β=0.25), the school social bond (β=–0.16), parental monitoring (β=–0.24), low self-control (β=0.17), and micro-place disorder (β=0.33).

After having described the direct effects of the factors that are considered causes of the causes of gang involvement and offending in the integrated theoretical framework, we now turn to the two key dependent variables, namely offending and gang involvement. Before describing the findings, a remark should be made concerning the temporal place of the variables in the model. We have chosen to draw a causal arrow from offending to gang involvement and not the other way around. This is justified by the knowledge that prior offending is related to the likelihood of gang involvement in most research. We do not suggest that no causal arrow could exist between gang involvement and offending, in fact there is a growing consensus that being involved temporarily increases offending.[13]

[13] Our choice is influenced by theoretical reasoning and backed up by a preliminary test of feedback loops (something that is technically not possible, when one variable is a count variable and the other a dichotomy, but still, we checked how the model would look if we assumed that the

Table 5.1 Descriptives (in original metrics)

	N	Min	Max	Mean	Std
Scale scores[a]					
Micro-place disorder	2443	0.00	29.00	7.48	5.36
Parental attachment	2476	4.00	20.00	17.05	3.25
Parental monitoring	2454	5.00	25.00	19.58	4.37
External locus of control	2400	3.00	15.00	8.31	3.08
Low self-control	2375	7.00	35.00	21.18	6.32
School social bond	2454	5.00	25.00	18.27	3.91
Legal cynicism	2461	4.00	20.00	9.94	4.35
Lifestyle risk	2382	−3.00	3.00	−1.47	1.32
Offending (variety scale)	2333	0.00	9.00	1.84	2.06
Gang involvement[b]	2476	0.00	1.00	0.08	0.27
Background characteristics					
Gender[b]	2485	0.00	1.00	0.49	
Immigrant background[b]	2486	0.00	10.00	0.45	
Valid *N* (listwise)	2172				

[a]Scales scores were all standardized in the multivariate analyses, with the exception of offending, which is a count variable

[b]Dichotomous items are presented as proportions

We argue that panel data are absolutely necessary to understand the co-evolution of offending and gang involvement (Melde and Esbensen 2011, 2014; Thornberry et al. 2003). We observed direct effects on offending from a series of variables: micro-place disorder (β=0.10), low self-control (β=0.14), parental monitoring (β=−0.10), lifestyle risk (β=0.24), and legal cynicism (β=0.34). We observed direct effects on gang involvement from the following variables: micro-place disorder (log-odds=0.38), parental monitoring (log-odds=−0.32), legal cynicism (log-odds=0.67), lifestyle risk (log-odds=0.27), and offending (log-odds=0.15).

Finally, we also examined the stability of the abovementioned key findings in multiple groups by gender and immigrant background combined (see Appendix 2). The main reason for performing these analyses by subgroups was to get insight into the stability of the results. General theories should be valid in different populations. Thus, there is no better way to test this key idea than by rerunning the model and comparing the findings. For all subgroups we observed significant direct effects of parental monitoring, legal cynicism, and lifestyle risk on gang involvement. Direct effects of offending on gang involvement were observed in the subgroup of Belgian boys. Micro-place disorder has a direct effect on gang involvement for all subgroups, except for Belgian girls. The subgroup of Belgian girls is unique in the way that low self-control directly affects gang involvement.

---

variables were metric). The result showed only a significant effect from offending to gang involvement and not the other way around. Our decision is thus partially a practical consequence of the limitation of the data.

Table 5.2 Path analyses of the CCE-model of gang involvement (best fitting model)

	Parental attachment	Parental monitoring	External locus of control	Low self-control	School social bond	Legal cynicism	Lifestyle risk	Offending	Gang involvement
Independent variables	β	β	β	β	β	β	β	B	Log odds
Micro-place disorder	–0.16	–0.19	0.20	0.20	–	–	0.33	0.10	0.38
Parental attachment		0.42	–0.16	–	0.22	–	–	–	–
Parental monitoring			–0.10	–0.21	0.13	–0.22	–0.24	–0.10	–0.32
External locus of control				0.41	–0.14	0.13	–	–	–
Low self-control					–0.23	0.39	0.17	0.14	–
School social bond						–0.12	–0.16	–	–
Legal cynicism							0.25	0.34	0.67
Lifestyle risk								0.24	0.27
Offending									0.15
(Pseudo-)R^2	0.03	0.24	0.11	0.35	0.27	0.43	0.37	0.51	0.47

Note: all path-coefficients are statistically significant at $p<0.01$ or better

5.6 Discussion and Conclusion

The purpose of this chapter was to present an integrative theoretical framework to explain individual differences in gang participation. To test the integrative theory, we used data from a large-scale youth survey that was conducted in Antwerp (Belgium) in 2005. Since this was a cross-sectional study, we do not know these adolescents' past childhood development, and we do not know how they have developed since they participated in the study. Therefore we cannot explain how these individual differences have emerged and cannot say how their current gang participation will affect their future lives. Unfortunately the cross-sectional study design poses some restrictions. While this research studied individual differences in involvement, it is paramount for future research to study involvement and disengagement seriously as separate concepts that may have a distinct etiology (Melde and Esbensen 2011; Sweeten et al. 2013).

In line with the integrated theory, micro-place disorder matters regarding personal and social control mechanisms (parental attachment, parental monitoring, external locus of control, and low self-control) and lifestyle risk. Parental monitoring had multiple direct effects on low self-control, external locus of control, the school social bond, legal cynicism, offending, and gang participation. The effect of external locus of control should, however, not be overestimated. There was no direct effect on gang involvement and offending when low self-control, legal cynicism, and school social bond were taken into account. Indeed, this may not be surprising, given the number of intervening mechanisms, but the number of studies that have empirically tested effects of locus of control in an integrative framework are limited. Does that mean that locus of control is irrelevant as an explanatory mechanism? We argue that this is not the case. Firstly, there exists a moderate bivariate correlation between external locus of control and gang involvement (0.30; $p<0.001$) and between external locus of control and offending ($r=0.30$; $p<0.001$). Secondly, we argued that it is of utmost importance to distinguish between causes and causes of the causes of gang involvement and offending. An external locus of control is one of the strongest direct predictors of low self-control and external locus of control is directly related to the school social bond and to moral beliefs. Locus of control logically fits into general integrated theoretical frameworks: external locus of control is a consequence of micro-place disorder and is negatively related to parental monitoring, also one of the important control mechanisms in control theories of gang involvement and offending.

Contrary to previous studies, this study did not find any direct effects of low self-control on gang involvement when lifestyle risk was taken into account. Adopting a street-oriented lifestyle affects the likelihood of becoming involved in a gang. That may be because youth groups actively recruit or because the risky lifestyle increases the likelihood of getting in contact. Theoretically a risky lifestyle can have a selection effect, a socialization effect and a facilitating effect. The risky lifestyle is especially related to low self-control and legal cynicism. Another issue that needs to be empirically studied in the Belgian context is the effect of risky lifestyles on victimization (in gang and non-gang youth). It is not clear to what extent this relationship that may be hypothesized from different theoretical frameworks (see, e.g., Guterman et al. 2009) also can be reproduced in the Belgian context.

We do not doubt the relevance of testing alternative models of gang involvement that incorporate mechanisms which are sometimes discussed, but rarely tested. But as we have tested a theory of youths using a cross-sectional model, this model is not able to fully capture what is going on over time. While the integrated theory is built on causal arrows that go in one direction, we believe for a number of reasons that this is an oversimplification. First of all, a number of longitudinal studies, such as the ones referred to by Thornberry and colleagues (2003) have demonstrated that there are reciprocal effects over time. It is unclear at the moment to what extent gang involvement in itself is related to the ecological, personal, social, and situational mechanisms over time. This is an interesting question that remains unanswered. It is plausible that a relationship exists between external locus of control and the length of an individual's career as a gang member. If such a relationship would exist, the strength of that relationship might depend on the nature of the group and the functions and social roles that the individual fulfils. Gang involvement is likely to reinforce legal cynicism over time, just like it intensifies offending (Melde and Esbensen 2011). As Ross and Mirowsky (2009) observed, external locus of control is higher in micro-places that are characterized by high levels of disorder. The negative world view that one is not in control (i.e., fatalism) is an additional mechanism in the development of legal cynicism and low self-control, which in turn has strong consequences for lifestyle risk and ultimately for gang involvement and offending. Most micro-place theories stress that micro-place effects are indirect through their impact on informal controls. We have tested an additional link. Future research might also want to study the effect of repeat victimization on external locus of control and might want to study reciprocal effects between locus of control, moral beliefs, and self-control. These reciprocal effects are not necessarily mediated by gang involvement and offending and these hypothesized reciprocal effects may even be slightly different in males and females or immigrant and non-immigrant youths. Clearly, only detailed empirical analyses can provide an answer to this question.

Despite these restrictions, our findings contribute to theory and practice. Also in Belgium a number of young adolescents self-reported gang involvement. In our sample the percentage was 8.1. This underscores the urgent need for effective gang resistance education programs and other primary and secondary prevention and intervention initiatives directed at youths in early adolescence, especially those that are prone to a risky lifestyle, have low self-control, and have high scores on legal cynicism and external locus of control. Additionally, the basic pattern holds in all subgroups (Belgian and non-Belgian girls and boys). The similarities by and large exceed the differences.[14] The magnitude of the coefficients is similar. The implication of our finding for theories of gang involvement is that we have demonstrated that the relationship between observed micro-place disorder and gang involvement

[14] The models differ with regard to the existence of direct effect of the "causes of the causes" of VYG and offending, not regarding the basic structure of the end-to-end integrative model.

is a matter of social controls, self-control, and lifestyle risk but also a matter of external locus of control. External locus of control or "subjective powerlessness" fits in as a concept in Wood and Alleyne's (2010) unified framework of gang membership but it may also fit in Thornberry's interactional theory. The justification for this statement is found in the strong direct effects on key causes of gang involvement and offending. In other words, control orientation is an important mechanisms that explains why some individuals develop the propensities they have (moral beliefs and self-control), which in turn have an impact on self-selection (i.e., why some individuals self-select the settings in which they are situationally triggered). This is what a deep causal explanation is all about in the analytical criminological framework we proposed. The principles of an analytical approach toward the theoretical and empirical study of gang involvement may stimulate the development and refinement of theoretical frameworks that previously existed. Theories are not static, but rather dynamic and should be adapted when new and stable findings emerge. Whether this is the case with the integrated framework we proposed should become clear after careful and critical tests in future studies.

Appendix 1: Constructs with Factor Loadings and Alpha Values

Scale construct	Item	Factor loading	Alpha value
Micro-place disorder	Neighborhood inhabitants quarrelling on the street	.549	.84
	Elder people being angry with youths	.515	
	Someone trying to hide something in a shopping bag in a local store to steal it	.612	
	Garbage and/or dirt being on the sidewalk	.515	
	A group of local youth harassing someone to get money or something else of value	.698	
	House fronts, doors, etc. being covered with graffiti	.467	
	A couple of men drinking alcohol (beer, etc.) in the street (e.g., at a bus-stop or local supermarket)	.605	
	Someone selling drugs (hash, marijuana, etc.) on the streets	.671	
	Someone being threatened with a weapon on the street (fire arm, knife, etc.)	.662	
	A youngster starting a fight because he or she has been challenged by another youth	.669	

(continued)

(continued)

Scale construct	Item	Factor loading	Alpha value
Parental attachment	I can get along well with my parents/caretakers	.730	.81
	I find the remarks from my parents important	.740	
	I like to be with my parents in my free time	.740	
	I can talk well with my parent/caretakers	.701	
Parental monitoring	My parents/caretakers know with whom I hang around when I am not at home	.645	.71
	My parents/caretakers know where I am when I am not at home	.743	
	My parents/caretakers know how I behave when I am not home	.625	
	When I have to go to school the next day, I need to be in bed on time	.439	
	If I am with friends, I need to be home at an agreed upon hour	.454	
External locus of control	I often have the feeling of getting into trouble beyond my control	.566	.59
	I believe that planning does not guarantee success	.615	
	Working hard is useless, its seldom pays off for me	.520	
Low self-control	Used items consists of two subscales: temper and impulsiveness		.78
Temper (anger management)	When I am angry, others had better stay out of my way	.637	.67
	When I am angry with someone, I'd rather hit then talk	.617	
	I get angry easily	.659	
Impulsiveness (immediate gratification)	I often do things without thinking	.583	.72
	If I can have fun immediately, I'll do it, even if I get in rouble later	.666	
	I say what I think, even if it is not smart	.586	
	I often do immediately what I feel like doing	.665	
School social bond	I do not make a serious effort to do homework	.601	.65
	I don't care for the remarks of my teachers	.519	
	I am not interested in getting high grades	.539	
Legal cynicism	Rules are made to be broken	.668	.78
	It is ok to break rules, as long as you don't get caught	.772	
	It is ok to fight if you are challenged	.639	
	If I don't succeed using honest methods, then I use unfair methods	.680	
Situational context	Exposure to criminogenic moral settings (people + places)		

(continued)

(continued)

Scale construct	Item	Factor loading	Alpha value
Peer delinquency (people)	How many of your friends have ever stolen something or taken away money?	.697	.72
	How many of your friends have ever hit someone with the consequence that this person needed medical care?	.684	
	How many of your friends have ever destroyed or damaged something?	.682	
Routines risk indicator questions (places)	Q1: How often are you spending your leisure time on street corners (−1 = never/0 = sometimes, 1 = often) +	–	–
	Q2: How often are you spending your leisure time in unsupervised settings (like parking lots, parks,…) (−1 = never/0 = sometimes, 1 = often)		
	Routine risk score = $q1 + q2$		
Overall exposure/ Lifestyle Risk Score	Summation of binned variable peer delinquency (−1 = lower quartile, 0 = medium, 1 = upper quartile) and routine risk score (see above), thus lifestyle risk = binned peer delinquency scale + routine risk score		

Appendix 2: Path Analyses of the CCE-Model of GANG Involvement by Gender and by Immigrant Background

Belgian boys (best fitting model, all parameters significant at $p < 0.05$ or better)

	Parental attachment	Parental monitoring	External locus of control	LSC	School social bond	Legal cynicism	Lifestyle risk	Offending	Gang involvement
Independent variables	β							*B*	Log odds
Micro-place disorder	–0.20	–0.14	0.14	0.13	–		0.26	0.15	0.44
Parental attachment		0.38	–0.19		0.20		–		–
Parental monitoring			–	–0.20	0.37	–0.16	–0.13	–0.11	–0.43
External locus of control				0.45	–0.22	0.09	–	–	–
Low self-control					–0.13	0.41	0.12	–	–
School social bond						–0.16	–0.14	–	–
Legal cynicism							0.28	0.48	0.99
Lifestyle risk								0.44	0.22
Offending									0.39

β standardized beta coefficient, *B* negative binomial coefficient, L.O. log-odds

RMSEA 0.045 CFI 0.98 X^2: 26.907 *df* 13 $p < 0.01$ (calculated from linear model)

Immigrant boys (best fitting model, all parameters significant at $p<0.05$ or better)

	Parental attachment	Parental monitoring	External locus of control	LSC	School social bond	Legal cynicism	Lifestyle risk	Offending	Gang involvement
Independent variables	β							B	L.O.
Micro-place disorder	–0.13	–0.19	0.22	0.17	–	–	0.30	–	0.42
Parental attachment		0.44	–0.12	–	0.21	–	–	–	–
Parental monitoring			–0.08	–0.13	0.13	0.23	–0.18	–0.10	–0.50
External locus of control				0.38	–0.09	0.13	–	–	–
LSC					–0.28	0.40	0.15	–	–
School social bond						–0.11	–	–	–
Legal cynicism							0.16	0.32	0.43
Lifestyle risk								0.43	0.64
Offending									–

β standardized beta coefficient, B negative binomial coefficient, L.O. Log-odds
RMSEA 0.019 CFI 0.99 X^2: 14.796 d*f* 12 $p<0.03$ (calculated from linear model)

Belgian girls (best fitting model, all parameters significant at $p < 0.05$ or better)

	Parental attachment	Parental monitoring	External locus of control	LSC	School social bond	Legal cynicism	Lifestyle risk	Offending	Gang involvement
Independent variables	β	β	β	β	β	β	β	B	L.O.
Micro-place disorder	–0.23	–0.18	0.16	0.21	–	–	0.24	–	–
Parental attachment		0.43	–0.21	–	0.25	–	–	–	–
Parental monitoring			–0.13	–0.20	0.19	–0.18	–0.25	–0.20	–0.23
External locus of control				0.52	–0.15	0.12	–	–	–
LSC					–0.26	0.32	0.13	0.48	0.99
School social bond						–0.25	–0.12	–	–
Legal cynicism							0.21	0.37	0.57
Lifestyle risk								0.61	1.27
Offending									–

β standardized beta coefficient, B negative binomial coefficient, L.O. log-odds
RMSEA = 0.047 CFI 0.98 X^2: 33.100 df 15 $p < 0.001$ (calculated from linear model)

Immigrant girls (best fitting model, all parameters significant at $p < 0.05$ or better)

	Parental attachment	Parental monitoring	External locus of control	LSC	School social bond	Legal cynicism	Lifestyle risk	Offending	Gang involvement
Independent variables	β							B	L.O.
Micro-place disorder	–0.16	–0.09	0.23	0.22		–	0.16	0.10	0.35
Parental attachment		0.49	–	–	0.18	–	–	–	–
Parental monitoring			–0.20	–0.29	0.11	–0.14	–0.24	–0.10	–0.32
External locus of control				0.35	–0.15	0.15	–	–	–
LSC					–0.16	0.37	0.18	0.14	–
School social bond						–0.14	–0.13	–	–
Legal cynicism							0.25	0.50	0.95
Lifestyle risk								0.64	0.91
Offending									–

β standardized beta coefficient, B negative binomial coefficient, L.O. log-odds
RMSEA = 0.047 CFI 0.98 X^2: 45.414 d*f* 18 < 0.000 (calculated from linear model)

References

Alleyne, E., & Wood, J. L. (2010). Gang involvement: Psychological and behavioral characteristics of gang members, peripheral youth, and nongang youth. *Aggressive Behavior, 36*(6), 423–436.

Bandura, A. (1986). *Social learning theory*. Englewood Cliffs, NJ: Prentice-Hall.

Bernasco, W., Ruiter, S., Bruinsma, G. J., Pauwels, L. J., & Weerman, F. M. (2013). Situational causes of offending: A fixed-effects analysis of space–time budget data. *Criminology, 51*(4), 895–926.

Bernburg, J. G., & Thorlindsson, T. (2005). Violent values, conduct norms, and youth aggression: A multilevel study in Iceland. *The Sociological Quarterly, 46*(3), 457–478.

Bjørgo, T., & Haaland, T. (2001). *Vold, konflikter og gjenger. En undersøkelse blant ungdomsskoleelever i Skedsmo kommune*. Oslo: NIBR-notat 2001, 1.

Bollen, K. A. (1996). An alternative two stage least squares (2SLS) estimator for latent variable equations. *Psychometrika, 61*(1), 109–121.

Bollen, K. A. (1998). *Structural equations with latent variables. Wiley series in probability and mathematical statistics*. New York: Wiley.

Braga, A. A., Papachristos, A. V., & Hureau, D. M. (2010). The concentration and stability of gun violence at micro places in Boston, 1980–2008. *Journal of Quantitative Criminology, 26*(1), 33–53.

Brutsaert, H. (2001). *Co-educatie: Studiekansen en kwaliteit van het schoolleven*. Leuven, Belgium: Garant.

Bunge, M. (2012). *Causality and modern science*. New York: Courier Dover. (Original work published 1959)

Byrne, B. M. (2011). *Structural equation modeling with Mplus: Basic concepts, applications, and programming*. New York: Routledge Academic.

Cloward, R. A., & Ohlin, L. E. (1960). *Delinquency and opportunity*. New York: Free Press.

Cohen, A. (1955). *Delinquent boys: The culture of the gang*. Glencoe, IL: The Free Press.

Colvin, M. (2000). *Crime and coercion: An integrated theory of chronic criminality*. New York: St. Martin's Press.

Curry, G. D., & Decker, S. H. (2003). *Confronting gangs: Crime and community*. Los Angeles, CA: Roxbury.

Decker, S. H., & Weerman, F. M. (Eds.). (2005). *European street gangs and troublesome youth groups* (Vol. 3). Oxford, England: Altamira Press.

Edling, C., & Hedström, P. (2005). *Analytical sociology in Tocqueville's democracy in America* (Working Paper No. 3). Department of Sociology Stockholm University.

Elliott, D. S., Ageton, S. S., & Canter, R. J. (1979). An integrated theoretical perspective on delinquent behavior. *Journal of Research in Crime and Delinquency, 16*(3), 3–27.

Esbensen, F.-A., & Deschenes, E. P. (1998). A multisite examination of youth gang membership: Does gender matter? *Criminology, 36*(4), 799–827.

Esbensen, F.-A., Peterson, D., Taylor, T. J., & Freng, A. (2010). *Youth violence: Sex and race differences in offending, victimization, and gang membership*. Philadelphia, PA: Temple University Press.

Esbensen, F.-A., & Winfree, L. T. (1998). Race and gender differences between gang and nongang youth: Results from a multisite survey. *Justice Quarterly, 15*(3), 505–525.

Esbensen, F.-A., & Maxson, C. (2012). *Youth gangs in international perspective. Results from the Eurogang program of research*. New York: Springer.

Esbensen, F.-A., & Weerman, F. M. (2005). Youth gangs and troublesome youth groups in the United States and the Netherlands: A cross-national comparison. *European Journal of Criminology, 2*(1), 5–37.

Felson, M., & Boba, R. L. (Eds.). (2010). *Crime and everyday life* (4th ed.). Thousand Oaks, CA: Sage.

Forde, D. R., & Kennedy, L. W. (1997). Risky lifestyles, routine activities, and the general theory of crime. *Justice Quarterly, 14*(2), 265–294.

Gottfredson, M., & Hirschi, T. (1990). *A general theory of crime*. Stanford, CA: Stanford California Press.
Grasmick, H. G., Tittle, C. R., Bursik, R. C., & Arneklev, B. J. (1993). Testing the core empirical implications of Gottfredson and Hirschi's general theory of crime. *Journal of Research in Crime and Delinquency, 30*(1), 5–29.
Gatti, U., Haymoz, S., & Schadee, H. M. (2011). Deviant youth groups in 30 countries: Results from the second international self-report delinquency study. *International Criminal Justice Review*. doi:1057567711418500.
Guterman, N. B., Lee, S. J., Taylor, C. A., & Rathouz, P. J. (2009). Parental perceptions of neighborhood processes, stress, personal control, and risk for physical child abuse and neglect. *Child Abuse & Neglect, 33*(12), 897–906.
Haaland, T. (2000). *Vold—konflikt og gjengdannelse : en undersøkelse blant ungdom i fire byer*. NIBR-rapport 2000,14. Oslo, Norway: NIBR.
Hayes, A. F. (2013). *Introduction to mediation, moderation, and conditional process analysis*. New York: Guilford.
Haymoz, S., Maxson, C., & Killias, M. (2014). Street gang participation in Europe: A comparison of correlates. *European Journal of Criminology, 11*(6), 659–682.
Haynie, D. L., & Osgood, D. W. (2005). Reconsidering peers and delinquency: How do peers matter? *Social Forces, 84*(2), 1109–1130.
Hedström, P., & Swedberg, R. (Eds.). (1998). *Social mechanisms: an analytical approach to social theory*. Cambridge, England: Cambridge University Press.
Hedström, P. (2005). *Dissecting the social: On the principles of analytical sociology*. Cambridge, England: Cambridge University Press.
Heitmeyer, W., Collmann, B., Conrads, J., Matuschek, I., Kraul, D., Kühnel, W., et al. (1995). *Gewalt: Schattenseiten der Individualisierung bei Jugendlichen aus unterschiedlichen Milieus*. München, Germany: Juventa.
Higgins, G. E., & Jennings, W. G. (2010). Is unstructured socializing a dynamic process? An exploratory analysis using a semiparametric group-based modeling approach. *Criminal Justice Review, 35*(4), 514–532.
Huizinga, D., & Schumann, K. F. (2001). Gang membership in Bremen and Denver: Comparative longitudinal data. In M. Klein, H.-J. Kerner, C. Maxson, & E. Weitekamp (Eds.), *The Eurogang paradox* (pp. 231–246). Dordrecht, The Netherlands: Kluwer.
Jones, S., & Lynam, D. R. (2009). In the eye of the impulsive beholder the interaction between impulsivity and perceived informal social control on offending. *Criminal Justice and Behavior, 36*(3), 307–321.
Jöreskog, K. G., & Sörbom, D. (1993). *LISREL 8 User's reference guide*. Chicago, IL: Scientific Software International.
Katz, C. M., & Fox, A. M. (2010). Risk and protective factors associated with gang-involved youth in Trinidad and Tobago. *Revista Panamericana de Salud Pública, 27*(3), 187–202.
Klein, M. W., Weerman, F. M., & Thornberry, T. P. (2006). Street gang violence in Europe. *European Journal of Criminology, 3*(4), 413–437.
Kornhauser, R. R. (1978). *Social sources of delinquency*. Chicago, IL: University of Chicago Press.
Lilly, J. R., Cullen, F. T., & Ball, R. A. (2014). *Criminological theory: Context and consequences*. Thousand Oaks, CA: Sage.
Matza, D. (1964). *Delinquency and drift*. New Brunswick, NJ: Transaction.
Maxfield, M. G. (1987). Lifestyle and routine activity theories of crime: Empirical studies of victimization, delinquency, and offender decision-making. *Journal of Quantitative Criminology, 3*(4), 275–282.
Maxson, C. L., & Klein, M. W. (1995). Investigating gang structures. *Journal of Gang Research, 3*(1), 33–40.
Melde, C., & Esbensen, F.-A. (2011). Gang membership as a turning point in the life course. *Criminology, 49*(2), 513–552.
Melde, C., & Esbensen, F.-A. (2014). The relative impact of gang status transitions: Identifying the mechanisms of change in delinquency. *Journal of Research in Crime and Delinquency, 51*(3), 349–376.

Miller, J., & Brunson, R. K. (2000). Gender dynamics in youth gangs: A comparison of male and female accounts. *Justice Quarterly, 17*(3), 801–830.

Miller, W. (1958). Lower class culture as a generating milieu of gang delinquency. *Journal of Social Issues, 14*(3), 5–20.

Mirowsky, J., & Ross, C. E. (2003). *Social causes of psychological distress* (2nd ed.). Hawthorne, NY: Aldine De Gruyter.

Muthén, B. (2011). *Applications of causally defined direct and indirect effects in mediation analysis using SEM in Mplus*. Retrieved from https://www.statmodel.com/download/causalmediation.pdf

Muthén, L. K., & Muthén, B. (2011). *Mplus user's guide* (6th ed.). Los Angeles, CA: Muthén & Muthén.

Oberwittler, D. (2004). A multilevel analysis of neighbourhood contextual effects on serious juvenile offending: The role of subcultural values and social disorganization. *European Journal of Criminology, 1*(2), 201–235.

Oberwittler, D., & Wikström, P.-O. (2009). Why small is better: Advancing the study of the role of behavioral contexts in crime causation. In D. Weisburd, W. Bernasco, & G. Bruinsma (Eds.), *Putting crime in its place* (pp. 35–59). New York: Springer.

Osgood, D. W., Wilson, J. K., O'Malley, P. O., Bachman, J. G., & Johnston, L. D. (1996). Routine activities and individual deviant behavior. *American Sociological Review, 61*(4), 635–655.

Pauwels, L. (2008). Geweld in groepsverband onder Antwerpse jongeren: de rol van schoolcontext en leefstijl. *Tijdschrift voor Criminologie, 50*(1), 3–16.

Pauwels, L. (2010). Violent youth group involvement in context: The case of Antwerp. In L. J. Pauwels, W. Hardyns, & M. Van de Velde (Eds.), *Social disorganisation, offending, fear and victimisation. Findings from Belgian studies on the urban context of crime*. Den Haag, The Netherlands: Boom Juridische Uitgevers.

Pauwels, L. (2012). Social disorganisation and adolescent offending in Antwerp. A multilevel study of the effect of neighbourhood disadvantage on individual involvement in offending. In P. Ponsaers (Ed.), *Social analysis of financial, economic and ecological crime, (in)security and (Dis)trust, public and private policing security* (pp. 133–166). Antwerpen, Belgium: Maklu.

Pauwels, L. (2013). Adolescent offending and disadvantage in urban neighbourhoods and schools. A cross-classified multilevel analysis. In D. Oberwittler, S. Rabold, & D. Baier (Eds.), *Städtische Armutsquartiere—Kriminelle Lebenswelten? Studien zu sozialräumlichen Kontexteffekten auf Jugendkriminalität und Kriminalitätswahrnehmungen* (pp. 117–140). Wiesbaden, Germany: VS Verlag für Sozialwissenschaften.

Pauwels, L. (2014). *Regelovertredend gedrag. Oorzakelijke mechanismen en verklaringsmodellen*. Gent, Belgium: Academia Press.

Pauwels, L., Hardyns, W., & Van de Velde, M. (Eds.). (2010). *Social disorganisation, offending, fear and victimisation: Findings from Belgian studies on the urban context of crime*. The Hague, The Netherlands: Boom Legal.

Pauwels, L., & Pleysier, S. (2009). Self-report studies in Belgium and the Netherlands. In R. Zauberman (Ed.), *Self-reported crime and deviance studies in Europe* (pp. 51–76). Brussels, Belgium: VUB-Press.

Pauwels, L., & Svensson, R. (2008). How serious is the problem of item nonresponse in scale constructs of delinquency and key social mechanisms? A cross-national inquiry of two classroom PAPI-self report studies in Antwerp and Halmstad. *The European Journal of Criminology, 5*(3), 289–309.

Pauwels, L., & Svensson, R. (2013). Troublesome youth group involvement, self-reported offending and victimization: An empirical assessment of an integrated informal control/lifestyle model. *European Journal of Criminal Policy & Research, 19*(4), 369–386. doi:10.1007/s10610-013-9205-7.

Pauwels, L., & Svensson, R. (2014). Micro-place disorder, subjective powerlessness and violent youth group involvement: testing an integrative control theory. *International Journal of Criminology & Sociology*. doi:10.6000/1929-4409.2014.03.18.

Pauwels, L., Weerman, F., Bruinsma, G., & Bernasco, W. (2011). Perceived sanction risk, individual propensity and adolescent offending: Assessing key findings from the deterrence literature in a Dutch sample. *European Journal of Criminology, 8*(5), 386–400.

Pratt, T. C., & Cullen, F. T. (2000). The empirical status of Gottfredson and Hirschi's general theory of crime: A meta-analysis. *Criminology, 38*(3), 931–964.
Pyrooz, D. C. (2014). From your first cigarette to your last dyin' day: The patterning of gang membership in the life-course. *Journal of Quantitative Criminology, 30*(2), 349–372.
Riley, D. (1987). Time and crime: The link between teenager lifestyle and delinquency. *Journal of Quantitative Criminology, 3*(4), 339–354.
Ross, C. E., & Mirowsky, J. (2009). Neighborhood disorder, subjective alienation, and distress. *Journal of Health and Social Behavior, 50*(4), 49–64.
Sampson, R. J., & Bartusch, D. J. (1998). Legal cynicism and (subcultural?) tolerance of deviance: The neighborhood context of racial differences. *Law and Society Review, 32*, 777–804.
Sampson, R. J., & Laub, J. H. (2003). Life-course desisters? trajectories of crime among delinquent boys followed to age 70. *Criminology, 41*(3), 555–592.
Sharp, C., Aldridge, J., & Medina, J. (2006). *Delinquent youth groups and offending behaviour: Findings from the 2004 Offending, Crime and Justice Survey*. Home Office Online Report 14/06. London, UK: Home Office.
Svensson, R., & Pauwels, L. J. R. (2010). Is a risky lifestyle always "risky"? The interaction between individual propensity and lifestyle risk in adolescent offending: A test in two urban samples. *Crime & Delinquency, 56*(4), 608–626.
Sweeten, G., Pyrooz, D. C., & Piquero, A. C. (2013). Disengaging from gangs and desistance from crime. *Justice Quarterly, 30*(3), 469–500.
Thorlindsson, T., & Bernburg, J. G. (2004). Durkheim's theory of social order and deviance: A multi-level test. *European Sociological Review, 20*(4), 271–285.
Thornberry, T. P. (1987). Toward an interactional theory of delinquency. *Criminology, 25*(4), 863–892.
Thornberry, T. P., Krohn, M., Lizotte, A. J., & Smith, C. A. (2003). *Gangs and delinquency in developmental perspective*. Cambridge, UK: Cambridge University Press.
Thornberry, T. P., Hawkins, J. D., & Krohn, M. D. (1998). *Gang membership, delinquent peers, and delinquent behavior*. Washington, DC: US Department of Justice, Office of Justice Programs, Office of Juvenile Justice and Delinquency Prevention.
Thrasher, F. M. (1927). *The gang*. Chicago, IL: University of Chicago Press.
Vowell, P. R. (2007). A partial test of an integrative control model: Neighborhood context, social control, self-control, and youth violent behavior. *Western Criminology Review, 8*(2), 1–15.
Weisburd, D. L., Groff, E. R., & Yang, S. M. (2012). *The criminology of place: Street segments and our understanding of the crime problem*. New York: Oxford University Press.
Weisburd, D., Groff, E. R., & Yang, S. M. (2014). Understanding and controlling hot spots of crime: The importance of formal and informal social controls. *Prevention Science, 15*(1), 31–43.
Weerman, F. M. (2005). Identification and self-identification: Using a survey to study gangs in The Netherlands. In S. H. Decker & F. M. Weerman (Eds.), *European street gangs and troublesome youth groups: Findings from the Eurogang research program* (pp. 165–188). Walnut Creek, CA: AltaMira Press.
Weerman, F. M., Lovegrove, P. J., & Thornberry, T. (2015). Gang membership and its consequences: exploring changes related to joining and leaving gangs in two countries. *European Journal of Criminology, 12*(1), 70–91.
Wikström, P.-O., & Butterworth, D. A. (2006). *Adolescent crime, individual differences and lifestyles*. Cullompton, Devon: Willan.
Wikström, P.-O., & Sampson, R. J. (2003). Social mechanisms of community influences on crime and pathways in criminality. In B. B. Lahey, T. E. Moffitt, & A. Caspi (Eds.), *Causes of conduct disorder and juvenile delinquency* (pp. 118–148). New York: Guilford.
Wikström, P.-O., Oberwittler, D., Treiber, K., & Hardie, B. (2012). *Breaking rules: The social and situational dynamics of young people's urban crime*. Oxford, England: Oxford University Press.
Wood, J., & Alleyne, E. (2010). Street gang theory and research: Where are we now and where do we go from here? *Aggression and Violent Behavior, 15*(2), 100–111.

Chapter 6
Gang Youth and Friendship Networks in California Correctional Facilities: Examining Friendship Structure and Composition for Incarcerated Gang and Non-Gang Youth

Shannon E. Reid and Cheryl L. Maxson

6.1 Introduction

Surveys of US correctional officials have long established that gangs and gang members are considered a critical threat to the safety and management of an institution (Camp and Camp 1985; Winterdyk and Ruddell 2010).[1] However, prison gangs are not necessarily a uniquely US problem, with research from the United Kingdom noting gang activity in their prison system (Wood et al. 2009; Wood 2006; Wood and Adler 2001). Gangs in prison continue to be a problem in US correctional institutions and, as the presence of gangs grows in Europe, gangs in prison may increasingly become an issue in Europe. Gangs in prison (whether they are street or prison oriented) bring a range of issues and complications into the correctional setting. Gangs are disruptive since they exert control over both individual prisoners and the larger prison environment through a range of gang-related activities, including violence and contraband distribution (Hagedorn 2005; Krienert and Fleisher 2001; Pyrooz et al. 2011). To many correctional officials and some scholars, gang membership is an organizing feature of prison life (Skarbek 2011).

Prison scholars have determined that gang membership is a major predictor of misconduct within a correctional institution (Blackburn and Trulson 2010; Cunningham and Sorensen 2007; DeLisi et al. 2004; Drury and DeLisi 2011; Gaes et al. 2002;

[1] Interestingly, prison officials often refer to gangs as "security threat groups." We retain the term "gang" as most appropriate for bridging the literature relevant to our work.

S.E. Reid (✉)
Department of Criminal Justice and Criminology, University of North Carolina at Charlotte, Charlotte, NC, USA
e-mail: s.reid@uncc.edu

C.L. Maxson
Department of Criminology, Law and Society, University of California, Irvine, Irvine, CA, USA
e-mail: cmaxson@uci.edu

C.L. Maxson, F.-A. Esbensen (eds.), *Gang Transitions and Transformations in an International Context*, DOI 10.1007/978-3-319-29602-9_6

Griffin 2007; Ireland and Power 2013; Jiang and Fisher-Giorlando 2002; Trulson 2007). Accordingly, correctional staff often utilizes gang designations for housing, treatment, and suppression actions within the facility. The relationship between gang members and misconduct has made the effective handling of gang members a main concern for prison administrators and staff (Carlson 2001; Huff and Meyer 1997). While the literature has focused on an individual's gang membership as a risk factor for misconduct, few have considered the group context of the gang and its members as a mechanism for behavioral problems within a correctional institution.

Since much of the institutional gang research has been conducted at the adult level, gangs in juvenile facilities are often ignored as a unique entity when compared to the gangs seen in prisons. Theoretical perspectives developed to explain adult behavior in prison may have less utility for youth correctional environments because they do not highlight the central role of peer influence on juvenile offending. The association between a youth's delinquent behavior and that of their friends has been consistently supported through decades of delinquency research (Akers et al. 1979; Haynie 2001; Haynie and Osgood 2005; Kandel 1978; Matsueda and Anderson 1998; Monahan et al. 2014; Warr 2005; Weerman 2011; Elliott et al. 1985). Peer studies within detention centers or group care facilities primarily focus on the negative effects of aggregating delinquent youth on future behavior and adult outcomes (Dishion et al. 1999; Leve and Chamberlain 2005). The aggregation of antisocial youth seems to provide a context that reinforces antisocial behaviors and attitudes (Leve and Chamberlain 2005). However, there is little discussion about the mechanisms behind this association. More research on the relationship between peers, gangs, and misconduct, beyond simple aggregation effects, would deepen our understanding of the group dynamics that can potentially affect individual risk factors for misconduct.

The current study uses the egocentric friendship networks from youth during their incarceration in the California Department of Corrections and Rehabilitation (CDCR) Division of Juvenile Justice (DJJ)[2] to examine how the structural and attribute characteristics of social networks vary between gang and non-gang youth. An egocentric network design consists of an *ego* (the focal actor), his or her set of alters (in this instance, friends) who are tied to the ego, and the measurements for the ties among the alters (Wasserman and Faust 1994). Egocentric networks focus on the personal networks of individuals rather than the entire social network of the facility. The goal of this chapter is to better understand gang membership as an organizing feature within juvenile facilities through the lens of the peer group. The study of gang and non-gang friendship network variation is the first step in considering the role of the peer group on differences in institutional behavior. An egocentric network design expands our understanding of institutional organization by building upon traditional studies of inmate culture by directly examining the structure and characteristics of a youth's friendship network. Since social network analysis offers the conceptual and methodological tools to study the patterns of relationships, it is ideal for undertaking the current project given the value placed on friendship during adolescence. This chapter explores whether gang members

[2] DJJ was previously called the California Youth Authority or CYA.

have distinctive egocentric networks and consider how these differences could be used to more effectively design prevention and intervention programs that target the gang-based peer group dynamics.

6.2 Background Literature and Hypotheses

6.2.1 Gangs in Correctional Settings

Gangs create two major issues within carceral settings. First, the presence of gangs disrupts the formal social control of the prison (Kalnich and Stojkovic 1985; Pyrooz et al. 2011; Ralph 1997). According to Fleisher and Decker (2001), prison gangs exploit the structural weaknesses in a prison, such as overcrowding and understaffing, for financial gain. Fleisher (1989) also points out that in a closed setting of a prison, competition for a limited number of customers for gang-related products or services can be problematic. Fong et al. (1992) discuss how overcrowding can also contribute to intergang competition. The presence of gangs has been found to increase racial tensions within a facility (Ross and Richards 2002). In California, the CDCR identifies eight gangs[3] active to varying degrees in its youth correctional facilities; most of these groups have distinct racial or geographic criteria about who can join (Skarbek 2011). Wood (2006) also noted that prisoners in the UK reported that prisoner groups formed along regional boundaries. Skarbek (2011) discusses how prison gangs leverage their power monopoly to administer governance services to the illicit markets present in California prisons. Similar gang dynamics were found in UK correctional institutions with both inmates and staff reporting that gang activity in the institution influenced their perceptions of how groups controlled events within the prison and decreased staff control (Wood 2006; Wood and Adler 2001).

The second concern is the relationship between the individual inmate's gang affiliation and their institutional behavior. The association between street gang membership and violence in the community is one of the most enduring findings of gang research (see Klein and Maxson 2006, for review). Similarly, inmate gang membership is positively associated with violent misconduct across a range of studies (Camp and Camp 1985; Fischer 2001; Gaes et al. 2002; Huebner 2003; Ireland and Power 2013). For example, Fischer (2001) determined that prison gang members were 74 % more likely than non-gang inmates to commit serious disciplinary violations. The overlap of peers and gang membership is underlined by Steiner et al.'s (2014) use of the terms antisocial peers and gang membership interchangeably in their review of the prison misconduct literature. While the juvenile correctional literature is much more limited than the adult misconduct literature, the connection between gangs and misconduct has been replicated in these studies. Using a sample of parolees from California's Youth Authority (previous name of DJJ), MacDonald

[3] Southerners, Northerners, Bulldogs, Crips, Bays/415, Bloods, Asians and Peckerwoods are the institutional gangs identified by DJJ.

(1999) determined that gang members were 30 % more likely to commit assorted acts of violence while incarcerated. Both Trulson (2007) and DeLisi et al. (2013) have found that gang members and/or those with gang-related family members were associated with higher levels of institutional misconduct.

6.2.2 Responding to Institutional Gangs

Correctional staff is tasked with controlling and minimizing the damage done by gangs in their facility. Administrative solutions to gang problems tend to focus on two main techniques: segregation and transfer (Pyrooz et al. 2011). Segregation refers to the removal of a gang member from the general population and isolating them in their cells for 23 h a day in an attempt to control their behavior and minimize their influence over other inmates. In Camp and Camp's (1985) survey of 33 agencies, both gang member segregation and gang leader segregation were cited 20 times. In a national study of 133 prison officials, Knox (2000) found that the majority of officials reported that the segregation policy did not meet antigang crime goals. However, a 2009 survey of 37 prison systems by Winterdyk and Ruddell (2010) identified segregation/isolation as the most commonly used strategy to manage gang issues and 75 % of their respondents considered the approach as very effective, the highest ranking among 13 strategies. Isolating gang members, and especially gang leaders, continues to be a popular control strategy.

A second strategy is the transferring of gang members to more secure or distant facilities. A Department of Justice (1992) report recommends the continual circulation of gang leaders between prisons to disrupt the group's leadership structure. Camp and Camp (1985) report that transfer was cited by 27 of the 33 agencies they surveyed. Other ways of managing the gang threat identified in surveys of corrections officials include: the use of informers; facility lockdowns; specialized housing units; restrictions on privileges; extension of prison sentences; increase in security classification; and interception of prison gang members' communications (Camp and Camp 1985; Winterdyk and Ruddell 2010). As seen from these surveys and reports, correctional administrators focus on either the individual or the larger group when attempting to manage the threat of institutional gangs. Focusing efforts on these two levels of intervention ignores the potential for behavior management at the smaller peer group or clique level.

6.2.3 Social Networks, Gangs, and Peers

In contrast to individual risk factor based studies of institutional behavior, social network methodology attempts to understand a youth's behavior as a function of their peer group structure. Network studies of friendship and offending groups are valuable since tie structure impacts the flow of information, social support, and social control. Within the broader criminological literature, network methodology has been used to investigate gang and co-offending networks. Weerman's (2003) study of Dutch youth determined that co-offending networks fluctuate over time. Sarnecki (2001) noted that in the Swedish town of Borlänge, 47 % of juvenile suspects were linked to one another in a single large network during a 6-month period. In a longitudinal egocentric network study, McGloin and Piquero (2010) found that higher levels of redundancy within a co-offender network were related to higher levels of specialized offending for group crimes. The application of social network methods to study gangs specifically is still fairly limited in the literature despite Fleisher's (2005) call to expand its use. When applying social network methodology to the study of gangs, scholars have focused on the group processes approach to gang research and gang violence (e.g., Fleisher 2006; McGloin 2005; Papachristos 2006, 2009). The continued growth of social network and gang research can only help elucidate our understanding of gang structure and its influence on individual members.

In the broader peer delinquency literature, social network studies have added nuance to the study of the relationship between peers and delinquency. Krohn and his colleagues (1986, 1988, 1993) were among the first to evaluate the degree to which delinquent behavior is influenced by an individual's network. These scholars determined that, while friends' delinquency is associated with an adolescent's own delinquency involvement, the structural characteristics of the friendship networks, such as its density and an adolescents' network position, influence the delinquency–peer connection. Haynie (2001) noted that the proportion of delinquent friends within an individual's network impacts delinquent behavior and Weerman (2011) reports that the average level of delinquency of one's friends influences individual behavior. Haynie (2001) found that the density of the peer network is an important component of the delinquency–peer association, in which very cohesive (dense) networks contain stronger delinquency–peer associations than those that are less cohesive. In the only network-based study of peer groups in a correctional setting, Clarke-McLean (1996) used social-cognitive mapping and found that youth were able to identify friendship clusters within the facility. While these association clusters do not address levels of intimacy within the group, they do show a peer group dynamic that creates clearly defined groups within the institution. Clarke-McLean (1996) also noted that these clusters showed stability despite the potential turnover present in a correctional setting. The integration of social network methodology into nontraditional settings, such as a correctional facility, offers the opportunity to understand misconduct beyond individual or institutional level risk factors by considering the role of the peer group and its structure.

6.2.4 *Gang Organization and Friendship Choice*

If gang membership is a primary organizing characteristic of a correctional facility, the peer group should reflect this association bias toward other gang members. This expectation is based in large part on the concept of homophily.

Homophily theories point to the behavioral and attitudinal similarities between individuals and their peer affiliations, the idea that "birds of a feather flock together" (Kandel 1978; Poulin et al. 1997; Urberg et al. 1998; Brechwald and Prinstein 2011). At the individual level, homophily theories hypothesize that people with similar characteristics are more likely to form a connection and those individuals who are already connected are more likely to share common attributes or statuses (Verbrugge 1977). In a correctional setting, there are administrative discussions of homogeneity along race/ethnicity and gang identities but this has not been systematically studied.

There are important implications of homophilous relationships at both the macro and micro level. At the macro level, homophily restricts the diffusion of information, resources, and other cultural material (McPherson et al. 1992). At the individual level, homophily on a particular behavior can serve as a reinforcer, which may contribute to undesirable behaviors such as aggression or depression (Dishion et al. 1991; Hartup and Moore 1990). Because of these behavioral and attitudinal implications, it is important to remember that homophily is seen as a recursive process. As stated by Erickson (1988) and reiterated in Kadushin (2012), the process of homophily means that people tend to associate with those who have similar attitudes and values as themselves, and if they associate with each other, they tend to have similar values and attitudes. When considering homophily among gang members, a peer group that consists of other gang members has important implications for behavioral and attitudinal outcomes within the facility.

In this chapter, we explore similarities and differences across gang and non-gang egocentric networks for youth incarcerated in California's DJJ. Based on previous gang research, the organizational expectations of a correctional staff, and theories of homophily, we investigate the following hypotheses:

Hypothesis 1 *Gang youth will have larger and denser networks than non-gang youth.*

Gang networks are expected to be larger than non-gang networks since their gang membership should ease their access into a pre-existing peer group from which to make friends. Their networks are also expected to be denser since gang members will know one another.

Hypothesis 2 *Gang networks will be demographically different than non-gang networks, with gang networks being more racially homogeneous, consist of more gang members, be younger and include fewer staff than non-gang networks.*

As mentioned earlier, the CDCR considers most of their prison gangs to have distinct racial or geographic distinctions about who can join (Skarbek 2011). For gang members, these distinct lines should be reflected in their peer networks. Skarbek (2011) also discusses the pride California gang members take in their affiliations and because of this their networks may be limited to their other gang member associates. It is also expected that gang members will have a younger group of friends due to the peak in gang membership being below age 18 (Esbensen and Carson 2012).[4] It is also expected that due to the gang's activity within the facility, youth will be less likely to build friendships with staff members.

Hypothesis 3 *Gang youth networks will have a longer history with their friends, will draw friends from throughout the facility, will spend more time together, and will rely on them more for assistance than non-gang youth.*

It is hypothesized that gang youth will have longer relationships with each other due to either (a) a longer incarceration history with more opportunity to meet other gang members in detention or state-run facilities and/or (b) a street gang connection to their peers who also have a higher risk for incarceration. It is also expected that they will spend more time together and be more likely to rely on their friends for help since there are potentially different expectations about gang-based friendship relationships.

Hypothesis 4 *Gang members will nominate more friends in their network who they perceive as involved in fighting and who they would be willing to fight for than non-gang youth.*

Incarcerated gang members are expected to participate in more misconduct than their non-gang counterparts. Based on theories of homophily, gang members should be more likely to build friendships with those who they perceive as more similar to themselves. Because of this, gang member youth should more often state that their friends are involved in fighting. Gang youth should also be more willing to intervene for their friends since this is a stronger behavioral expectation among gang youth than non-gang youth.

6.3 Research Methods

This chapter uses egocentric network data gathered from youth who were incarcerated in the five youth facilities operated by the DJJ during mid-September 2010. Access to these locations was gained as part of the remedial plan put in place after the settlement of *Farrell v Allen*, a 2004 lawsuit accusing California Youth Authority (now DJJ) of failing to protect wards from violence and abuse by staff and other wards. As a result of this lawsuit, DJJ was required to consult with nationally recognized experts to design strategies to reduce the gang and racial violence present in DJJ institutions. Data gathered by the larger project provided the foundation for policy recommendations (Maxson et al. 2012).

Over the decade prior to the initiation of the study, the number of youth held in state placements declined dramatically, from 7761 to 1602 at the time we drew our sample (Office of Research 2010). In addition to declining youth arrests, changes in

[4] DJJ can hold youth past their 18th birthday, so the population is not limited to 18 and under.

legislative policy made it far more costly for local authorities to send youth to DJJ institutions. In 2007, the California legislature constrained the type of conviction offenses for which youth were eligible for placement in DJJ. At the time of this study, only youth convicted of violent or serious felonies (defined under PC 707b) that *could* result in prosecution in adult court or certain sex crimes (which require registration as defined in PC 290) may be committed to DJJ (Office of Research 2010). While youth convicted by the juvenile court may be housed in DJJ facilities until age 25, current policy now requires all adult court commitments to be transferred to a CDCR facility (state prison or fire camp) at age 18. Thus, the period immediately preceding—and during which we conducted—the study, was marked by a decreasing population of increasingly serious offenders and a series of facility closures that challenged the corrections officials charged with maintaining safety and security for both staff and youth.

At the time we drew our interview sample, 71 % of the DJJ population was officially designated as a gang member. This percentage represents a modest decrease in the proportion of officially designated gang members. In 1995, 56.6 % of the DJJ population was an officially designated gang member compared to 82.4 % in 2006 (Parker et al. 2008). A Gang Information Coordinator (GIC) in each institution interviews youth within a few days of arrival to determine gang status.[5] The youth completes a gang disclosure form and is inspected for gang tattoos. Along with information contained in the youth's file, the GIC records the name of the youth's street gang and also the name of the institutional gang with which the youth is expected to affiliate. DJJ recognizes eight institutional gangs that are racially[6] and geographically distinct. Some youth reported to us that they only identified with their street gang, but this is not recognized in the official record: every youth with a street gang affiliation is also attributed an institutional gang affiliation. We were able to identify no instance wherein DJJ staff removed an official gang designation or reclassified an individual as inactive, or former, gang member. The current study utilizes membership in a street and/or institutional gang as reported by the youth to us during a confidential interview.

6.4 Network Instrument

The network prompt was focused on eliciting the names of close friends within the facility from a random sample of respondents. The network instrument was developed specifically for this project to study and gain an understanding of friendship within the closed setting of a juvenile correctional institution. The network instrument collected both more traditional demographic characteristics of each of the friends and a range of questions unique to the correctional experience.

[5] See Maxson et al. (2012), for a more thorough description of the official designation practice.

[6] See Goodman (2008), for a study of the racialized sorting process in adult prison reception centers in California.

The network prompt was adapted from the General Social Survey network prompt to focus on close friendships within the facility (Burt 1984). The current prompt states: *This section asks about the people you get support from here. Looking back at the time spent during your current stay, think about the people you would consider close friends, such as those whom you might discuss a personal matter with.* Since the network instrument was aimed at capturing friendship networks of youth during their period of incarceration, the prompt was restricted to friendships during both their current stay and current facility. The name generator consisted of an open-ended friendship prompt. This was a purposeful decision aimed at building upon previous juvenile network research by not artificially limiting or inflating the number of friends a youth might nominate.

The network instrument included a range of alter/friend demographics and relational history questions. These domains were aimed at testing homophily within the network and understanding any history between a youth and their friend(s). These network questions include the friend's age, race/ethnicity, gang membership, adult court commitment status, whether or not the friend is a staff member, and if the friend is housed in the same unit. Historical questions include if the ego knew the friend prior to their current incarceration and whether the ego knew the friend from the street or a previous incarceration, as well as how long the ego has known the individual. In order to explore some of the behavioral similarities and expectations within the friendship network, the instrument included several behavioral questions focused on fighting behavior.

6.5 Data

A random sample of 306 males, stratified by facility, was interviewed in confidential settings during the fall of 2010. The participation rate was 83 % and the sample closely approximates the DJJ male population (Maxson et al. 2012). Interviews took an average of 43 min. The network questions occurred at the very end of the interview and there was considerable attrition due to wanting or needing to return to other activities (e.g., meals, work, or recreation).

The institutional friendship prompt resulted in 144 male youth who nominated at least one friend and 69 youth who stated that they had no close friendships within the facility. These 213 youth were distributed across all five facilities operating during the time of the study. The network sample was not significantly different from those that did not complete the network portion on demographic or behavioral measures. This chapter focuses on the 144 youth who nominated at least one friend in the facility.

More than half (54 %) of the youth that reported at least one friend are Hispanic, and just over a quarter (29 %) are black; white youth constitute just 10 % of the sample and Asian or other race/ethnicity is 7 %. Reflecting our earlier description of the DJJ policy of retaining juvenile jurisdiction up until the age of 25, the mean age of the responding youth is 18.8 years (standard deviation = 2.1; range = 14.6–24.1). About two thirds (67 %) of those reporting at

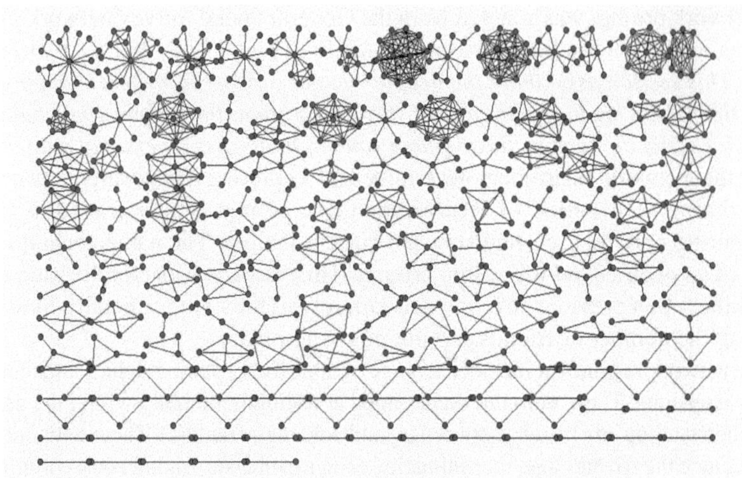

Fig. 6.1 Sociograms for youth's egocentric networks

least one friend were committed for a violent, non-sexual offense[7]; approximately one-quarter (28 %) for a sexual offense; and 5 % for some other offense. Just 13 % of this sample was committed to DJJ by an adult court. Finally, 67 % of the youth self-reported current gang membership.

6.6 Analysis

In order to analyze the youth networks, we created a matrix format dataset from the hand-drawn networks. The matrix dataset documents the ego/friend and friend/friend ties designated in the ego's network. Once this matrix was created, it was entered into UCINet (Borgatti et al. 2002) for analysis. Figure 6.1 shows the network drawings created in Pajek[8] (Batagelj and Mrvar 1999). The network drawings are a visual demonstration of the network arrangements. One can see the range from the one friend configurations to the larger networks at the top of the figure. The smallest networks were those where the ego only nominated one friend; the largest was an ego who nominated 16 friends. The average network is around four friends, and the majority of the egos nominated between two and five friends. On average, the density of these networks is 0.52 indicating that about half of all possible ties are present.

This chapter examines potential differences in how youth organize their friendship groups structurally and their perceptions of their friends' demographic characteristics and their friends' behavior. In order to do so, we test the hypotheses

[7] These were primarily for assault and robbery but 11 % of the sample was convicted of murder.

[8] While the pictures show some friend's friend connections, these were removed for final analysis.

presented earlier with a series of simple bivariate comparisons on a range of network structural and attribute variables.

6.7 Measures

We report the measures of variables included in the bivariate comparisons below. In some instances, such as age and fighting behavior, two different variables were used in the analysis in order to test potential differences. For example, since researchers have determined that both the count (Warr 1993a, b) and the proportion of delinquent peers (Haynie 2001) have an impact on behavior, we included both in analyses of fighting behavior.

Size: The count of friends a youth nominates in their network.

Density: Density of egocentric networks is calculated as the proportion of possible connections between friends that are actually present in the network, ranging from zero (no connections between friends) to one (all connections present) (Wasserman and Faust 1994).

Proportion same race or ethnicity: The proportion of a youth's total network that the youth identified as the same race or ethnicity as the youth.

Average age: The average age of friends in the youth's network.

Proportion under 18: The total number of friends under the age of 18 included in the youth's network.

Proportion gang member: The proportion of a youth's total network that the youth identified as a gang member (both street and institutional gangs included).

Total adult court commitments: The total number of youth sentenced through the adult court system that is included in the youth's network. Total number of youth rather than proportion is used for this variable since some facilities have very low numbers of adult court committed youth.

Total staff members: The total number of staff members included in the youth's network.

Total same housing unit: The number of friends in a youth's network that are housed in the same unit as the youth.

Previous knowledge of friends: A summary variable of the number of friend(s) a youth knew prior to their current incarceration.

Amount of time youth spends with friends: An average of the scaled responses to the question: "How often do you hang out or talk with [friend]? Would you say: everyday, most days, occasionally, rarely, never." This variable is coded from 1 to 5 (Never–Everyday).

Proportion youth goes to for help: The proportion of a youth's total network to which they responded positively to the question: "If you needed something, would you ask [friend] to help you get it?"

Proportion that fights: The proportion of friends in a youth's network that the youth answered affirmatively to the question "Is [initials] ever involved in fighting in this facility?"

Total friends that fight: The total number of friends in a youth's network that the youth answered affirmatively to the question "Is [initials] ever involved in fighting in this facility?"

Proportion that you would fight for: The proportion of a youth's network that the youth answered affirmatively to the question "Is there anyone on this paper who, if they got jumped and you saw it, you would jump in?" Staff friends were removed from this calculation.

Proportion you would fight for (without seeing incident): The proportion of a youth's network that the youth answered affirmatively to the question "Is there anyone on this paper who you would get into a fight for if you heard they were jumped but didn't see the fight?" Staff friends were removed from this calculation (Table 6.1 lists the descriptive statistics).

Table 6.1 Descriptive statistics of friendship network characteristics

Variable	Obs	Mean	SD	Min	Max
Network size	144	3.88	2.69	1	16
Network density[a]	124	0.52	0.42	0	1
Proportion same race/ethnicity	144	0.67	0.39	0	1
Average age of friends	142	20.34	5.71	15	50
Proportion under 18	144	0.14	0.23	0	1
Proportion gang member	139	0.51	0.43	0	1
Total adult court commitments	144	0.52	0.88	0	5
Total staff members	144	0.44	1.11	0	7
Proportion same housing unit[b]	137	0.65	0.35	0	1
Previous knowledge of friend(s)	144	1.19	1.50	1	9
Amount of time spent with friends	141	4.53	0.87	1	5
Proportion go to for help[b]	137	0.83	0.32	0	1
Proportion that fights	141	0.41	0.40	0	1
Total involved with fighting	144	1.59	2.07	0	13
Proportion fight for[b]	137	0.71	0.41	0	1
Proportion fight for[b] (did not see fight)	144	0.44	0.46	0	1

[a]Density was not calculated for the 20 out of 144 networks that had only an ego and one friend
[b]Does not include staff friends (there were 7 all staff networks)

Table 6.2 Network structural characteristics and friend demographic results

	Self-reported gang youth ($n=96$)		Self-reported non-gang youth ($n=48$)		
	M	SD	*M*	SD	*t*-test
Size	3.83	2.40	3.95	3.22	ns
Density[a] ($n=124$)	0.50	0.43	0.56	0.41	ns
Proportion same race	0.73	0.36	0.55	0.41	**
Proportion gang members ($n=139$)	0.62	0.41	0.25	0.05	***
Average age ($n=142$)	19.9	4.92	21.1	6.97	ns
Total under 18	1.51	1.79	0.89	1.24	*
Total staff members	0.39	1.02	0.52	1.27	ns
Total adult court commitments	0.60	0.94	0.35	0.69	*t*

t $p<.10$ *$p<0.05$ **$p<0.01$ ***$p<0.001$

[a]Density is only calculated for networks with two or more friends

Table 6.3 Friend relationships

	Self-reported gang youth ($n=96$)		Self-reported non-gang youth ($n=48$)		
	M	SD	*M*	SD	*t*-test
Total friends known previously	1.42	1.64	0.75	1.04	**
Total known from community	0.98	1.92	0.52	1.65	*t*
Length of time previously known (months)	24.53	23.59	22.52	34.78	ns
Proportion go to for help	0.91	0.25	0.82	0.34	*
Total same housing unit ($n=137$)	1.97	1.41	2.84	2.49	**
Amount friends hang out together	4.50	0.09	4.64	0.13	ns

t $p<.10$ *$p<0.05$ **$p<0.01$ ***$p<0.001$

6.8 Results

The next stage of our analysis explores whether gang and non-gang youth report networks with different structures and friend attributes. We begin by asking whether network structures and demographics vary between the two groups. As shown in Table 6.2, we find no significant differences in the size or density of the egocentric networks reported by gang and non-gang youth. Some of the demographic variables are significant, and suggest greater homophily among gang networks. For example, gang members have a significantly higher proportion of friends of the same race or ethnicity as themselves as well as a higher proportion of gang members in their networks. Gang members also have more friends under the age of 18. There is no difference in the average age of the friends reported by gang and non-gang youth,

Table 6.4 Friendship and fighting

	Self-reported gang youth ($n=96$)		Self-reported non-gang youth ($n=48$)		
	M	SD	*M*	SD	*t*-test
Proportion that fights	0.505	0.39	0.233	0.33	***
Total friends that fight	1.98	2.27	0.79	1.27	***
Proportion that you would fight for (no staff)	0.79	0.38	0.64	0.44	*
Proportion that you would fight for (without seeing) (no staff)	0.50	0.50	0.34	0.53	*

t $p<.10$ *$p<0.05$ **$p<0.01$ ***$p<0.001$

but gang members had—marginally—more adult court commitments in their networks.

Table 6.3 displays the comparison of features of personal relationships between a youth and their friends for gang and non-gang respondents. Gang youth knew significantly more of their friends prior to their current stay. Of the friends they knew prior to their incarceration, gang youth knew marginally more from the community. Gang youth also reported that, on average, they had a higher proportion of friends that they would go to for help. There are no differences in how long a youth had known their friends prior to incarceration or in how much time they spend with their friends in the facility. Non-gang youth reported significantly more friends from their own housing unit.

The final set of results (Table 6.4) focuses on the fighting behavior of a youth's friends and the youth's willingness to fight for their friends. Gang youth have a significantly higher proportion and total number of friends that they stated participate in fighting within the facility. Gang youth also report a larger proportion of friends within their networks that they would fight for if they saw them in a fight or if they heard their friend had been in a fight.

6.9 Discussion

This chapter examined differences in the structure and composition of gang and non-gang youth friendship networks. We hypothesized a range of differences in structure (gang larger and more dense), demographics (gang younger and more homogeneous regarding race/ethnicity, gang affiliation and staff friends), relationships (gang known longer, hang out more, rely more for assistance, and draw friends from throughout the facility), and fighting behaviors (gang friends more involved in fighting and willing to fight for). The results of the bivariate analyses highlight the differences in friendship groups between gang and non-gang youth. While we expected some differences in the structure and size of gang networks compared to non-gang networks, this did not prove to be the case. The lack of differences in the structural variables may be due to the constraints of the environment. Considering the closed nature of the facility, the limited population, and the range of opportunities for interaction between youth, it was perhaps unrealistic of us to expect differences in the density of the networks. The size of gang friendship networks may be determined by the number of members of the same gang placed in that facility whereas their non-gang counterparts may have more freedom of friendship choices.

Nevertheless, the composition of networks varied between the two groups on demographic, relationship, and fighting dimensions. Regarding the group of demographic characteristics, as hypothesized, gang youth had a significantly higher proportion of friends of the same race/ethnicity. It should be noted that over half of both gang and non-gang networks were of the same race/ethnicity as the respondent. Given the expectedly racialized nature of friendship selection in correctional institutions, it is interesting that these networks are not exclusively mono-racial/ethnic. While gang and non-gang youth show some racial preferences within their networks (and gang members more than others), both groups display racial/ethnic diversity. Gang youth also had a significantly higher proportion of gang members among their friendship networks (0.62 compared to 0.25). While gang membership in DJJ is highly racialized, we noted that the vast majority of youth listed their friends' street gang membership, rather than the more race/ethnicity-based institutional gang designation. This pattern suggests that gang members in an institution surround themselves with other gang members within their close personal friendship networks. The potential of these other gang-involved youth to influence institutional behavior needs to be investigated further.

Gang members also had more friends under the age of 18 and a higher proportion of adult court commitments. These two variables may be correlated because the majority of adult court commitments are transferred to adult prison on their 18th birthday. Future analyses might examine this in a multivariate context in order to better understand this relationship. The increased presence of younger friends may also have behavior implications since those youth may be earlier in their offending trajectories and more prone to adolescent behavioral issues. While number of friends under 18 years old differentiates the two groups of youth, mean age of friends did not and this held whether or not networks included staff friends. This finding may be due to the limited age range of the facilities and both gang and non-gang youth's willingness to befriend staff members. It is also interesting to note that neither gang nor non-gang youth showed a preference for staff members. Both groups of youth were willing to build friendships with staff (with or without it being reciprocated) and these relationships may offer opportunities for behavioral interventions with youth.

Our analyses revealed some differences in the nature of relationships between a youth and their friends. Gang youth knew more friends prior to their current incarceration and about twice as many from the community. Presumably, gang members' home networks may put them in contact with other delinquent youth who may end up in DJJ. Gang members also reported a significantly higher proportion of friends that they would go to for help with a problem. There are several potential reasons why gang members may go to their friends for help more often than non-gang youth. There may be a higher expectation of help when one is in a gang, a gang member may consider their friends to have more resources within the institution, or perhaps their previous knowledge of their friends has built trust for help-seeking efforts. Non-gang youth drew a significantly higher proportion of friends from their same housing unit, suggesting that gang youth rely less on proximity for friendship selection. Since non-gang youth knew fewer of their friends prior to the current incarceration, the creation of friendships may be more reliant on propinquity, which being in the same housing unit would provide. There were no differences between gang and non-gang youth in the amount of time that they reported hanging out with their friends. Considering the setting in which this study took place, this finding is unsurprising since youth spend all of their time in the presence of others. Even a decision to avoid someone would be difficult to implement since youth are expected to participate in a range of activities during the day.

The final set of variables we investigated in this chapter focused on the fighting behavior of networks. Gang youth reported both significantly more and a higher proportion of their friends were involved in fighting behavior. Past research has revealed that the perceptions of friend's attitudes and behavior can influence one's behavior (Metzler et al. 1994; Prinstein et al. 2001; Rai et al. 2003). Both groups also reported a high proportion of friends for whom they would physically intervene if they saw them being attacked, with gang members having a significantly higher proportion. Gang members also had a significantly higher proportion of friends for whom they stated they would fight if they heard that their friend had been jumped or assaulted. These findings confirm some of our expectations about gang members and their willingness to participate in fighting. It is worth noting that both groups had a high proportion of friends for whom they would fight (0.79 compared to 0.64) highlighting the violent offending histories of those currently incarcerated in DJJ and behavioral expectations within a correctional setting (Scott 2014).

6.10 Conclusion

In this chapter, we examined the egocentric networks of incarcerated youth in order to investigate whether there are significant structural and attribute characteristic differences between gang and non-gang youth friendship networks. The results indicate that there are significant differences in the peer groups for these two subsets of youth. Institutionalized gang youth appear to form deeper, more committed friendships than their non-gang counterparts, perhaps in response to the threat they experience as gang members. Gang members' networks reveal some dimensions of greater homophily. These qualities suggest that gang members' friendship networks may be difficult to disrupt even while their friends likely have a negative influence on a youth's institutional behavior.

Correctional officials' concern about the deleterious effect of gang membership on the safety of youth and staff is quite justified. Decades of research on responses to street gangs in the USA leave us with little guidance regarding effective interventions. As gangs become more recognized in Europe and are subjected to US-style suppression techniques (Shute et al. 2012), we predict that gang activity in European correctional institutions will become an increasing concern. Social network methods offer an opportunity to chart this development and bring new insights into gang processes and friendship selection in these highly constrained environments. Following Fleisher (2005), we encourage our European colleagues to utilize social network analysis to further our understanding of friendship formation and peer influence in a variety of settings.

References

Akers, R. L., Krohn, M. D., Lanza-Kaduce, L., & Radosevich, M. (1979). Social learning and deviant behavior: A specific test of a general theory. *American Sociological Review, 44*(4), 636–655.

Batagelj, V., & Mrvar, A. (1999). *Pajek program for analysis and visualization of large networks reference manual list of commands with short explanation version BE.*

Blackburn, A. G., & Trulson, C. R. (2010). Sugar and spice and everything nice? Exploring institutional misconduct among serious and violent female delinquents. *Journal of Criminal Justice, 38*(6), 1132–1140.

Borgatti, S. P., Everett, M. G., & Freeman, L. C. (2002). *Ucinet for windows: Software for social network analysis*. Harvard, MA: Analytic Technologies.

Brechwald, W. A., & Prinstein, M. J. (2011). Beyond homophily: A decade of advances in understanding peer influence processes. *Journal of Research on Adolescence, 21*(1), 166–179.

Burt, R. (1984). Network items and the General Social Survey. *Social Networks, 6*(4), 293–339.

Camp, G.M., & Camp, C.G. (1985). *Prison gangs: Their extent, nature, and impact on prisons*. US Department of Justice, Office of Legal Policy, Federal Justice Research Program.

Carlson, P. M. (2001). Prison interventions: Evolving strategies to control security threat groups. *Corrections Management Quarterly, 5*(1), 10–22.

Clarke-McLean, J. G. (1996). Social networks among incarcerated juvenile offenders. *Social Development, 5*(2), 203–217.

Cunningham, M. D., & Sorensen, J. R. (2007). Predictive factors for violent misconduct in close custody. *The Prison Journal, 87*(2), 241–253.

DeLisi, M., Berg, M. T., & Hochstetler, A. (2004). Gang members, career criminals and prison violence: Further specification of the importation model of inmate behavior. *Criminal Justice Studies, 17*(4), 369–383.

DeLisi, M., Spruill, J. O., Peters, D. J., Caudill, J. W., & Trulson, C. R. (2013). "Half in, half out:" Gang families, gang affiliation, and gang misconduct. *American Journal of Criminal Justice, 38*(4), 602–615.

Dishion, T. J., McCord, J., & Poulin, F. (1999). When interventions harm: Peer groups and problem behavior. *American Psychologist, 54*(9), 755.

Dishion, T. J., Patterson, G. R., & Kavanagh, K. A. (1991). An experimental test of the coercion model: Linking theory, measurement, and intervention. In J. McCord & R. Tremblay (Eds.), *The interaction of theory & practice: Experimental studies of intervention* (pp. 253–284). New York: Guilford.

Drury, A. J., & DeLisi, M. (2011). Gangkill: An exploratory empirical assessment of gang membership, homicide offending, and prison misconduct. *Crime & Delinquency, 57*(1), 130–146.

Elliott, D., Huizinga, D., & Ageton, S. (1985). *Explaining delinquency and drug use*. Beverly Hills, CA: Sage.

Erickson, B. H. (1988). The relational basis of attitudes. In B. Wellman & S. D. Berkowitz (Eds.), *Social structures: A network approach* (pp. 99–121). Cambridge, England: Cambridge University Press.
Esbensen, F.-A., & Carson, D. C. (2012). Who are the gangsters? An examination of the age, race/ethnicity, sex and immigrant status of self-reported gang members in a seven-city study of American youth. *Journal of Contemporary Criminal Justice, 28*(4), 462–478.
Fischer, D. R. (2001). *Arizona Department of Corrections: Security Threat Group (STG) program evaluation, final report.* Washington, DC: US Department of Justice, Office of Justice Programs, National Institute of Justice.
Fleisher, M. S. (1989). *Warehousing violence*. Newbury Park, CA: Sage.
Fleisher, M. S. (2005). Fieldwork research and social network analysis: Different methods creating complementary perspectives. *Journal of Contemporary Criminal Justice, 21*(2), 120–134.
Fleisher, M. S. (2006). Youth gang social dynamics and social network analysis: Applying degree centrality measures to assess the nature of gang boundaries. In J. F. Short & L. A. Hughes (Eds.), *Studying youth gangs* (pp. 85–98). Lanham, MI: Altamira Press.
Fleisher, M. S., & Decker, S. H. (2001). An overview of the challenge of prison gangs. *Corrections Management Quarterly, 5*(1), 1–9.
Fong, R. S., Vogel, R. E., & Buentello, S. (1992). Prison gang dynamics: A look inside the Texas Department of Corrections. In P. J. Benekos & A. V. Merlo (Eds.), *Corrections: Dilemmas and directions* (pp. 57–77). Cincinnati, OH: Anderson.
Gaes, G. G., Wallace, S., Gilman, E., Klein-Saffron, J., & Suppa, S. (2002). The influence of prison gang affiliation on violence and other prison misconduct. *The Prison Journal, 82*(3), 359–385. doi:10.1177/003288550208200304.
Goodman, P. (2008). "It's just black, white or Hispanic": An observational study of racializing moves in California's segregated prison reception centers. *Law and Society Review, 42*(4), 735–770.
Griffin, M. (2007). Prison gang policy and recidivism: Short term management benefits, long-term consequences. *Criminology & Public Policy, 6*(2), 223–230.
Hagedorn, J. M. (2005). The global impact of gangs. *Journal of Contemporary Criminal Justice, 21*(2), 153–169.
Hartup, W. W., & Moore, S. G. (1990). Early peer relations: Developmental significance and prognostic implications. *Early Childhood Research Quarterly, 5*(1), 1–17.
Haynie, D. (2001). Delinquent peers revisited: Does network structure matter? 1. *American Journal of Sociology, 106*(4), 1013–1057.
Haynie, D. L., & Osgood, D. W. (2005). Reconsidering peers and delinquency: How do peers matter? *Social Forces, 84*(2), 1109–1130.
Huebner, B. M. (2003). Administrative determinants of inmate violence: A multilevel analysis. *Journal of Criminal Justice, 31*(2), 107–117.
Huff, C. R., & Meyer, M. (1997). Managing prison gangs and other security threat groups. *Corrections Management Quarterly, 1*(4), 10–18.
Ireland, J. L., & Power, C. L. (2013). Propensity to support prison gangs: Its relationship to gang membership, victimisation, aggression and other disruptive behaviours. *Psychology, Crime & Law, 19*(9), 801–816.
Jiang, S., & Fisher-Giorlando, M. (2002). Inmate misconduct: A test of the deprivation, importation, and situational models. *The Prison Journal, 82*(3), 335–358.
Kadushin, C. (2012). *Understanding social networks: Theories, concepts, and findings*. New York: Oxford University Press.
Kalnich, D. B., & Stojkovic, S. (1985). Contraband: The basis for legitimate power in a prison social system. *Criminal Justice and Behavior, 12*(4), 435–451.
Kandel, D. B. (1978). Homophily, selection, and socialization in adolescent friendships. *American Journal of Sociology, 84*(2), 427–436.
Klein, M. W., & Maxson, C. L. (2006). *Gang structures, crime patterns, and police responses*. Los Angeles, CA: Social Science Research Institute, University of Southern California.

Knox, G. W. (2000). A national assessment of gangs and security threat groups (STGs) in adult correctional institutions: Results of the 1999 Adult Corrections Survey. *Journal of Gang Research, 7*(3), 1–45.
Krienert, J. L., & Fleisher, M. S. (2001). Gang membership as a proxy for social deficiencies: A study of Nebraska inmates. *Corrections Management Quarterly, 3*(1), 47–58.
Krohn, M. (1986). The web of conformity: A network approach to the explanation of delinquent behavior. *Social Problems, 33*(6), 601–613.
Krohn, M., Massey, J., & Zielinski, M. (1988). Role overlap, network multiplexity, and adolescent deviant behavior. *Social Psychology Quarterly, 51*(4), 346–356.
Krohn, M. D., Thornberry, T. (1993). Network theory: A model for understanding drug abuse among African-American and Hispanic youth. In M. R. De La Rosa & J.-L. Recio Adrados (Eds.) *Drug Abuse among minority youth: Advances in research and methodology* (pp. 102–28). NIDA research monograph 130. Washington, DC: U.S. Department of Health and Human Services.
Leve, L. D., & Chamberlain, P. (2005). Association with delinquent peers: Intervention effects for youth in the juvenile justice system. *Journal of Abnormal Child Psychology, 33*(3), 339–347.
MacDonald, J. M. (1999). Violence and drug use in juvenile institutions. *Journal of Criminal Justice, 27*(1), 33–44. doi:10.1016/S0047-2352(98)00033-6.
Matsueda, R. L., & Anderson, K. (1998). The dynamics of delinquent peers and delinquent behavior. *Criminology, 36*(2), 269–308.
Maxson, C., Bradstreet, C., Gascón, D., Gerlinger, J., Grebenkemper, J., Haerle, D., et al. (2012). *Gangs and violence in California's youth correctional facilities: A research foundation for developing effective gang policies*. Report submitted to the California Department of Corrections and Rehabilitation's Division of Juvenile Justice.
McGloin, J. (2005). Policy and intervention considerations of a network analysis of street gangs. *Criminology & Public Policy, 4*(3), 607–635.
McGloin, J. M., & Piquero, A. R. (2010). On the relationship between co-offending network redundancy and offending versatility. *Journal of Research in Crime and Delinquency, 47*(1), 63–90.
McPherson, J. M., Popielarz, P. A., & Drobnic, S. (1992). Social networks and organizational dynamics. *American Sociological Review, 57*(2), 153–170.
Metzler, C. W., Noell, J., Biglan, A., Ary, D., & Smolkowski, K. (1994). The social context for risky sexual behavior among adolescents. *Journal of Behavioral Medicine, 17*(4), 419–438.
Monahan, K. C., Rhew, I. C., Hawkins, J. D., & Brown, E. C. (2014). Adolescent pathways to co-occurring problem behavior: The effects of peer delinquency and peer substance use. *Journal of Research on Adolescence, 24*(4), 630–645.
Office of Research. (2010). *Juvenile justice outcome evaluation report*. California Department of Corrections and Rehabilitation.
Papachristos, A. V. (2006). Social network analysis and gang research: Theory and methods. In J. F. Short Jr. & L. Hughes (Eds.), *Studying youth gangs* (pp. 99–116). Lanham, MD: AltaMira Press.
Papachristos, A. V. (2009). Murder by structure: Dominance relations and the social structure of gang homicide. *American Journal of Sociology, 115*(1), 74–128.
Parker, R. N., Negola, T., Haapanen, R., Miranda, L., & Asencio, E. (2008). Treating gang-involved offenders. In R. D. Hoge, N. G. Guerra, & P. Boxer (Eds.), *Treating the juvenile offender* (pp. 171–192). New York: Guilford.
Poulin, F., Cillessen, A. H., Hubbard, J. A., Coie, J. D., Dodge, K. A., & Schwartz, D. (1997). Children's friends and behavioral similarity in two social contexts. *Social Development, 6*(2), 224–236.
Prinstein, M. J., Boergers, J., & Spirito, A. (2001). Adolescents' and their friends' health-risk behavior: Factors that friend or add to peer influence. *Journal of Pediatric Psychology, 26*(5), 287–298.

Pyrooz, D., Decker, S., & Fleisher, M. (2011). From the street to the prison, from the prison to the street: Understanding and responding to prison gangs. *Journal of aggression, conflict and peace research, 3*(1), 12–24.
Rai, A. A., Stanton, B., Wu, Y., Li, X., Galbraith, J., Cottrell, L., et al. (2003). Relative influences of perceived parental monitoring and perceived peer involvement on adolescent risk behaviors: An analysis of six cross-sectional data sets. *Journal of Adolescent Health, 33*(2), 108–118.
Ralph, P. H. (1997). From self-preservation to organized crime: The evolution of inmate gangs. In J. W. Marquart & J. R. Sorensen (Eds.), *Correctional contexts: Contemporary and classical readings* (pp. 182–186). Los Angeles, CA: Roxbury.
Ross, J. I., & Richards, S. C. (2002). *Behind bars: Surviving prison*. New York: Penguin.
Sarnecki, J. (2001). *Delinquent networks: Youth co-offending in Stockholm*. Cambridge, England: Cambridge University Press.
Scott, D. W. (2014). Attitude is everything: Youth attitudes, gang involvement, and length of institutional gang membership. *Group Processes & Intergroup Relations, 17*(6), 704–709.
Shute, J., Aldridge, J., & Medina, J. (2012). Loading the policy blunderbuss. *Criminal Justice Matters, 87*(1), 40–41.
Skarbek, D. (2011). Governance and prison gangs. *American Political Science Review, 105*(04), 702–716.
Steiner, B., Butler, H. D., & Ellison, J. M. (2014). Causes and correlates of prison inmate misconduct: A systematic review of the evidence. *Journal of Criminal Justice, 42*(6), 462–470.
Trulson, C. R. (2007). Determinants of disruption institutional misconduct among state-committed delinquents. *Youth Violence and Juvenile Justice, 5*(1), 7–34.
United States Department of Justice. (1992). *Management strategies in disturbances and with gangs/disruptive groups*. Washington, DC: U.S. Government Printing Office.
Urberg, K. A., Degirmencioglu, S. M., & Tolson, J. M. (1998). Adolescent friendship selection and termination: The role of similarity. *Journal of Social and Personal Relationships, 15*(5), 703–710.
Verbrugge, L. M. (1977). The structure of adult friendship choices. *Social Forces, 56*(2), 576–597.
Warr, M. (1993a). Parents/peers, and delinquency. *Social Forces, 72*(1), 247–264.
Warr, M. (1993b). Age, peers, and delinquency. *Criminology, 31*(1), 17–40.
Warr, M. (2005). Making delinquent friends: Adult supervision and children's affiliations. *Criminology, 43*(1), 77–106.
Wasserman, S., & Faust, K. (1994). *Social network analysis: Methods and applications*. New York: Cambridge University.
Weerman, F. M. (2003). Co-offending as social exchange. Explaining characteristics of co-offending. *British Journal of Criminology, 43*(2), 398–416.
Weerman, F. M. (2011). Delinquent peers in context: A longitudinal network analysis of selection and influence effects. *Criminology, 49*(1), 253–286.
Winterdyk, J., & Ruddell, R. (2010). Managing prison gangs: Results from a survey of US prison systems. *Journal of Criminal Justice, 38*(4), 730–736.
Wood, J. (2006). Gang activity in English prisons: The prisoners' perspective. *Psychology, Crime & Law, 12*(6), 605–617.
Wood, J., & Adler, J. (2001). Gang activity in English prisons: The staff perspective. *Psychology, Crime & Law, 7*(1–4), 167–192.
Wood, J., Moir, A., & James, M. (2009). Prisoners' gang-related activity: The importance of bullying and moral disengagement. *Psychology, Crime & Law, 15*(6), 569–581.

Chapter 7
Israeli and US Gangs in the Virtual World: The Sociocultural Context of Gang Members' Online Activity

Revital Sela-Shayovitz, David C. Pyrooz, and Scott H. Decker

7.1 Introduction

Recent changes in digital technology have had a powerful impact on daily lives. The Internet has become the dominant communication medium of modern life, and impacts a wide range of routine activities such as news consumption, social networking, obtaining information, entertainment, and shopping. Indeed, Internet access and use have become nearly ubiquitous around the globe (Boonaert and Vettenburg 2011; Moule et al. 2013; Silverblatt 2004; Pyrooz et al. 2015). Global Internet usage grew by nearly sevenfold between the years 2000 and 2014 (Internet World Stats 2014). Clearly this provides evidence of the continued integration of the Internet into everyday lives, especially in technologically advanced nations. More than 90 % of American youths are Internet users (Horrigan 2010), and 74 % of American adolescents have access to the Internet on cell phones or tablets (Madden et al. 2013). Furthermore, 82 % of the youths in European countries are online and have social networking sites (Livingstone and Helsper 2010). In Israel, 91 % of the youths are online (Israel Internet Association 2014). In a cross-national report of children and youth activity, it was found that Israel is placed second among European countries with regard to the extent of youths using of the Internet (Harel-Fisch et al. 2009).

R. Sela-Shayovitz (✉)
David Yellin Academic College and Institute of Criminology, The Hebrew University of Jerusalem, Jerusalem, Israel
e-mail: revital28s@gmail.com

D.C. Pyrooz
Department of Sociology, University of Colorado—Boulder, Boulder, CO, USA
e-mail: David.Pyrooz@colorado.edu

S.H. Decker
School of Criminology and Criminal Justice, Arizona State University, Tempe, AZ, USA
e-mail: Scott.Decker@asu.edu

C.L. Maxson, F.-A. Esbensen (eds.), *Gang Transitions and Transformations in an International Context*, DOI 10.1007/978-3-319-29602-9_7

The Internet also has opened new venues and opportunities for criminal activities. This is largely due to the convenient opportunities to obtain immediate information, develop and sustain criminal networks, maintain anonymity, operate with no borders, and limited regulation (Holt 2007; Maratea and Kavanaugh 2012; Pyrooz et al. 2015; Weimann 2004). As a consequence, cybercrime has become a rapidly expanding global phenomenon (Interpol 2014). Cybercrime consists of a wide range of offenses that can be divided into three main areas: (1) cyber-attacks against computer hardware and software (e.g. viruses, botnets, malware); (2) online violence and abuse offenses (e.g. hacking, harassment, stalking); and (3) financial crimes such as online fraud (Holt and Bossler 2013; Interpol 2014), but also include the migration of traditional forms of property crime to the web. These may include drug dealing and sales of illicit goods (firearms) and stolen property on sites such as Craigslist or eBay. In addition, criminal organizations have also taken advantage of the web to expand their criminal activities and increase their profits (Interpol 2014). Further, the criminal possibilities associated with the Internet are not confined to online space and may cascade into offline space (Holt and Bossler 2013; Pyrooz et al. 2015; Yar 2005). The possible uses of the web for violence go so far as to include the waging of war (Arquilla and Ronfeldt 1997) among other things.

It is not surprising that gangs and individual gang members would engage the web for criminal and non-criminal purposes, particularly as we have witnessed the "globalization" of gangs (Decker and Pyrooz 2010, 2011; Hagedorn 2008) as well as the widespread involvement of gang members in crime. Furthermore, in an era when there is concern that immigration plays a role in spreading knowledge of gangs and gang behavior (Decker et al. 2009) in Europe, it is easy to surmise that the Internet would be similarly suited to do so. The Internet may provide additional outlets for their criminal activity and expand it to online offending. Indeed, the web can fulfill instrumental and symbolic needs for gangs. Recent studies indicate that collective and group identity exists in the virtual arena (Van Hellemont 2012; Morselli and De'Cary-Hetu 2012; Patton et al. 2013; Pyrooz et al. 2015; Sela-Shayovitz 2012a). In addition, gang members in the USA are more involved in online deviance than their non-gang peers (Pyrooz et al. 2015). Although there is growing interest in the use of the web by gangs, the difference between gangs in the virtual setting and on the street has been largely neglected (Moule et al. 2014). Furthermore, because sociocultural conditions can influence online behaviors, it is important to pay attention to the diversity of gang members' activities on the Internet across cultures. Indeed, comparative research across countries is a central purpose of the Eurogang research program (Esbensen and Maxson 2012; Klein 2005) and seems appropriate for behavior such as Internet use that spans country boundaries.

This chapter addresses this important issue by examining the differences and similarities in the online behaviors and criminal activities among gang members in the USA and Israel. In addition to individual-level activities, the study focuses on the online behaviors and processes of the gangs to which these individuals belong. The study draws on routine activity theory to explore the role of gang members' online routines in online offending. Accordingly, three research hypotheses will be tested quantitatively, the first of which is a convergence hypothesis: there are similarities in gang members' online activities between the two countries due to the comparable characteristics in the extent of youth Internet usage and online behaviors across countries. The counterpart to the expectation of similarities between the two countries is found in our second hypothesis where we assess divergence, that is, there will be differences in the online activities of gang members due to cultural, institutional, and structural differences. Finally, based on routine activities theory, we anticipate that—across both countries—online routines are positively related to online offending and gang-level activities. Answering these questions will provide insight into the role of the sociocultural context of gang members' online activity.

7.2 Youth Online Activities

The advance of digital technologies markedly changes social interactions and information access in daily lives. While in some sense the Internet might be a "new way of doing old things" (Tyler 2002), the web offers a portal for a wide range of entertainment and communication channels. Young people, who are often called the "net-generation" or "digital natives" (i.e., were born during or after the expansion of the Internet), are more likely to adopt digital technologies. These terms aim to emphasize high technological capacity and engagement, and to distinguish the young people from "digital immigrants," namely those who adopted the Internet later in life and commonly lack computer skills (Mesch 2009; Moule et al. 2013; Prensky 2001; Pyrooz et al. 2015). There is a wide debate regarding the cultural and social influences of the Internet on the "digital natives." The Internet has led young people to develop new ways of expression, communication, and motivation (Mesch 2009; Prensky 2001).

Although young people are more inclined to use the Internet, there are "digital inequalities" in its use. While the "digital divide" refers to inequality of Internet use and adoption between age, sex, social class, and race (Moule et al. 2013; Rogers 2005; Van Dijk and Hacker 2003), "digital inequalities" recognize that, even among demographic and socioeconomic groups, there are serious differences in levels of computer knowledge (Gui and Argentin 2011; Hargittai 2008; Prensky 2001). The level of education and lifestyle are key factors for understating the use and adoption of the Internet. Individuals with a high level of education are more likely to utilize the benefits of the web than are individuals with a low level of education (Schradie 2012; Van Deursen and Van Dijk 2010). Furthermore, the lifestyle, interests, and attitudes of students are predictors of Internet use and adoption (Chan and Leung 2005). However, involvement in criminal lifestyles, mainly street crime, increased the likelihood of spending time on social networking sites, while association with a gang was negatively related to Internet adoption (Moule et al. 2013). This study draws from routine activity theory as a way to assess how digital inequalities relate to online offending among gang members in the USA and Israel.

7.2.1 Theoretical Framework

Routine activity theory (Cohen and Felson 1979) provides a theoretical perspective for understanding youth involvement in online deviance and crime. This perspective posits that lifestyle and routine activity play a key role in the possibility of occurrence of crime and criminal victimization. Cohen and Felson (1979) identified three core elements to explain patterns of offending: an accessible target, a motivated offender, and the absence of capable guardians. Thus, the convergence of target, offenders, and absence of capable guardianship in particular spaces and specific times can explain the possibility and likelihood of criminal activity or victimization (Cohen and Felson 1979; Felson 1995; 2002).

Osgood and colleagues (1996) extended routine activity theory to understand the role of spending time with peers on the etiology of deviant behaviors. According to this approach, unstructured socializing with peers in the absence of authority figures creates situational inducements for deviance. Recent studies have applied this concept to the virtual setting, and demonstrated that the amount of virtual time spent socializing plays a key role in both online victimization (Pratt et al. 2010) and deviant behaviors (McCuddy and Vogel 2014; Meldrum and Clark 2013). However, the virtual time spent with peers has a weaker relationship with delinquency than time spent with peers in public without supervision (Weerman et al. 2013). This unsupervised time with peers is a key link to delinquent involvement, something that underlies most online behavior because the digital sphere is largely unregulated and without guardians.

7.2.2 Online Behaviors Across Cultures: Convergence or Divergence?

The debate about globalization processes raises the question of whether there is convergence or divergence in online behaviors across countries in Internet use. Studies to date provide mixed evidence on these hypotheses; thus the issue is far from settled. Analyses of Internet use among youths in the United Kingdom and Bahrain revealed that digital media consumption appears to be similar, although culturally gendered perspectives play an important role in the restrictions upon Internet usage (Davidson and Martellozzo 2013).

Examination of online risk behaviors among adolescents and children across 25 European countries has found cultural and cross-national differences (Lobe et al. 2011). The study indicated that the GDP per capita has a significant and positive effect on online risks. In countries that use more strategies to counter online risks (like England, Ireland, and Portugal), the level of involvement in online risks was low. On the other hand, in countries with high press freedom and less Internet censorship (like Scandinavian and Baltic countries), youths are more likely to be involved in online risk behaviors (Lobe et al. 2011). Analysis of the differences in hacking behaviors between Chinese and American students revealed that moral beliefs about hacking were strong predictors of hacking in both countries. However, self-control and risk-seeking were better predictors of hacking among American students, whereas, the tendency to lose one's temper, and playing computer and team games were strong predictors of hacking among the Chinese students (Hu et al. 2013).

7.2.3 Deviant Groups and the Web

The unique features of the Internet (e.g., anonymity, no borders, large audiences, and limited regulation) facilitate the use of the Internet by radical and extremist groups. Indeed, the Internet and attendant social media are agnostic to ideology. Consequently, extreme groups such as cults (Dawson and Hennebry 1999), terrorist groups (Weimann 2004; Weimann 2006), and hate and racial supremacy groups (Corb 2011; Gerstenfeld et al. 2003; Sela-Shayovitz 2012b) have become widespread and mainly appeal to the young. The Internet provides an efficient infrastructure for these groups to broadcast their ideology and propaganda and to recruit new members (Corb 2011; Reid and Chen 2002; Sela-Shayovitz 2012b). The Internet may facilitate the formation of new deviant subcultures that had not existed previously such as websites that are designed to promote and support eating disorders or cutting and other forms of self-harm (Boniel-Nissim and Latzer 2011). Certainly terrorist groups such as ISIL and Al Queda use the web to their advantage (Conway 2010). However, the web can also contribute to the creation of deviant online subcultures that traditionally were defined as "loners" or "isolated deviants" (Maratea and Kavanaugh 2012).

7.2.4 Youth Gangs and the Internet

Gang members' daily online routine activities are similar to non-gang peers in terms of access, prevalence of activities, and participation in social networking (Decker and Pyrooz 2011; Pyrooz et al. 2015). Examination of the online routine activities and criminal behaviors of 418 current and former gang members in the USA has showed that they spend more hours on the web than their non-gang peers (7.7 h vs. 6 h per week, respectively) and that their computer technological skills were similar to those of youths who were not in gangs (Pyrooz et al. 2015). Sela-Shayovitz (2012a) interviewed 30 gang members in Israel and found that they were highly reliant on the Internet and had collective online activities. Furthermore, some reported a high level of technological competency, including hacking (13.3 %), and one-third of the respondents stated that the Internet played a vital role in their group activities (Sela-Shayovitz 2012a).

The Internet can provide the gang and gang members an avenue to fulfill both instrumental and symbolic collective needs for maintaining their prestige or responding to status threats. Gang members frequently use websites to generate respect for their group; they coordinate action, broadcast threats, brag, and upload fights on YouTube (Decker 1996; Decker and Pyrooz 2011; Hanser 2011; Van Hellemont 2012; King et al. 2007; Patton et al. 2013). Gang members also post online messages that reflect their group's street behavior (Pyrooz et al. 2015). Recent findings indicate that higher levels of gang organization increase the probability of gang-level online activities such as having a website, posting videos, and recruiting online (Moule et al. 2014). Morselli and De'Cary-Hetu (2012) conducted a qualitative study of systematic keywords for analyzing the presence of gangs in Canada in social networking sites such as Facebook, Myspace, and Twitter. The search included additional terminology of gangs such as violence, crime, and drugs. The study revealed that the gang presence dramatically rose between 2010 and 2011. Furthermore, the presence of gangs was primarily linked to gang promotion or street culture through individual displays. Similarly, analysis of social networking sites of *Sureno* gangs and Mexican drug cartels shows that websites of gang members were mostly used to maintain respect. Gang members commonly uploaded pictures and videos with macho images such as holding guns, flashing tattoos, and presenting hand signs (Womer and Bunker 2010). Densley (2012) has noted that some gangs use the web to showcase "strength in numbers." This is consistent with the "Big Gang" theory (Felson 2006) assumption that gangs create myths in order to exaggerate their size to display strength (see also Decker and Van Winkle 1996; Densley 2012; Pyrooz et al. 2015).

Gangs can take advantage of Internet opportunities to expand their criminal activities. The web can exacerbate their involvement in violent crime with rival gangs or contribute to the development of new conflicts. In addition, it can facilitate drug distribution, sale of stolen property, or gun acquisitions. Pyrooz et al. (2015) found that gang members were more involved in online deviant activity than were non-gang peers. Therefore, there is a link between street deviant behavior and online deviant activity, and the effect of the web has led to enhancement of delinquency in online settings, consistent with the theoretical models proposed by Thornberry and colleagues (1993) yet transferred to digital spheres. Importantly, these findings highlight the influence of online interaction on social facilitation processes. Taken together, these studies indicate that gang members' online activities are related to offending.

Nevertheless, computer skills were found to be a key factor for understanding gang members' engagement in online delinquency and cybercrime: gang members who have technological competency are more likely to engage in online deviance and crime. Thus, it appears that once gang members acquire more computer skills, their online criminal activity increases and converges with offline settings (Pyrooz et al. 2015; Sela-Shayovitz 2012b). However, it is important to note that a low level of involvement in online offending is also related to the gang members' concerns about police surveillance of the web (Densley 2012; Sela-Shayovitz 2012b).

In summary, although there is similarity in the online behaviors of youth, there are also cultural and cross-national differences across countries. Previous studies provide evidence that collective and gang identity exists on the web. Furthermore, computer skills and group organization are key factors for gangs' online activities. The current study adds to the research knowledge through analysis of differences in the Internet usage and gang-related online behaviors between gang members in the USA and Israel. The study draws on routine activity theory for better understanding the role of online routines in online offending and online gang-level activities.

7.3 Methods

7.3.1 Data

The sample in this study was drawn from two countries: Israel and the USA. Both samples were generated using purposive sampling strategies in order to learn more about the online activities of gangs and gang members based on surveys administered to 192 active gang members. Only respondents who self-reported being an active member of a gang were included in the present study because—consistent with the aim of the Eurogang program of research—our goal was to make cross-national comparisons in the level and correlates of the online activities of gangs and gang members. The Eurogang methodology was used in the Israel sample to determine gang membership, while self-nomination was used in the US sample (see Decker et al. 2014; Esbensen et al. 2001; Matsuda et al. 2012). None of our prior research using these data has focused on uncovering the correlates of online activities among active gang members, let alone having a comparative focus (Decker and Pyrooz 2011; Moule et al. 2013; 2014; Pyrooz et al. 2015; Sela-Shayovitz 2012a).

The Israeli sample consisted of 57 respondents from Jerusalem, the largest city in Israel (population 850,000). Data were gathered from respondents in four youth clubs, and interviews were conducted over the course of 2010, 2011, and 2014.[1] Two of the clubs were situated within the city center and were designed for school dropouts. The other clubs were located in community centers of two large neighborhoods. All of the clubs were operated by the city Youth Advancement Unit and include prevention and intervention programs. These clubs, however, were independent from the criminal justice system and designed to be a safe haven for youth. Many youth from different gangs attended the clubs. It should be noted that in Israel, the common expression is "band," which is less stigmatizing, and the term "gang" has been used only for youth groups that were involved in serious violent crime, which is common also in other countries (Decker and Pyrooz 2010; Weerman et al. 2009).

[1] Examination of the differences between the 2 years of the Israeli sample shows that patterns of Internet usage and technological skills were mostly similar and no problem was found to pool them together.

The American sample consisted of 136 respondents from five cities in the USA who were interviewed in 2011–2012: Cleveland, OH; Fresno, CA; Los Angeles, CA; Phoenix, AZ; and St. Louis, MO. Respondents report varying levels of involvement in gangs and the criminal justice system. In Cleveland, respondents were the clients of outreach workers and were individuals at high risk for involvement in crime. The respondents in Los Angeles and Phoenix were participants in street outreach programs that aimed to work with gang members and former offenders seeking to change their lives. In Fresno, interviews were conducted with a jail population, representing a deep end sample that had been arrested and processed by the criminal justice system. The St. Louis interviews were conducted with individuals in the community who were on probation or parole and under active supervision by the criminal justice system.

For both samples, members of the research project staff conducted interviews in private settings, such as classrooms or attorney rooms. Refusal to participate was rare (<10 %), although some respondents declined to answer some questions. In Israel, the interviews were semi-structured and lasted approximately 1.5 h. In the USA, because this was part of a larger project, both structured and semi-structured interview formats were used. The current study is based on the structured survey, which lasted approximately 45 min. Of course, there are age, geographic, and cultural differences between the two samples. However, given the overlap between the samples in the historical time period of the interviews, the purposive sampling strategy, and the questions asked of the respondents (described next), this serves as a strong basis for a comparative study of the online activities of gang members.

7.3.2 Dependent Variables

Our key dependent variable in this study is an *online offending* variety score. Seven questions were included in the survey with regard to whether the respondents engaged in several different forms of criminal and deviant activities mediated by the Internet, including (1) illegally downloading media such as music or computer software, (2) selling stolen property on websites such as eBay or Craigslist, (3) setting up drug sales or purchasing drugs online, (4) harassing or threatening someone on social media sites such as Facebook or Twitter, (5) coordinating assaults through email or social media, (6) posting or uploading videos of fights or threats on sites like YouTube, and (7) targeting or attacking someone in the street because of events occurring online. A key methodological difference between the samples is that the Israeli respondents were asked to self-report on these activities over the last 12 months, while the US respondents were asked to self-report over the last 6 months.

All seven of the criminal and deviance items are binary variables and have been studied in prior research on cybercrime (Pyrooz et al. 2015; Holt et al. 2012; Skinner and Fream 1997; Tcherni et al. 2015; Wolfe et al. 2014). Respondents were assigned a "0" if they had not engaged in the activity and 1 if they had. The items were then summed to create a variety score that ranged from 0 (no criminal/deviant activity) to 7 (endorsed all items). Much like offending in street settings, the battery of items hung together with a mean inter-item correlation of 0.33 (alpha=0.77). However, the internal consistency of the items was stronger among the US sample (inter-item $r=0.39$, alpha=0.81) than the Israel sample (inter-item $r=0.15$, alpha=0.56). Because we use a variety score, we interpret our findings as the individual propensity to engage in online crime and deviance.

7.3.3 *Independent Variables*

7.3.3.1 Demographics

Age (in years), *female* (=1, "male"=0), and *foreign born* (=1, "born in Israel/US"=0) were included in the analysis. These variables are not only associated with the digital divide, but are also known correlates of gang and criminal activity (Bersani 2014; Esbensen and Carson 2012; Pyrooz 2014; Sweeten et al. 2013). We also report for descriptive purposes the minority group statuses for Latinos and African-Americans in the US sample and Russians and Ethiopians in the Israel sample but exclude these country-specific distinctions from the analysis. Age is centered at 18 in the regression analysis to make the intercept interpretable.

7.3.3.2 Online Routine Activities

A series of questions related to the digital profiles of the respondents were included in the study. *Hours spent online* measures the weekly number of hours respondents estimate they spend on the Internet, ranging from 0 to 30 h. In the US sample, responses were mean-adjusted based on five categories (e.g., 5–10 h=7.5 h online) to approximate a meaningful distribution, while no fixed response categories were provided to the Israel sample. If offenders are committing crimes in digital settings, we would expect that these behaviors are at least partially a function of exposure to such opportunities. *YouTube user* is a binary item asking if respondents "go on YouTube or other sites to watch videos" ("yes"=1, "no"=0). YouTube is a convergence space for the transmission of gang culture and a staging ground for intimidation, threats, and violence (Densley 2013; Pyrooz et al. 2015). *Social network user* is a binary item asking if respondents have accounts and use social networking websites such as Facebook, Myspace, Twitter, and other social network sites ("yes"=1, "no"=0). *Technological ability* tapped respondents' "knowledge and skills in using computers" and ranged from 0 ("I do not use them unless I absolutely have to") to 3 ("I can use Linux, most software, and fix most computer problems") (Holt and Bossler 2008). We would expect that at least some forms of offending, such as piracy (Wolfe et al. 2008), should be facilitated by the ability to navigate digital space.

7.3.3.3 Online Gang Activities

Much like how gang-level organizational and structural characteristics influence the criminal offenses of gangs and gang members (Bouchard and Spindler 2010; Decker et al. 2008; Klein and Maxson 2006; Pyrooz et al. 2012), we expect that the digital profiles of gangs will be differentially related to the online criminal and deviant activities of gang members. Therefore, we examine several characteristics of the online existence and importance of the gangs in which our respondents were involved, including *gang has a website* (or social media page), *gang organizes online* (e.g., meetings, drug sales, parties, assaults), gang posts videos online (music or intimidation or fights), and the *Internet is important to the gang*. Because gangs are not equally active in online settings (Moule et al. 2014), these measures give us a chance to understand if and how they are related to the online criminal and deviant behaviors of gang members.

7.3.3.4 Analytic Strategy

This study begins by examining the descriptive statistics of the study variables. We partition the sample by country to determine if Internet-mediated criminal and deviant activities, as well as the explanatory variables, are different among gang members in Israel and the USA. The next stage of the study examines the interrelationships among the study variables in each country to provide a preliminary understanding of how demographics, online routine activities, and online gang activities are related to crime and deviance online. The final portion of the analysis involves multivariate regression models predicting individual propensity to engage in crime and deviance. Given that our dependent variable is a count of offending types, a Poisson model is appropriate and overdispersion in the dependent variable was not problematic (likelihood ratio test of alpha $p > .05$). The models were first estimated separately for each country. We then compare the coefficients to determine if they perform differently in sign, significance, and magnitude in Israel and the USA. Importantly, given the small sample sizes in each site, the findings should be interpreted with caution because there is limited power to detect statistical differences. All of the analyses were run in Stata 12.0 and all regression models report robust standard errors.

7.4 Results

7.4.1 Descriptive and Bivariate Statistics

Table 7.1 reports the descriptive statistics for the pooled and partitioned samples. The Israel sample was younger than the US sample, as a consequence of the differences in the purposive sampling strategies. Both samples were comprised overwhelmingly of males—none of the Israel sample and one-fifth of the US

Table 7.1 Descriptive characteristics of the study sample by country ($N = 192$)

	Israel	US	Stat
% (N)	30 % (57)	70 % (136)	sig.
Demographics			
Age	18.02 (1.2)	25.18 (7.70)	*
Female	0 %	20 %	#
Foreign born	18 %	8 %	#
Latino	–	32 %	
African-American	–	62 %	
Russian	14 %	–	
Ethiopian	5 %	–	
Online routine activities			
Hours spent online	21.29 (8.2)	7.70 (7.76)	*
YouTube user	95 %	86 %	#
Social network user	86 %	80 %	
Technological ability	1.64 (1.0)	1.24 (0.76)	*
Online gang activities			
Gang has a website	13 %	24 %	#
Gang organizes online	9 %	13 %	
Gang posts videos	20 %	51 %	*
Internet is important	18 %	23 %	
Criminal and deviant activities			
Illegal downloads	43 %	33 %	
Sell stolen property	4 %	4 %	
Drug sales	5 %	7 %	
Harassment/threats	9 %	12 %	
Coordinate assaults	7 %	8 %	
Upload deviant videos	11 %	14 %	
Online-street assaults	9 %	13 %	
Online variety score	0.88 (1.2)	0.91 (1.5)	

Note: "Stat. sig." refers to statistical significance using χ^2 and independent sample *t*-tests. Means and percentages are reported in the cells. Standard deviations are reported in parentheses
$^{\#}p < .10$; $^{*}p < .05$ (two-tailed test)

sample were female. More respondents were foreign born in Israel than in the USA; in Israel immigrants were mostly of Russian or Ethiopian origins while in the USA, the foreign born were all Latino.

The respondents spent a good amount of time online, although the Israel sample reported a much higher rate of Internet usage. Both samples reported a high rate of social media usage, including YouTube and social networking sites. The US sample appears to be more digitally engaged. Indeed, one-quarter of active gang members in the US sample reported that their gang had a website or social media page, compared to one-eighth of the Israel sample. Similarly, while both samples reported high usage of YouTube and other video sharing sites, the majority of the US sample indicated that their gang posted videos on such sites compared to one-fifth of the Israel sample. This was among the key factors that distinguished the USA from the Israel sample. Neither of the samples reported high rates of using the Internet for organizing activities, which is consistent with the Internet being more central to symbolic rather than instrumental goals.

Perhaps the most interesting set of findings to emerge from Table 7.1 is the comparison of online offending among gang members from the USA with gang members from Israel. The online offending rates were practically identical. Both samples engaged in online piracy at relatively high rates, while also engaging in several other forms of crime and deviance at rather low rates (<10 %), including selling stolen property online, organizing drug sales/purchases, and coordinating assaults. The remaining forms of crime and deviance—all of which were endorsed at a rate hovering around 9 and 14 %—are what we think is key to computer-mediated gang conflict: harassment and threats in digital forums, the posting of videos, and online provocations translating into street conflicts. Importantly, despite a recall period in Israel (12 months) that was twice as great as the USA (6 months), there were no differences across each of the individual items or overall in the online variety score.

Table 7.2 displays the zero-order correlations for the study variables by country. Age was a discriminating factor across many of the variables for the US sample, but not the Israel sample, which was confined to a smaller cross section of youth and young adults. Respondents who spent more time online were also more likely to report greater technological ability in both countries. Each of the gang-level online activities measures was correlated in sign and significance, and moderate in magnitude in both countries—an inter-item correlation of 0.45 in Israel and 0.38 in the USA. In other words, endorsing one form of gang-level online activity was associated with the likelihood of endorsing another form of gang-level online activity.

Notably, the bottom row (US) and the rightmost column (Israel) report the bivariate relationship between the independent variables and the online variety score. There was no convergence between the countries regarding the role of demographic factors in accounting for differences in the online variety score. In terms of online routines, all of the factors were related positively to online offending in the USA, while only technological ability was statistically significant and in the expected direction in Israel. Gang-level online activities exhibited the most consistency between the two countries, where gang website, gang organizes online, and gang posts videos were related positively to online offending. The key difference was the importance of the Internet to gangs, which was unrelated to offending in Israel but strongly related to offending in the USA. Given the interrelationships across the study variables, it is important to turn to multivariate models to better understand how these factors are related to online forms of crime and deviance.

Table 7.2 Zero-order correlations for the study variables by country ($N=192$)

		Israel ($N=57$)											
		Age	Male	Foreign born	Hours spent online	YouTube user	Social network user	Tech. ability	Gang has a website	Gang organizes	Gang posts videos	Internet is important	Online variety score
US ($N=136$)	Age	–	.	0.11	0.03	–0.13	–0.08	–0.10	–0.19	–0.11	–0.16	–0.01	0.07
	Male	–0.09	–	–	–	–	–	–	–	–	–	–	–
	Foreign born	0.04	0.08	–	0.06	0.11	0.19	0.03	–0.18	–0.15	0.00	0.15	–0.23#
	Hours spent online	–0.22*	–0.12	0.06	–	–0.00	–0.04	0.32*	0.23#	0.04	0.08	0.16	0.12
	YouTube user	–0.43*	0.17	0.02	0.14	–	–0.10	0.08	0.09	0.07	0.12	0.11	0.11
	Social network user	–0.26*	–0.20*	–0.12	0.24*	0.17#	–	0.27*	0.15	–0.05	0.07	0.06	–0.01
	Tech. ability	–0.20*	0.06	–0.10	0.29*	0.18#	0.19*	–	0.42*	0.24	0.37*	0.27*	0.32*
	Gang has a website	–0.06	0.02	0.03	0.07	0.00	0.06	–0.04	–	0.64*	0.36*	0.53*	0.24#
	Gang organizes	–0.11	0.08	–0.11	0.16#	0.05	0.19*	0.11	0.47*	–	0.63*	0.34*	0.27*
	Gang posts videos	–0.34*	0.18*	–0.09	0.26*	0.19#	0.14	0.23*	0.26*	0.28*	–	0.24#	0.39*
	Internet is important	–0.25*	0.08	–0.16	0.34*	0.08	0.21*	0.24*	0.43*	0.43*	0.41*	–	–0.02
	Online variety score	–0.35*	–0.03	–0.11	0.40*	0.23*	0.24*	0.19*	0.27*	0.51*	0.25*	0.52*	–

Notes: Bivariate correlations are reported separately for the US sample (*bottom left*) and the Israel sample (*upper right*)
# $p<.10$; * $p<.05$ (two-tailed test)

7.4.2 Multivariate Regression Models

Table 7.3 presents the results of the Poisson regression models that are partitioned by country. In the Israel model, the only determinants of online offending were demographic and gang-level factors. Older respondents and those born in Israel were responsible for a greater amount of online offending than younger respondents and those born outside of Israel. Also, individuals who reported that their gang posts videos online engaged in higher rates of online crime and deviance, holding other demographic, online routines, and gang-level factors constant. In the US sample, the covariates used in the regression model do a better job at differentiating individuals across their levels of online crime and deviance. Indeed, the pseudo R2 was nearly twice as great in the US sample than in the Israel sample. And factors across each of the three explanatory domains explained at least some portion of the variance in online offending, including demographic factors (age, gender), online routines (hours spent online, YouTube user, social network user), and online gang-level activities (organizes online, Internet is important to gang). Because there is a great deal of interrelatedness among the gang-level factors in both countries, it is not surprising to see some degree of saturation in the explanation of the variance of online offending.

Table 7.3 Poisson regression models predicting online crime and deviance variety score in Israel ($N=57$) and the USA ($N=136$)

	Israel		US		Coefficient differences	
	Coefficient	(SE)	Coefficient	(SE)	(US–Israel)	(SE)
Age	0.21	(0.08)*	–0.07	(0.02)*	–0.28	(0.08)*
Female	–	–	0.56	(0.27)*	–	–
Foreign born	–1.04	(0.50)*	–0.43	(0.44)	0.61	(0.66)
Hours spent online	–0.00	(0.02)	0.03	(0.01)*	0.03	(0.03)
YouTube user	0.86	(0.69)	2.05	(0.84)*	1.19	(1.08)
Social network user	–0.30	(0.46)	0.79	(0.43)#	1.08	(0.63)#
Technological ability	0.31	(0.22)	0.04	(0.16)	–0.27	(0.28)
Gang has a website	0.65	(0.50)	0.26	(0.27)	–0.39	(0.57)
Gang organizes online	–0.41	(0.51)	0.89	(0.30)*	1.30	(0.59)*
Gang posts videos	0.97	(0.40)*	–0.25	(0.28)	–1.22	(0.48)*
Internet is important	–0.69	(0.44)	0.64	(0.33)#	1.33	(0.55)*
Constant	–1.41	(0.89)	–3.28	(0.98)*	–1.86	(1.32)
Wald χ^2	40.1*		201.6*			
Pseudo R^2	16.9 %		32.4 %			

Notes: Country-level interactions were used to determine statistical significance in coefficient differences

#$p<.10$; * $p<.05$ (two-tailed test)

SE robust standard error

The final column in Table 7.3 compares the performance of the coefficients across the Israel and the US models. Positive and negative signs indicate that the association of the covariate with online offending is stronger or weaker, respectively, in the USA than it is in Israel. Among the 10 covariates, along with the constant, there were five coefficients that differed statistically across the two countries. Out of all of the covariates, only age operated in statistically significant and opposite directions—positive in Israel and negative in the USA. As mentioned above, this could be due to several factors. Social network usage was statistically different between the two countries, null in Israel yet marginally significant and positive in the USA. Similarly, two of the gang-level factors—gang organizes online and Internet is important to gang—were null in Israel but positively related to online offending in the USA. Finally, the coefficient for the gang-level posting of videos was different statistically, positively related to online offending in Israel but null in the USA.

7.5 Discussion

Researchers, policy makers, and enforcement groups have paid more attention to the online activities of gangs in recent years. Indeed, the digital world offers new opportunities for expanding the variety and extent of criminal activities by gangs. The Internet helps gangs to maintain their prestige, display strength, and can even exacerbate their involvement in violent crime with rivals (Densley 2013; Hanser 2011; Van Hellemont 2012; King et al. 2007; Morselli and De'Cary-Hetu 2012; Moule et al. 2014; Pyrooz et al. 2015; Sela-Shayovitz 2012a). Drawing on routine activity theory, our results extend this line of research and compare routine online activities between gang members in the USA and in Israel. Several findings were particularly noteworthy.

First, the majority of gang members in Israel and the USA are actively engaged with digital activities and reported involvement in criminal and deviant activities. These findings are consistent with a convergence hypothesis. Gang members reported a high rate of social media usage and spent a considerable amount of time online. Furthermore, those who spent more time online in both samples reported greater technological ability. Thus, gang members rely heavily on the Internet, as expected from their membership in the "net-generation" (Mesch 2009; Prensky 2001). These findings are compatible with prior research on gangs and the web (Madden et al. 2013; Pyrooz et al. 2015; Sela-Shayovitz 2012b). Gang members in Israel reported more virtual time and a higher level of technological knowledge than the US sample. The results suggest that there are "digital inequalities" in levels of computer knowledge between gangs across countries that may be a result of social and cultural differences. However, it can be assumed that the age difference between the two samples might contribute to these differences. Furthermore, some of the Israel interviews were collected in 2014 while the US data were all collected in 2011–2012. Thus, given the rapid changes in technology and adoption of tech, it can be suggested that this might be a contributing factor for the "digital inequalities" in computer knowledge. Patterns of online offending were similar across countries. The analysis indicates that level of online piracy was relatively high, while the level of involvement in other forms of online crime and deviance was low (<10 %). Thus, gang members' online activities are marginally related to crime, which indicates that overall they are still far from fully utilizing the benefits of the Internet for offending (Pyrooz et al. 2015; Sela-Shayovitz 2012b).

Second, the main difference between the two samples is related to the symbolic web presence of gang identity (gang's website) and online collective activities. The rates of gangs' websites and video posting were significantly higher in the American sample than the Israeli sample. This suggests that the symbolic side of gang membership may be more salient to gang members in the USA. However, there is limited evidence of online gang organization in both countries. Thus, in a similar vein to online offending, it seems that most gang members are unlikely to exploit the Internet opportunities to further their collective goals, including involvement in crime. The differences in collective online gang activities may reflect the differences in gang culture between the two countries. These results suggest that gang members in the USA are more likely to be motivated by symbolic goals than their Israeli counterparts. Prior research indicated that gang members in Israel are less motivated to "show off" or "floss," and mainly use the Internet for communication and to track rival groups. As one of the gang members said: "We don't need the Internet or Facebook so that people know who we are. Whoever knows us, knows, and believe me, people know who we are and know not to mess with us" (Sela-Shayovitz 2012a, p. 399). It is also feasible that the divergence in collective online activities derives from different perceptions about police online surveillance across countries. Previous research has shown that most gang members in Israel reported that they were concerned about police online surveillance. However, those who had a high level of computer knowledge seem less concerned about police and tend to take online risks (Sela-Shayovitz 2012a). In this context, it is important to note that there were a few cases of violent crimes in Israel that were identified through the Israeli police computer unit and received extensive media coverage. Thus, these cases may have a deterrent effect on gang members' online activities. Indeed, the level of involvement in online delinquency is also related to gang members' concerns about police online monitoring (Densley 2012). Another possible explanation is that gang members utilize other forms of communication (i.e., cell phones and email) that are less monitored by law enforcement (Decker et al. 2012).

The results are consistent with routine activities theory (Cohen and Felson 1979) in that virtual time spent socializing, YouTube usage, and online gang organization play an active role in the individual tendency to engage in online offending and deviance in the American sample, although only posting videos online increases the likelihood of online offending in the Israeli sample. The findings from both countries are consistent with the facilitation and enhancement models (Thornberry et al. 1993, 2003) in the virtual world (Pyrooz et al. 2015), yet the divergence in the correlates of these digital behaviors requires further consideration and may be due to several factors. First, gang members in Israel are younger than those in the American sample. This may influence their tendency to engage in online offending, especially given the age restriction in the Israeli sample. Second, the divergence may result from cultural differences and structural characteristics between the countries. Another explanation is related to measurement differences between the two samples. As mentioned, there was a key methodological difference with regard to the recall period between the two samples. Finally, as we mentioned above, this could be due to the culture of gangs in the two countries, although any further empirical investigation into this divergence goes beyond the scope of our analysis. A next step would be to better understand the frequency with which the Internet and social media contribute to gang activities on the street, as well as inhibit such activities due to digital engagement; lest the consequences of the Internet be confined solely to digital spheres, we find such a conclusion unlikely.

This study also demonstrates the continuing vitality of the Eurogang research platform. As envisioned in its initial formulation by Malcolm Klein, Eurogang was to be comparative. The web, a platform that does not conform to the boundaries of countries, is particularly well suited to be addressed in this context. Given the high levels of web use and criminal involvement among the age groups that typically include gangs, this topic merits further examination. Policymakers and law enforcement groups are monitoring illegal behavior online, including (among others) that of gangs and gang members. In this regard, the web represents a paradox: On the one hand, it is part of the problem, yet on the other hand, it may be part of the solution. A number of problem behaviors—anorexia, cutting, substance abuse—have viable web-based responses that provide tangible prevention and intervention for individuals involved in such activities. Developing such responses should be a high priority for schools, community groups, clubs, and the like. Chat rooms, online games, and accurate information presented in age-appropriate contexts may provide useful alternatives to gang recruitment. iKeepSafe.org represents one such effort.

In the end, although globalization processes have had an influence on the online behaviors of gangs and gang members, the sociocultural context appears to play an important role in the online collective activities of gangs. Thus, further comparative research is required on gangs in the virtual setting. Expanding the analysis to other countries and other forms of telecommunication would provide a better insight into this field.

References

Arquilla, J., & Ronfeldt, D. (1997). *In Athena's camp: Preparing for conflict in the information age*. Santa Monica, CA: Rand.

Bersani, B. E. (2014). An examination of first and second generation immigrant offending trajectories. *Justice Quarterly, 31*(2), 315–343.

Boniel-Nissim, M., & Latzer, Y. (2011). The characteristics of pro-ana community. In D. Stein & Y. Latzer (Eds.), *Treatment and special issue of eating disorders* (pp. 73–84). New York: Nova Science.

Boonaert, T., & Vettenburg, N. (2011). Young people's internet use: Divided or diversified? *Childhood, 18*(1), 554–566.

Bouchard, M., & Spindler, A. (2010). Groups, gangs, and delinquency: Does organization matter? *Journal of Criminal Justice, 38*(5), 921–933.

Chan, J., & Leung, L. (2005). Lifestyles, reliance on traditional news media and online news adoption. *New Media & Society, 7*(3), 357–382.
Cohen, L. E., & Felson, M. (1979). Social change and crime rate trends: A routine activity approach. *American Sociological Review, 44*(4), 588–608.
Conway, M. (2010). Terrorism and the internet: A review of the history, issues, and responses. In P. Reich (Ed.), *Cybercrime and security*. Oxford, England: Oxford University Press.
Corb, A. (2011). *Into the minds of mayhem: White supremacy, recruitment, and the internet*. Cambridge, England: Google Ideas.
Davidson, J., & Martellozzo, E. (2013). Exploring young people's use of social networking sites and digital media in the internet safety context. *Information, Communication & Society, 16*(9), 1456–1476.
Dawson, L. L., & Hennebry, J. (1999). New religions and the internet: Recruiting in a new public space. *Journal of Contemporary Religion, 14*(1), 17–39.
Decker, S. H. (1996). Collective and normative features of gang violence. *Justice Quarterly, 13*(2), 243–264.
Decker, S. H., Katz, C. M., & Webb, V. J. (2008). Understanding the black box of gang organization: Implications for involvement in violent crime, drug sales, and violent victimization. *Crime & Delinquency, 54*(1), 153–172.
Decker, S. H., & Pyrooz, D. C. (2010). Gang violence around the world: Context, culture and country. In G. McDonald (Ed.), *Small arms survey* (pp. 128–155). London: Oxford University Press.
Decker, S. H., & Pyrooz, D. C. (2011). Gangs, terrorism, and radicalization. *Journal of Strategic Security, 4*(4), 151–166.
Decker, S. H., & Pyrooz, D. C. (2012). Gang offending and online behavior. *JRSA Forum 30*(3), 1–4.
Decker, S. H., Pyrooz, D. C., Sweeten, G., & Moule, R. K. (2014). Validating self-nomination in gang research: Assessing differences in gang embeddedness across non-, current, and former gang members. *Journal of Quantitative Criminology, 30*(4), 577–598.
Decker, S. H., Van Gemert, F., & Pyrooz, D. (2009). Gangs, migration and crime: The changing landscape in Europe and the United States. *Journal of International Migration and Immigration, 10*(1), 393–408.
Decker, S. H., & Van Winkle, B. (1996). *Life in the gang: Family, friends and violence*. New York: Cambridge University Press.
Densley, J. A. (2012). Street gang recruitment. *Social Problems, 59*(3), 301–321.
Densley, J. (2013). *How gangs work: Ethnography of youth violence*. New York: Palgrave Macmillan.
Esbensen, F.-A., & Carson, D. C. (2012). Who are the gangsters? An examination of the age, race/ethnicity, sex, and immigration status of self-reported gang members in a seven-city study of American youth. *Journal of Contemporary Criminal Justice, 28*(4), 465–481.
Esbensen, F.-A., & Maxson, C. L. (2012). *Youth gangs in international perspective. Results from the Eurogang program of research*. New York: Springer.
Esbensen, F.-A., Winfree, L. T., He, N., & Taylor, T. J. (2001). Youth gangs and definitional issues: When is a gang a gang, and why does it matter? *Crime & Delinquency, 47*(1), 105–130.
Felson, M. (1995). Those who discourage crime. In J. E. Eck & D. Weisburd (Eds.), *Crime and place* (pp. 53–66). Monsey, NY: Criminal Justice Press.
Felson, M. (2002). *Crime and everyday life* (3rd ed.). Thousand Oaks, CA: Sage.
Felson, M. (2006). The street gang strategy. In M. Felson (Ed.), *Crime and nature* (pp. 305–324). Thousand Oaks, CA: Sage.
Gerstenfeld, P. B., Grant, D. R., & Chiang, C. (2003). Hate online: A content analysis of extremist internet sites. *Analyses of Social Issues and Public Policy, 3*(1), 29–44.
Gui, M., & Argentin, G. (2011). Digital skills of internet natives: Different forms of digital literacy in a random sample of northern Italian high school students. *New Media & Society, 13*(6), 963–980.
Hagedorn, J. (2008). *A world of gangs: Armed young men and gangsta culture*. Minneapolis, MN: University of Minnesota Press.
Hanser, R. D. (2011). Gang-related cyber and computer crimes: Legal aspects and practical points of consideration in investigations. *International Review of Law, Computers, and Technology, 25*(1–2), 47–55.

Harel-Fisch, Y., Korn, I., Fogel-Grinvald, H., Ben- David, I., & Nave, S. (2009). *Youth in Israel: Social welfare, mental health, and risk behavior*. Ramat Gan, Israel: Bar Ilan University press (Hebrew).
Hargittai, E. (2008). Whose space? Differences among users and non-users of social network sites. *Journal of Computer-Mediated Communication, 13*(1), 276–297.
Holt, T. J. (2007). Subcultural evolution? Examining the influence of on- and off-line experiences on deviant subcultures. *Deviant Behavior, 28*(2), 171–198.
Holt, T. J., & Bossler, A. M. (2008). Examining the applicability of lifestyle-routine activities theory for cybercrime victimization. *Deviant Behavior, 30*(1), 1–25.
Holt, T. J., & Bossler, A. M. (2013). Examining the relationship between routine activities and malware infection indicators. *Journal of Contemporary Criminal Justice, 29*(3), 420–436.
Holt, T. J., Bossler, A. M., & May, D. C. (2012). Low self-control, deviant peer associations, and juvenile cyber deviance. *American Journal of Criminal Justice, 37*(3), 378–395.
Horrigan, J. (2010). *Broadband adoption and use in America OBI working paper series*. Federal Communications Commission. Retrieved from http://online.wsj.com/public/resources/documents/FCCSurvey.pdf.
Hu, Q., Xu, Z., & Yayla, A. A. (2013). *Why college students commit computer hacks: Insights from a cross culture analysis*. Retrieved from http://beta.orionsshoulders.com/Resources/articles/26_22254_%20().pdf.
Internet World Stats. (2014). *World Internet users and population stats*. Retrieved from http://www.internetlivestats.com/internet-users.
Interpol. (2014). *Cybercrime report*. Retrieved from http://www.interpol.int/Crime-areas/Cybercrime/Cybercrime.
Israel Internet Association. (2014). *A survey of internet usage among Israeli youth*. Retrieved from http://data.isoc.org.il/data/563.
King, J. E., Walpole, C. E., & Lamon, K. (2007). Surf and turf wars online—Growing implications of internet gang violence. *Journal of Adolescent Health, 4*(6), 66–68.
Klein, M. W. (2005). The value of comparisons in street gang research. *Journal of Contemporary Criminal Justice, 21*(2), 135–152.
Klein, M. W., & Maxson, C. M. (2006). *Street gang patterns and policies*. New York: Oxford University Press.
Livingstone, S., & Helsper, E. (2010). Balancing opportunities and risks in teenagers' use of the internet: The role of online skills and internet self-efficacy. *New Media & Society, 12*(2), 309–329.
Lobe, B., Livingstone, S., Ólafsson, K., & Vodeb, H. (2011). *Cross-national comparison of risks and safety on the Internet*. London School of Economics and Political Science. Retrieved from http://www.lse.ac.uk/media@lse/research/EUKidsOnline.
Madden, M., Lenhart, A., Duggan, M., Cortesi, S., & Gasser, U. (2013). *Teens and technology*. The Berkman Center for Internet & Society, Harvard University. Retrieved from http://www.pewinternet.org/2013/03/13/teens-and-technology-2013.
Maratea, R. J., & Kavanaugh, P. K. (2012). Deviant identity in online contexts: New directives in the study of a classic concept. *Sociological Compass, 6*(2), 102–112.
Matsuda, K. N., Esbensen, F.-A., & Carson, D. C. (2012). Putting the 'gang' in 'Eurogang': Characteristics of delinquent youth groups by different definitional approaches. In F.-A. Esbensen & C. L. Maxson (Eds.), *Youth gangs in international perspective: Results from the Eurogang program of research* (pp. 17–33). New York: Springer.
McCuddy, T., & Vogel, M. (2014). More than just friends: Online social networks and offending. *Criminal Justice Review, 6*(1), 1–21.
Meldrum, R. C., & Clark, J. (2013). Adolescent virtual time spent socializing with peers, substance use, and delinquency. *Crime & Delinquency, 20*(1), 1–23.
Mesch, G. S. (2009). The internet and youth culture. *Hedgehog Review, 11*(1), 50–60.
Morselli, C., & De'Cary-Hetu, D. (2012). Crime facilitation purposes of social networking sites: A review and analysis of the "cyberbanging" phenomenon. *Small Wars and Insurgencies, 24*(1), 152–170.
Moule, R. K., Pyrooz, D. C., & Decker, S. H. (2013). From 'What the F#@% is a Facebook?' to 'Who Doesn't use Facebook?': The role of criminal lifestyles in the adoption and use of the internet. *Social Science Research, 42*(6), 1411–1421.

Moule, R. K., Pyrooz, D. C., & Decker, S. H. (2014). Internet adoption and online behavior among American gangs: Integrating gangs and organizational theory. *British Journal of Criminology, 54*(6), 1186–1206. doi:10.1093/bjc/azu050.
Osgood, D. W., Wilson, J. K., Bachman, J. G., O'Malley, P. M., & Johnston, L. D. (1996). Routine activities and individual deviant behavior. *American Sociological Review, 61*(4), 635–655.
Patton, D. U., Eschmann, R. D., & Butler, D. A. (2013). Internet banging: New trends in social media, gang violence, masculinity and hip-hop. *Computers in Human Behavior, 29*(5), 54–59.
Pratt, T. C., Holtfreter, K., & Reisig, M. D. (2010). Routine online activity and internet fraud targeting: Extending the generality of routine activity theory. *Journal of Research in Crime & Delinquency, 47*(3), 267–296.
Prensky, M. (2001). Digital natives, digital immigrants (part 1). *On the Horizon, 9*(5), 1–6.
Pyrooz, D. C. (2014). "From your first cigarette to your last dyin' day": The patterning of gang membership in the life-course. *Journal of Quantitative Criminology, 30*(2), 349–372.
Pyrooz, D. C., Decker, S. H., & Moule, R. K. (2015). Criminal and routine activities in online settings: Gangs, offenders, and the internet. *Justice Quarterly, 32*(3), 471–499.
Pyrooz, D. C., Fox, A. M., Katz, C. M., & Decker, S. H. (2012). Gang organization, offending, and victimization: A cross-national analysis. In F.-A. Esbensen & C. L. Maxson (Eds.), *Youth gangs in international perspective: Results from the Eurogang program of research* (pp. 85–105). New York: Springer.
Reid, E., & Chen, H. (2002). Internet-savvy U.S. and middle eastern extremist groups. *Mobilization: An International Quarterly Review, 12*(2), 177–192.
Rogers, E. (2005). *The diffusion of innovation* (5th ed.). New York: Simon and Schuster.
Schradie, J. (2012). The trend of class, race, and ethnicity in social media inequality. *Information, Communication and Society, 15*(4), 555–571.
Sela-Shayovitz, R. (2012a). Gangs and the web: Gang members' online behavior. *Journal of Contemporary Criminal Justice, 28*(4), 389–405.
Sela-Shayovitz, R. (2012b). The impact of globalization, migration, and social group processes on neo-Nazi youth gangs. In F.-A. Esbensen & C. L. Maxson (Eds.), *Youth gangs in international perspective: Results from the Eurogang program of research* (pp. 295–310). New York: Springer.
Silverblatt, A. (2004). Media as social institution. *American Behavioral Scientist, 48*(1), 35–41.
Skinner, W. F., & Fream, A. M. (1997). A social learning theory analysis of computer crime among college students. *Journal of Research in Crime and Delinquency, 34*(4), 495–518.
Sweeten, G. A., Piquero, R., & Steinberg, L. (2013). Age and the explanation of crime, revisited. *Journal of Youth and Adolescence, 42*(6), 921–938.
Tcherni, M., Davies, A., Lopes, G., & Lizotte, A. (2015). The dark figure of online property crime: Is cyberspace hiding a crime wave? *Justice Quarterly*. doi:10.1080/07418825.2014.994658.
Thornberry, T. P., Krohn, M. D., Lizotte, A. J., Smith, C. A., & Tobin, K. (2003). *Gangs and delinquency in developmental perspective*. Cambridge, MA: Cambridge University Press.
Thornberry, T. P., Krohn, M. D., Lizotte, A. J., & Chard-Wierschem, D. (1993). The role of juvenile gangs in facilitating delinquent behavior. *Journal of Research in Crime and Delinquency, 30*(1), 55–87.
Tyler, T. R. (2002). Is the internet changing social life? It seems the more things change, the more they stay the same. *Journal of Social Issues, 58*(1), 195–205.
Van Deursen, A., & Van Dijk, J. (2010). Internet skills and the digital divide. *New Media & Society, 11*(1), 1–19.
Van Dijk, J., & Hacker, K. (2003). The digital divide as a complex and dynamic phenomenon. *The Information Society, 19*(4), 315–326.
Van Hellemont, E. (2012). Gangland online: Performing the real world of gangstas and ghettos in Brussels. *European Journal of Crime, Criminal Law and Criminal Justice, 20*(1), 159–173.
Weerman, F. M., Bernasco, W., Bruinsma, G. J., & Pauwels, L. J. (2013). When is spending time with peers related to delinquency? The importance of where, what, and with whom. *Crime & Delinquency*. doi: 10.1177/0011128713478129.

Weerman, F., Maxson, C., Esbensen, F.-A., Aldridge, J., Medina, J., & van Gemert, F. (2009). *Eurogang program manual*. Eurogang Network. Retrieved from http://www.umsl.edu/ccj/eurogang/EurogangManual.pdf.

Weimann, G. (2004). Www.terror.net*: How modern terrorism uses the Internet* (Special report 116). Washington, DC: United States Institute of Peace.

Weimann, G. (2006). Virtual disputes: The use of the internet for terrorist debates. *Studies in Conflict & Terrorism, 29*(7), 623–639.

Wolfe, S. E., Higgins, G. E., & Marcum, C. D. (2008). Deterrence and digital piracy: A preliminary examination of the role of viruses. *Social Science Computer Review, 26*(3), 317–333.

Wolfe, S. E., Marcum, C. D., Higgins, G. E., & Ricketts, M. L. (2014). Routine cell phone activity and exposure to sex messages: Extending the generality of routine activity theory and exploring the etiology of a risky teenage behavior. *Crime & Delinquency*. doi: 10.1177/0011128714541192.

Womer, S., & Bunker, R. J. (2010). Surenos gangs and Mexican cartel use of social networking sites. *Small Wars and Insurgencies, 21*(1), 81–94.

Yar, M. (2005). Computer hacking: Just another case of juvenile delinquency? *The Howard Journal, 44*(4), 387–399.

Part II
Transitions and Gang Transformation

Chapter 8
Motivations for Leaving Gangs in the USA: A Qualitative Comparison of Leaving Processes Across Gang Definitions

Dena C. Carson and Finn-Aage Esbensen

8.1 Introduction

Knowledge regarding gangs and gang members has increased significantly in the past several decades. Research in this arena is both multi-national, spanning North America, Europe, and Latin America, and multi-disciplinary with work being contributed by anthropology, sociology, psychology, and criminology. From this research we have amassed a great deal of information surrounding risk factors for gang joining, consequences of membership, group processes and gang behavior, and prevention and intervention strategies as well as knowledge on defining gang membership (Decker et al. 2013).

Recent research has examined the processes surrounding leaving the gang. Studies on gang desistance stem from the consistent finding that youth are able to leave their gangs and that membership typically lasts 1 year or less (Decker and Lauritsen 2002; Esbensen and Huizinga 1993; Hill et al. 1999; Moore 1991; Vigil 1988). Research in this arena focuses on the motivations, methods, and consequences of leaving the gang as well as variations in these factors based on level of gang embeddedness (Bolden 2012; Carson et al. 2013; Horowitz 1983; Pyrooz et al. 2013; Spergel 1995; Sweeten et al. 2013; Vigil 1988), demographics

D.C. Carson (✉)
School of Public and Environmental Affairs, Indiana University Purdue University Indianapolis, Indianapolis, IN, USA
e-mail: carsond@iupui.edu

F.-A. Esbensen
Department of Criminology and Criminal Justice, University of Missouri-St. Louis, St. Louis, MO, USA
e-mail: esbensen@umsl.edu

C.L. Maxson, F.-A. Esbensen (eds.), *Gang Transitions and Transformations in an International Context*, DOI 10.1007/978-3-319-29602-9_8

(Carson et al. 2013; Decker and Lauritsen 2002; Hagedorn 1994; Moloney et al. 2011; Moore 1991; O'Neal et al. 2014; Peterson 2012; Pyrooz and Decker 2011; Quicker 1999; Vigil 1988), and definitional issues (Carson et al. 2013; Decker and Lauritsen 2002; Pyrooz and Decker 2011; Sweeten et al. 2013).

Motivations for leaving the gang come in many forms and can be used to inform policies surrounding gang interventions and prevention efforts. That said, discussions of policy across these contexts are often hampered by differences in the conceptualization of gangs. One aim of the current study is to further explore the differences and similarities across conceptual definitions by comparing motivations for leaving the gang among youth who self-nominate as gang members, those who fit the Eurogang definition, and multi-definitional youth who fit both classifications. In order to make these comparisons, this chapter draws on prospective survey data with gang and Eurogang-involved youth as well as a linked sample of retrospective qualitative interviews. A second aim of this study is to compare prospective and retrospective motivations for leaving the gang.

8.2 Research Comparing Definitional Approaches

Social science researchers have employed varying conceptual and operational definitions of gangs. This is apart from the various classifications used by law enforcement and policy makers to identify gang members. These definitional issues have resulted in considerable debate over what constitutes a gang or gang member, which is further complicated in an international context. American gang researchers typically rely on a self-nomination of gang membership (i.e., are you now in a gang?), which has been shown to be a reliable and valid measure (Esbensen et al. 2001). However, the term "gang" does not always translate in an international context, leading to what Klein and colleagues (2001) referred to as the "Eurogang Paradox" or the false notion that gangs and gang-like groups do not exist in Europe. The Eurogang definition of gang membership was created as a response to this paradox and classifies youth gangs as any group that is durable, street-oriented, and whose involvement in illegal activity is part of their group identity (Weerman et al. 2009).

Several studies have attempted to assess the validity of the self-nomination and Eurogang approach. In a cross-national comparison, Esbensen and Weerman (2005) compared youth fitting the Eurogang definition (the Dutch sample) with youth who self-nominated as belonging to a gang (the US sample). Findings indicated that risk factors and offending were similar across the measures of gang membership. Other research, however, has identified a lack of convergent validity. Matsuda and colleagues (2012) found only a 4 % overlap between self-nomination and Eurogang-defined youth. Despite this low convergent validity, the study finds that these youth are at higher risk than youth not involved in a gang-like group. In other words, youth who self-report gang membership and youth who meet the Eurogang definition participate in higher levels of offending and have more risk factors than non-gang involved youth. While these conceptual definitions are similar when compared to non-gang youth, there is evidence that gang members still differ by how they are defined. Matsuda and colleagues (2012) found that youth who self-nominate were more delinquent when compared with Eurogang youth at the bivariate level. In addition, the Eurogang sample captures youth who are typically underrepresented by other definitions (i.e., female, white, and older gang members).

In another study, Esbensen and colleagues (2009) compared three groups of gang-involved youth: (1) self-nominated; (2) Eurogang; and (3) multi-definitional youth (i.e., those fitting both gang definitions). This work found that youth who self-nominate into a gang and also met the Eurogang definition were more committed to negative peers, reported less guilt, and participated in higher levels of offending than youth who met only one of those definitions or were not gang-involved (Esbensen et al. 2009). This is not only further evidence that self-nominated gang and Eurogang youth are significantly different from non-gang involved youth, but also indicates that youth who fit both definitions are more at risk for offending. The current study seeks to compare multi-definitional youth with self-nominated and Eurogang-defined youth to determine if there is a relationship between the higher risk lifestyle of multi-definitional youth and motivations for leaving the gang.

8.3 Motivations for Desistance

Prior research has classified motivations for leaving the gang as either *push* or *pull* factors. Push factors are internal to the gang or individual and serve to push an individual out of gang life (Bjorgo 2002; Pyrooz and Decker 2011). Push factors have the potential to "facilitate or hasten" the desistance process because they paint the gang environment as unappealing (Pyrooz and Decker 2011). Conversely, pull factors are external to the individual and serve to pull him/her away from the gang. Pull factors tend to present gang members with more appealing alternatives to gang life. It is important to note that these factors are often intertwined and it is usually an accumulation of both that results in gang desistance (Decker and Lauritsen 2002; Vigil 1988).

Research on leaving the gang has identified a number of push factors, with the most common being disillusionment. Disillusionment occurs when gang members lose faith in the inner workings of the gang, perceive that the gang is unsupportive (i.e., not visiting in jail/prison or protecting one another from rival gang threats), or when they believe they are being taken advantage of by their gang peers (Bjorgo 2002; Decker et al. 2014; Hagedorn 1994; Padilla 1992; Thrasher 1927/1963; Vigil 1988). Research often categorizes statements such as "I just felt like it" or "it wasn't my type of life" as motivations associated with disillusionment (Carson et al. 2013; Decker and Lauritsen 2002; Padilla 1992; Pyrooz and Decker 2011).

The role of violence in gang life is also thought to generate feelings of disillusionment and is often discussed as a motivation for leaving the gang (Carson et al. 2013; Decker and Pyrooz 2011; Pyrooz and Decker 2011; Vecchio 2014). Motivations associated with violence can range from fear of future violence and vicarious victimization (i.e., victimization of a friend, family member, or fellow gang member) to direct experiences with violence (e.g., getting beaten, stabbed, and shot). The accumulation of violent experiences may result in violence fatigue (Bjorgo 2002; Decker and Van Winkle 1996; Spergel 1995; Vigil 1988).[1]

Push factors, while sufficient reasons to leave the gang, may work in tandem with pull factors as the impetus of gang desistance. Pull factors can come in many forms and typically represent life-course transitions or "hooks for change." Prior research has identified pull factors such as experience with official sanctions (Carson et al. 2013; Decker and Pyrooz 2011; Decker et al. 2014; Hagedorn 1994; Horowitz 1983; Moore 1991; Sanchez-Jankowski 1991; Spergel 1995; Vigil 1988); being encouraged by teachers, parents, or other influential adults to leave the gang (Carson et al. 2013; Decker et al. 2014; Padilla 1992; Vigil 1988); spirituality and religious conversion (Decker et al. 2014; Spergel 1995); gainful employment (Bjorgo 2002; Decker and Lauritsen 2002; Decker et al. 2014; Decker and Van Winkle 1996; Hagedorn 1994; Moore 1991; Padilla 1992; Sanchez-Jankowski 1991; Spergel 1995; Vigil 1988); romantic relationships (Bjorgo 2002; Decker and Lauritsen 2002; Decker and Pyrooz 2011; Hagedorn 1994; Horowitz 1983; Moore 1991; Thrasher 1927/1963; Vigil 1988); parenthood (Decker and Pyrooz 2011; Decker et al. 2014; Fleisher and Krienert 2004; Hagedorn 1994; Moloney et al. 2009, 2011; Moore 1991; Varriale 2008); moving to a new neighborhood, city, or school (Carson et al. 2013; Decker and Lauritsen 2002; Decker and Van Winkle 1996; Hagedorn 1994; Padilla 1992; Spergel 1995; Vigil 1988) and, finally, the dissolution of the gang (Decker and Pyrooz 2011; Horowitz 1983; Quicker 1999; Spergel 1995; Thrasher 1927/1963; Vigil 1988).

While sometimes occurring independently, it is more often the case that push and pull factors work together in the desistance process. Gang youth most commonly become disillusioned by their involvement in the gang, in combination with maturation or violence fatigue, which is often accompanied by significant life events or "hooks for change" outside of the gang. No doubt a number of intertwining factors play into the decision to begin the desistance process from the gang and, given this, it is unlikely that this progression occurs rapidly.

While prior research typically finds a lack of variation in desistance motivations across gender (Carson et al. 2013; Moore 1991; O'Neal et al. 2014; Peterson 2012; Quicker 1999) or race/ethnicity (Carson et al. 2013; Decker and Lauritsen 2002; Hagedorn 1994; Hagedorn and Devitt 1999; Horowitz 1983; Vigil 1988), there appear to be some differences by age. This is not surprising as some external pulls are age-graded (i.e., marriage, military involvement, employment) (Decker and Lauritsen 2002; Moore 1991; Pyrooz and Decker 2011). However, other research indicates that older gang members are more likely to report motivations associated

[1] This may be surprising given that prior research typically finds that violence serves to increase the solidarity and cohesion of the gang (Decker 1996; Hagedorn 1988; Klein 1971; Padilla 1992; Vigil 1988); however, these divergent findings might be due to the origin of the violence. Violence among gang members or occurring within the gang context may be more salient to members, thus facilitating a sense of disillusionment and violence fatigue. Violence that occurs between gangs or between gang members, however, may intensify the bonds of membership (Decker and Van Winkle 1996).

with violence (Carson et al. 2013) and to experience official sanctions (Vigil 1988). Apart from demographics, variation in reasons for leaving the gang is also found across levels of gang embeddedness. Youth who are more embedded (i.e., core members) find it more difficult to leave (Horowitz 1983; Pyrooz et al. 2013; Sweeten et al. 2013) and are more likely to report motivations associated with disillusionment, but peripheral members are more likely to name violence as a key motivation for leaving the gang (Carson et al. 2013). Relatedly, it is reasonable to expect that gang youth who are more heavily involved in offending and more frequently victimized are likely to report motivations associated with violence, but research on this topic produces mixed results (Carson et al. 2013; Pyrooz and Decker 2011). Finally, few studies have examined motivations across differing gang definitions. Carson and associates (2013) compared three increasingly restrictive operational definitions of gang desisters and found few differences in motivations. We hope to expand on work by Carson and colleagues by comparing motivations for gang leaving across three distinct conceptual definitions of gang desisters.

8.4 Summary and Current Study

Prior research has identified a number of motivational factors associated with gang desistance that have been shown to be relatively stable across demographics and operational definitions of desistance. Less is known, however, about how these motivations may vary across conceptual definitions of gang membership. The first aim of the current study is to explore this issue by comparing desistance motivations across youth who self-nominate gang membership, youth who fit the Eurogang definition (but do not self-nominate), and multi-definitional youth who fit both definitions. We explore whether there are differences in motivations associated with demographic characteristics (sex, race/ethnicity, age) and whether there are differences based on how gang membership is determined (i.e., self-nominated, Eurogang, or both).

In this study we integrate prospective quantitative survey data with a linked sample of retrospective qualitative interviews to compare desistance motivations across self-identified gang youth, Eurogang youth, and multi-definitional youth. This mixed-methods framework also allows for a comparison of prospective and retrospective motivations that gang youth give for leaving their gang, which is the second aim of the current work. Prior research has demonstrated little overlap when comparing prospective and retrospective self-reports of experiences (Fivush 1993; Henry et al. 1994; Kruttschnitt and Dornfeld 1992; Wagenaar and Groeneweg 1990; Yarrow et al. 1970). This lack of consistency could be related to recall issues and retrospective reinterpretation, as well as concern about social desirability (Bradburn et al. 1987; Henry et al. 1994; Ross 1989; Squire 1989). However, youth may be better able to remember events that are more salient like violence or life transitions, but less able to recall those that are vague such as disillusionment or receiving encouragement from an adult in their life. Henry and colleagues (1994), for example, compared prospective and retrospective accounts of psychological and behavioral variables, finding that retrospective accounts of injuries, delinquent behaviors, and arrests were all moderately more accurate than would be expected by chance. However, they found little agreement between prospective and retrospective measures of their psychological variables. This study contributes to this body of research by examining the extent to which the retrospective and prospective accounts of gang leaving tell the same story.

8.5 Methods

The current study uses a mixed-methods approach to examine motivations for leaving the gang across three conceptual definitions of gang membership. This section provides an overview of both the quantitative and qualitative data sources and then discusses how the two data sources were combined for analysis.

8.5.1 Prospective Quantitative Sample

The quantitative data used in this study come from the National Evaluation of the G.R.E.A.T. (Gang Resistance Education and Training) Program, a longitudinal panel study (2006–2013) of a school-based gang prevention program that took place in seven cities across the USA (see Esbensen et al. 2013, for more detail about the evaluation design). The G.R.E.A.T. program is an American gang prevention program taught by law enforcement officers targeting middle school youth (i.e., 11 and 12 year olds). Cities were chosen to participate in the evaluation based on the existence of an established G.R.E.A.T. program, geographic and demographic diversity, and presence of gang activity. The final seven sites represent a wide range of cities from the east to the west coast and include the following: Albuquerque, New Mexico; Chicago, Illinois; Greeley, Colorado; Nashville, Tennessee; Philadelphia, Pennsylvania; Portland, Oregon; and a city in the Dallas/Fort Worth, Texas area.

All students in the selected classrooms were eligible to participate in the evaluation. A total of 4905 students were enrolled in the 195 participating classrooms in the 31 middle schools at the beginning of the data collection process. After a thorough active parental consent process, 89 % (N=4372) of youth returned consent forms, and 78 % (N=3820) were given permission by a parent or guardian to participate in the evaluation (11 % of parents declined) (see Esbensen et al. 2008 for a detailed description of procedures and factors related to active consent). In 2006, students completed pretest and posttest (Waves 1 and 2) self-report surveys with completion rates of 98.3 % and 94.6 %, respectively.[2] The sample also completed four annual follow-up surveys (Waves 3, 4, 5, and 6),

[2] Due to an under-representation of African American youth in Chicago schools obtained in the 2006 sampling effort, two additional schools were included in the evaluation, beginning during the 2007–2008 school year (Esbensen et al. 2013).

with participation rates of 87 %, 83 %, 75 %, and 73 %, respectively. These completion rates are very good, especially given the mobility of the sample. While the evaluation began in 31 schools, by Wave Four, the research team surveyed students in 219 different schools.

8.5.2 Retrospective Qualitative Sample

The qualitative data come from a subsample of the G.R.E.A.T. study; youth who reported being in a gang ($N=512$) or who met the Eurogang definition ($N=697$) in one or more of the G.R.E.A.T. surveys were eligible to participate in the second study. The research design called for an examination of both stable and transient gang youth. Stable gang members were identified as those who self-reported involvement in a gang in two or more consecutive waves ($N=156$). Transient members were those youth who reported gang membership in at least one of the six waves of data: this includes youth who reported gang membership in 2 or more non-consecutive years ($N=356$). Participants were selected using a purposive oversampling of stable youth ($N=131$) and a random sampling of both transient gang youth ($N=198$) and youth who fit the Eurogang definition ($N=97$).[3] This resulted in a sampling frame of 426 gang and Eurogang youth. As expected, however, interviewers encountered a number of youth that had moved (27.7 %), parents and/or youth who declined to participate (5.3 %), continuous non-contact with anyone in the household in spite of repeated visits to the address (20.2 %) (interviewers were instructed to visit each address a minimum of three different times and on different days), as well as other reasons for non-participation (e.g., incarceration) (4.2 %). The youth in the G.R.E.A.T. evaluation were highly mobile; therefore, it was not surprising that a number of the gang youth had moved to a different home, particularly given that respondents were contacted almost 2 years after the end of the G.R.E.A.T. study. Therefore, approximately 42 % of youth in the selected sample completed an interview. This resulted in a final sample of 142 self-nominated gang youth and 38 Eurogang youth.

Information was collected during the summer of 2012 via in-depth face-to-face interviews with these youth and was retrospective in nature. It is important to note that in some cases youth may have been asked to recall gang membership from as far back as 2006. The interview guide included questions about gangs in neighborhoods and schools, but focused on peer group transitions, especially those associated with gang joining and gang leaving. All interviews were recorded and conducted in a confidential location by trained interviewers. The majority of interviews lasted approximately 1 h and youth were paid $20 for their participation.

---

[3] It is important to point out that for the purposes of this sample youth were not included in the pool of Eurogang youth if they self-nominated as a gang member at any wave of the G.R.E.A.T. evaluation.

8.5.3 Combined Analysis Sample and Operationalization of Desisted Youth

Gang desistance was operationalized uniquely across the quantitative and qualitative data sets. In the quantitative data set, youth were separated into three definitional categories. First, are the respondents who "self-nominate" as a gang member by answering "yes" to the question "Are you now in a gang?" Second, the Eurogang approach included youth who had a group of friends that fit the following criteria: (1) had three or more people, (2) consisted of people mostly between the ages of 12 and 25, (3) spends a lot of time in public places, (4) been in existence for more than 3 months, and (5) accepted and actually participated in illegal activity. Third, youth were defined as multi-definitional if they met both of these definitions within the same reporting wave. Youth were considered desisted from the gang if they met one of these gang definitions in one wave and met none in the next consecutive wave. In the full quantitative data, there were approximately 753 respondents that could be classified as desisters. This included mutually exclusive categories of desisters: 292 self-nomination gang youth, 344 Eurogang youth, and 117 multi-definitional gang youth.

Of the 180 youth in the qualitative gang sample, 127 retrospectively reported belonging to a gang-like group (102 Gang and 25 Eurogang). A total of 53 youth self-reported gang membership in the quantitative survey, but later denied gang involvement in the qualitative interview. Of the 127 youth that reported involvement, 107 can be classified as having desisted from a gang-like group on the basis of responding affirmatively to questions regarding desistance from their group. Since our interest is in motivations for gang desistance, we limit our subsequent analyses to those youth who were classified as desisters in both the qualitative and quantitative data sets: this resulted in an analysis sample of 82 youth spanning three mutually exclusive categories: Eurogang only ($N=20$), gang only ($N=35$), and multi-definitional youth ($N=27$).[4] Motivations for desistance were examined for consistencies and deviations both within and across conceptual definitions using descriptive and bivariate analysis.[5] Qualitative interviews were analyzed using a grounded theory approach and open line-by-line coding. Themes were then matched with the quantitative responses.

[4]Analysis comparing the full sample of desisters to the final analysis sample revealed no differences in desistance motivations across youth classified as self-nominated or multi-definitional. Youth classified as belonging to a Eurogang in the full sample were significantly older than those included in the analysis sample; however, there were no other demographic differences across the samples within each group.

[5]Differences in demographics and motivations were compared across the three conceptual definitions using Fisher's exact test. This significance test is typically used in place of X^2 in the presence of small sample sizes, which can violate the X^2 assumption that the expected value in a cell is greater than 5. That said, when examining differences in age via ANOVA analysis we tested for equal variances using both Levene's test of equal variances and Welch's robust test. In terms of post hoc analyses, Games–Howell's test was used as the variances were not assumed to be equal. This is a modified test that allows for unequal variances as well as unequal sample sizes.

8.5.4 *Motivations for Desistance*

In the quantitative data, youth were asked to self-report on their subjective reasons for leaving their gang and were asked to "circle all that apply" from a list of motivations. These questions were only asked of youth who self-reported gang membership and, therefore, responses are not available for youth who only fit the Eurogang definition. In the in-depth interviews, however, all youth were asked to discuss why they left their gang or group so comparisons can be made across all three definitions in these data.

Quantitative motivations were categorized as those associated with disillusionment, violence, adult interventions, and life transitions. Youth who circled that they "just left" their gang or that the gang "wasn't what they thought it was going to be" were coded as experiencing disillusionment. Motivations such as "A friend was hurt or killed," "A family member was hurt or killed," and "I was hurt" were classified as violent motivations. Adult intervention motivations included "I got into trouble with the police," "An adult encouraged me to get out," and "My parents made me leave the gang." Finally, youth who "made new friends" or "moved to a new home or school" were coded as experiencing reasons associated with life transitions.

Qualitative analysis identified a variety of themes associated with motivations for leaving the gang, many of which correspond to the subjective reasons provided in the quantitative surveys. When comparing prospective and retrospective responses, however, we will only draw on similar themes in order to make more accurate comparisons. Importantly, the motivations listed above are not an exhaustive list of reasons given in the qualitative data.

8.6 Findings

8.6.1 *Comparing Conceptual Definitions*

Descriptive demographic data are presented in Table 8.1. There were no significant differences across sex, but the Eurogang group included the largest proportion of females. There were also no differences in race/ethnicity across definitions. Substantively, however, there are more minorities present in gang only and multi-definitional categories. Multi-definitional youth were significantly older than Eurogang youth.

Table 8.2 presents the motivations for desistance given by youth in both the quantitative and qualitative data. Comparisons of the pulls and pushes associated with leaving the gang can be made between youth categorized as gang desisters and multi-definitional desisters only in the quantitative data and there were no significant differences between these two groups of desisters. Both categories of youth reported experiencing external pulls and internal pushes to leave the gang, but multi-definitional youth were not significantly more or less likely to report

Table 8.1 Descriptive statistics

	Eurogang only desisters	Gang only desisters	Multi-definitional desisters
N	20	35	27
Sex (male) (%)	9 (45.0)	20 (57.1)	18 (66.7)
Race (%)			
White	7 (35.0)	5 (14.3)	4 (14.8)
African-American	3 (15.0)	13 (37.1)	5 (18.5)
Hispanic	6 (30.0)	13 (37.1)	16 (59.3)
Other	4 (20.0)	4 (11.4)	2 (7.4)
Wave 1 Age (SD)[a]	11.32 (0.82)	11.56 (0.71)	12.00 (0.87)

[a]Significant difference between Eurogang and Multi-definitional desisters using Games-Howell post-hoc test for unequal variances

Table 8.2 Motivations for gang desistance

	Quantitative motivations		Qualitative sample		
	Gang only desisters	Multi-definitional desisters	Eurogang only desisters	Gang only desisters	Multi-definitional desisters
N	35	27	20	35	27
External pulls					
Adult interventions	11 (31.4)	10 (37.0)	3 (15.0)	14 (40.0)	13 (48.1)
Trouble with police	10 (28.6)	10 (37.0)	0 (0.0)	1 (2.9)	4 (14.8)
Adult encouraged	7 (20.0)	5 (18.5)	0 (0.0)	4 (11.4)	5 (18.5)
Parent encouraged	6 (17.1)	3 (11.1)	3 (15.0)	11 (31.4)	10 (37.0)
Life transitions	12 (34.3)	7 (25.9)	18 (90.0)	28 (80.0)	18 (66.7)
Made new friends*	12 (34.3)	6 (22.2)	4 (20.0)	10 (28.6)	1 (3.7)
Moved home/school	4 (11.4)	1 (3.7)	17 (85.0)	23 (65.7)	15 (55.6)
Internal pushes					
*Violence**	15 (42.9)	11 (40.7)	0 (0.0)	5 (14.3)	10 (37.0)
Friend hurt or killed*	11 (31.4)	7 (25.9)	0 (0.0)	4 (11.4)	7 (25.9)
Family hurt or killed	5 (14.3)	5 (18.5)	0 (0.0)	0 (0.0)	1 (3.7)
I was hurt	10 (28.6)	6 (22.2)	0 (0.0)	2 (5.7)	3 (11.1)
Disillusionment	12 (34.3)	10 (37.0)	2 (10.0)	4 (11.4)	9 (33.3)
I just felt like it	12 (34.3)	9 (33.3)	0 (0.0)	1 (2.9)	3 (11.1)
Not what I thought	8 (22.9)	4 (14.8)	2 (10.0)	3 (8.6)	7 (25.9)

Note: Individual motivations will not be equal because youth were instructed to "circle all that apply"

*Denotes a significant difference ($p<0.05$) in the qualitative sample based on Fisher's exact

these motivations than gang only desisters. Full comparisons across conceptual definitions can be made in the qualitative interviews; there were few significant differences across conceptual definitions. External pulls to leave the gang were experienced by all categories of youth, but those who desisted from a Eurogang only group were substantively less likely to experience adult interventions. Youth classified as multi-definitional desisters were the least likely to experience life transitions as a motivation. Within the life transitions category, it was common for youth, particularly among Eurogang youth, to state that they desisted from their gang via residential or school mobility. For example, Destiny, a Eurogang desister, stated "...some people moved away, some people, some people went to the neighborhood high school, some people didn't..." Youth classified as having desisted from a multi-definitional gang were significantly less likely to report meeting new friends as a motivation. This motivation was most commonly reported by youth who self-nominated, like Jordan, who said, "Yeah, I also met other people, or other people met me and that was that."

In terms of internal pushes, violent experiences were only discussed by self-nominated and multi-definitional desisters. Multi-definitional desisters were significantly more likely to report experiencing indirect forms of violence, such as having a friend hurt or killed. Indirect violent experiences were often characterized by statements like the following:

> Andre (gang only desister): "Um, my man got killed last uh May...And...it was somebody among the group that did it, so like, that was just my cue to get away from them, so I just separated myself from them after that."
>
> Mitch (multi-definitional desister): "My friend actually got uh, got jumped right by my mom's apartment and um broke ribs and all that and that just scared the living crap out of me and I was like 'oooh.'"

While direct experiences with violence (i.e., "I was hurt") were discussed by both multi-definitional and self-nominated youth, it is important to note that they were rare in the qualitative interviews overall with only five youth discussing direct violence as a motivation. For example, Angel, a multi-definitional desister, states, "I've been, I haven't been stabbed but I've been sliced with a box cutter." Also, Michael, a self-nominated gang desister, describes his experience with violence:

> I dunno, ever since I got shot at, 'cause with my old group a homies a couple of them shot at me and I was like oh, whoa, I dunno, it just like pissed me off. So it's like I just kick it with my family ya know. I dunno I just don't really bang no more.

Internal pushes associated with disillusionment did not significantly vary across conceptual definitions. These motivations were classified in the quantitative data by response categories such as "I just felt like it" and "It wasn't what I thought it was going to be." Similar statements could be found in the qualitative data as well, such as Felicia, a multi-definitional desister, who indicated, "Just like I didn't feel like hanging with them" or Jacob, a Eurogang desister, who stated, "Well what happened was at first everyone was like really nice to you...but eventually over time, they started showing their true colors as people. They were kind of douche bags."

Overall, the results demonstrate that external pulls, particularly in the form of mobility, for leaving the gang are more common than internal pushes across all three groups. Eurogang desisters, similar to the other categories, most commonly discussed motivations associated with moving to a new home or school. The most frequently reported motivations by both gang only and multi-definitional desisters were reasons associated with moving homes or school, followed by those associated with their parents encouraging them to leave the gang.

8.6.2 Comparison of Prospective and Retrospective Motivations

We now turn our attention to the second aim of this study, to compare the prospective and retrospective motivations for leaving the gang. Given the limitations of the quantitative data (see above), comparisons were only made between youth categorized as gang only or multi-definitional ($N=62$). Furthermore, the sample only includes youth who reported a motivation in a specific category. Note, however, that the modal condition in both the qualitative and quantitative studies was for youth not to report a motivation in a particular category. Table 8.3 compares prospective and retrospective results for those youth who reported that particular motivation in either study. Results were deemed to be inconsistent when there was a mismatch between affirmative and negative responses across the qualitative and quantitative samples. For example, if a youth reported a violent motivation in the quantitative data, but not in the qualitative data, or vice versa, he/she was counted as inconsistent. Responses were classified as consistent, for example, if a youth reported a violent motivation in both the quantitative and qualitative samples.

The results clearly indicate that youth are frequently inconsistent in their prospective and retrospective accounts. The largest amount of consistency occurs with motivations associated with violence such as having a friend hurt or killed or being directly victimized as well as motivations associated with adult interventions such as having a parent or other adult encourage gang desistance. That said, the sample

Table 8.3 Prospective versus retrospective consistency in motivations

	N	Inconsistent	Consistent
External pulls			
Adult interventions			
Trouble with police	23	21 (91.3)	2 (8.7)
Adult encouraged	19	17 (89.5)	2 (10.5)
Parent encouraged	27	24 (88.9)	3 (11.1)
Life transitions			
Made new friends	28	27 (96.4)	1 (3.6)
Moved home/school	40	37 (92.5)	3 (7.5)
Internal pushes			
Violence			
Friend hurt or killed	24	19 (79.2)	5 (20.8)
Family hurt or killed	11	11 (100)	0 (0)
I was hurt	19	17 (89.5)	2 (10.5)
Disillusionment			
I just felt like it	24	23 (95.8)	1 (4.2)
Not what I thought	21	20 (95.2)	1 (4.8)

Please note that this table only includes youth who reported a motivation in a given category. The modal response was to not report a specific motivation

sizes are so small that it is difficult to draw any concrete conclusions. Unsurprisingly, there was less consistency among the more vague motivations like disillusionment, but, again, there were small sample sizes here as well. Overall, youth were rarely consistent in their retrospective motivations with five desisters, at most, reporting consistent reasons for leaving the gang across the two samples.[6]

8.7 Discussion and Conclusions

In this chapter we drew on prospective survey data with gang and Eurogang-involved youth as well as a linked sample of retrospective qualitative interviews to accomplish two goals. The first was to explore the differences and similarities in motivations across three conceptual definitions of desisted youth, those who fit the Eurogang definition, self-nominated gang youth, and multi-definitional youth who fit both. The second goal of this study was to compare the prospective and retrospective motivations for leaving the gang.

Demographic results revealed that all three conceptual definitions captured similar youth in terms of sex and race/ethnicity. However, youth who were classified as fitting both self-nominated gang and Eurogang definitions (i.e., multi-definitional youth) were significantly older. Recall that the quantitative sample was limited to youth who self-nominated and were multi-definitional gang desisters. Comparison of motivations for leaving the gang across these two groups demonstrated a high degree of consistency across definition; that is, there were no statistically significant differences between the two groups. In the qualitative data, however, we did find some variation in motivations across the three definitions. Eurogang youth had less variation in their responses and no youth classified as a Eurogang desister discussed motivations associated with violence. In addition, youth who were classified as multi-definitional desisters more frequently reported experiencing indirect violence. Overall, though, there was a large degree of similarity in motivations across the three definitions with few significant differences present in both the quantitative and qualitative data.

Consistent with prior research on motivations for leaving the gang it was more common for youth to report motivations that were not associated with direct and indirect violence. In the qualitative accounts, for instance, it was particularly common for youth to state that they left their gang because of external pulls, such as moving to a new home or school. Other commonly discussed motivations include those associated with adult interventions in the form of parental encouragement. That said, it is important to note that violence is more likely to play a role in youth who were classified as multi-definitional desisters, perhaps representing their more violent lifestyles.

[6] Importantly, given the difference in recall period associated with the qualitative interviews, we found no differences in the consistency of motivations for leaving the gang between the "recent" and "distant" gang desisters.

Turning attention to the comparison of prospective and retrospective motivations, prior research in the social science arena suggests a lack of consistency in prospective and retrospective results (Menard et al. 2016). The results demonstrated here are consistent with this prior research when examining prospective and retrospective responses on motivations for leaving the gang. This lack of consensus between retrospective and prospective accounts may be due to the subjective nature of the motivations. Youth may have had time to reinterpret their motivations as well as give more credence to certain motivations over others. While still low, more consistency was found when examining salient life events like direct violence and mobility. The lack of consistency between prospective and retrospective responses begs the question, which method provides more valid information? We might expect, given prior research on recall error and retrospective interpretation, that the prospective data would be more valid. Others, however, have argued that retrospective accounts are more appropriate when attempting to understand significant events in the life-course (i.e., turning points) as well as when examining attitudes and emotions (Baxter and Bullis 1986; Metts et al. 1991; Surra et al. 1988). While these retrospective accounts allow respondents to apply meaning to their experiences, it may also be the case that individuals re-interpret prior events to be consistent with their current self-image, thereby introducing measurement error into these retrospective accounts. It is also possible that the lack of consistency presented here is due to memory decay as suggested by Menard and colleagues (1990, 2016) in their assessment of the validity of self-reported delinquency measures. One possible solution to this dilemma is to incorporate open-ended probes into prospective interviews, a strategy some researchers suggest provides more accurate recall than self-administered surveys (Sudman and Bradburn 1973).

While this study advances our understanding of motivations for leaving the gang, it is not without limitations. First, one of the most consistent themes that emerged in the qualitative data was centered on mobility as a reason for leaving the gang. While often discussed as a reason *why* youth leave their gang or peer group, changing schools or residences could also be a method of gang desistance or *how* youth left their gang. Future research should be careful in the interpretation of this motivation and try to parse out whether or not its discussion is in the context of motivating factors or methods of leaving the gang. Second, the qualitative findings indicate that youth were not likely to report violence as a motivation for leaving the gang. While this is an important finding and one that has implications for policy, it is important for readers to be aware of selection bias in the qualitative sample due to the nature of the sampling strategy. When sampling we relied on addresses provided at least 1 year prior to data collection; therefore, it is likely that we sampled and interviewed youth who were less mobile or easier to locate. Due to this, the youth in the sample are likely to be more prosocial than those youth who were more difficult to locate. Finally, the current study only examined motivations for leaving a gang. Given these findings it would be worthwhile for future research to examine differences in methods and consequences of leaving the gang across these three conceptual definitions.

The results presented in this chapter are able to inform prior and future research on variations in motivations for leaving the gang as well as increase understanding of prospective and retrospective accounts of salient life events. While there was low consistency across the quantitative and qualitative data in motivations for leaving the gang, both sets of results are able to inform prior research regarding motivations for leaving the gang. The gang desistance literature suggests that, when leaving the gang, youth typically become disillusioned with gang life and begin to drift away from their gang friends. In addition, while youth in both the quantitative and qualitative sample report motivations associated with the violent nature of gang life, they were often reported in conjunction with other, nonviolent, motivations. This seems to indicate, consistent with prior literature, that there may be an upper limit to the amount of violence youth are willing to withstand as part of gang life. The most commonly reported nonviolent motivation for leaving the gang was moving to a new home or school. This points to the idea that even minor relocations such as moving to a new neighborhood can make a difference in the lives of gang youth.

References

Baxter, L. A., & Bullis, C. (1986). Turning points in developing romantic relationships. *Human Communication Research, 12*(4), 469–493.

Bjorgo, T. (2002). *Exit Neo-Nazism: Reducing recruitment and promoting disengagement from racist groups*. Paper 627. Norwegian Institute of International Affairs.

Bolden, C. L. (2012). Liquid soldiers: Fluidity and gang membership. *Deviant Behavior, 33*(3), 207–222.

Bradburn, N. M., Rips, L. J., & Shevell, S. K. (1987). Answering autobiographical questions: The impact of memory and inference on surveys. *Science, 236*(4798), 157–161.

Carson, D. C., Peterson, D., & Esbensen, F.-A. (2013). Youth gang desistance: An examination of the effect of different operational definitions of desistance on the motivations, methods, and consequences associated with leaving the gang. *Criminal Justice Review, 38*(4), 510–534.

Decker, S. H. (1996). Collective and normative features of gang violence. *Justice Quarterly, 13*(2), 245–264.

Decker, S. H., & Lauritsen, J. L. (2002). Leaving the gang. In C. R. Huff (Ed.), *Gangs in America* (3rd ed., pp. 51–67). Thousand Oaks, CA: Sage.

Decker, S. H., Melde, C., & Pyrooz, D. C. (2013). What do we know about gangs and gang members and where do we go from here. *Justice Quarterly, 30*(3), 369–402.

Decker, S. H., & Pyrooz, D. C. (2011). *Leaving the gang: Logging off and moving on*. Council on Foreign Relations.

Decker, S. H., Pyrooz, D. C., & Moule, R. K., Jr. (2014). Disengagement from gangs as role transitions. *Journal of Research on Adolescence, 24*(2), 268–283.

Decker, S. H., & Van Winkle, B. (1996). *Life in the gang: Family, friends, and violence*. New York: Cambridge University Press.

Esbensen, F.-A., & Huizinga, D. (1993). Gangs, drugs, and delinquency in a survey of urban youth. *Criminology, 31*(4), 565–589.

Esbensen, F.-A., Melde, C., Taylor, T. J., & Peterson, D. (2008). Active parental consent in school-based research: How much is enough and how do we get it? *Evaluation Review, 32*(4), 335–362.

Esbensen, F.-A., Osgood, D. W., Peterson, D., Taylor, T. J., & Carson, D. C. (2013). Short- and long-term outcome results from a multisite evaluation of the G.R.E.A.T. program. *Criminology and Public Policy, 12*(3), 375–411.
Esbensen, F.-A., Taylor, T. J., & Peterson, D. (2009). *The validity of the filtering and funneling methods of defining gang membership.* Paper presented at the European Society of Criminology, Ljubljana, Slovenia.
Esbensen, F.-A., & Weerman, F. M. (2005). Youth gangs and troublesome youth groups in the United States and the Netherlands: A cross-national comparison. *European Journal of Criminology, 2*(1), 5–37.
Esbensen, F.-A., Winfree, J., Thomas, L., He, N., & Taylor, T. J. (2001). Youth gangs and definitional issues: When is a gang a gang and why does it matter? *Crime & Delinquency, 47*(1), 105–130.
Fivush, R. (1993). Developmental perspectives on autobiographical recall. In G. S. Goodman & B. L. Bottoms (Eds.), *Child victims, child witnesses: Understanding and improving testimony* (pp. 1–24). New York: Guilford Press.
Fleisher, M. S., & Krienert, J. L. (2004). Life-course events, social networks, and the emergence of violence among female gang members. *Journal of Community Psychology, 32*(5), 607–622.
Hagedorn, J. M. (1988). *People and folks: Gangs, crime, and the underclass in a rustbelt city.* Chicago, IL: Lakeview Press.
Hagedorn, J. M. (1994). Homeboys, dope fiends, legits, and new jacks. *Criminology, 32*(2), 197–219.
Hagedorn, J. M., & Devitt, M. L. (1999). Fighting female: The social construction of female gangs. In M. Chesney-Lind & J. M. Hagedorn (Eds.), *Female gangs in America: Essays on gender and gangs* (pp. 256–276). Chicago, IL: Lakeview Press.
Henry, B., Moffitt, T. E., Caspi, A., Langley, J., & Silva, P. A. (1994). On the "Remembrance of Things Past": A longitudinal evaluation of the retrospective method. *Psychological Assessment, 6*(2), 92–101.
Hill, K. G., Howell, J. C., Hawkins, J. D., & Battin-Pearson, S. R. (1999). Childhood risk factors for adolescent gang membership: Results from the Seattle social development project. *Journal of Research in Crime and Delinquency, 36*(3), 300–322.
Horowitz, R. (1983). *Honor and the American dream.* New Brunswick, NY: Rutgers University Press.
Klein, M. (1971). *Street gangs and street workers.* Englewood Cliffs, NJ: Prentice Hall.
Klein, M., Kerner, H.-J., Maxson, C. L., & Weitekamp, E. G. M. (Eds.). (2001). *The Eurogang paradox: Street gangs and youth groups in the U.S. and Europe.* Dordrecht, The Netherlands: Kluwer.
Kruttschnitt, C., & Dornfeld, M. (1992). Will they tell? Assessing Preadolescents' reports of family violence. *Journal of Research in Crime and Delinquency, 29*(2), 136–147.
Matsuda, K. N., Esbensen, F.-A., & Carson, D. C. (2012). Putting the "gang" in "Eurogang" characteristics of delinquent youth groups by definitional approaches. In F.-A. Esbensen & C. L. Maxson (Eds.), *Youth gangs in international perspective: Results from the Eurogang program of research* (pp. 17–34). New York: Springer.
Menard, S., Bowman-Bowen, L. C., & Lu, Y.-F. (2016). Self-reported crime and delinquency. In T. S. Bynum, & B. M. Huebner (Eds.), *The handbook of measurement issues in criminology & criminal justice.* New York: Wiley.
Menard, S., & Elliott, D. S. (1990). Longitudinal and cross-sectional data collection and analysis in the study of crime and delinquency. *Justice Quarterly, 7*(1), 11–55.
Metts, S., Sprecher, S., & Cupach, W. R. (1991). Retrospective self-reports. In B. M. Montgomery & S. Duck (Eds.), *Studying interpersonal interaction* (pp. 162–178). New York: Guilford Press.
Moloney, M., Hunt, G. P., Joe-Laidler, K., & MacKenzie, K. (2011). Young mother (in the) hood: Gang girls negotiation of new identities. *Journal of Youth Studies, 14*(1), 1–19.

Moloney, M., MacKenzie, K., Hunt, G. P., & Joe-Laidler, K. (2009). The path and promise of fatherhood for gang members. *British Journal of Criminology, 49*(3), 305–325.

Moore, J. W. (1991). *Going down to the barrio: Homeboys and homegirls in change*. Philadelphia, PA: Temple University Press.

O'Neal, E. N., Decker, S. H., Moule Jr., R. K., & Pyrooz, D. C. (2014). Girls, gangs, and getting out: Gender differences and similarities in leaving the gang. *Youth Violence and Juvenile Justice*. doi:10.1177/1541204014551426.

Padilla, F. M. (1992). *The gang as an American enterprise*. New Brunswick, NJ: Rutgers University Press.

Peterson, D. (2012). Girlfriends, gun-holders, and ghetto-rats? Moving beyond narrow views of girls in gangs. In S. Miller, L. D. Leve, & P. K. Kering (Eds.), *Delinquent girls: Contexts, relationships, and adaptations* (pp. 71–84). New York: Springer.

Pyrooz, D. C., & Decker, S. H. (2011). Motives and methods for leaving the gang: Understanding the process of gang desistance. *Journal of Criminal Justice, 39*(5), 417–425.

Pyrooz, D. C., Sweeten, G., & Piquero, A. R. (2013). Continuity and change in gang membership and gang embeddedness. *Journal of Research in Crime and Delinquency, 50*(2), 239–271.

Quicker, J. C. (1999). The Chicana gang: A preliminary description. In M. Chesney-Lind & J. M. Hagedorn (Eds.), *Female gangs in America: Essays on girls, gangs, and gender* (pp. 46–48). Chicago, IL: Lakeview Press.

Ross, M. (1989). Relation of implicit theories to the construction of personal histories. *Psychological Review, 96*(2), 341–357.

Sanchez-Jankowski, M. (1991). *Islands in the street: Gangs and urban American society*. Berkeley, CA: University of California Press.

Spergel, I. A. (1995). *The youth gang problem: A community approach*. Oxford, England: Oxford University Press.

Squire, L. (1989). On the course of forgetting in very long-term memory. *Journal of Experimental Psychology: Learning, Memory, and Cognition, 15*(2), 241–245.

Sudman, S., & Bradburn, N. M. (1973). Effects of time and memory factors on response in surveys. *Journal of American Statistical Association, 68*(344), 805–815.

Surra, C. A., Arizzi, P., & Asmussen, L. A. (1988). The association between reasons for commitment and the development and outcome of marital relationships. *Journal of Social and Personal Relationships, 5*(1), 47–63.

Sweeten, G., Pyrooz, D. C., & Piquero, A. R. (2013). Disengaging from gangs and desistance from crime. *Justice Quarterly, 30*(3), 469–500.

Thrasher, F. M. (1963). *The gang: A study of one thousand three hundred thirteen groups in Chicago*. Chicago: University of Chicago Press. (Original work published 1927)

Varriale, J. A. (2008). Female gang members and desistance: Pregnancy as a possible exit strategy. *Journal of Gang Research, 15*(4), 35–64.

Vecchio, J. M. (2014). *The role of violence within and across self-identified gang youth*. Doctoral Dissertation, University of Missouri, St. Louis.

Vigil, J. D. (1988). *Barrio gangs: Street life and identity in Southern California*. Austin, TX: University of Texas Press.

Wagenaar, W. A., & Groeneweg, J. (1990). The memory of concentration camp survivors. *Applied Cognitive Psychology, 4*(2), 77–87.

Weerman, F. M., Maxson, C., Esbensen, F.-A., Aldridge, J., Medina, J., & van Gemert, F. (2009). *Eurogang Program manual: Background, development, and use of the Eurogang instruments in multi-site, multi-method comparative research*.

Yarrow, M. R., Campbell, J. D., & Burton, R. V. (1970). Recollections of childhood: A study of the retrospective method. *Monographs of the Society for Research in Child Development, 35*(5), 1–83.

Chapter 9
Dutch Crips Run Dry in Liquid Society

Frank van Gemert, Robby Roks, and Marijke Drogt

9.1 Introduction

Since the early 1990s Crips and Bloods were reported in the Netherlands (HOF 1994; Van Stapele 1998). The Hague was the stomping ground of several groups that named themselves after the notorious American west coast gangs and drew attention, apart from their appearance, because of criminal activities. Today there still are Crips in The Hague, as well as in Amsterdam, but after more than two decades much has changed. The majority of these groups have disappeared and the remaining average Crip member is much older now.

In the Netherlands gangs have become an important issue. Towards the end of the century the Ministry of Justice pushed for the introduction of an inventory instrument for youth groups (Beke et al. 2000). Even though the word "gang" is avoided and this instrument only refers to "troublesome," "nuisance," and "criminal" youth groups, it is safe to say that the third category comes close to the Eurogang definition (Van Gemert 2012; Van Gemert and Weerman 2013, 2015). Since 2008,

F. van Gemert (✉)
Department of Criminal Law & Criminology, VU University Amsterdam,
Amsterdam, The Netherlands
e-mail: f.h.m.van.gemert@vu.nl

R. Roks
Department of Criminology, School of Law, Erasmus University Rotterdam,
Rotterdam, The Netherlands
e-mail: Roks@law.eur.nl

M. Drogt
Department of Applied Psychology, Hogeschool Leiden, University of Applied Sciences,
Leiden, The Netherlands
e-mail: Marijkedrogt@gmail.com

C.L. Maxson, F.-A. Esbensen (eds.), *Gang Transitions and Transformations in an International Context*, DOI 10.1007/978-3-319-29602-9_9

this inventory presents results throughout the country and these are available for everyone on the internet. Since 2009 the number of groups has declined (Ferwerda and Van Ham 2010, 2011, 2012).

The Dutch Crips, for their part, have also gone through change. In the late 1980s, the stereotypical American west coast gang became a style icon for youth in the Netherlands. Black youth from the former Dutch colonies of Suriname and the Antilles[1] especially were drawn to the gang images portrayed in movies like *Colors* (1988), *Boyz n the Hood* (1991), and *Menace II Society* (1993). Copying the American examples, youth on the street could distinguish themselves from others by wearing baseball caps, baggy pants, blue shirts, or bandanas, but they would also use symbols like hand signs, slang, and graffiti. Apart from the movies, popularity of the gang youth style was especially boosted through gangsta rap and the masculine "boasting" hiphop subgenre found, for instance, in N.W.A.'s classic album *Straight Outta Compton* (1988). Parental advisory stickers about "explicit lyrics" that were intended to protect youth from bad influence probably had an opposite effect (Shank 1996; Wermuth 2002). As youth styles come and go, the popularity of the gang style and rap music reached its peak some years later. The various elements of the gang style, especially clothing and music, have diffused into mainstream youth culture and the symbols have lost most of their significance since young people use them at will (Van Gemert 2005).

In 2015, Crips still exist in Dutch cities, but the phenomenon seems to be fading away. The members are involved in criminal activities and known to claim certain neighborhoods as their territory. A number of these gang members are now in their 40s. According to gang literature that is old and thus atypical. Some of them are original gangsters, OGs, who were part of the gang from the beginning. In this chapter, we focus on these older individuals. In reviewing more than two decades of Crips in the Netherlands, it is possible, to some extent, to reconstruct their careers. We describe how they got involved and became Crips members, but especially we try to shed light on the process of desistance.

Apart from some official reports, the data for this chapter are drawn from qualitative research. Most important are sources on the emergence of Crips in the city of The Hague (Van Gemert 1998, 2001; Van Stapele 2003), on the development of Crips in this city that took place afterwards (Roks and Staring 2008; Roks 2007, 2016), and on the history and the current situation of Crips in Amsterdam (Drogt 2014). In both cities we pay special attention to a few individuals that played a leading and pivotal role in the gang over a longer period of time.

[1] Suriname became independent in 1975. That year, inhabitants were to choose between the Surinamese and the Dutch nationality. Many decided for the latter option and as a consequence they migrated to the Netherlands. In the 1980s youth from Surinamese descent drew attention because of integration difficulties that coincided with the introduction of heroin in the major Dutch cities. The Antilles consist of six islands in the Caribbean area that are part of the Dutch Kingdom. Citizens can travel freely between the isles and the Netherlands. Some of the isles have a "status aparte," but formally they are still part of the Dutch kingdom. Currently, youngsters of Surinamese descent seem well integrated in Dutch society. Even though their number is smaller, Antillean youth play a more problematic role, as police statistics show.

9.2 Gang Identity and Life Course in a Changing Context

Bauman (2000, 2003, 2005) wrote three books that are centered around a single word: liquid. In late modernity society is constantly changing. While "solid society" refers to *Gemeinshaft* or mutual involvement, "liquid society" is characterized by detachment, evasion, and a hopeless search for identity (Bauman 2000, p. 120). This change could be very relevant for gang studies, because a number of gang stereotypes refer to elements that are "solid" in the sense that they are stable, permanent, or steadfast. Membership is said to be "4 life"; "Blood in, blood out" refers to strict rules for entering and for leaving the gang, as members have to be "jumped in" as well as "jumped out"; territory is part of group identity and gangs can relate to this in their name (for example: "18th Street"; "Eight Tray Gangster Crips"; "White Fence"); various symbols such as colors, tattoos, and graffiti are of great significance and for that reason they are targeted by rival gangs. These elements constitute the masculine gang identity. Among Crips in the Netherlands respected members are referred to as "solid soldiers." These words are carried as tattoos and often used in clips (e.g., https://youtu.be/Wpl47IoSxYQ).

It is not a coincidence then, that given the change to liquid modernity, recent studies have challenged the "solid" characteristics of gangs. Even though he does not refer to Bauman, Bolden (2012) chose the title "Liquid soldiers" for an article in which he points to "affiliates and associates" in order to show that the lines of inclusion for gangs are becoming increasingly unclear. "Liquid city" is used by Ilan (2013) to describe the fluent use of space of a group of young men he studied in Dublin. "Street life in the liquid city is not always amenable to the stable structures and hierarchies of the traditionally conceived street gang, nor the well-defined spaces of the solid city" (Ilan 2013, p. 22).

It is said that gang stereotypes are the cause of misunderstanding the gang phenomenon altogether. Modern media have dispersed these stereotypes that were largely based on US west coast gangs such as Crips and Bloods. All over the world these stereotypes have become the main model for what a gang is, but research has shown that in reality the stereotypes only apply for a limited number of US gangs. So, when in Germany, Russia, or the Netherlands the word "gang" is used, the point of reference may not be realistic. Klein (2001) has labelled this "the Eurogang Paradox."

On the other hand, for people to give meaning to their lives it is not only reality that counts. Some people hold on to tradition, but others create new stories of their own or adopt new practices and identities based on what they see and to what they are attracted (Appadurai 1996). Films were important for supplying these practices and identities and currently the internet plays an important role. In liquid society the construction of gang life is not just the outcome of what is "real."

Since Thrasher (1927), Whyte (1943), Cohen (1955), and Cloward and Ohlin (1960) three themes are dominant in American gang theory: migration, marginalization, and neighborhood. These classical themes derived from monumental studies certainly are relevant, but they are incomplete for understanding the contemporary phenomenon of gangs in European countries like the Netherlands. Just like Crips, other infamous American gangs such as Latin Kings (Brotherton 2007; Feixa et al. 2008) and MS13 (Johnson and Muhlhausen 2005; McGuire 2007; Papachristos 2005; Savenije 2007; Ward 2013) have been reported well outside the USA. Considering countries in Central America such as El Salvador, Guatemala, and Honduras, the migration and repatriation of gang members is a fact. But, as Maxson (1998) has pointed out for the proliferation within the USA, gang members that come from other cities have minimal influence on the emergence of gangs. The idea of gang proliferation through a kind of franchising is a myth (Howell 2007). In order to understand the existence of Crips in cities of European countries such as Italy, Spain, or the Netherlands, one has to look at gangs as brands that offer young people a strong identity they can use to stand their ground in the streets (Van Gemert 2008; Van Gemert and De Jong 2010).

The transmission of gang culture needs to be added to classical themes in order to understand how preexisting local problems in the Netherlands could lead to the emergence of gangs such as the Crips (Van Gemert and Weerman 2015). For young marginalized people with a migrant background the masculine roles and images of American gangs are especially attractive. Gang stereotypes may be false, but at the same time they hold powerful symbols. One can understand how they provide seductive identities for young people. Next, the question arises: how do individuals deal with these identities when they leave the gang? Do they need to get rid of them?

In this chapter, we focus on old members who left the gang. In the life course approach in criminology three periods can be distinguished relative to crime: onset, continuity, and desistance (Sampson and Laub 1993; Farrington 2003). This three-period-model can also be applied to gangs. There is abundant literature on why young people join gangs and on (criminal) behavior of active gang members, but until recently desistance and leaving the gang was seldom the reason for study. Decker and Lauritsen (2002) discuss two patterns. The first is based on the concept of "knifing off": purging off one's previous ways, social roles, including associates, disadvantage, stigma, and opportunities (cf. Elder 1998; Maruna 2001). The second pattern is the more gradual departure from the gang during which a member can "simply drift away." Where the first seems abrupt and clear, the second pattern is vague and often gradual. Individuals may have left the gang, but they still have ties with active members with whom they hang out, drink, or play sports. Thus, desistance becomes a process of disengagement (Decker and Lauritsen 2002; cf. Bjorgo 2009). In this process there are lingering ties to the gang that bind (Pyrooz et al. 2010). People move away from the gang, but have not yet fully disengaged. It is in this lapse before post-exit validation that pushes and pulls from within the gang and from other groups make individuals most vulnerable to re-engagement (Decker et al. 2014).

So, when the older individuals are in the process of leaving the gang, how do they deal with a change in identity? Do they "knife off" all the contacts with the Crips and stop "being a Crip?" Can they "simply drift away" from the gang and do they drift away from identity too? As stated previously the influence of gang culture in the Netherlands reached its peak a while ago, and one would expect the gang stereotypes to fade away and be replaced again by what is currently "hot." On the other hand, young people are resilient towards trends and mode and ready to adopt what is new, while older people may have more at stake and are said to be more conservative. Does a general rule like this apply to the Dutch Crips?

9.3 Methods

Apart from various official documents and media accounts of gang activities, the data for this chapter are drawn from qualitative research. The three authors each conducted research that focuses on Dutch Crips, but their research was done separately. In this chapter we combine the findings.

In 1997, during a meeting at the Ministry of Justice in The Hague, there was discussion of how youth groups should be dealt with in the Netherlands. Two examples of groups that had been active in the city of The Hague were discussed. According to the police, these were gangs. Both groups were said to be Crips, but at that time this did not mean much to most people present at the meeting. In order to get a better understanding of this phenomenon, it was agreed the groups should be studied. A third group from Rotterdam, also Crips, was to be included in a study. Frank van Gemert participated in the discussion and was asked to write a research proposal that was later accepted by the Ministry of Justice. Since members of these three groups were brought to trial, it was believed that the groups no longer existed and that field research was impossible. However, the police and justice reports on the groups were extensive. The main data consisted of documents that had to be read and analyzed in the courts of The Hague and Rotterdam. Van Gemert conducted additional interviews with police who had worked on the cases and with the public prosecutor of The Hague, who had first brought these groups to attention and who was present at the initial meeting in 1997. The report was published in 1998 (Van Gemert 1998) and later an English chapter was included in the first Eurogang Volume (Van Gemert 2001).

The book "Crips.nl" (Van Stapele 2003) was Robby Roks' introduction to the Dutch Crips. An e-mail address on the back of the book formed the basis of an enduring contact with leader and founder Keylow. Roks reconstructed the criminal career of Keylow for his master thesis by spending time with and around Keylow for almost 7 months, conducting several in-depth interviews and observing Keylow and his "homies" in The Hague (Roks 2007). He returned to The Hague and from January 2011 to December 2013 he conducted intensive fieldwork in the same neighborhood where these Crips lived (Roks 2016). The focus of this ethnographic research was on the embeddedness of crime, in particular on how the Crips were part of the local and larger community. During fieldwork, 150 informants, consisting of (former) members of the Crips, residents, youngsters hanging around the neighborhood, local police officials, and youth workers became part of the research network. In-depth material about their lives and/or criminal careers was collected from 60 individuals through interviews, informal conversations, and observations. Apart from that, the activities on social media (Facebook, Twitter, and Instagram) from 40 youngsters from the network were monitored and analyzed.

In 2013 and 2014 Marijke Drogt conducted ethnographic fieldwork on the 241 Gangster Crips, a gang in the neighborhood of Gein in Amsterdam Southeast. Drogt lives in the area and contact was established in a natural way. After meeting Mhythy Base (MB) at a party, she found out he was a Crips member. This led to the idea to write a criminology assignment about him. MB agreed to this and later she would conduct additional research for writing her master thesis (Drogt 2014). Because biography was central to the thesis, two men in particular, MB and Original Gangster Bita (OGB), were followed to collect their life histories. Using a symbolic interactionist framework, Drogt was especially interested in the difference of their presentation front stage and back stage (Goffman 1959). At that time, the 241 Gangster Crips consisted of 15–20 men. None of them had a regular job, none paid taxes and, so it comes as no surprise, most participated in criminal activities to make ends meet. The fieldwork consisted mainly of hanging out and observing them on the streets in Gein. Drogt was invited to occasional barbecues and she was present during music clip shoots. These clip shoots were very relevant for the research, because here the individuals would take on masculine poses and use boasting language. This front stage behavior differed, to some extent, from what was observed during the endless hours of hanging out and what was said in conversations (back stage). All of these occasions were written down in fieldnotes to be coded and analyzed afterwards. In a later stage of the research, 16 of the men were interviewed in a more formal manner. The main focus though, stayed on MB and OGB. The internet was used to chat, find out what was going on and watch music clips of the group or to trace specific members.

To ensure the promised confidentiality and protection of identities, we make use of either street or gang names (in the case of Keylow, Original Gangster Bita and Mhythy Base) or a pseudonym (in the case of Tyrell, Daniel, Jermaine, and Kerim) to refer to the Dutch gang members in this chapter.

9.4 The Emergence of Crips in The Hague

In 1983, Keylow and a few friends formed a group that they called "CUC"; this was short for "Call Us Cool." This group of local youngsters, mostly from Surinamese descent, was involved in breakdancing and music, but they were also known for picking fights and getting involved in some minor delinquent activities like petty theft and vandalism. After watching *Colors* in 1988, Keylow and his friends adopted the identity of the Crips and became one of the first such groups in the Netherlands. Since CUC already carried a double C in its name, it was easy to rebrand the group as "Crazy Undaground Crips" (Van Stapele 2003; Roks 2007). One can only guess what would have happened if the former group's name had started with a "B."

Around 1993 gangs became an issue in the city of The Hague. Different sets of youngsters emerged dressed in blue or red, calling themselves "Crips" and "Bloods." In a newspaper article the local police of The Hague estimated that some 250 youngsters were active members in 15 different gangs (Abels and Dwarkasing 1994). When it turned out that some Crips were getting involved in criminal activities, it became more urgent to learn about these groups that were apparently in some way similar to American gangs. For this reason, the police from The Hague started doing research on youth groups and gangs (Gruter 1997; Gruter et al. 1996; Van Oosterwijk et al. 1995; for an overview see Van Gemert 2012).

The groups carried American sounding names like Kings Crips, Eight Tray Crips, 90-C, and East Side Crips and the symbols used by these Dutch youngsters were clearly copied from the stereotypical west coast "gangsta" style as portrayed in rap songs and videos. Dress codes and hand signs were imitated and the lyrics of N.W.A. provided them with new, exciting words like "packing," "jacking," and "strapped." Apart from movies and gangsta rap, the gang stereotypes on Crips and Bloods were also transmitted via a few specific books. "Do or Die" (Bing 1992), a book written by a journalist, played a role in bringing the street codes from Los Angeles gang life to the Netherlands. Likewise, the autobiography "Monster" (Shakur 1993) presented the personal story of an infamous leader of the Eight Tray Gangster Crips to the youth in The Hague.

It is not a coincidence then that Dutch copies of these books were found in the houses of arrested Dutch members of the Eight Tray Gangsters. These youngsters had not only adopted the name from the specific Crips set for their own group, but by reading the books they had also learned about initiation. In order to become a member of the Eight Tray Crips individuals had to do a "Jackmove," which means that they had to rob someone on the street while other members were present as witnesses. During some of these initiation acts, violence was used and so it happened that members of the newly formed gang were arrested after beating a man unconscious with a steel pipe (Viering 1994; Van Gemert 1998, 2001).

9.5 Reputation and Identity

While police action ended the Eight Tray Crips and the East Side Crips in The Hague, media attention added to the reputation of Keylow (Roks 2007). Being 24 years old and leader and founder of CUC, Keylow was interviewed for the weekly *Panorama* to comment on this disturbing new gang phenomenon in the Netherlands (Viering 1994). Keylow dismissed the Eight Tray Crips as "peewees" and "wannabes" and claimed that his set was "the oldest and most powerful gang of The Hague and the Netherlands." When the journalist challenged him that he was imitating the Los Angeles based Crips and bragging and boasting, Keylow proclaims: "Don't mistake our lives for a game or romance, the life of a Crip is hard. If we would live in America, in LA, several of us would have been arrested or killed a long time ago" (Viering 1994, p. 41).

This interview kick-started an enduring relationship between these Dutch Crips and the media, with Keylow acting as frontman and spokesperson (Roks and Staring 2008). Other magazine interviews including (cover) photos followed (Van Stapele 1998), as did items in popular television shows and the publication of the book "Crips.nl" (Van Stapele 2003). Some years later, the media attention culminated in "Strapped'n Strong" (Van der Valk 2009), a 90 min documentary on the criminal lifestyle of the gang. Keylow was keen to make the right impression. At the time the documentary was filmed he drove a small Fiat Panda. In front of the camera though, Keylow was behind the steering wheel of the Mercedes that belonged to the cameraman. Later, when he visited his fellow gang members from the Rollin 40s in Los Angeles, Keylow insisted that a Hummer was rented and the director had to pick up the bill (Joost van der Valk, personal communication).

Over the years the gang changed, rebranded, and updated its name from the "Crazy Undaground Crips" to the "Criminal Undaground Crips" to the "Main Triad Crips" and eventually to "Rollin 200 Crips." Currently, these Crips refer to their neighborhood as "h200d" and they call themselves "h200dstas" (for explanation of the various names, see Roks 2016). Crime became a more central part of the gang identity, as criminal activities from individual members were mentioned in the media. The book Crips.nl (Van Stapele 2003) shows a transition from street crime to organized forms of crime, most notably violent drug transactions. In 1994, Keylow was convicted of masterminding a helicopter hijacking to free a convict from prison and spent 4 years in prison. The spectacular nature of this rescue attempt generated media publicity and contributed to the street reputation of the Crips.

Reputation and media attention played an important role in attracting new young members to join the gang. In the early years, growing popularity of Crips in the Netherlands was connected to the Los Angeles stereotypes, but these no longer constitute the only frame of reference that provide a powerful gang identity. A Turkish youngster from the neighborhood stated: "I learned about the Crips from being right here, from hanging around the neighborhood. Later I found out that you also have Crips in Los Angeles, in the United States" (May 31, 2013, interview Kerim).

9.6 Gang Economy and Desistance

During the 1990s CUC was predominantly a local group of brothers, relatives, and friends from a specific neighborhood. Over the years, friends of friends joined the set and eventually also prison became a place where new members were recruited. This resulted in the Rollin 200 Crips being no longer exclusively comprised of gang members from the locality (Roks 2016).

In 2011, the Rollin 200 Crips consisted of some 50 active members, ranging in age from 15 to 40 years old, predominantly with a Surinamese background. Several of these members were incarcerated at some point, because of their involvement in stabbings, assault of police officers, possession of illegal drugs, and weapon charges. Furthermore, the Rollin 200 Crips manufactured marijuana in residential housing, while several individual members sold various illegal narcotics on the street. However, a substantial part of these gang members combined their criminal activities with a formal (often low paying) job, school, or they collected unemployment benefits to make ends meet.

Towards the end of fieldwork in 2013, the number of Rollin 200 Crips members was declining rapidly. In a period of 18 months almost 20 members left the set. The stereotypical association of violence with leaving a gang was also embedded in the subcultural repertoire of the Rollin 200 Crips. There were stories about former members who were "jumped out" of the gang, but reality was different. Some "h200dstas" gradually departed over the course of a couple of months, but in other cases the break was rather abrupt with members deleting contact information and never showing their face in the "h200d" again. Tyrell, leaving the gang after being a member for years, felt compelled to give his side of the story.

> When I came to the block it was like: Tyrell, go stand over there, you know? I'm like: what the fuck, you know? Always this kinda bullshit. At least I came, you know? And then he treats me like this? And you know what Keylow did? You know what he did? He grabbed me by the throat and hit me. He started hitting me, you know? He beat the shit out of me. He said: you better start explaining what the fuck you guys are up to! I started crying right there, I'm being real with you. I couldn't understand what was happening you know? I always did everything they said. If they said A, I did A, you know what I mean? I always did what the fucking big homies told me. And still it was like: no, you did that wrong and you didn't do this right. Whatever man. With all the homies, all of the homies, we put in so much work for the h200d and now we're bitches? Now we're bitchass niggas?" (May 10, 2013, interview Tyrell).

The day-to-day reality of being a member of a Dutch Crips gang differed greatly from the Rollin 200 Crips imagery and stories. What actually happened within the set did not match the expectations of most members and increasingly they were becoming disenchanted with the situation. This brought them closer to leaving the gang. The network of the Rollin 200 Crips revealed imbalanced power relations and made members vulnerable to exploitation in the context of crime. Several younger members told stories about committing criminal activities for the set, without receiving any financial compensation for their work. Daniel, a 26-year-old former member, sheds light on how inner workings of the gang bring desistance closer.

> You would think that someone would start questioning after so many people bouncing, you know. They can't logically see that shit. I tried to tell them, like: listen, I have to make money. I can't stand here like this you know? My life is basically standing still you know? Not paying no bills, not paying nothing. No fucking mail coming in, you know what I'm saying? No money coming in at all. Living hand to mouth. The little bit of money that I get, I spend on food, weed and cigarettes. And you know what? Half the fucking hood is smoking my cigarettes and my weed (March 15, 2013, interview Daniel).

Members joined the Crips because of the attraction of the gang images and reputation of the gang. They were proud to be a Crip and many of them have earned tattoos that testify to their dedication to the gang. The position of the core members may be powerful, but until now they have not been able to establish a successful criminal enterprise that is rewarding to its members. On the contrary, they use their power to exploit new members. Many of these younger "h200dstas" hoped for some form of reciprocity for their gang banging, but after they learned this was an illusion, they turned their back on the gang. For the youngsters this process is clear, but for older members like 44-year-old Jermaine it felt like betrayal.

> It took me a while before I was at peace with my decision to stop banging, even though I knew it was the right thing to do. But leaving my cuzzo's, my homies like that, it felt like betrayal. That Crip shit was so deep and it's still a huge part of me. When friends ask me what goes on with Rollin 200 and if I still see them, I explain that I left and that I'm trying to find a job and a house. They're glad to hear that I took a different turn in life, but they always ask me: you are no longer banging, but you still wear blue? You know what, I will always wear blue. I'm no longer active, but I will always be a Crip. I made that choice back in 1994 and it's on my body: Tru Blue Till My Casket Drops. Cripping cost me too much. It took my freedom, it fucked up my relationship with women and my kids. So yeah, I will always wear blue, because that shit just cost me too much (November 27, 2013, interview Jermaine).

9.7 Branche in Amsterdam

Mythy Base (MB) and Original Gangster Bita (OGB) were both born in 1974. They are of Surinamese descent and both were raised in Amsterdam Southeast. On the streets they formed a group of friends and during their teenage years criminal activities became part of their street identity. Both have been incarcerated as juveniles and they have serious criminal records.

In 2007, the 241 Gangster Crips was formed. At that time the key person was Sin Quin, a man that was in contact with the Rollin 200 Crips from The Hague. Together with OGB, Sin Quin decided to start a set in Amsterdam. For them this was not a complex transformation, but rather a logical step to add the Crips identity after being a group for many years. By wearing the characteristic blue colors and using the other symbols, they started representing Crips in Gein. There was a certain hierarchy within the group, consisting of leaders and soldiers, with Sin Quin being the president these first years.

On a hot summer night in August 2012, Sin Quin was shot and killed in his own neighborhood of Gein. The perpetrator was not found and the motive for the killing remains unclear. In a national television program that collaborates with the police, Sin Quin's criminal network was mentioned as a cause for the violence, but private circumstances were not ruled out (Editorial 2012). The 241 Gangster Crips lost their president, but it turned out that Sin Quin also had ties to motor club Satudarah, as a large number of members of this club came to pay their respect at his funeral.

Another man, Iron Mike, also had a significant part in the rise of the set. He was a central person in the group and was loved by many, considering his actions to keep the group together. In an early interview with a website Iron Mike said: "Brotherhood is the reason why I am part of the Crips set. There are people who support you and have your back" (Editorial 2013). In 2007, Mike was shot during a fight. Again this happened in the streets of Gein. He survived, but in the years to follow his battered body never fully recovered. Iron Mike died in 2013, and it is believed this is still the effect of the shooting. Both men are remembered and honored by the Amsterdam Crips in a number of clips.

After these prominent Crips left the scene, in 2012, OGB and MB fulfilled the roles of president and general of the 241 Gangster Crips, respectively. When asked, they want to leave no doubt that they take their task seriously. "We lead the younger men. We don't want to take advantage of them," says OGB. After becoming general, in an interview MB states that he is a "solid soldier." He claims that in the past he has proved to be ready for leading a group because of the street reputation that he has built. Both men agree that the Crips are about loyalty, respect, willpower, motivation, and discipline. They stress that this is a solid group and listening to their words brotherhood and military characteristics come to mind. But, these are words.

Again, identity is a key issue. Claiming Crip means that stereotypes are stressed over and again. Wearing blue and using boasting language in clips is obvious front stage behavior. The fact that two important members were killed adds to the significance of local gang myths. On the other hand, life in Gein is quiet. Even though violent events have taken place, lethal shootings are very rare in the neighborhood. During fieldwork it became clear that the daily routine of these men has little to do with dodging bullets. There are no rival gangs to compete with, but within the group there is a struggle between young and old members and, just like in The Hague, there is no money and lots of waiting. The Crips spend much time representing in streets that can be cold and wet. They look back and remember lost honored friends, but this doesn't bring food to the table.

9.8 Alternative Identity

In 2014, OGB and MB get in contact with people from the motorcycle club, BlackJack. Both men become members of this club and afterwards some of their fellow Crip members decide to do the same. In recent years motorcycle clubs are a rapidly growing phenomenon. For several decades Hells Angels was the only one in the Netherlands, but now Satudarah, No Surrender, and Bandidos all have chapters in several Dutch cities and the media mentions wars as well as alliances across European borders (Editorial 2015; "Timeline" 2015; Van den Heuvel and Thimister 2015). The older members are tapping into a popular phenomenon that provides them with a new identity.

This is not the end of the 241 Gangster Crips. The new motorcycle club identity is combined with being a Crips member. The club brings a new kind of brotherhood and OGB and MB decide to start a chapter in Amsterdam. Again, they become leaders. OGB is the president, MB the vice president. Another hierarchy, not in blue but with a leather jacket is established. They state that the motorcycle club is more organized and they consider this group to be more an adult collective than what they had with the Crips. Again, respect and loyalty are key values.

But then, despite their years of friendship, OGB and MB get into a conflict over money and respect. They break up and OGB turns in his leather jacket and leaves the motorcycle club. From now on he will focus only on the Crips. MB on the other hand, sees his future in the MC. "I'm getting too old for banging," MB says, as he refers to the Crips. "The world is so much bigger than hanging on the corner, drinking and smoking. I'm too old for that." In his role as Vice President of the Amsterdam chapter, he is leading a new group. This identity now seems to have replaced the old one of the Crips. He still sees himself as "Crip for life" though, but no longer in an active role. "Since the death of both brothers, the set is frozen and it moves in no direction." He looks down on the group that he left. "The only danger those guys know is the bottle of alcohol they drink every day."

OGB has a different position, but his perspective is similar. "I can't deny Sin Quin and Iron Mike gave their lives for this group and it's my duty to keep it alive." OGB describes the Crips today as the same group, even though men have left. "Our set is not outdated. It's just that a few are no longer welcome. Apart from that, nothing has changed." His opinion on the members that left is straightforward. "I don't have time for games, some people are born to stay stupid forever." So, both men still consider themselves Crips even though they chose to go different directions.

9.9 Conclusion

In the Netherlands, Crips gangs have been important for supplying a gang identity and street reputation for a number of people. But over a longer period we witness the turning of the tide. The phenomenon started emerging in the late 1980s and in 2015 it is fading.

Nowadays, the Rollin 200 Crips in The Hague are still active, but the gang is stripped down to the core members that constitute the founding fathers of CUC. These OGs are in their 40s and have been "Cripping" since the late 1980s. In Amsterdam, two important members of the 241 Gangster Crips are dead, while two other senior members, who share a long history together, have become separated. OGB and MB both still claim to be Crip, but one of them has moved away from the gang and spends time in a motorcycle club.

Even though core members claim to be loyal to the Crip identity, a larger number of younger members have left the gang after participating for various periods of time. Part of the explanation is economic by nature. Only few members, if any, seem to have benefited from being in the gang in an economic sense. The gang lifestyle blocks social mobility via regular routes. It is difficult if not impossible to get a regular job with little education and a proud attitude of not working for a boss. At the same time, the revenues from crime never have been high enough to sustain a stable lifestyle. More recently, the balance is even more negative as exploitation of younger members has become an issue.

Furthermore, different from gang members in the United States and Latin America, in the Netherlands there is no (acute) necessity for gang members regarding personal safety or survival for joining or staying in a gang. The streets are not dangerous and there seldom are rival gangs to deal with. The regular, mainstream economy and the Dutch welfare system provide young men with more certainty and security than street life (Van Gemert and Weerman 2015). So it comes as no surprise that, after leaving the Rollin 200 Crips, a number of former members went looking for a formal job and eventually found regular employment, often based on flexible and temporal job contracts (Roks 2016).

Classical American gang studies have pointed to migration, marginalization, and neighborhood as key themes (Thrasher 1927; Whyte 1943; Cohen 1955; Cloward and Ohlin 1960), and over and again these have reoccurred since. For understanding the situation in a European country such as the Netherlands, the transmission of gang culture must be included. Looking at the Dutch Crips we have seen how this gang culture was of influence, but we can also see how this influence is now fading. This coincides with a declining number of youth groups being reported via the police inventory, as was mentioned in the introduction.

Young men were attracted to stereotypical gang images that supplied them with a powerful and attractive masculine identity. In liquid society however, identities are not a static entity. Neither do they have to be composed of "real" ingredients. This makes the fact that gang stereotypes are to some extent not based on reality irrelevant. Young people construct their identity from what they feel attracted to. Gang movies and gangsta rap played an important role especially for the emergence of gangs in the neighborhoods of The Hague and Amsterdam. In cultural criminology the importance of the transmission of images through media has long been recognized. "The screen scripts the street" (Ferrell et al. 2008, p. 129 e.v.). The Dutch Crips, especially Keylow and his men, have created images and stories of their own that, in turn, give rise to new constructions. "Strapped'n Strong" is a clear example of where we see a loop become a spiral: "the screen scripts the street and the street scripts the screen."

While in the late 1980s a relatively small number of movies were important for transmitting the American gang stereotypes, in 2015 modern media plays a role that is much larger and more complex (Pyrooz et al. 2013). People are no longer dependent on movie images, stereotypical or not, that are provided to them. In liquid society, they use the internet, Twitter, Instagram, and other new media to create the identities they desire (see Chap. 7, this volume). Communication has become much more direct and effective.

No wonder then, that young members left the gang. The older OGs, who have tattoos that testify as to their dedication for being Crip, remain. The Crip identity is part of their body and interwoven with their life. Not only do these Dutch OGs still use much gang argot in their daily conversation, there is another clear indication that they remain "true to blue." Crips from The Hague have named their children after the set in the last couple of years, of which RolliNCy and Triad (after the formerly used name of the set) serve as the most powerful examples. For these senior Crips, it will be "Crip till the casket" or "Crip 4 life," as the tattoos on their bodies say. They may stay "true to blue," but younger members disengage from the gang. Street reputation is valued, but the gang identity based on American stereotypes is less appealing to a new generation.

References

Abels, R., & Dwarkasing, A. (1994, June 18). Crips en Bloods, de padvinders van de grote stad. *Trouw*.

Appadurai, A. (1996). *Modernity at large: Cultural dimensions of globalization*. Minneapolis, MN: University of Minnesota Press.

Bauman, Z. (2000). *Liquid modernity*. Cambridge, MA: Polity Press.

Bauman, Z. (2003). *Liquid love: On the frailty of human bonds*. Cambridge, MA: Polity Press.

Bauman, Z. (2005). *Liquid life*. Cambridge, MA: Polity Press.

Beke, B. M., Van Wijk, A. P., & Ferwerda, H. B. (2000). *Jeugdcriminaliteit in groepsverband ontrafeld. Tussen rondhangen en bendevorming*. Amsterdam: SWP.

Bing, L. (1992). *Gangs, jeugdbendes in Los Angeles*. Utrecht, The Netherlands: Luitingh Sijthoff.

Bjorgo, T. (2009). Processes of disengagement from violent groups of the extreme right. In T. Bjorgo & J. Horgan (Eds.), *Leaving terrorism behind: Individual and collective disengagement* (pp. 30–48). London: Routledge.

Bolden, C. L. (2012). Liquid soldiers: Fluidity and gang membership. *Deviant Behavior, 33*(3), 207–222.

Brotherton, D. C. (2007). Proceedings from the Transnational Street Gang/organization Seminar. *Crime, Media and Culture, 3*(3), 372–381.

Cloward, R. A., & Ohlin, L. B. (1960). *Delinquency and opportunity. A theory of delinquent gangs*. New York: Free Press.

Cohen, A. K. (1955). *Delinquent boys: The culture of the gang*. Glencoe, IL: Free Press.

Decker, S. H., & Lauritsen, J. (2002). Leaving the gangs. In C. R. Huff (Ed.), *Gangs in America* (pp. 51–67). Thousand Oaks, CA: Sage.

Decker, S. H., Pyrooz, D., & Moule, R. (2014). Disengagement from gangs as role transitions. *Journal of Research on Adolescence, 24*(2), 268–283.

Drogt, M. (2014). *Rollin' met mannen die de straat kennen*. Retrieved from http://www.boxpress-education.nl/rollin-met-mannen-die-de-straat-kennen.html

Editorial. Friends shot Sin Quin threaten killer in clip [Editorial]. (2012, September 18). *Ad.nl*. Retrieved from http://www.ad.nl/ad/nl/1041/Amsterdam/article/detail/3318320/2012/09/18/Vrienden-doodgeschoten-Sin-Quin-bedreigen-moordenaar-in-clip.dhtml

Editorial. Rapper Iron Mike overladen [Editorial]. (2013, January 12). *Crimesite Camilleri*. Retrieved from http://www.camilleri.nl/2013/01/rapper-iron-mike-overleden/

Editorial. Tension between motorcycle clubs in border runs again [Editorial]. (2015, August 15). *1Limburg*. Retrieved from. http://www.1limburg.nl/spanning-tussen-motorclubs-grensstreek-loopt-weer-op

Elder, G. H. (1998). The life-course as developmental theory. *Child Development, 69*(1), 1–12.

Farrington, D. P. (2003). Developmental and life-course criminology: Key theoretical and empirical issues—The 2002 Sutherland Award Address. *Criminology, 41*(2), 221–256.

Feixa, C., Canelles, N., Porzio, L., Recio, C., & Giliberti, L. (2008). Latin kings in Barcelona. In F. van Gemert, D. Peterson, & I.-L. Lien (Eds.), *Street gangs, migration and ethnicity* (pp. 63–78). Cullompton, England: Willan.

Ferrell, J., Hayward, K., & Young, J. (2008). *Cultural criminology*. London: Sage.

Ferwerda, H., & Van Ham, T. (2010). *Problematische jeugdgroepen in Nederland; Omvang en aard en politieproces beschreven*. Arnhem, The Netherlands: Bureau Beke.

Ferwerda, H., & Van Ham, T. (2011). *Problematische jeugdgroepen in Nederland; Omvang en aard in het najaar van 2010*. Arnhem, The Netherlands: Bureau Beke.

Ferwerda, H., & Van Ham, T. (2012). *Problematische jeugdgroepen in Nederland; Omvang en aard in het najaar van 2011*. Arnhem, The Netherlands: Bureau Beke.

Goffman, E. (1959). *The presentation of self in everyday life*. London: Allen Unwin.

Gruter, P. (1997). *Problematische jeugdgroepen in de regio Haaglanden anno 1997. Een hernieuwde inventarisatie onder wijkagenten en jeugdrechercheursen jeugdrechercheurs*. Den Haag, The Netherlands: Politie Haaglanden.

Gruter, P., Baas, M., & Vegter, D. (1996). *Problematische jeugdgroepen in de regio Haaglanden. Een inventarisatie onder wijkagenten en jeugdrechercheurs*. Den Haag, The Netherlands: Politie Haaglanden.
HOF. (1994). *Tussen mode en menens; Crips en Bloods in Nederland*. Den Haag, The Netherlands: Haagse Ondersteunings Functie.
Howell, J. C. (2007). Menacing or mimicking?: Realities of youth gangs. *Juvenile and Family Court Journal, 58*(2), 39–50.
Ilan, J. (2013). Street social capital in the liquid city. *Ethnography, 14*(1), 3–24.
Johnson, S., & Muhlhausen, D. B. (2005). *North American transnational youth gangs: Breaking the Chain of violence*. The Heritage Foundation. Retrieved July 10, 2015, from http://www.heritage.org/Research/UrbanIssues/bg1834.cfm
Klein, M. W. (2001). Resolving the Eurogang paradox. In M. W. Klein, H. J. Kerner, C. L. Maxson, & E. G. M. Weitekamp (Eds.), *The Eurogang paradox: Street gangs and youth groups in the U.S. and Europe* (pp. 7–19). Dordrecht, The Netherlands: Kluwer.
Maruna, S. (2001). *Making good: How ex-convicts reform and rebuild their lives*. Washington, DC: American Psychological Association.
Maxson, C. L. (1998). *Gang members on the move*. Washington, DC: US Department of Justice, Office of Juvenile Justice and Delinquency Prevention.
McGuire, C. M. (2007) *Working paper on Central American Youth Gangs in the Washington D.C. Area*. Washington Office on Latin America (WOLA). Retrieved July 10, 2015, from http://www.wola.org/index.php?option=com_content&task=viewp&id=272&Itemid=2
Papachristos, A. V. (2005). Gang world. *Foreign Policy, 147*(March/April), 49–55.
Pyrooz, D. C., Decker, S. H., & Moule, R. K. (2013). Criminal and routine activities in online settings: Gangs, offenders, and the internet. *Justice Quarterly, 32*(3), 471–499.
Pyrooz, D. C., Decker, S. H., & Webb, V. J. (2010). The ties that bind: Desistance from gangs. *Crime & Delinquency, 60*(4), 491–516.
Roks, R. A. (2007). *Het is hier toch geen Amerika?' Reconstructie van de criminele carrière van een Nederlandse 'gangsta'*. Rotterdam, The Netherlands: Erasmus University Rotterdam.
Roks, R. A. (2016). *In de h200d. Een eigentijdse etnografie over de inbedding van criminaliteit en identiteit*. Rotterdam, The Netherlands: Erasmus University Rotterdam.
Roks, R. A., & Staring, R. J. H. M. (2008). Crime, Rhyme en de Media: een eigentijdse levensgeschiedenis van een Haagse Gangsta. In D. Siegel, F. van Gemert, & F. Bovenkerk (Eds.), *Culturele criminologie* (pp. 161–173). Den Haag, The Netherlands: Boom Juridische Uitgevers.
Sampson, R. J., & Laub, J. H. (1993). *Crime in the making: Pathways and turning points through life*. Cambridge, MA: Harvard University Press.
Savenije, W. (2007). Las pandillas transnacionales o "Maras": Violencia urbana en Centroamérica. *Foro Internacional 189, 47*(3), 637–659.
Shakur, S. (1993). *Monster. De autobiografie van een Crips leider*. Amsterdam: Luitingh Sijthoff.
Shank, B. (1996). Fears of the white unconscious: Music, race, and identification in the censorship of 'cop killer'. *Radical History Review, 66*, 124–145.
Thrasher, F. M. (1927). *The gang: A study of 1,303 gangs in Chicago*. Chicago, IL: University of Chicago Press.
Timeline: Rising tensions between motorcycle clubs Limburg. (2015, May 27). *RTL Nieuws*. Retrieved from http://www.rtlnieuws.nl/nieuws/binnenland/tijdlijn-oplopende-spanningen-tussen-motorclubs-limburg
Van den Heuvel, J., & Thimister, B. (2015, August 17). Leaders motorcycle clubs are on death list. *De Telegraaf*. Retrieved from http://www.telegraaf.nl/binnenland/24382734/__Leiders_motor-clubs_op_dodenlijst__.html
Van der Valk, J. (2009). *Strapped'n strong*. Documentary. Retrieved from http://www.documentairenet.nl/review/crips-strapped-n-strong/
Van Gemert, F. (1998). *Crips in drievoud; Een dossieronderzoek naar drie jeugdbendes*. Amsterdam: Regioplan.
Van Gemert, F. (2001). Crips in orange; Gangs and groups in the Netherlands. In M. W. Klein, H.-J. Kerner, C. J. Maxson, & E. G. M. Weitekamp (Eds.), *The Eurogang paradox: Street gangs and youth groups in the U.S. and Europe* (pp. 145–152). Boston, MA: Kluwer.

Van Gemert, F. (2005). Gangsta rap: De controverse voorbij. *Justitiële Verkenningen, 31*(4), 68–81.
Van Gemert, F. (2008). MS13; Over transnationale gangs en sterke merken. In D. Siegel, F. van Gemert, & F. Bovenkerk (Eds.), *Culturele criminologie* (pp. 135–146). Den Haag, The Netherlands: Boom juridisch uitgevers.
Van Gemert, F. (2012). Five decades of defining gangs in The Netherlands: The Eurogang paradox in practice. In F.-A. Esbensen & C. Maxson (Eds.), *Youth gangs in international perspective: Results from the Eurogang Program of Research* (pp. 69–84). New York: Springer.
Van Gemert, F., & De Jong, J. D. (2010). Migrant Boyz'n the Hood: Over transnationale en buurtgebonden jeugdbendes. In F. Bovenkerk, M. Easton, L. Gunther Moor, & P. Ponsaers (Eds.), *Policing in Multiple Communities* (pp. 197–215). Cahiers Politiestudies 15.
Van Gemert, F., & Weerman, F. (2013). Youth groups and street gangs in the Netherlands. In EU Street Violence. Youth Groups and Violence in Public Spaces (pp. 203–227). Paris: European Forum for Urban Security (Efus).
Van Gemert, F., & Weerman, F. (2015). Understanding European gangs. In S. H. Decker & D. Pyrooz (Eds.), *Handbook gangs*. Chichester, England: Wiley.
Van Oosterwijk, C., Gruter, P., & Versteegh, P. (1995). *Haagse jeugdbendes en Amerikaanse gangs. Een vergelijkend onderzoek naar jeugdbende criminaliteit in de regio Haaglanden*. Den Haag, The Netherlands: Politie Haaglanden.
Van Stapele, S. (1998). Crips. *Nieuwe Revu*, 43–47.
Van Stapele, S. (2003). *Crips.nl: 15 jaar gang cultuur in Nederland*. Amsterdam: Vassallucci.
Viering, P. (1994). Straatroof, inbraak, doodslag. *Panorama, 3*, 37–42.
Ward, T. (2013). *Gangsters without borders: An ethnography of a Salvadoran street gang*. Oxford, England: Oxford University Press.
Wermuth, M. (2002). *No sell out: De popularisering van een subcultuur*. Amsterdam: Aksant.
Whyte, W. F. (1943). *Street corner society: The social structure of an Italian slum*. Chicago: University of Chicago Press.

Chapter 10
Why Do Flemish Youth Participate in Right-Wing Disruptive Groups?

Maarten De Waele and Lieven J.R. Pauwels

10.1 Introduction

There has been a long-standing tradition for gang research in criminological inquiries (Decker and Weerman 2005; Klein and Maxson 2006; Esbensen and Maxson 2012). While studies of troublesome youth groups in Belgium are still limited in comparison to other countries in Europe such as The Netherlands (Esbensen and Weerman 2005), there has been a mounting interest in the topic in Belgium (Pauwels et al. 2011; Pauwels and Svensson 2013; Van Hellemont 2013; Vettenburg et al. 2013). Research on participation in right-wing extremist groups, however, has attracted relatively little attention in Belgium. Therefore, the present study aims to fill this gap by presenting and testing an integrative model that is capable of explaining why extreme-right young people participate in disruptive groups (henceforth, RWD group participation).

Qualitative studies on neo-Nazi gangs and racist groups have supplied us with detailed information concerning motives for entry (Bjorgo 2002; Sela-Shayovitz 2012). This current contribution adopts a different perspective and analyzes the role of a series of social-psychological mechanisms in prompting participation in right-wing extremist groups. Previously, Bouhana and Wikström (2010) argued that studies of terrorism and violent extremism suffer from a poor understanding of causal mechanisms and lack integration of explanatory levels. Bouhana and Wikström were not alone with this criticism, as a comparable

M. De Waele (✉)
VVSG, The Association of Flemish Cities and Municipalities, Brussels, Belgium
e-mail: maarten.dewaele@vvsg.be

L.J.R. Pauwels, Ph.D.
Department of Criminology, Criminal Law and Social Law, Ghent University, Ghent, Belgium

C.L. Maxson, F.-A. Esbensen (eds.), *Gang Transitions and Transformations in an International Context*, DOI 10.1007/978-3-319-29602-9_10

statement was made earlier by Mudde (2002, p. 10) on the state of studies on right-wing extremism[1]: this lack of knowledge "[...] has been partly caused by the fact that the term is not only used for scientific purposes but also for political purposes." The social construction of this politically sensitive concept is shaped by multiple actors, including politicians, academics, and the media. Although this elusive concept has been a subject of interesting debate and calls for clarification from a criminological viewpoint, the present study is not aimed at extending the debate on how right-wing extremism can and should be best defined: our focus is on presenting and validating an integrated model which combines elements from social psychological and sociological traditions that have previously been applied to the study of violent youth groups. Previously, Decker and Pyrooz (2015) argued that much can be learned from 100 years of gang research when we test theories of violent extremism. This study can thus be seen as a modest attempt in this regard. By integrating fragmented insight, we hope to stimulate theoretical elaborations and the development of more comprehensive perspectives that can throw new light on preventing or tackling the problem of right-wing extremist violence.

In this chapter, we first describe the integrated framework that has been used. Then, we introduce the sample, outline the methods, and explain the data. Next, we present the results of path analyses and finally, discuss the findings.

10.2 An Integrative Mechanism-Based Approach

In criminology the idea that a single theoretical framework does not provide a salient explanation for offending and for participation in troublesome youth groups has long been acknowledged (Bernard and Snipes 1996). Elliott et al. (1979) indicated as early as in the late 1970s that theoretical reliance on variables from one theory (cf. strain, self-control, etc.) for the explanation of offending has limited results in view of the moderate level of explanatory power for crime or criminal behavior. Furthermore, competitive testing of theories on criminal behavior did not yield conclusive results (Bernard and Snipes 1996; Liska et al. 1989). Nevertheless, theoretical integration does not come without restrictions. Some scholars have warned about creating theoretical mush by which the fundamental purpose of theory constructions is neglected (Thornberry 1989). Besides, an integrative approach requires discovering communalities in seemingly competing theories rather than focusing on differences. Therefore, integration should build on an internal causal logic to explain phenomena, by which theoretical causation, human agency, and the person–environment interaction should be duly considered to advance knowledge, detect causes, and take preventive actions. This implies that it is important to gain insights into both the proximate and the remote causes of RWD group participation (Wikström 2010).

[1] For more detail on the definition of right-wing extremism, see, e.g., De Waele (2013).

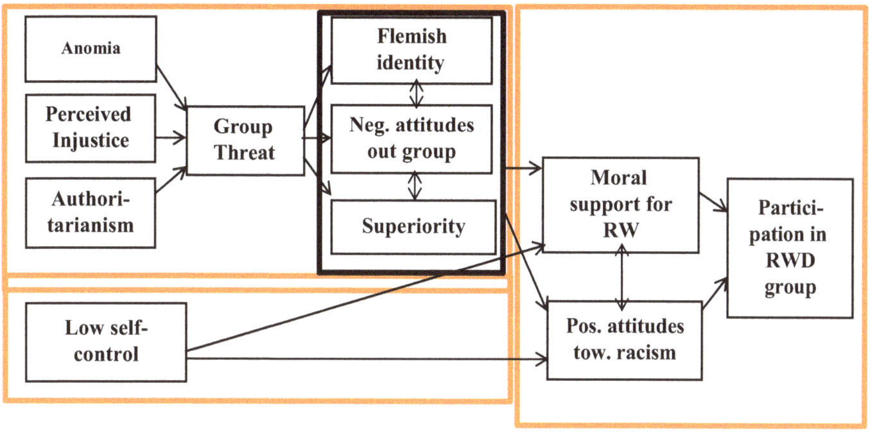

Fig. 10.1 Conceptual model for the explanation of right-wing disruptive participation

Integrated theories have also been used in gang research (e.g., Thornberry et al. 1993; Esbensen et al. 2010; Alleyne and Wood 2014). The conceptual framework presented in Fig. 10.1 elaborates on the existing models and integrates concepts from three different traditions: (1) perceived injustice/relative deprivation literature, (2) self-control, and (3) moral beliefs favorable to right-wing extremism and racist peer exposure.

We assert that perceived injustice, anomia, and authoritarianism (the strain initiated model) on the one hand, and thrill-seeking behavior (low self-control) on the other, have consequences for RWD group participation through different routes. Social psychological mechanisms that represent discontent affect RWD group participation through a series of psychological mechanisms that have been identified in social identity theory, while thrill-seeking behavior affects the membership through the development of attitudes favorable to right-wing extremism and through the selection of racist peers. Both racist peers and moral support for RW extremism are considered proximate causes of RWD group participation.

10.2.1 Strain Initiated Model

Since the 1960s, studies of violent left-wing extremism have pointed to the effect of root causes which criminologists would label as strains. Within the field of criminology, it has especially been considered the merit of Agnew's general strain theory to stress the importance of perceived injustice. Agnew's General Strain Theory (GST) argues that negative feelings may cause strain, which can pressure adolescents into crime (by stimulating negative emotions and violent beliefs) (Agnew

2006, 2011). In this respect, crime is a coping strategy. Subjective strains such as perceived injustice and feelings of political powerlessness (anomia[2]) may act as stressors that may trigger one's involvement in disruptive groups. The latter feelings of strain, together with authoritarianism, can pave the way for developing moral support for the use of violence by right-wing extremist groups (henceforth, moral support for right-wing extremism). In the next paragraphs, we explain how we conceive each of these strain-related concepts.

10.2.1.1 Perceived Injustice and Anomia as Strain

Perceived injustice corresponds to the feeling of being treated unfairly as a result of the perception that the person itself or the group to which one belongs ("reference group," see Merton 1957) are unjustly disadvantaged compared with other individuals or groups in society. This term thus highlights the subjective perception and experience of it (Van den Bos et al. 2009). Runciman (1966) first introduced the term of relative deprivation in his study on attitudes of social inequality and his work inspired Gurr (1970) to operationalize the concept as a state of deprivation by which persons compare their own situation with that of others. Gurr particularly deserves the credit for translating this idea into the realm of studies of political violence. From the social psychological standpoint, Van den Bos et al. (2009) indicated in their study of Dutch native and immigrant youths that (the perception of) negative treatment indirectly leads to negative emotions towards out-groups, and that societal disconnectedness or anomia was a very important mediator.

As regards social disconnection, Srole (1956) suggested that people with high scores on the anomia scale tend to feel helpless, alone, powerless, and alienated from society. Previous studies have found that especially the dimension of political powerlessness[3] strongly correlates with support for right-wing ideology, and, indirectly, influences right-wing extremist violence and vandalism (Hagedoorn and Janssen 1983; Boehnke et al. 1998; De Groof et al. 1999; De Witte 2001; De Waele 2014). In addition, based on a large-scale Belgian survey conducted in Flanders and Wallonia, Pauwels et al. (2014) demonstrated that perceived injustice and alienation were strong predictors for moral support for left-wing extremism, religious extremism, right-wing extremism, and political violence. A more detailed analysis of the

---

[2] 'Anomie' was originally defined by Durkheim and Merton as a state of society (macro) and "the breakdown of moral norms that limit desires and aspirations" (Deflem 1989, p. 629). It was later modified by Srole (1956), who described "anomia" as a state of mind expressed by individuals with "*a* subjective feeling responding to societal dysfunctions" (Van de Velde and Pauwels 2010, p. 112).

[3] Srole indicated that the concept of anomia contains five strongly interrelated subdimensions. In this chapter the concept is limited to the dimension of political powerlessness, given the political-related nature of the dependent variable. Furthermore, previous research in this field has indicated that right-wing extremist ideology mainly seems to correlate with this dimension (Scheepers et al. 1989; Van de Velde and Pauwels 2010; De Witte 1999). For more information on this topic see De Waele (2013, p. 28).

Flemish data revealed that the direct effect of perceived injustice declined when the researcher controlled for other direct effects (De Waele 2014). However, the above-mentioned studies were not designed to study the effects of social identity related concepts (e.g., group threat, Flemish identity, negative attitudes towards out-groups, and superiority feelings). The present study therefore extends previous research and aims to advance the understanding of the negative consequences of perceived injustice. We hypothesize that the effect of perceived injustice and anomia on RWD group participation is indirect, mediated by the effect of group threat.

10.2.1.2 Authoritarianism as an Exogenous Variable

Besides perceived injustice, the strain-initiated model also incorporates authoritarianism as one of the first explanations for right-wing participation. Developed by Adorno et al. (1950) in their seminal work on "The Authoritarian Personality," the concept of authoritarianism was a relatively stable intrapersonal trait which results from enduring intrapersonal conflicts rooted in childhood experiences of harsh education. Adorno et al. argued that authoritarians consider others—out of dissatisfaction with their own position—as weak or immoral (Adorno et al. 1950; Whitley and Ægisdóttir 2000). In contrast, Altemeyer (1998) disagreed with that view and instead rejected the idea of authoritarianism as a personality characteristic. He rather believed that authoritarianism consists of a set of coherent attitudes learned from peer groups and similar socializing agents (Altemeyer 1981, 1998). Altemeyer thus reconceptualized authoritarianism as a value syndrome that comprises three distinct elements: (1) conventionalism, which is a high level of compliance with social norms; (2) an emphasis on hierarchy and submission to authority; and (3) a "law and order" mentality which legitimizes anger and aggression against those who deviate from social norms. Authoritarians are often supporters of nationalism and share ethnocentric attitudes. Research even indicated that people with high scores for authoritarianism are showing displays of biological racism and fear things that differ from the traditional role relationship, such as homosexuality (De Witte 1999). Therefore, it is plausible to assume that people having high levels of authoritarianism are more likely to exhibit higher levels of group threat.

10.2.1.3 Perceived Group Threat as Mediator of Perceived Strains

Researchers often indicate the strong effects of group threat on forming prejudice against out-groups. Manifestations of prejudice are explained as a coping mechanism to establish group privilege (Blumer 1958). This point is especially stressed in the Integrated Threat Theory (Stephan et al. 2000). The theory was modeled after Pettigrew's theory of intergroup contact (Pettigrew 1998) and focuses on the conditions that lead to perceptions of threat, which in turn have an impact on attitudes and behavior (Wagner et al. 2008). In their experiment on threatening information about ethnic out-groups, Cohrs and Ibler (2009) demonstrated that high levels of right-wing authoritarian (RWA) feelings increased the likelihood of prejudicial attitudes (Heylen and Pauwels 2015). Perceptions of threat may endorse people to engage in violent activities to reduce feelings of anxiety and threat. Three dimensions of perceived threat have been identified in the literature, i.e., symbolic threat, realistic threat, and intergroup anxiety (Stephan et al. 2002; Doosje et al. 2013). The first refers to the threat to the respondent's culture, which in our study is a threat to the Flemish/Belgian culture. Realistic threat, on the other hand, indicates the economic conditions and the influence of immigrant groups. Quillian (1995) maintained in his study that while threat is perceived by individuals, the effect of prejudice is largely experienced in the context of intergroup relations between dominant and subordinate social groups. On the basis of these opinions, we hypothesize that perceived group threat has an indirect effect on participation in right-wing extremist groups through its effect on ethnocentrism and feelings of superiority.

10.2.1.4 Ethnocentrism and Superiority as Consequences of Perceived Group Threat

Integrated threat theory provides the reason for which perceived threat results in bias-motivated behavior: it may foster ethnocentrism and feelings of superiority. In their research, Pennings and Brants (1985) stated that right-wing extremism is characterized by strong contra-identification with leftist opinion, multiculturalism, and internationalism. In contrast, as indicated by the historical roots of Flemish nationalism, right-wing militancy is mostly connected with strong Flemish identity. Nevertheless, this relationship can by no means be seen as a causal relationship.[4] Tajfel and Turner (1974) worked on the influence of social identity and contended that shared experiences, values, and norms of the group are crucial for the development of social identity and status of the group in relation to enemies. They referred to the social-psychological process of in-group socialization when individuals enter a certain group. On the other hand, not only a positive identification, but also a negative identification with the "out-group" (contra-identification) needs to be mentioned (Scheepers and Eisinga 1989; Hogg and Terry 2000; Hooghe and Reeskens 2006). This "in-/out-group" relation allows people to break down the barriers of illegality (Heitmeyer 2003; Van der Valk and Wagenaar 2010). Applied to the current study, in-group identification was measured as a strong identification with the Flemish people. In contrast, the contra-identification was derived from the negative attitudes towards the out-group (immigrants in general, Muslims, and Jews). It is hypothesized in our study that both

[4] Although there is considerable overlap between Flemish nationalism and support for a right-wing ideology, it is clear that the one does not imply the other. For instance, currently Flanders deals with some right-wing national solidarist groups, who tend to focus less on the subnational context but more on geopolitical nationalist issues. Vice versa, there are also Flemish nationalist movements, without political orientation, aiming to gather a broad Flemish public regarding linguistic and cultural matters.

aspects of ethnocentrism have an impact on moral support for right-wing extremism and the exposure to racist comments by peers (henceforth, peer racism).

Connected to the sense of strong Flemish in-group identification is the feeling of superiority among the Flemish people or the so-called superior race. Results from Scandinavian research on former members of extreme right-wing groups have indicated that various extremists were convinced that they belonged to a superior group (Kimmel 2007). These feelings of superiority can have an effect on positive attitudes towards the use of violence against Muslims (Van den Bos et al. 2009). Therefore, we hypothesize that superiority has a positive significant effect on moral support. Likewise, we assume that people with higher feelings of superiority run a bigger risk of being exposed to racist comments by peers. This assumption is supported by the social selection effect worded as "birds of a feather flock together" by Glueck and Glueck (1950), who said that people join groups in which they can recognize themselves. Van der Valk and Wagenaar (2010) illustrated this as the mirror effect with which individuals connect with people who have similarities.

10.2.2 Low Self-Control Initiated Model

While the perceived injustice model has caught considerable interest, the role of self-control is by no means less important. Despite the fact that self-control theory was not originally developed to explain individual differences in right-wing extremist groups, Gottfredson and Hirschi (1990) claimed their theory was a general theory of crime. The central assumption in Gottfredson and Hirschi's General Theory of Crime is that low self-control increases the risk of offending, as well as other deviant and imprudent behaviors. A large number of studies have tested this proposition and empirical research has shown that low self-control is associated with offending among different samples (e.g., youth, college students, adults, males vs. females, criminals) and in different designs (Burton et al. 1998; Pratt and Cullen 2000). More recently, attention has been paid to the concept of self-control in the explanation of troublesome youth group involvement (Kissner and Pyrooz 2009; Esbensen and Weerman 2005; Hope and Damphousse 2002). Therefore, it is important to test empirically whether thrill-seeking behavior is an additional mechanism that exerts an independent effect on RWD group participation. Ethnographic studies have revealed that new members are often motivated by their own opportunistic or thrill-seeking motives (Bjorgo 2002; Watts 2001). Although ideological motivations are important in understanding acts of politically motivated violence, ideology is not always crucial for entering extremist groups. The search for adventure, i.e., thrill-seeking behavior, is one of the reasons frequently mentioned by (former) members of extremist groups. A pure self-control-based explanation would consider the lack of self-control to be the ultimate cause of right-wing extremist group involvement. Moral support for right-wing extremism, exposure to racist peers, and participation in a right-wing extremist group would therefore all be common consequences of low self-control.

10.2.3 Proximate Causes

10.2.3.1 Moral Support for Right-Wing Extremism

The concept of moral support for right-wing extremism refers to the individual's favorable attitude towards the use of violence by right-wing extremist groups. Radicalization is often defined as the process whereby individuals acquire moral support for violence used in a means-to-an-ends fashion. Moral support for right-wing extremist violence constitutes a personal moral belief that favors the use of violence by right-wing extremist groups. In the perceived injustice induced model, moral support for violence is seen as the key mechanism by which perceived injustice, group threat, authoritarianism, anomia, feelings of superiority, Flemish identity, and ethnocentrism are translated into RWD group participation. A multitude of studies have found that measures of antisocial moral beliefs are positively related to offending and gang membership, while those of prosocial moral beliefs are negatively related to offending and troublesome youth group involvement (Esbensen et al. 2010; Hill et al. 1999; Svensson et al. 2010; Weerman and Esbensen 2005) and political violence and vandalism (Hagan et al. 1995; Pauwels and De Waele 2014).

10.2.3.2 Exposure to Racist Peers

The role of peers is especially prominent in social learning theories (Akers 1998; Bruinsma 1992; Warr 2002) but highly contested in control theories (Gottfredson and Hirschi 1990; Kornhauser 1978; Hirschi 1969). Peer delinquency is one of the strongest predictors of self-reported delinquency, and therefore, it is expected to help explain right-wing extremist group participation. Differential association with racist groups provides two specific contexts of exposure to settings in which the use of violence is supported or considered as a means of justifying the ideological goals of the group. Differential associations are important not only in social learning theory, but also in routine-activities/lifestyle theory (Laub and Sampson 2003; Wikström and Butterworth 2006; Pauwels and Svensson 2013). Reasoned from a routine activities/lifestyle perspective, racist peers are important as they may be responsible for the situational instigation to commit an act of (politically motivated) violence or become involved in a right-wing extremist group. In the present study we take into account exposure to peer racism as an important indicator of exposure to criminogenic moral settings, which shapes the individual's routines and risky lifestyle. In short, we summarize the hypotheses that are derived from the integrated approach as outlined in Fig. 10.1: the conceptual model.

- H1: Group threat is determined by authoritarianism, anomia, and perceived injustice
- H2: Flemish identity, ethnocentrism, and superiority are determined by group threat
- H3: Moral support for right-wing extremism is determined by superiority, Flemish identity, ethnocentrism, and thrill-seeking behavior

- H4: Exposure to racist peers is directly related to thrill-seeking behavior, ethnocentrism, and moral support for right-wing extremism
- H5: RWD group participation is directly related to moral support for right-wing extremism, exposure to racist peers, and thrill-seeking behavior

10.3 Data and Method

10.3.1 Method and Sample

Between December 2012 and April 2013 a self-administered questionnaire was made available online. In this study, we used a convenience sample of students. The basic idea was that as students differ on political attitudes and behavior, we would need to find a way that guaranteed maximum variation in terms of right-wing extremism. Therefore, a link to the online questionnaire was placed on different web pages for targeting extreme-right youngsters on chat rooms of Neo-Nazi groups and extreme-right Flemish nationalist student organizations. In addition, the survey was spread through social media and online forums of universities and university college students. It is therefore not surprising that our survey contains an overrepresentation of students in the population (94.7 %), which implies that our sample is not representative, even for the population among adolescents and young adults between the ages of 18 and 25. However, we do not claim to make any generalization about the prevalence of RWD group participation. On the contrary, our aim is to analyze the proximate and remote causes of RW extremist group participation. This sampling approach allowed us to have a good grasp of the extreme-right population in Flanders. We were aware of other ways to possibly gain insight into the political preferences of the Belgian population, as some representative surveys on sociocultural attitudes are drawn every second year in Flanders. However, those surveys were not targeted at discovering RWD group participation. Overall, we were able to receive completed online questionnaires from 723 respondents. The majority of the respondents were female (64.3 %), student (94.7 %), and either Catholic (45.6 %) or atheist (47.3 %). In terms of the place of origin, the majority was from the eastern part of Flanders (64 %), with 34.7 % and 29.3 % of the respondents coming from the provinces of Limburg and Antwerp, respectively. The remaining respondents lived in Flemish Brabant and the Brussels Capital (10.1 %), East Flanders (16.7 %), and West Flanders (9.3 %).

While the survey may not be seen as a nationally representative survey, its goal was to test a general theory, and therefore the sample can be seen as a test of the theory, particularly based on Popper's idea of developing potential falsifications for theories (Popper 1963; Opp 2009). This idea holds that if a theory is to be seen as a general theory, it should be applicable in different subsamples. However, we are trying to falsify the hypotheses stated above (Henrich et al. 2010). Although an online survey has some advantages, it cannot ensure that researchers completely monitor the processes of response selection and that the condition of the questionnaire is verified completely (e.g., presence of others and anonymity). As a result, the motivation to participate is left entirely to the respondent, and therefore, data could have a selection bias. In this regard, it is important to recognize the impossibility of monitoring response selection, self-selection, and under-coverage (internet availability). However, it should be mentioned that these drawbacks, including preparedness to answer survey questions, the willingness to report, and too limited information on the participants, are also discernible in the more traditional survey modes (Dillman 1978). Yet, we remain confident about the advantages of the online survey method: it is low in cost and is also easily analyzed with the aid of software programs, such as SPSS and Mplus. Furthermore, web surveys are especially useful for explanatory research in studying the causes and correlates rather than the prevalence of the phenomenon for lack of randomization. Despite this restriction, the percentage (4.1 %) is very similar to the percentages found in studies on political preferences (Maxson and Klein 1995).

10.3.2 Measurement of Constructs

In the present study, numerous scale constructs were used to assess the relation between exogenous variables, mediators, and dependent variables. In view of the extensive nature of concepts employed, a brief overview of the scale constructs is presented below. A more detailed overview of the scales can be found in Appendix 1, in which question wording, descriptives, and the measure of scale reliability, i.e., Cronbach's alpha, are included. All exogenous and independent constructs achieve an acceptable reliability coefficient of .62–.92.

10.3.2.1 Dependent Variable

Since there are no existing scales available on RWD group participation, we attempted to develop a measure of RWD group participation on the basis of the idea of funneling, which is paramount to the Eurogang definition of street gang membership. The Eurogang group provides a consensus definition which constitutes a gang as any durable, street-oriented youth group whose involvement in illegal activity is part of its group identity (Weerman et al. 2009; Esbensen and Maxson 2012). Therefore, this contribution adopts aspects of the latter definition, and applies it to the context of right-wing extremism.

Our aim was to follow the Eurogang definition as closely as possible. We made a distinction between the essential elements of a gang definition (gang definers) and specific characteristics of the gang (gang descriptors) (Esbensen and Maxson 2012, p. 6). With regard to the disruptive group, we chose to work with parts of the Eurogang definition. The duration and size of the non-informal group were determined, and in accordance with the Eurogang definition, the group was restricted to respondents who were members of a group containing three or more persons for longer than 3 months (Decker and Weerman 2005). This approach made it feasible to identify "active individuals" with an acceptable minimum time period. However, different from the Eurogang definition, we did not focus on street-orientation. Although some overlap may exist between street gangs and right-wing extremist groups, the focus of the present study is on detecting young adults who can be placed on the far-right, and who are affiliated with right-wing social movements or subcultural networks which combine the political ideology with illegal acts. Despite the fact that many right-wing groups often partake in (illegal) political protest and occasionally "hang around" on the street, they cannot be seen as RWD group participants.

As mentioned earlier, RWD group participation was measured with the funneling technique. This means that we combined answers to one filter question and four follow-up questions to measure self-reported group participation, further narrowing the answers down with an additional question about right wing orientation and other group characteristics. The leading question was "do you consider yourself to be a member of a group of friends (not an organization or association) that frequently meets and considers itself as a group?" (1 = yes, 0 = no). The four follow-up questions were: (1) How long have you been a member of the group? (2) How big is your group? (3) Do members of this group get involved in fights with other cliques? (4) Are members of this group involved in law breaking? The last two questions were dichotomies (1 = yes, 0 = no). Respondents were categorized as involved in a "disruptive group" if they answered affirmatively to the leading question, (1) were members for more than 3 months and (2) the group consisted of more than 3 persons. Regarding question 3 and 4, it was sufficient to score positive on one of the two follow-up questions. To the introductory question ($n=295$), 40.8 % of the total sample answered positively, while ($n=70$), 9.7 % answered positively to the follow-up questions. In addition, the members were asked to position themselves on a left (0) to right (7) scale. From the latter group 30 respondents (4.1 %) positioned themselves at the extreme right spectrum (6–7). This latter group of 30 respondents is consequently regarded as disruptive group members with an extreme-right attitude, henceforth referred to as RWD group participation. Although we are aware of the fact that the operationalization does not necessarily make these groups extremist, we assume the group's acceptance of extreme-right members is an indication of tolerance towards the extreme-right ideology.

10.3.2.2 Exogenous and Independent Variables

Perceived injustice refers to the extent to which respondents feel they have been treated unjustly by others. In this survey, the others are not linked to specific persons (see Appendix 1). The questions are intended to measure the overall perception of both personal and group discrimination, and personal negative treatment. The combined scale measures items on personal discrimination, group discrimination, and personal treatment and has a Cronbach's alpha of 0.62. *Perceived personal discrimination* indicates one's feelings of being discriminated against in relation to other people in society. An example of the latter scale is, "It makes me angry when I think of how I am treated in comparison to others." *Perceived group discrimination* refers to discrimination against the group to which the respondent belongs. Group discrimination is measured through questions, such as: "If I compare the group to which I belong with other groups in Belgium, I think we are treated unfairly." The last dimension of the perceived injustice scale is *Personal treatment* which raises questions about everyday treatment of people by others, such as: "I think that if I have complaints about anything, that, normally, people listen to my opinion." The items were originally used in a Dutch survey of attitudes towards extremism conducted by Van den Bos et al. (2009) and validated in a study by Pauwels and Schils (2014).

In the present study, a number of *attitudes/beliefs* that intervene in the relationship with perceived injustice are studied. These intervening mechanisms are authoritarianism, anomia, ethnocentrism, Flemish identity, superiority, and thrill-seeking behavior. *Authoritarianism* was measured by using 11 items based on the three elements of Altemeyer's (1998) authoritarianism scale (conventionalism, hierarchy and submission, and law and order mentality). One example question to measure the construct is: "Can people be divided into two distinct classes: the weak and the strong?"

As indicated in the theoretical section, *Ethnocentrism* was measured on the basis of both in-group, i.e., Flemish identity, and out-group orientation, i.e., negative attitude towards the out-group—in this case, migrants. The scale was derived from the research of Van den Bos et al. (2009) and the Social Cohesion in Flanders (SCIF) questionnaire (for more information see Appendix 1). Since Flemish identity is operationalized as a strong form of Flemish preference, we asked questions assessing how important it was for them to be Flemish or how proud they were to be Flemish. In contrast to the in-group questions, more negative attitudes were measured regarding the out-group, operationalized here as immigrants. For instance, one negative statement was: "Immigrants come here to exploit our social security." A few positive statements were also included in this category, for example, "We should welcome the immigrants who want to live in Belgium"(R).[5]

Derived from Srole's (1956) study of personal alienation, *anomia* was operationalized on the dimension of perceived political powerlessness. Questions were phrased as to the extent to which respondent (dis)believed that, for instance, there is no sense in voting, because the parties do what they want to do anyway.

In the present study, we also incorporated Gottfredson and Hirschi's (1990) conceptualization of self-control through the notion of thrill-seeking behavior (the tendency to seek adventure and kicks). The items were taken from the attitudinal self-control scale used by Bursik and Grasmick (1993). This scale has been frequently used in many delinquency studies (Pratt and Cullen 2000). The tendency to seek adventure was operationalized by statements such as: "I sometimes find it exciting to do things that could be dangerous."

Personal superiority was operationalized as the fact that someone perceives him/herself as better than others. For instance, respondents were asked how strongly

[5] The *R* indicates that the scores for this item were reversed.

they (dis)agreed with the statement: "When people think differently, they are less valuable to me." *Perceived group threat* was derived also from the study of Van den Bos et al. (2009) and adapted to the Flemish context. It was measured regarding three out-groups, i.e., the immigrant in general, Muslims, and Jews. However, the three categories of out-groups strongly correlated. The construct was operationalized in items probing to what extent respondents agreed that "Belgians do not get the respect that they deserve from Jews" or the reversed question "In Belgium, people from other countries have the right to be more important than Belgians."

Moral support for right-wing extremism was measured through items from a scale that measures attitudes towards the use of violence by right-wing extremists in order to reach political goals. The items were taken from a larger scale used in a study by Van den Bos et al. (2009). Three questions were asked, and one of them stated: "To what extent do you understand that some right-wing extremists use violence against the people who have the power in Belgium?" *Positive attitudes towards racism* were measured via the scale from Van den Bos et al. (2009). The exposure was operationalized as the near environment of the respondents. Therefore, questions were asked relating to the extent to which respondents believe their friends think it is OK if they participate in, for example, violent behaviors; i.e., "Do you think your friends would think it is OK if you would fight with an immigrant without any reason?" More information can be found in Appendix 1.

10.3.3 Analysis Plan

To test the integrated theoretical model, a series of structural equation models were run in order to identify the direct and indirect effects. As the dependent variables are dichotomous, a logistic path model was tested using Mplus (Muthén and Muthén 2012). The results are shown in Fig. 10.2 in which only the direct effects of the best fitting model are presented. These direct effects between the scale variables are standardized regression coefficients (β). All independent variables were standardized before entering into the equation. The direct relationships between independent variables (i.e., Moral support for RWE and positive attitudes towards racism) and the dependent variable (i.e., RWD group participation) are log-odds and should be interpreted as the one standard deviation change in the log-odds of the dependent variable as the independent variables change with one standard deviation.

10.4 Results

The results are shown in two ways. First, a detailed overview of the specific direct effects on the independent variables and the dependent variable is given in Table 10.1. In addition, Fig. 10.2 displays the best fitting model to explain RWD group participation. Starting with the effects of the exogenous variables, it is noted

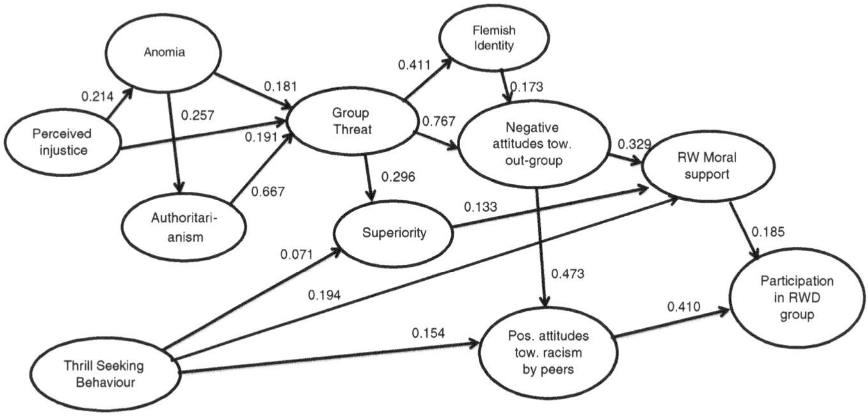

Fig. 10.2 Merged model for the explanation of participation in right-wing disruptive groups, RMSEA=0.062. All parameters are statistically significant at the $p<0.05$ level or better

that perceived injustice (β=0.129), anomia (β=0.241), and authoritarianism (β=0.515) have strong effects on group threat. In total, the model indicates R^2 of 0.433, indicating that 43.3 % of the total variation of group threat is explained by the model. Although it was proposed in the conceptual model that anomia and authoritarianism were seen as exogenous variables, results also indicated positive direct effects towards the other exogenous variables. However, the coefficient of determination R^2 is much lower for perceived injustice (R^2=0.048), anomia (R^2=0.095), and authoritarianism (R^2=0.071). A similar R^2 is measured for the fourth exogenous variable, thrill-seeking behavior. In line with our conceptual model, the results confirm that our exogenous variables are to a large extent explained by factors that are not included in this model.

Another confirmation of our proposed conceptual model is found in regard to the outcome variables of group threat (i.e., Flemish identity, negative attitudes towards out-group, and superiority). Results confirm that group threat can be seen as a common cause of the three variables. Regarding the interrelationship of the three outcome variables, a strong relationship is found between the measures of ethnocentrism, i.e., Flemish identity (identification) and negative attitudes towards out-group (contra-identification). Furthermore, both measures indicate a reasonable to good fit of the coefficient of determination R^2, respectively, 0.317 and 0.618. No positive significant relationship was found between superiority and ethnocentrism. Negative significant effects were measured from both anomia (β=–0.189) and superiority (β=0.086) towards Flemish identity.

The proximate causes (moral support for RWE and positive attitudes to racism by peers) were strongly influenced by the negative attitudes towards out-groups. The effect of the latter variable on positive attitudes towards racism (β=0.272) and moral support for RWE (β=0.227) was positive. In contrast, no positive effect was found from this form of contra-identification towards the dependent variable of RWD group participation. A similar common cause of the proximate causes was

Table 10.1 Specific direct effects of the independent variables

Independent variables (x)	Perceived injustice	Anomia	Authoritarianism	Group threat	Flemish identity	Negative attitudes tow. out-group	Superiority	Thrill-seeking behavior	Positive attitudes towards racism	Moral support for RWE	Participation in RWD group
	β	β	β	β	β	β	β	β	β	β	Log Odds
Perc. Injust.	–	0.174***	0.082**	0.129***	–0.058	0.028	0.088*	0.114**	0.095**	0.034	0.001
Anomia	0.183***	–	0.238***	0.241***	–0.189***	0.101***	0.005	0.052	–0.022	0.010	–0.137
Authoritarianism	0.084*	0.232***	–	0.515***	0.346***	0.209***	0.195***	0.053	0.077	–0.035	0.043
Group threat	–	–	–	–	0.102*	0.488***	0.160**	0.129*	0.089	0.060	0.103
Flemish ident.	–	–	–	–	–	0.189***	–0.111**	0.055	–0.022	0.005	0.119
Negative att. tow. out-group	–	–	–	–	0.339***	–	0.032	–0.185**	0.272***	0.227***	0.127
Superiority	–	–	–	–	–0.086**	0.014	–	0.054	0.002	0.140***	0.032
TSB	–	–	–	–	0.039	–0.074**	0.050	–	0.114**	0.171***	0.150
Pos. att. tow. racism	–	–	–	–	–	–	–	–	–	0.108**	0.239**
Moral support for RWE	–	–	–	–	–	–	–	–	0.103**	–	0.049
R-square	0.048	0.095	0.071	0.433	0.317	0.618	0.119	0.042	0.234	0.197	0.270

Notes: All effects are standardized beta coefficients, except for the direct effect on RWD membership. *$p<0.1$; **$p<0.01$; ***$p<0.001$

found in the exogenous variable of thrill-seeking behavior. Regarding the effects on the dependent variable, only one significant effect was measured, namely that of positive attitudes towards racism ($\beta=0.239$).

Figure 10.2 presents the best fitting model of the SEM path analysis (RMSEA=0.062). As hypothesized, anomia ($\beta=0.214$), perceived injustice ($\beta=0.191$), and authoritarianism ($\beta=0.667$) are directly related to perceived group threat. Perceived injustice and anomia have both direct and indirect significant effects on group threat (see Appendix 2). The best fitting model indicates that perceived injustice has a positive effect on anomia ($\beta=0.214$) and anomia has a positive effect on authoritarianism ($\beta=0.257$).

Furthermore, there is a direct path from perceived group threat to Flemish identity ($\beta=0.411$), negative attitudes towards out-groups (0.767) and feelings of superiority ($\beta=0.296$). The pathway of group threat on the dependent variable may run through the concept of ethnocentrism, involving both the in-group identification (Flemish identity) and the contra-identification with the out-group (negative attitudes towards out-groups). In line with the results of the direct effects in Table 10.1, the results indicate a direct effect of contra-identification ($\beta=0.329$), and no significant effect of in-group identification, on moral support for RWE. The effect of Flemish identity might be mediated by contra-identification which has an independent effect on negative attitudes towards out-groups ($\beta=0.173$). A positive significant effect is evident from contra-identification on positive attitudes towards racism by peers ($\beta=0.473$). Likewise, no direct effect is found from Flemish identity on positive attitudes towards racism.

In line with the previous results, group threat operates as a common cause of both ethnocentrism and superiority. However, in contrast to the previous results, the best fitting model indicates a small, but significant effect of thrill-seeking behavior ($\beta=0.071$). Both contra-identification ($\beta=0.133$) and superiority ($\beta=0.140$) indicated a positive significant effect on moral support. Nevertheless, no effect occurred from superiority on positive attitudes of peers in regard to racism. The effect on the latter variable might be suppressed by the strong effect of negative attitudes towards the out-group.

Thrill-seeking behavior exhibits a direct effect on exposure to racist peers ($\beta=0.154$), but not on RWD group participation. Interestingly, in the best fitting model, there is no direct relationship between moral support for right-wing extremism and positive attitudes to racism by peers. In line with a key assumption of self-control theory, thrill-seeking behavior is a common cause of both moral support ($\beta=0.194$) and positive attitudes towards racism.

There are only two direct effects on RWD group participation: moral support for right-wing extremism (log-odds[6]: 0.210) and exposure to racist peers (log-odds: 0.482). For interpretation, we calculate the odds ratio by taking the inverse

[6] Log odds reflect the increase in the change in the dependent variable (participation in RWD group vs. no participation in RWD group) with respect to the value of the independent variable. The higher the value of the log odds is, the greater effect there is. A positive value indicates a positive effect, while a negative value denotes a negative effect.

log function. Results indicate that a one-standard deviation increase on moral support for RWE increases the likelihood of RWE participation with a factor of 1.23 (odds-ratio). Moreover, a one-standard deviation increase in exposure to racist peers increases the probability of RWD group participation with a factor of 1.62 (odds-ratio) (Menard 2011).

10.5 Discussion and Conclusion

The results have shown that RWD group participation partially stems from perceived injustice, group threat, authoritarianism, and anomia. This is consistent with previous research that recognizes the triggering of feelings of both perceived and procedural justice by the lack of social integration with school and/or family (De Waele 2014; Pauwels and Schils 2014). Past studies have also confirmed that perceived injustice impacts respondents' feelings of legitimacy about democratic institutions, such as the police. Such feelings of distrust might lower the threshold for illegal behavior and, likewise, support the motivation to RWD group participation.

Nevertheless, feelings of injustice do not directly trigger RWD group participation (see Table 10.1). The results supported our hypothesis that group threat may trigger feelings of superiority and ethnocentrism (identification and contra-identification). Contra-identification, in particular, plays a major role in further translating the aforementioned strains into RWD group participation. These mechanisms derived from the social identity theory and the intergroup threat theory are directly related to moral support for right-wing extremism. Regarding our result that no direct effect was observed from in-group identification on moral support, Billiet et al. (2003) obtained similar results, and they attributed this result to the fact that strong identification with national identity does not necessarily require a strong contra-identification with foreigners. In addition, our research only measured the contra-identification with immigrants and not with other related out-groups, including leftist or the political establishment. Therefore, it can be inferred from respondents who feel aligned with the Flemish people and the nation that there exists a different in-/out-group connotation. Billiet et al. (2003) argued that national identity and attitudes toward immigrants are determined by the social representation of "nation." The in-group is, thereby, built through shared images and beliefs about the national in-group and its relationship to other groups or foreigners. In addition, the results also indicated a negative effect of anomia, as measured by political powerlessness, on Flemish identity. This indicates that persons who strongly identify with Flanders do not necessarily identify as a result of disillusionment with the political system. In contrast, it can be argued that political awareness and interest in politics could trigger Flemish identification.

On the other hand, thrill-seeking behavior is an additional important exogenous mechanism: it affects both moral support for right-wing authoritarianism and exposure to racist peers. We find both the perceived injustice model and the self-control initiated model highly compatible with each other: our study reveals that both models share common intervening mechanisms leading to RWD group participation. While this revelation is found to be the case for right-wing extremism, it remains to be seen if it would be applicable to the study of religious Islamic extremism and left-wing extremism. Future studies should attempt to gain an insight into the general character of these mechanisms.

Based on previous empirical tests of general models (see, e.g., Van den Bos et al. 2009), the present study integrated a social-psychological model with a self-control initiated model, leading to different paths that explain RWD group participation. These findings are in line with those from past research (Pauwels and De Waele 2014) but more importantly, they have extended our knowledge by stressing the importance of additional routes from social identity theory and intergroup threat theory. By discovering the different routes, we have contributed to a more thorough understanding of individual differences in RWD group participation. Future research, in consonance with the gang research, could explore the amplifying effect of RWD group participation on the development and persistence of violent behavior.

However, some limitations of the present study should be acknowledged. First of all, our theoretical model has been applied to explain individual differences in RWD group participation among students. Future research should investigate to what extent the model also applies to the explication of RWD group participation in adults and in non-student populations. Second, the measure of RWD group participation is a constructed combination of personal ideological positioning and gang identifiers. In this research we assumed that tolerating right-wing extremist participants was a measure of RWD group participation. However, to capture the total concept of RWD groups, future research might also include additional measures of ideological group positioning. Third, the study is cross-sectional and therefore not optimal for studying causal inferences, as causes and effects are measured simultaneously. Finally, our results are based on a large-scale web survey, and it is unclear to what extent our results are biased by this method of data collection.

Research into the domain of RWD group participation and political violence is important not only for the development and evaluation of criminological theories, but also within the framework of prevention of political violence. It is in this regard that studies of violent extremism and gang research can benefit from a vigorous definition that can enlighten us about aspects of political extremist groups, which live on the edge of mainstream society. In their recent work, Decker and Pyrooz (2011, 2015) point out how the study of terrorism, extremism and radicalization and gang research could mutually benefit from each other by comparing the similarities and contrasting the differences. First, they argue that in gang research, political belief and ideology are barely touched upon. Therefore, it may be worthwhile to consider combining the research concerns of Eurogang with the interest in left/right identification. When we apply the gang definition to RWD group participation, inquiries into the political beliefs of the group could then be undertaken and illuminated. Second, Decker and Pyrooz specify that the motivation of violence could differ between the two groups. We agree with this statement, but concurrently recognize that although the motivation could be different, the causal mechanisms of political violence might not. The strong effect of thrill-seeking behavior, identified in the current research and past studies regarding political violence, underlines the prominence of Bjorgo's statement (1997) that ideology is far from the determining factor in joining right-wing groups (De Waele 2014; Pauwels and De Waele 2014). Finally, some scholars also indicate that there is a difference between the international aspect of terrorism and local gang activity. This brings us to the already cited view that the street oriented level of the definition of gangs cannot be applied to the research of RWD group participation. Although this aspect of street orientation could be a descriptor of some disruptive groups, it cannot be seen as a general definer (Esbensen and Maxson 2012). Therefore, future research should consider the Eurogang definition in combination with inquiries into the political preferences by which the ideological connotation constitutes a part of the subcultural context. The continuation of work on a more comprehensive definition in the field of radicalization could also draw inspiration from the traditional research on gangs, together with other traditional fields of political violence and political protest (e.g., Opp 2009), so as to produce more profound research.

Appendix 1: Question Wording and Scale Construct

Perceived injustice (five-point scale translated from Van den Bos et al. 2009): "It makes me angry when I think of how I am treated in comparison to others," "I think I am worse off than others in Belgium," "I have the feeling of being discriminated," "If I compare myself with others in Belgium than I feel unfairly treated." "I think the group to which I belong is worse off than other people in Belgium," "It makes me angry when I think of how my group is treated in comparison to other groups in Belgium," "I have the feeling that the group to which I belong is discriminated," "If I compare the group to which I belong with other groups in Belgium, I think we are treated unfair." "I think I am being treated with justice" (R), "I think I am being treated with respect" (R), "I think that, most of the time, I am being treated fairly" (R), "I think that if I have complaints about anything, that, normally, people listen to my opinion" (R).

Group threat (five-point scale translated from Van den Bos et al. 2009): "In Belgium, Muslim themselves as better than Belgians," "Most Muslims in Belgium will never understand how Belgians are," "In Belgium, people from other countries do not understand what is written in the Belgian constitution (for instance, that everyone can say what he or she thinks and everyone has to be treated equally)," "In Belgium, people from other countries have the right to be more important than Belgians," "People from other countries get to much money from the Belgian government in comparison to the Belgians," "Non-Muslims in Belgium do not get the respect that they deserve from Muslims," "In Belgium, people from other countries do not understand how Belgian see the world," "In Belgium, Muslims have, in comparison to Non-Muslims, other values about their work," "If you do business with the Jews, you have to be extremely careful," "Belgians do not get the respect that they deserve from Jews," "Jews want to dominate everything," "Most Jews think that they are better than others," "Muslims should not try to change the norms and values of Belgians," "In Belgium, people from other countries have other norms and values than Belgians," "Many companies in Belgium will prefer to work with people from other countries, instead of Belgians, even if Belgians are more suitable for the job," "Jews incite war and give us the blame."

Superiority (five-point scale translated from Van den Bos et al. 2009): "What I think is the truth," "I think that if everyone would properly reflect, they would think the same as me," "I think that everyone should be like me," "When people think differently, they are less valuable to me," "it scares me if people think different than me," "I actually never met people who think different than me."

Anomia (five-point scale from Srole's study of personal alienation 1956, dimension of political powerlessness) "There is no sense in voting, the parties do what they want to do anyway," "Parties are only interested in my vote, not in my opinion," "So many people vote in elections that my vote doesn't make any difference," "During the elections parties promise things, but eventually nothing changes," "Most politicians promise a lot, but nothing is done," "Politicians have never learned to listen to people like me," "Actually there is not even one politician that I would trust," "In general, we can support on our political leaders to take the best decisions" (R).

Negative attitudes towards the out-group (in this case immigrants) (five-point scale derived and translated from the SCIF[7] questionnaire): "Immigrants come here to exploit our social security," "Immigrants are a threat to our culture and customs," "In general, immigrants can't be trusted," "If the number of jobs decreases, the immigrants should be sent back to their own countries," "The presence of different cultures in is an enrichment for our society"(R), "Immigrants contribute to the wealth of our country"(R), "We should welcome the immigrants who want to live in Belgium."

Authoritarianism (five-point scale derived from Altemeyer 1998): "obedience and respect for authority are the two most important virtues children have to learn," "young people are often rebellious, but the will have to adapt as they get older," "what we need most, more than laws and institutions, is a few courageous and devoted leaders in whom people can put their faith," "People can be divided into two distinct classes: the weak and the strong," "Sex crimes, such as rape and attacks on children, deserve more than mere imprisonment; such criminals ought to be publicly whipped, or worse," "Most of our social problems would be solved if we could somehow get rid of the immoral, crooked, and feebleminded people," "If people would talk less and work more, everybody would be better off," "People should have more respect for our national heritage and habits," "those who break the law must be strongly punished to learn what is right and wrong," "Laws need to be executed, especially regarding rioters and revolutionaries."

Flemish identity (five-point scale, translated from Van den Bos et al. 2009): "It is important to me to be Flemish," "I am proud of being Flemish," "The fact that I am

[7] Social cohesion indicators in Flanders (SCIF).

Flemish is totally not important to me" (R), "I think that there can only be a beautiful world if everyone is proud to be Flemish," "It makes me scared that people are not proud to be Flemish."

Moral Support for right-wing extremism (five-point scale translated from Van den Bos et al. 2009): "I understand that some right-wing extremists use violence against the people who have the power in Belgium," "I can understand right-wing extremists who disrupt the order," "I can understand right-wing extremists who use violence against others."

Positive attitudes towards racism (four-point scale, derived and translated from Van den Bos et al. 2009): Do you think your friends would think it is OK if … "you would say that you don't want to have anything to do with immigrants?", "you would write 'stop immigration' on a public wall," "you would fight with an immigrant without any reason."

Thrill-seeking behavior (five-point scale derived from Grasmick et al. 1993): "I sometimes find it exciting to do things that could be dangerous," "I often do things without thinking of the consequences," "Sometimes I will take a risk just for the fun of it."

Left/Right identification (seven-point scale from extreme left to extreme right): Where do you position yourself on a scale from (1) extreme-left to (7) extreme-right.

Participation in disruptive groups (five-point scale derived from the Eurogang definition and left-right identification questionnaire): "Do you consider yourself to be a member of a group of friends (no organisation or association) that frequently meets and considers itself as a group?" (1 = yes, 0 = no). Four follow-up questions were (1) How long have you been a member of the group? (2) How big is your group? (3) "Do members of this group get involved in fights with other cliques?" (4) "Are members of this group involved in law-breaking?" To maintain the right-wing disruptive group respondents need to score positive on the introduction question, question (1) and (2) and question (3) or (4). Furthermore they had to indicate a score 6 or 7 on the left/right scale (Tables 10.2 and 10.3).

Appendix 2: Indirect Effects

Total indirect effects of independent variables on the dependent variable (Table 10.4).
Strongest specific indirect effects

- *Perceived injustice* (0.067***)
  Perceived injustice>Group Threat>Negative attitudes towards out-group>Positive attitudes towards racism>Participation in RWD groups (0.033**)
- *Anomia* (0.089***)
  Anomia>Authoritarianism>Group Threat>Negative attitudes towards out-group>Positive attitudes towards racism>Participation in RWD groups (0.029***)
- *Authoritarianism* (0.170***)
  Authoritarianism>Group Threat>Negative attitudes towards out-group>Positive attitudes towards racism>Participation in RWD groups (0.155***)

Table 10.2 Overview of scale constructs and reliabilities

Scale construct	Cronbach's alpha	Scale construct	Cronbach's alpha
Positive attitudes towards racism by peers	0.85	Group threat	0.76
Perceived injustice	0.62	Authoritarianism	0.92
Flemish identity	0.83	Superiority	0.76
Moral support for right-wing extremism	0.87	Low self-control	0.71
Anomia	0.87	Negative attitudes towards out-group	0.88

Table 10.3 Descriptive statistics

Variable	Min	Max	Mean	Std
Perceived injustice	−1.02	4.28	0	1
Authoritarianism	−2.65	2.93	0	1
Anomia	−2.48	2.78	0	1
Group threat	−2.69	3.17	0	1
Flemish identity	−1.94	1.75	0	1
Negative attitude towards out-group	−2.24	3.01	0	1
Superiority	−1.25	3.79	0	1
Thrill-seeking behavior	−1.54	3.21	0	1
Positive attitudes towards racism	−1.83	2.99	0	1
Moral support for right-wing extremism	−1.45	4.16	0	1

- *Group threat* (0.266***)
  Group Threat>Negative attitudes towards out-group>Positive attitudes towards racism>Participation in RWD groups (0.179***)
- *Negative attitudes towards out-group* (0.295***)
  Negative attitudes towards out-group>Positive attitudes towards racism>Participation in RWD groups (0.225***)
- *Flemish identity* (0.050**)
  Flemish identity>Negative attitudes towards out-group>Positive attitudes towards racism>Participation in RWD groups (0.038**)
- *Superiority* (0.028*)
  Superiority>Moral support for RW extremism>Participation in RWD groups (0.028*)
- *Thrill seeking behavior* (0.115***)
  Thrill seeking behavior>Positive attitudes towards racism>Participation in RWD groups (0.072**)

Table 10.4 Total indirect effect (and significance level) of the independent variables on RWD group participation

Independent variables	Perceived injustice	Anomia	Authoritarianism	Group threat	Flemish identity	Negative attitudes tow. out-group	Superiority	TSB	Moral sup. for RWE	Positive attitudes towards racism
RWD group participation	0.067 (0.000)	0.089 (0.000)	0.170 (0.000)	0.266 (0.000)	0.050 (0.001)	0.295 (0.000)	0.028 (0.029)	0.115 (0.000)	/	/

References

Adorno, T. W., Levinson, D. J., Horkheimer, M., Aron, B., & Frenkel-Brunswik, E. (1950). *The authoritarian personality*. New York: Harper & Brothers.

Agnew, R. (2006). *Pressured into crime: An overview of general strain theory*. Oxford. MA: Oxford University Press.

Agnew, R. (2011). Revitalizing merton: General strain theory. In F. T. Cullen, C. L. Jonson, A. J. Meyer, & F. Adler (Eds.), *The origins of American criminology* (Vol. 16, pp. 137–158). New Brunswick, NJ: Transaction Publishers.

Akers, R. L. (1998). *Social structure and social learning*. Los Angeles, CA: Roxbury.

Alleyne, E., & Wood, J. L. (2014). Gang involvement: Social and environmental factors. *Crime & Delinquency, 60*(4), 547–568. doi:10.1177/0011128711398029.

Altemeyer, B. (1981). *Right-wing authoritarianism*. Winnipeg, Manitoba, Canada: University of Manitoba Press.

Altemeyer, B. (1998). The other "authoritarian personality". *Advances in Experimental Social Psychology, 30*, 47–92.

Bernard, T. J., & Snipes, J. B. (1996). Theoretical integration in criminology. *Crime and Justice, 20*, 301–348.

Billiet, J., Maddens, B., & Beerten, R. (2003). National identity and attitude toward foreigners in a multinational state: A replication. *Political Psychology, 24*(2), 241–257.

Bjorgo, T. (1997). *Racist and right-wing violence in Scandinavia: Patterns, perpetrators, and responses*. Sats: Tano Aschehoug.

Bjorgo, T. (2002). Exit neo-nazism: Reducing recruitment and promoting disengagement from racist groups. *Norwegian Institute of International Affairs (NUPI) Working Papers, 627*, 3–33.

Blumer, H. (1958). Race prejudice as a sense of group position. *Pacific Sociological Review, 1*(1), 3–7.

Boehnke, K., Hagan, J., & Merkens, H. (1998). Right-wing extremism among German adolescents: Risk factors and protective factors. *Applied Psychology, 47*(1), 109–126.

Bouhana, N., & Wikström, P.-O. H. (2010). Theorizing terrorism: Terrorism as moral action. *Contemporary Readings in Law and Social Justice, 2*(2), 9–79.

Bruinsma, G. J. N. (1992). Differential association theory reconsidered: An extension and its empirical test. *Journal of Quantitative Criminology, 8*(1), 29–49.

Bursik, R., & Grasmick, H. G. (1993). *Neighborhoods and crime: The dimensions of effective community control*. New York: Lexington Books.

Burton, V. S., Cullen, F. T., Evans, T. D., Alarid, L. F., & Dunaway, R. G. (1998). Gender, self-control, and crime. *Journal of Research in Crime and Delinquency, 35*(2), 123–147.

Cohrs, J. C., & Ibler, S. (2009). Authoritarianism, threat, and prejudice: An analysis of mediation and moderation. *Basic and Applied Social Psychology, 31*(1), 81–94.

De Groof, S., Debusscher, M., Derks, A., & Elchardus, M. (1999). *Zonder maskers: Een actueel portret van jongeren en hun leraren*. Gent, Belgium: Globe.

De Waele, M. (2013). Flemish youngsters and right-wing extremist groups: Status quaestionis. In A. Crawford, J. de Maillard, J. Shapland, A. Verhage, & P. Ponsaers (Eds.), *Crime, violence, justice and social order: Monitoring contemporary security issues* (pp. 15–51). Antwerpen, Belgium: Maklu.

De Waele, M. (2014). Political violence among Flemish adolescents: The impact of moral support for right-wing extremism. In J. Shapland, J. De Maillard, S. Farrall, A. Groenemeyer, & P. Ponsaers (Eds.), *Desistance, social order and responses to crime. Today's security issues* (pp. 134–166). Antwerpen, Belgium: Maklu.

De Witte, H. (1999). 'Alledaags' racisme in Belgie. Een overzicht van de onderzoeksliteratuur over racistische opvattingen en een interpretatie van de betekenis van het opleidingsniveau. *Migrantenstudies, 15*(1), 2–27.

De Witte, H. (2001). *Rechts van de democratie: Enkele lacunes in onderzoek naar rechts-extremisme opgevuld*. Brussel: Vereniging voor sociologie.

Decker, S. H., & Pyrooz, D. (2011). Gangs, terrorism, and radicalization. *Journal of Strategic Security, 4*(4), 151–166.

Decker, S. H., & Pyrooz, D. C. (2015). "I'm down for a Jihad": How 100 years of gang research can inform the study of terrorism, radicalization and extremism. *Perspectives on Terrorism, 9*(1), 104–112.

Decker, S. H., & Weerman, F. M. (Eds.). (2005). *European street gangs and troublesome youth groups*. Oxford, England: AltaMira Press.

Deflem, M. (1989). From anomie to anomia and anomic depression: A sociological critique on the use of anomie in psychiatric research. *Social Science & Medicine, 29*(5), 627–634.

Dillman, D. A. (1978). *Mail and telephone surveys* (Vol. 3). New York: Wiley.

Doosje, B., Loseman, A., & Van den Bos, K. (2013). Determinants of radicalization of Islamic youth in the Netherlands: Personal uncertainty, perceived injustice, and perceived group threat. *Journal of Social Issues, 69*(3), 586–604.

Elliott, D. S., Ageton, S. S., & Canter, R. J. (1979). An integrated theoretical perspective on delinquent behavior. *Journal of Research in Crime and Delinquency, 16*(1), 3–27.

Esbensen, F.-A., & Maxson, C. L. (Eds.). (2012). *Youth gangs in international perspective: Results from the Eurogang program of research*. Dordrecht, The Netherlands: Springer.

Esbensen, F.-A., Peterson, D., Taylor, T., & Freng, A. (2010). *Youth violence: Sex and race differences in offending, victimization, and gang membership*. Philadelphia: Temple University Press.

Esbensen, F.-A., & Weerman, F. M. (2005). Youth gangs and troublesome youth groups in the United States and the Netherlands: A cross-national comparison. *European Journal of Criminology, 2*(1), 5–37.

Glueck, S., & Glueck, E. T. (1950). *Unraveling juvenile delinquency*. Cambridge, MA: Harvard University Press.

Gottfredson, M. R., & Hirschi, T. (1990). *A general theory of crime*. Stanford, CA: Stanford University Press.

Grasmick, H. G., Tittle, C. R., Bursik, R. J., & Arneklev, B. J. (1993). Testing the core empirical implications of Gottfredson and Hirschi's General Theory of Crime. *Journal of Research in Crime and Delinquency, 30*(1), 5–29.

Gurr, T. R. (1970). *Why men rebel*. Princeton, NJ: Princeton University Press.

Hagan, J., Merkens, H., & Boehnke, K. (1995). Delinquency and disdain: Social capital and the control of right-wing extremism among East and West Berlin youth. *American Journal of Sociology, 100*(4), 1028–1052.

Hagedoorn, L., & Janssen, J. (1983). *Rechts-ommekeer. Rechtsextreme opvattingen bij leerlingen van middelbare scholen*. Baarn, The Netherlands: Amoboeken.

Heitmeyer, W. (2003). Right-wing extremist violence. In W. Heitmeyer & J. Hagan (Eds.), *International handbook of violence research* (pp. 399–436). Dordrecht, The Netherlands: Kluwer.

Henrich, J., Heine, S. J., & Norenzayan, A. (2010). The weirdest people in the world? *Behavioral and Brain Sciences, 33*(2–3), 61–83.

Heylen, B., & Pauwels, L. J. R. (2015). The social roots of contemporary prejudice. *International Journal of Criminology and Sociology, 4*, 28–35.

Hill, K. G., Howell, J. C., Hawkins, J. D., & Battin-Pearson, S. R. (1999). Childhood risk factors for adolescent gang membership: Results from the Seattle Social Development Project. *Journal of Research in Crime and Delinquency, 36*(3), 300–322.

Hirschi, T. (1969). *Causes of delinquency*. Berkeley: University of California Press.

Hogg, M. A., & Terry, D. I. (2000). Social identity and self-categorization processes in organizational contexts. *Academy of Management Review, 25*(1), 121–140.

Hooghe, M., & Reeskens, T. (2006). Kerkelijke betrokkenheid, vertrouwen en etnocentrisme: een vergelijkende studie onder christelijke gelovigen in Europa. *Tijdschrift voor sociologie, 27*(3), 263–284.

Hope, T. L., & Damphousse, K. R. (2002). Applying self-control theory to gang membership in a non-urban setting. *Journal of Gang Research, 9*(2), 41–61.

Horgan, J. (2005). *The psychology of terrorism*. New York: Routledge.

Kimmel, M. (2007). Racism as adolescent male rite of passage. *Journal of Contemporary Ethnography, 36*(2), 202–218.
Kissner, J., & Pyrooz, D. C. (2009). Self-control, differential association, and gang membership: A theoretical and empirical extension of the literature. *Journal of Criminal Justice, 37*(5), 478–487.
Klein, M. W., & Maxson, C. L. (2006). *Street gang patterns and policies*. New York: Oxford University Press.
Kornhauser, R. R. (1978). *Social sources of delinquency: An appraisal of analytic models*. Chicago: University of Chicago Press.
Laub, J. H., & Sampson, R. J. (2003). *Shared beginnings, divergent lives: Delinquent boys to age 70*. Harvard: Belknap Press.
Liska, A. E., Krohn, M. D., & Messner, S. F. (1989). *Strategies and requisites for theoretical integration in the study of crime and deviance* (Theoretical integration in the study of deviance and crime: Problems and prospects). Albany: State University of New York.
Maxson, C. L., & Klein, M. (1995). Investigating gang structures. *Journal of Gang Research, 3*(1), 33–40.
Menard, S. (2011). Standards for standardized logistic regression coefficients. *Social Forces, 89*(4), 1409–1428.
Merton, R. K. (1957). *Social theory and social structure* (revth ed.). New York: Free Press.
Mudde, C. (2002). *The ideology of the extreme right*. Manchester, England: Manchester University Press.
Muthén, L. K., & Muthén, B. O. (2012). *Mplus user's guide. Statistical analysis with latent variables. Version 7*. Los Angeles, CA: Muthén & Muthén.
Opp, K.-D. (2009). *Theories of political protest and social movements: A multidisciplinary introduction, critique, and synthesis*. New York: Routledge.
Pauwels, L., Brion, F., Schils, N., Laffineur, J., Verhage, A., De Ruyver, B., et al. (2014). *Explaining and understanding the role of exposure to new social media on violent extremism. An integrative quantitative and qualitative approach*. Ghent, Belgium: Academia Press.
Pauwels, L., & De Waele, M. (2014). Youth involvement in politically motivated violence: Why do social integration, perceived legitimacy, and perceived discrimination matter? *International Journal of Conflict and Violence, 8*(1), 135–153.
Pauwels, L., & Schils, N. (2014). Differential online exposure to radical content and political violence. Testing the relative strength of social learning and competing perspectives. *Terrorism and Political Violence*. 1–29. doi:10.1080/09546553.2013.876414
Pauwels, L. J. R., & Svensson, R. (2013). Violent youth group involvement, self-reported offending and victimisation: An empirical assessment of an integrated informal control/lifestyle model. *European Journal on Criminal Policy and Research, 19*(4), 1–18.
Pauwels, L., Vettenburg, N., Gavray, C., & Brondeel, R. (2011). Societal vulnerability and troublesome youth group involvement: The mediating role of violent values and low self-control. *Journal of International Criminal Justice, 21*(3), 283–296.
Pennings, P., & Brants, K. (1985). *Rechts-extreme jongeren: theorie en praktijk van politiek randgedrag*. Amsterdam, The Netherlands: Universiteit van Amsterdam; Vakgroep Collectief politiek Gedrag.
Pettigrew, T. F. (1998). Intergroup contact theory. *Annual Review of Psychology, 49*(1), 65–85.
Popper, K. (1963). *Conjectures and refutations: The growth of scientific knowledge*. London, England: Routledge & Kegan Paul.
Pratt, T. C., & Cullen, F. T. (2000). The empirical status of Gottfredson and Hirschi's general theory of crime: A meta-analysis. *Criminology, 38*(3), 931–964.
Quillian, L. (1995). Prejudice as a response to perceived group threat: Population composition and anti-immigrant and racial prejudice in Europe. *American Sociological Review, 60*(4), 586–611.
Runciman, W. G. (1966). *Relative deprivation & social justice: Study attitudes social inequality in 20th century England*. Berkeley: University of California Press.

Scheepers, P. L., & Eisinga, R. N. (1989). *Etnocentrisme in Nederland: Theoretische en empirische modellen*. Nijmegen: Inst. voor Toegepaste Sociale Wetenschappen.

Scheepers, P., Felling, A., & Peters, J. (1989). Ethnocentrism in the Netherlands: A typological analysis. *Ethnic and Racial Studies, 12*(3), 289–308.

Sela-Shayovitz, R. (2012). The impact of globalization, migration, and social group processes on neo-Nazi youth gangs. In F.-A. Esbensen & C. L. Maxson (Eds.), *Youth gangs in international perspective: Results from the Eurogang program of research* (pp. 211–223). Dordrecht, The Netherlands: Springer.

Srole, L. (1956). Social integration and certain corollaries: An exploratory study. *American Sociological Review, 21*(6), 709–716.

Stephan, W. G., Boniecki, K. A., Ybarra, O., Bettencourt, A., Ervin, K. S., Jackson, L. A., et al. (2002). The role of threats in the racial attitudes of Blacks and Whites. *Personality and Social Psychology Bulletin, 28*(9), 1242–1254.

Stephan, W. G., Diaz-Loving, R., & Duran, A. (2000). Integrated threat theory and intercultural attitudes—Mexico and the United States. *Journal of Cross-Cultural Psychology, 31*(2), 240–249.

Svensson, R., Pauwels, L., & Weerman, F. M. (2010). Does the effect of self-control on adolescent offending vary by level of morality? A test in three countries. *Criminal Justice and Behavior, 37*(6), 732–743.

Tajfel, H. T., & Turner, J. C. (1974). The social identity theory of intergroup behavior. In S. Worchel & W. G. Austin (Eds.), *Psychology of intergroup relations* (pp. 7–24). Chicago: Nelson-Hall.

Thornberry, T. P. (1989). Reflections on the advantages and disadvantages of theoretical integration. In S. F. Messner, M. D. Krohn, & A. E. Liska (Eds.), *Theoretical integration in the study of deviance and crime: Problems and prospects* (pp. 51–60). Albany: State University of New York.

Thornberry, T. P., Krohn, M. D., Lizotte, A. J., & Chard-Wierschem, D. (1993). The role of juvenile gangs in facilitating delinquent behavior. *Journal of Research in Crime and Delinquency, 30*(1), 55–87.

Van de Velde, M., & Pauwels, L. (2010). Institutional distrust in Flanders: What is the role of social capital and dimensions of discontent? In M. Cools et al. (Eds.), *Safety, societal problems and citizens' perceptions. New empirical data, theories and analyses* (Vol. 3, pp. 109–133). Antwerpen, Belgium: Maklu.

Van den Bos, K., Loseman, A., & Doosje, B. (2009). Waarom jongeren radicaliseren en sympathie krijgen voor terrorisme: onrechtvaardigheid, onzekerheid en bedreigde groepen. https://www.wodc.nl/onderzoeksdatabase/jongeren-aan-het-woord-over-radicalisme-en-terrorisme.aspx

Van der Valk, I., & Wagenaar, W. (2010). *Monitor Racisme & Extremisme: The extreme right: Entry and exit*. Amsterdam, The Netherlands: Amsterdam University Press.

Van Hellemont, E. (2013). Research project: Black African gangs in Brussels: Understanding the seductiveness of youth gangs in a late modern metropolis (in progress)

Vettenburg, N., Gavray, C., Brondeel, R., & Pauwels, L. J. R. (2013). Societal vulnerability and adolescent offending: The role of violent values, self-control and troublesome youth group involvement. *European Journal of Criminology, 10*(4), 444–461.

Wagner, U., Tropp, L., Finchilescu, G., & Tredoux, C. (Eds.). (2008). *Improving intergroup relations: Building on the legacy of Thomas F. Pettigrew*. Malden, MA: Blackwell.

Warr, M. (2002). *Companions in crime: The social aspects of criminal conduct*. New York: Cambridge University Press.

Watts, M. W. (2001). Aggressive youth cultures and hate crime. *American Behavioral Scientist, 45*(4), 600–615.

Weerman, F. M., & Esbensen, F.-A. (2005). A cross-national comparison of youth gangs: The Netherlands and United States. In F. M. Weerman & S. H. Decker (Eds.), *European street gangs and troublesome youth groups* (Vol. 3). Dordrecht, The Netherlands: Springer.

Weerman, F. M., Maxson, C. L., Esbensen, F., Aldridge, J., Medina, J., & Van Gemert, F. (2009). Eurogang program manual background, development, and use of the Eurogang instruments in

multi-site, multi-method comparative research. https://www.umsl.edu/ccj/Eurogang/EurogangManual.pdf
Whitley, B. E., & Ægisdóttir, S. (2000). The gender belief system, authoritarianism, social dominance orientation, and heterosexuals' attitudes toward lesbians and gay men. *Sex Roles, 42*(11), 947–967.
Wikström, P.-O. H. (2010). Explaining crime as moral actions. In S. Hitlin & S. Vaisey (Eds.), *Handbook of the sociology of morality* (pp. 211–239). Dordrecht, The Netherlands: Springer.
Wikström, P. H., & Butterworth, D. A. (2006). *Adolescent crime: Individual differences and lifestyles*. Devon: Willan.

Chapter 11
Youth Gang Members' Transitions into and Within US Prisons

Beth M. Huebner and Kristina Thompson Garrity

11.1 Introduction

A crucial component of criminal justice policy and practice is determining why individuals become involved in crime. As gang activity is associated with higher rates of crime, and often more serious forms of crime, understanding the underlying mechanisms that influence gang membership is a critical starting point for criminal justice practitioners. Indeed, a number of risk factors have been identified as important precursors to gang membership (see Klein and Maxson 2006). Risk factors are often organized into individual, peer, family, and ecological domains, and they range from negative experiences in an individual's life (such as abuse or death in the family) to neighborhood gang presence (see O'Brien et al. 2013, for review). Research in this area has indicated that the number of risk factors present and the extent to which they exist in multiple domains are important for determining who ultimately joins the gang (Esbensen et al. 2009; Thornberry et al. 2003). While knowing these risk factors informs us about *who* is at risk, it does not necessarily illuminate *why* individuals join gangs. In other words, for the clearest understanding of how youths become gang-involved, it is important to consider motivations for joining, as well as how these motivations may mediate the relationship between risk factors and gang membership.

Many researchers have grappled with the complexities of why youth may end up as gang members. Work in this area often characterizes motivations as the "pushes" and "pulls" that introduce youths to gangs (Decker and Van Winkle 1996). These motivations vary from the allure of money and possessions (a pull) (Taylor 1990) to the perceived need for protection in the neighborhood (a push) (Decker and Curry

B.M. Huebner (✉) • K.T. Garrity
Department of Criminology and Criminal Justice, University of Missouri-St. Louis, St. Louis, MI, USA
e-mail: huebnerb@umsl.edu

C.L. Maxson, F.-A. Esbensen (eds.), *Gang Transitions and Transformations in an International Context*, DOI 10.1007/978-3-319-29602-9_11

2000). Such influences do not exist in a vacuum. For this reason, some researchers also consider how these motivations shift over time and across context. For example, in a multi-site investigation of youth gangs, Esbensen and Winfree (2013) note that reasons for joining the gang vary by location. Furthermore, some studies that examine desistance have indicated that the pushes that make gangs attractive at the time of joining may wane over time (Pyrooz and Decker 2011; Scott 2014).

In considering motivations that produce gang involvement in prison, it is important to understand how these gangs may differ characteristically from their street gang counterparts. Of particular importance is the extent to which gangs are organized. While a majority of street gangs have fluid membership and little organizational differentiation (Spergel 1990; Thornberry et al. 1993), some ethnographic accounts suggest that prison gangs reside on the more highly structured end of the organizational spectrum (Fong 1990; Mendoza 2005; Varese 2005). For example, Fong's (1990) case study of the Texas Syndicate and Mexican Mafia gangs within the Texas prison system indicates that prison gangs can be hierarchically structured in ways that parallel military organization. More recently, Varese (2005) described prison gang members in Russian gulags, noting that the gang operated as an organized crime group, with well-defined codes of conduct and membership requirements. Despite these depictions of prison gangs as distinctively organized, some research has indicated that differences may not be so marked. Specifically, Maxson's (2012) examination of youth gangs in carceral settings reveals that such groups operate in ways that are characteristically consistent with youth street gangs. In other words, gang activities within youth correctional facilities were not dissimilar to youth street gang activities. With these things in mind, researchers have suggested that the level of prison gang organization is reflective of the extent to which extra-legal governance is permitted to exist. In essence, those prisons with more formal governance by prison management, like those found in the United Kingdom, are likely to have fewer problems with prison gangs (Skarbek 2014). In this way, street gangs and prison gangs may not be all that different, with both types evolving into more organized entities as a response to lack of order in their neighborhoods (Taylor 1990).

Perhaps as a consequence of the organizational and membership qualities that characterize prison gangs, it is not surprising that their presence has important implications for prison environments. Most notably, prior literature has established that misconduct is significantly higher for those who identify as prison gang members (Gaes et al. 2002; Huebner 2003), although it is not entirely clear if gang membership is a cause of misconduct or a consequence of joining a gang. Furthermore, prison-level investigations have indicated that prisons have much higher reports of homicide when they house higher proportions of prison gangs (Reisig 2002). Taken as a whole, these facts highlight the necessity to elucidate the factors that contribute to prison gang involvement.

This chapter will focus on the motivations that draw youths into gang involvement as indicated by prior research. Furthermore, this chapter will consider how "push" and "pull" frameworks might be useful in understanding how individuals continue gang involvement in prison. Understanding these mediating mechanisms in the transition from youth street gangs to adult prison gangs has important implications for criminal justice practitioners and researchers alike.

11.2 Joining the Gang

When criminologists refer to youths being pushed into gang life, they are talking about the outside forces that make gang life attractive. While a number of criminological theories have been applied to this conceptualization, general strain theory provides a useful background for understanding pushes. Agnew describes strains as events or conditions that individuals view as negative (Agnew 1992). Crime, or in this case, gang membership, is seen as a way to lessen these strains. In general, negative life experiences, sometimes characterized as school or family stress, are significant predictors of gang involvement (Decker and Van Winkle 1996; Esbensen et al. 1993; Esbensen et al. 2009; LeBlanc and Lanctôt 1998; Thornberry et al. 2003). This perspective is also reflected in a number of ethnographic accounts. For instance, Vigil notes that racial and cultural marginalization, along with economic disadvantage, are critical conditions that may push Hispanic youths into gangs (Vigil 1988). This claim finds some support in Krohn and colleagues' work (2011), which suggests that social structural disadvantage, when coupled with shifting cultural customs, can impact the likelihood of Hispanic gang membership. In addition to strain as it relates to race, an important line of inquiry has examined how gender-specific strains may contribute to gang involvement. Those who have investigated female gang involvement find that girls involved in gangs often experienced victimization in the home (Campbell 1984; Joe and Chesney-Lind 1995; Miller 2001; Moore 1991).

Although the "pushes" outlined above are important considerations, it should be noted that motivations for gang involvement are often characterized as a combination of pushes and pulls (Thornberry et al. 2003). Pulls are described as those things specific to gangs that encourage membership. Gangs may appeal to youth for a variety of reasons. Early research argued that the gang's ability to provide some sort of status for those who feel unable to achieve middle-class goals is attractive to those youths (Cohen 1955). The concept of status is closely related to broader notions of identity attainment in criminological literature. Most notably, the symbolic interaction framework has informed how gangs may provide reflected appraisals of self for their members. Matsueda and Heimer (2004) do this most explicitly, examining how individuals might use their membership to define themselves and provide meaning for their lives. Esbensen and Winfree (2013) describe myriad factors that draw youth into gangs highlighting social reasons like friendship connections and instrumental reasons like the need for respect and protection. Further, the authors highlight the potential role that social context factors like economic disadvantage have on the motivations for gang joining.

In addition to individual-level interactions, research has also considered how group-level conflicts and identities can be meaningful. Prior research has suggested that intergroup conflict can provide a sense of identification for individuals (Simmel 1955). In other words, the building of an "us versus others" narrative provides a means for establishing identity in a neighborhood or community. Furthermore, Zatz and Portillos (2000) note that gang membership can be intricately entwined with familial and neighborhood loyalties. Thus, even with intra-gang conflict, for those youths who feel isolated, the gang offers an attractive and often times romanticized means of connection to others.

These concepts frame research that looks at youth involvement in gangs, and they can also be useful in discussing how involvement may be escalated to prison gang involvement upon incarceration. As prison gangs present a unique set of challenges for criminal justice actors, it is important to investigate the overlap of certain risk factors for street and prison gang involvement.

11.3 Youth Gang Members and the Transition to Prison

When examining how youths transition to prison, some research has found pre-incarceration characteristics to be important for determining a prisoner's behavior. For instance, DeLisi et al. (2011) link early life events to behaviors while incarcerated, which suggests that a life-course perspective is necessary for understanding why individuals may join prison gangs. From this importation model, we can think of joining the prison gang as simply a natural extension of street gang involvement. In consensus with Felson (2006), some researchers note that the gang's role in providing self-identity does not cease upon entrance into prison, and in fact, pre-incarceration gang socialization likely informs behaviors once behind bars (Fleisher and Decker 2001; Irwin 1980; Jacobs 1977). Likewise, some argue that romanticized ideas and myths about gangs may inform street gang members as to how they survive in the prison context (Pyrooz et al. 2011). Jacobs (1974) participant observation study of Chicago street gang members in prison offered early support for these ideas. Specifically, he finds that social organizations observed in prisons reflect the behaviors, beliefs, and organizational characteristics of the street gangs that are represented within them. This linkage has been supported in broader discussions of belief systems outside of and within the prison system. For example, Mears et al. (2013) find that "code of the street" belief systems follow individuals from the street to the prison. This finding, although not explicitly linked to gang membership, likely informs the behaviors of gang members. In other words, the code of conduct that resides in street gang culture likely has important outcomes once members find themselves incarcerated. Indeed, Scott (2014) finds street code values to be more prevalent in incarcerated gang youths than their non-gang counterparts. And yet, some research has suggested that distal causes may be more central to prison gang involvement. Most notably, Wood et al. (2014) find empirical evidence in contrast to Jacobs' work, noting that early characteristics matter for individual transition into prison gangs, but street gang involvement does not.

In addition to the importation of gang behaviors into prison settings, there are a number of different stressors that may push youths into prison gangs. The deprivation model contends that prison environments induce criminal behavior by their very nature (Clemmer 1940; Sykes 1958). That is, prisons are not only unfamiliar environments in which prisoners have lost autonomy, but they also house hyper-masculine and violent cultures. This inducement has parallels to the "pushes" of street gangs in that the strains experienced in the prison context push prisoners to become involved in gang activity. Certainly, prison environments may sometimes be places that contribute to strain. Most notably, victimization rates are found to be higher for prison populations than the general population (Wolff et al. 2009; Wooldredge 1998). Furthermore, environmental details such as overcrowding have been found to contribute to mental and physical health deteriorations (Paulus 1988). Determining how this translates to prison gang involvement is more difficult. Some research suggests that 11.6 % of males and 3.7 % of female inmates first joined gangs while incarcerated (Knox 2005). This means that there is a small subset of prisoners who are not importing past-gang behaviors into the prison setting; rather, they are acquiring involvement over the course of their imprisonment. The reasons behind these behaviors remain unclear. Decker and Van Winkle (1996) indicate that street gang members often cite protection as a reason for joining gangs, despite the increased risk for victimization associated with gang involvement (Melde et al. 2009). Prison life may operate similarly. In other words, fear of victimization in the prison environment may encourage individuals to seek out prison gangs as a form of protection. Some research supports this perspective. For instance, Lindegaard and Gear's (2014) ethnographic account of prisoners in South Africa reveals that joining gangs may be an adaptation to avoid victimization in oppressive prison settings. Specifically, prisoners reported joining gangs as a way to lessen themselves as targets for victimization. Furthermore, the decision to join a prison gang was linked to feeling a sense of control over ones' life. These themes are echoed in Ireland and Power's (2013) work, which focused on how a sample of Canadian prisoners crafted their opinions about prison gangs as well as their decision to join. The researchers find that despite the fact that prison gang affiliation or support was associated with higher rates of victimization, many individuals supported prison gangs on the basis that they functioned to provide safety to their members.

Extant research has demonstrated that the impetus for joining the gang varies greatly both for youths on the street and those that become incarcerated. Following the form of prior literature, this section has organized these motivations as "pushes" and "pulls" that may induce gang involvement. These reasons for involvement have been better understood in the context of street gang involvement, yet, prison gangs have received less attention regarding why individuals choose to join them. Furthermore, prison gang involvement may be derived directly from street gang experiences, meaning that there may not have been a discrete choice to join the gang upon incarceration. Rather, street gang involvement is simply extended once imprisoned. Because clear motivations remain ambiguous, there is a need for qualitative examination of those who end up as prison gang members. This study offers first-hand narratives of these individuals.

11.4 Current Study

The data for this study come from one-time, in-depth interviews with 17 male gang members who were serving time on parole in the Eastern District of Missouri in June of 2012. Members of the sample were recruited from a specialized caseload of gang members. Interviews occurred in private offices at each location and lasted 90 min on average.[1] We used a semi-structured interview guide modeled after prior research of this type (see Visher et al. 2004). The interview guide covered a range of topics including prison life and re-entry, housing, employment, gang involvement, and mental health.

The sample was predominantly men of color who self-identified histories of gang membership. In total, most sample members identified as African American men ($n=15$), and the average age of the sample was 27. Sample members averaged 7 months in the community at the time of the interview and had spent an average of 82 months in prison before parole. They predominately served time for gun-related or drug crimes, and all members of the sample indicated that they carried a gun prior to incarceration. At the time of the interview, 35 % ($n=6$) were employed and 47 % ($n=8$) had completed their GED or graduated high school. All but one of the men in the sample had dependent children, and 82 % ($n=14$) had histories of serious drug abuse.

All sample participants self-identified as a gang member at some point in their life, and 23 % ($n=4$) indicated that they were a member of the gang at the time of the interview. An additional 23 % indicated that they still maintained contact with the gang after prison even though they did not describe themselves as an active member. Finally, 46 % ($n=8$) of the sample indicated that they were active in prison gangs. Individuals joined gangs at an early age, with 12.5 as the average age of gang joining. When describing their gang, one-third indicated that the gang had regular meetings, 62 % noted that the group had rules, and all reported that the gang had colors, symbols, signs, or clothes. This sample is different than many traditional youth gang samples as it includes older gang members who have more extensive criminal justice histories which include a relatively long stay in federal prison. The sample had low levels of educational attainment prior to prison and substantial histories of drug use and abuse. As DeLisi et al. (2011) note, inmates import criminal behaviors and gang embeddedness into prison; therefore, the results presented here are partially a function of both long-term criminal embeddedness and gang membership that occurred before imprisonment.

11.4.1 Analysis

Interview data were imported into the qualitative software program NVivo for coding and analysis (QSR International Software NVivo 10, 2012). NVivo allows for coding to be done electronically while corralling like themes and patterns into "nodes." The analysis followed a grounded theory approach, which allows for themes to emerge from within the data. Open coding involves reading the interview transcripts and identifying and assigning codes to actions, descriptions, or events that emerge organically (Charmaz 2006). After broad themes were outlined, a focused coding technique was used to further refine concepts and domains. After

[1] At the beginning of each interview, offenders were given information regarding the study, assured confidentiality of their responses, and signed a consent form. Interviews were digitally recorded, transcribed, and pseudonyms assigned to each offender. An incentive of $20 for offenders was provided.

the initial open and focused coding, memos of single themes, or multiple themes within a broader topic, were compiled and re-read to detail and refine the analysis by identifying additional subthemes or divergent cases. Data analysis also consisted of a constant comparative technique which involves comparing statements within and across interviews to demonstrate further patterns and themes.

11.5 Results

11.5.1 Joining the Gang

Members of the sample indicated that they had been involved in gang membership before going to prison. For most of the sample, gang membership was a way of life. Jayden describes that gang membership was a part of his early life, and he made the transition to the gang in adolescence. "You know, cause it's different from most cities, there's no you get jumped in the gang, nothing like that, it's mainly like how we grew up you know, we all went to school together, my brother hung out with his brother, and things like that, so we young so now we all hang around with each other, you know." Gang membership was common in his neighborhood, and it was a part of the adolescent experience.

Similarly, Ethan indicates that he joined the gang at the age of 14, but he watched friends and family in the gang at a young age and tried to imitate behaviors as he grew up, "by the time I was 14, I was full-fledged." At the age of 12, I was watching so the next couple years, it was basically like a "be like me thing." He indicates that even though some members of his family warned him against associating with delinquent peers, friends soon "pulled" him into gang membership:

> OK, you sit back and you're young and your grandma tell you "don't go hanging with those guys, they're bad" this and that. The same people they tell you is bad you sort of like you learn how to be—they kind of become your role models.

Many members of the sample felt that they were influenced by neighborhood characteristics. The dangerousness of the community pushed many sample members into seeking solace and perceived protection in the gang. When Josiah was asked to describe his community, he noted, "I guess like every other neighborhood in the city, gang-related. I mean I actually stay in my neighborhood so gang-related." He further explained, "gang-related meaning like, the neighborhood I grew up in, we all know each other. We don't pick no extra friends, we just deal with nothing but our neighborhood. We got a big neighborhood so it's a lot of us." Gang membership isolated the members of the sample from others, but most indicated they felt safer in the confines of the gang.

The respondents, overall, took similar pathways into gangs and these pathways vary little from most modern street gang research. Although it is not clear from the data why these individuals continued to stay in the gang for a longer period than most, the group reported importing many of the behaviors from the street into prison.

11.5.2 Gang Membership Inside Prison

Consistent with research of this type (Fong 1990; Pyrooz et al. 2011), members of the sample indicated that the prison gang experience varied significantly from the structure of the street gangs. Like life in the community, prison gang members felt that they were more likely to be protected within the gang, yet many reported being physically assaulted in prison. Respondents indicated that violence was a way of life in the prison gang. When asked how they became accepted members of the prison gang, Caleb indicated that:

> When it's time to put in work, you gone put in work whether it's fighting. Whether it's stabbing or whatever the situation may be. You gone put in work or you gone get off the yard. That's how the gangs work versus the streets.

He explains further the difference between street and prison gangs. In street gangs, "see everybody ain't called to put in work on the streets. Only selective ones that they known to put in work. Everybody be used for different purposes but they can still be gang members." This narrative validates extant research that suggests that prison gangs require more violence and loyalty than typical street gangs (Decker and Pyrooz 2015; Pyrooz et al. 2011). Dean expresses similar sentiments:

> If you ain't violent, you gone have to get violent basically 'cause that's the atmosphere of jail versus the streets. Or if you ain't violent and you got money, you gone have to be productive and produce for the cause of the gang. If he ain't got it and you got it, you gone have to make sure he straight. That's part of being a brother.

The gang member narratives also reflect the deprivation of security that has been a common narrative in prison literature overall (Sykes 1958). At the same time, some respondents did provide examples to illustrate the organizing role of the prison gang. For example, gang members helped fellow inmates when they entered prison. Ben describes the ritual of providing goods from the canteen for new inmates that did not have the means to participate in commissary.

> Every month, all[members of the gang] got to bring something to put in this bag 'cause there might be another Crip that comes off this bus that don't got nothing 'cause everybody ain't selling drugs…you got to take care of your brother. You got to make sure he got shower shoes, radios, jogging suits, tennis shoes, food to eat. He might not have no money to call his family. So every month, everybody got to pay, even the shot caller. I had to put things in, as we call it, the box. I had to do it.

The sample included individuals who were released from federal prison, but most of the sample had done time in state prison as well. As such, the sample members recalled a different structure of gang membership in federal prison. Gang members associated with individuals of the same race, city, and community gang affiliation—even if they were not initially tied with that gang when in the community. For example, although Alex was a Crip in St. Louis, he indicated he did not affiliate with other Crips in prison. He notes, "I was in the St. Louis car," and people from the same area and race stay together. Respondents felt that associating with people from the same race and geographic region helped them adapt to prison life and brought a piece of home to the institution. Ruben described, "it help pass the time being around guys that come from the same thing you come from."

The respondents frequently mentioned the "politics" of life in federal prison. Respondents felt that there was more friction in the federal prison because individuals were less likely to have other people to vouch for them, and individuals found it difficult to find associates and linkages in the prison community because of the diverse population. Gabriel describes:

> Mexican gangs, black gangs, white gangs. It's more politics in the Feds as far as being a gang member than it is in the state. See in the state you around people that you know versus you around people from different states that's saying they this and they represent what they represent, different from the way you representing so it's like it's friction there.

At the same time, some respondents felt that prison gangs were more organized than on the street, and the politics of the prison were important for maintaining homeostasis in a very charged environment where violence was always near the surface. Marc describes his conception of politics in the prison gang structure:

> You know politics, like you know what I'm saying it's like you have to, it's say for instance, like this person over here you can't just go off and start fighting, because then it start a whole war with his people and your people, so you have to tell somebody you know, "I need you to go holler to head off his call so we go and get this off our chest," so it was mainly you can't do what you want to do, and that's what I had a problem with, I wanna do what I wanna do you know?

Marc wanted to solve problems as he had on the street, but he felt constrained by the gang organization in prison. The gang leaders instead tried to work out conflicts as to prevent further violence in the prison.

Gang leadership was particularly important when parolees described recreation and yard time. Older members of the gang ran the yard because they had the most experience and knew the rules of doing time. Yard leaders also provided intelligence on new members of the gang and provided initiation into the rules and mores of gang life. Milton explains:

> So whoever been there gone be like the voice, the spokesman for that yard, whoever been there the longest that knew that yard. As far as the administration. As far as the inmates. You gone get the whole script on everything. Oh he super calm or he such and such or she be doing this. You gone get the whole script 'cause he been there for some years to study the yard.

The narratives provide an introduction into the dualities of prison gang life. Although all sample members reported gang violence in prison, and many suggested it was more prevalent than gang-involved street crime, most indicated that the prison gang provided an organizing structure to everyday life.

11.6 Summary

The goal of the current study was to describe the pathways to gang membership and the experiences in the institution among a sample of inmates who had completed a term of incarceration in a federal institution and paroled to St. Louis. Given recent trends in incarceration, the study of prison gangs remains centrally important for theory and practice. Current estimates by the National Gang Intelligence Center suggest that approximately 230,000 gang members are incarcerated in federal and state prisons throughout the United States (National Gang Intelligence Center 2011), translating to 15 % of American prisoners (Glaze 2011). Recent scholarship using self-report data from institutional samples suggests that approximately 6–20 % of all inmates are involved in a prison gang (Huebner 2003; Olson et al. 2004). The numbers vary widely given the lack of agreement on a measure of prison gang membership, but the results suggest that a focus on this institution subpopulation is prudent.

Several findings deserve note. Gang members in the current study followed similar pathways to gang membership as those reported in street gang scholarship. Gang members felt the pull of gang life through the excitement of peers and the need for money and goods, and violence in the neighborhood also drew men into gangs looking for protection. Although it is beyond the scope of this research, it is important to understand how the pathways into gang membership may influence some gang members to continue to stay involved with violence and eventually become imprisoned while others desist. In particular, it is important to study the individual, group, and community processes that underlie desistance from gangs and criminality (McGloin 2007). There is evidence that gang leaving is a process, and that many youth leave gangs because they become disillusioned with the general environment or experienced a negative event (Decker and Lauritsen 2002; Carson et al. 2014; Sweeten et al. 2013). Even less is known about how and if gang leaving is linked to desistance from crime given that group embeddedness and leaving is a complex process (Pyrooz et al. 2013).

The research also suggests that gangs are central to understanding behaviors within the prison environment. As noted, many street gang members imported criminal connections from the street into prison. Similarly, most members of the current sample indicated that they felt the need to join a gang in prison for protection; yet, violence was a hallmark of prison life among this group, more so than in the community. The results from the current research comports with scholarship that has found that prison gangs have been associated with higher rates of institutional violence when compared with non-gang inmates. The violence and tension associated with gang membership can undermine correctional policies and authority, support criminogenic values that hamper rehabilitative efforts, and encourage criminal enterprises (Winterdyk and Ruddell 2010).

Overall, the current work highlights the utility of studying the pathways into prison gangs and the gang-offender experience once in prison. Given the small sample of federal inmates, it is not possible to generalize this research to the larger prison gang population. Future research is needed to examine the relationship between street and prison gangs and the degree to which street gangs influence prison gangs and prison gangs influence street gangs. As important is a better understanding of how and why individuals desist from gangs and crime while in prison and the community. There is a broad body of work that has documented the risk factors associated with gang joining (see Decker et al. 2013), but the next phase of research should continue to explore the process of leaving gangs.

References

Agnew, R. (1992). Foundation for a general strain theory of crime and delinquency. *Criminology, 31*(1), 47–88.

Campbell, A. (1984). *The girls in the gangs*. Oxford, England: Blackwell.

Carson, D. C., Peterson, D., & Esbensen, F.-A. (2014). Youth gang desistance: An examination of the effect of different operational definitions of desistance on the motivations, methods, and consequences associated with leaving the gang. *Criminal Justice Review, 38*(4), 510–534.

Charmaz, K. (2006). *Constructing grounded theory: A practical guide through qualitative analysis*. Thousand Oaks, CA: Sage.

Clemmer, D. (1940). *The prison community*. Boston, MA: Christopher Publishing House.

Cohen, A. K. (1955). *Delinquent boys: The culture of the gang*. New York: Free Press.

Decker, S. H., & Curry, G. D. (2000). Addressing key features of gang membership. Measuring the involvement of young members. *Journal of Criminal Justice, 28*(6), 473–482.

Decker, S., & Lauritsen, J. L. (2002). Leaving the gang. In C. R. Huff (Ed.), *Gangs in America* (pp. 51–67). Thousand Oaks, CA: Sage.

Decker, S. H., Melde, C., & Pyrooz, D. C. (2013). What do we know about gangs and gang members and where do we go from here. *Justice Quarterly, 30*(3), 369–402.

Decker, S. H., & Pyrooz, D. C. (2015). The real gangbanging is in prison. In J. Wooldredge & P. Smith (Eds.), *Oxford handbook on prisons and imprisonments*. New York: Oxford University Press.

Decker, S. H., & Van Winkle, B. (1996). *Life in the gang: Family, friends, and violence*. New York: Cambridge University Press.

DeLisi, M., Trulson, C. R., Marquart, J. W., Drury, A. J., & Kosloski, A. E. (2011). Inside the prison black box: Toward a life course importation model of inmate behavior. *International Journal of Offender Therapy and Comparative Criminology, 55*(8), 1186–1207.

Esbensen, F.-A., Huizinga, D., & Weiher, A. (1993). Gang and non-gang youth: Differences in explanatory factors. *Journal of Contemporary Criminal Justice, 9*(2), 94–116.

Esbensen, F.-A., Peterson, D., Taylor, T. J., & Freng, A. (2009). Similarities and differences in risk factors for violent offending and gang membership. *Australian and New Zealand Journal of Criminology, 42*(3), 310–335.

Esbensen, F.-A., & Winfree, T. L., Jr. (2013). Motivations for gang joining: Does context matter? In K. Boers, T. Feltes, J. Kinzig, L. W. Sherman, F. Streng, & G. Trueg (Eds.), *Criminology, crime policy, and penal law: Festschrift for Hans-Juergen Kerner on the occasion of his 70th birthday* (pp. 70–90). Tuebingen, Germany: Mohr Publishing.

Felson, M. (2006). *Crime and nature*. Thousand Oaks, CA: Sage.

Fleisher, M. S., & Decker, S. H. (2001). An overview of the challenge of prison gangs. *Corrections Management Quarterly, 5*(1), 1–9.

Fong, R. S. (1990). The organizational-structure of prison gangs: A Texas case-study. *Federal Probation, 54*(1), 36–43.

Gaes, G. G., Wallace, S., Gilman, E., Kelin-Saffran, J., & Suppa, S. (2002). The influence of prison gang affiliation on violence and other prison misconduct. *The Prison Journal, 82*(3), 359–385.

Glaze, L. E. (2011). *Correctional populations in the United States, 2010*. Washington, DC: US Department of Justice, Office of Justice Programs, Bureau of Justice Statistics.

Huebner, B. M. (2003). Administrative determinants of inmate violence: A multilevel analysis. *Journal of Criminal Justice, 31*(2), 107–117.

Ireland, J. L., & Power, C. L. (2013). Propensity to support prison gangs: Its relationship to gang membership, victimization, aggression, and other disruptive behaviours. *Psychology, Crime, and Law, 19*(9), 801–816.

Irwin, J. (1980). *Prisons in Turmoil*. Boston, MA: Little, Brown.

Jacobs, J. B. (1974). Street gangs behind bars. *Social Problems, 21*(3), 395–409.

Jacobs, J. B. (1977). *Stateville: The penitentiary in mass society*. Chicago: University of Chicago Press.

Joe, K. A., & Chesney-Lind, M. (1995). "Just every mother's angel": An analysis of gender and ethnic variations in youth gang membership. *Gender & Society, 9*(4), 408–431.

Klein, M. W., & Maxson, C. L. (2006). *Street gang patterns and policies*. New York: Oxford University Press.
Knox, G. W. (2005). The problem of gangs and security threat groups (stg's) in American prisons today: Recent research findings from the 2004 prison gang survey. http://www.ngcrc.com/corr2006.html
Krohn, M. D., Schmidt, N. M., Lizotte, A. J., & Baldwin, J. M. (2011). The impact of multiple marginality on gang membership and delinquent behavior for Hispanic, African American, and white male adolescents. *Journal of Contemporary Criminal Justice, 27*(1), 18–42.
LeBlanc, M., & Lanctôt, N. (1998). Social and psychological characteristics of gang members according to gang structure and its subcultural and ethnic makeup. *Journal of Gang Research, 5*(3), 15–28.
Lindegaard, M. R., & Gear, S. (2014). Violence makes safe in South African prisons: Prison gangs, violent acts, and victimization among inmates. *Focaal, 2014*(68), 35–54.
Matsueda, R. L., & Heimer, K. (2004). A symbolic interactionist theory of role-transitions, role-commitments, and delinquency. In T. P. Thornberry (Ed.), *Developmental theories of crime and delinquency* (Vol. 7, pp. 163–214). New Brunswick, NJ: Transaction.
Maxson, C. L. (2012). Betwixt and between street and prison gangs: Defining gangs and structures in youth correctional facilities. In F. A. Esbensen & C. Maxson (Eds.), *Youth gangs in international perspective: Results from the Eurogang Program of Research*. New York: Springer.
McGloin, J. M. (2007). The continued relevance of gang membership. *Criminology and Public Policy, 6*(2), 231–240.
Mears, D. P., Stewart, E. A., Siennick, S. E., & Simons, R. L. (2013). The code of the street and inmate violence: Investigating the salience of imported belief systems. *Criminology, 51*(3), 695–728.
Melde, C., Taylor, T. J., & Esbensen, F.-A. (2009). "I got your back": An examination of the protective function of gang membership in adolescence. *Criminology, 47*(2), 565–594.
Mendoza, R. (2005). *Mexican mafia: From alter boy to hitman*. Corona, CA: Ken Whitley and Associates.
Miller, J. (2001). *One of the guys: Girls, gangs, and gender*. New York: Oxford University Press.
Moore, J. (1991). *Going down to the barrio: Homeboys and homegirls in change*. Philadelphia: Temple University Press.
National Gang Intelligence Center. (2011). *2011 National Gang Threat Assessment: Emerging Trends*. Washington, DC: NGIC. Retrieved February 8, 2015, from http://www.fbi.gov/stats-services/publications/2011-national-gang-threat-assessment/2011-national-gang-threat-assessment--emerging-trends
O'Brien, K., Daffern, M., Chu, C. M., & Thomas, S. D. M. (2013). Youth gang affiliation, violence, and criminal activities: A review of motivational, risk, and protective factors. *Aggression and Violent Behavior, 18*(4), 417–425.
Olson, D. E., Dooley, B., & Kane, C. M. (2004). *The relationship between gang membership and inmate recidivism*. Chicago, IL: Illinois Criminal Justice Information Authority.
Paulus, P. (1988). *Prisons crowding: A psychological perspective*. New York: Springer.
Pyrooz, D. C., & Decker, S. H. (2011). Motives and methods for leaving the gang: Understanding the process of gang desistance. *Journal of Criminal Justice, 39*(5), 417–425.
Pyrooz, D. C., Decker, S. H., & Fleisher, M. (2011). From the street to the prison, from the prison to the street: Understanding and responding to prison gangs. *Journal of Aggression, Conflict and Peace Research, 3*(1), 12–24.
Pyrooz, D. C., Sweeten, G., & Piquero, A. R. (2013). Continuity and change in gang membership and gang embeddedness. *Journal of Research in Crime and Delinquency, 50*(2), 239–271.
QSR International Pty Ltd. (2012). NVivo qualitative data analysis software, Version 10.
Reisig, M. D. (2002). Administrative control and inmate homicide. *Homicide Studies, 6*(1), 84–103.
Scott, D. W. (2014). Attitude is everything: Youth attitudes, gang involvement, and length of institutional gang membership. *Group Processes and Intergroup Relations, 17*(6), 780–798.
Simmel, G. (1955). *Conflict and the web of group affiliations*. New York: Free Press.
Skarbek, D. (2014). *The social order of the underworld: How prison gangs govern the American penal system*. New York: Oxford University Press.
Spergel, I. A. (1990). *Gang organization and migration: Drugs, gangs and law enforcement*. Sacramento, CA: Office of the Attorney General.

Sweeten, G., Pyrooz, D. C., & Piquero, A. R. (2013). Disengaging from gangs and desistance from crime. *Justice Quarterly, 30*(3), 469–500.

Sykes, G. (1958). *The society of captives: A study of maximum security prison*. Princeton, NJ: Princeton University Press.

Taylor, C. S. (1990). *Dangerous society*. East Lansing: Michigan State University Press.

Thornberry, T. P., Krohn, M. D., Lizotte, A. J., Smith, C. A., & Tobin, K. (2003). *Gangs and delinquency in developmental perspective*. New York: Cambridge University Press.

Thornberry, T. P., Krohn, M. D., Lizotte, A. J., & Chard-Wierschem, D. (1993). The role of juvenile gangs in facilitating delinquent behavior. *Journal of Research in Crime and Delinquency, 30*(1), 55–87.

Varese, F. (2005). *The Russian mafia: Private protection in a new market economy*. New York: Oxford University Press.

Vigil, J. D. (1988). *Barrio gangs*. Austin: University of Texas Press.

Visher, C. A., LaVigne, N. G., & Travis, J. (2004). *Returning home: Understanding the challenges of prisoner reentry, Maryland pilot study: Findings from Baltimore*. Washington, DC: Urban Institute, Justice Policy Center.

Winterdyk, J., & Ruddell, R. (2010). Managing prison gangs: Results from a survey of US prison systems. *Journal of Criminal Justice, 38*(4), 730–736.

Wolff, N., Shi, J., & Siegel, J. (2009). Understanding physical victimization inside prisons: Factors that predict risk. *Justice Quarterly, 26*(3), 445–475.

Wood, J. L., Alleyne, E., Mozova, K., & James, M. (2014). Predicting involvement in prison gang activity: Street gang membership, social and psychological factors. *Law and Human Behavior, 38*(3), 203–211.

Wooldredge, J. (1998). Inmate lifestyles and opportunities for victimization. *Journal of Research in Crime and Delinquency, 35*(4), 480–502.

Zatz, M. S., & Portillos, E. L. (2000). Voices from the barrio: Chicano/a gangs, families, and communities. *Criminology, 38*(2), 369–401.

Part III
Fostering Gang Transition and Transformation: Strategies for Prevention and Intervention

Chapter 12
A Brief Review and Meta-Analysis of Gang Intervention Trials in North America

Stanley J. Huey Jr., Gabrielle Lewine, and Miriam Rubenson

12.1 Introduction

After more than 50 years of gang intervention research, the field remains divided regarding best practices for reducing gang membership and gang-related crime in high-risk populations. For example, in their review of the literature a decade ago, Klein and Maxson (2006) argued that results were indeterminate concerning gang prevention and intervention effects because most programs were unevaluated or poorly evaluated. By contrast, Howell (2007, 2010) argued that this view was too pessimistic, and noted that a number of promising and effective gang-related prevention and intervention programs do exist.

Fortunately, controlled outcome research has increased in recent years (e.g., Wong et al. 2012), which allows for the use of robust data synthesis methods to discern whether gang interventions are effective. In this chapter, we address three primary questions regarding gang-related intervention programs. First, what are key characteristics of controlled evaluations of gang interventions? Second, are interventions generally effective at preventing and reducing gang involvement and antisocial behavior? Third, what challenges arise in efforts to synthesize this literature?

S.J. Huey Jr. (✉) • G. Lewine • M. Rubenson
Department of Psychology, University of Southern California, Los Angeles, CA, USA
e-mail: hueyjr@usc.edu

C.L. Maxson, F.-A. Esbensen (eds.), *Gang Transitions and Transformations in an International Context*, DOI 10.1007/978-3-319-29602-9_12

12.2 Method

12.2.1 Literature Search

As an initial step, we conducted an electronic literature search using the following databases: ERIC, Library and Information Science Abstracts (LISA), ProQuest Dissertations and Theses, ProQuest Research Library, PsycArticles, PsycCritiques, PsycInfo, Social Services Abstracts, and Sociological Abstracts (years 1950 through June 2014). Terms representing gangs (e.g., *gang, gangs*), intervention (e.g., *intervention, treatment, prevention*), and controlled evaluation (e.g., *control, controlled, random*) were utilized. This search yielded 219 studies, and the titles and abstracts were screened for eligibility.

The electronic search was supplemented with reference lists from gang-focused meta-analyses and reviews (e.g., Esbensen 2000; Wong et al. 2012), as well as unpublished, *in press*, and published studies recommended by gang researchers.

12.2.2 Inclusion Criteria

In this chapter, we include a brief descriptive review (i.e., a summary of study characteristics and treatment effects) and meta-analysis (i.e., a quantitative summary of effect sizes). Studies were eligible if they included predominantly gang-affiliated individuals, focused on the prevention or reduction of gang involvement, assessed gang-related outcomes, or included gang affiliation as a predictor or moderator of intervention outcomes. Moreover, studies had to: (1) include a control or comparison group; (2) assess gang-related or antisocial behavior as intervention outcomes; (3) report posttreatment or follow-up outcomes for individual participants; and (4) be published or written in English. Finally, for the meta-analysis, studies were eligible only when they included data necessary to calculate effect sizes (e.g., outcome means and standard deviations, or proportions). Excluded were intervention studies that included no control/comparison conditions, made no reference to the gang involvement of participants, or only included outcomes at the neighborhood or community level. Overall, 38 controlled evaluations described in 36 papers met criteria for our descriptive review; of these, only 26 evaluations met criteria for our meta-analytic review.

12.2.3 Coding of Studies

For descriptive purposes, the following variables were coded for each study: predominant age level of participants (children, adolescents, or adults), predominant gender, predominant ethnicity (Black, Hispanic/Latino, White, Indigenous, minority, or not reported), country of origin (US vs. other), publication status (published vs. unpublished), whether the study was primarily prevention-oriented or treatment-oriented (i.e., focused more on prevention or rather remediating antisocial behavior and/or gang involvement), and study design (retrospective quasi-experimental, prospective quasi-experimental, or randomized trial).

12.2.4 Effect Size Estimation

The effect size statistic represents the standardized difference in outcomes between a treatment and comparison group at posttreatment or follow-up. For continuous variables, comparisons were calculated using the standardized mean difference statistic (d), with the pooled standard deviation as the denominator. For dichotomous variables (e.g., arrest or gang membership status), the log odds ratio was calculated then converted to d to create a common effect size index. A positive effect size indicates that the intervention is more beneficial than control, whereas a negative effect size indicates that control is more beneficial.

To avoid violating assumptions of statistical independence, only one effect size per study was included in any particular analysis (Lipsey and Wilson 2001). When multiple indices measured a particular outcome within a study (which occurred in the majority of studies), similar constructs were averaged to form a single effect size coefficient (e.g., if number of juvenile offenses and arrest rate were both recorded within a study, these were averaged to form a composite "antisocial behavior" effect size). To avoid problems related to combining conceptually distinct constructs (Borenstein et al. 2009), we presented outcomes separately for antisocial behavior and gang involvement.

12.2.5 Analysis

Because studies varied in terms of participant demographics, intervention characteristics, and setting features, heterogeneity of effects was expected. A random effects model was chosen for effect size analysis since this approach assumes that true effects vary systematically across studies (Borenstein et al. 2009).

The Q statistic (Hedges and Olkin 1985) was calculated to test for homogeneity of effects across studies. A significant Q statistic indicates a heterogeneous distribution and suggests that study characteristics, rather than sampling error, explain differences between studies. However, given that Q may be poor at detecting true heterogeneity when sample sizes are small, the I^2 index was also reported (Borenstein et al. 2009; Higgins et al. 2003). I^2 is the percentage of total variation across studies due to heterogeneity (versus chance), and is considered an index of *inconsistency* across study results. According to Higgins et al. (2003), an I^2 value of 25 % represents low heterogeneity, 50 % moderate heterogeneity, and 75 % high heterogeneity.

12.3 Characteristics of the Studies

The 38 controlled gang-focused evaluations included in this review are briefly summarized in Table 12.1. Thirty-four percent were randomized trials, 40 % prospective quasi-experimental, and 26 % retrospective quasi-experimental. Forty percent of the evaluations were reported in published journal articles, while 8 % were included in chapters or books, 8 % in unpublished dissertations, and 45 % in reports (published or unpublished). Thirty-seven percent were prevention-oriented trials whereas 63 % were treatment-oriented.

More than half of the studies included predominantly adolescents (58 %), 29 % children under 13, and 13 % adults. Males were the majority in most studies (84 %), females predominated in 8 %, males and females were equally represented in 5 %, and 3 % did not report gender. Hispanics were the majority in 26 % of studies, African Americans in 21 %, indigenous groups in 8 %, Whites/Caucasians in 13 %, and diverse or unspecified ethnic minorities in 26 %; 5 % of studies did not indicate the ethnicity of participants. Most studies were conducted in the United States (92 %), with the remainder based in Canada. Thus, despite evidence that European gang involvement has pernicious effects on antisocial behavior (Klein et al. 2006), as yet no gang intervention evaluations have emerged from Europe.

12.4 Results

Two methods were utilized to determine whether gang interventions are effective overall. First, we used a "vote counting" approach (Borenstein et al. 2009) by simply summing the number of controlled gang evaluations that reported *any* significant positive effects and comparing this with the number reporting nonsignificant effects. Figure 12.1 shows the proportion of studies reporting positive or null effects for our two target outcomes. Approximately 42 % of studies reported positive effects for antisocial behavior, whereas a somewhat larger percentage (45 %) reported null or *negative* effects; the remainder did not assess antisocial behavior. For gang-related outcomes, only 21 % reported positive effects whereas 42 % reported null effects; 37 % did not assess gang-related outcomes.

Figure 12.2 presents results only from the 19 studies that evaluated both antisocial behavior and gang outcomes. This figure shows that 21 % of studies found significant, positive effects for *both* outcomes. Approximately 32 % of studies found positive effects for antisocial behavior but not gang outcomes, whereas 10 % reported positive effects for gang outcomes but not antisocial behavior. The largest block of trials (37 %) showed significant effects for neither outcome.

However, this vote counting approach has several limitations (Borenstein et al. 2009). First, many studies in this review had fairly small sample sizes (e.g., under 50 per condition), with low power to detect significant intervention effects. For this reason, the large number of "null effect" studies may partly result from the prevalence of underpowered studies. Second, vote counting approaches allow small

Table 12.1 Summary of controlled gang intervention trials

Study	Sample	Intervention	Intervention Effects
Abreton and McClahan (2005). Prevention site	589 Youth in gang communities. Mostly male, African American	Targeted gang prevention through Boy/Girls Club of America	*Antisocial*: No. *Gang*: No
Abreton and McClahan (2005). Intervention site	175 Predominantly "high-risk" teens. Mostly male, ethnic minorities	Targeted gang intervention through Boy/Girls Club of America	*Antisocial*: No. *Gang*: No
Agopian (1990)	158 Adult, gang offenders. Mostly male and Black	Intensive supervision probation	*Antisocial*: Yes, but negative. *Gang*: Not assessed
Braga et al. (2009)	417 Adult inmates. All male and mostly non-White	Boston Reentry Initiative Intervention	*Antisocial*: Yes. *Gang*: Not assessed
Cohen et al. (1995)	528 Youth (inclusion criteria unclear). Mostly male and minority	Youth gang drug prevention program	*Antisocial*: Not assessed. *Gang*: No
Di Placido et al. (2006)	160 Adult, gang and nongang incarcerated offenders. All male, mostly Canadian aboriginal	High intensity cognitive-behavioral program	*Antisocial*: Yes. *Gang*: Not assessed
Dole (2005)	20 Aggressive/violent high school students. ½ male, mostly minority	Balance program (a social skills intervention)	*Antisocial*: No. *Gang*: No
Esbensen and Osgood (1999) [GREAT study #1]	5935 eighth graders. ½ male and mostly ethnic minorities	Gang Resistance Education and Training (GREAT) life skills prevention	*Antisocial:* Yes, positive. *Gang:* No
Esbensen et al. (2001) [GREAT study #2]	3568 Seventh graders. Gender and ethnicity not reported	GREAT life skills prevention	*Antisocial:* Yes, positive. *Gang:* No
Esbensen et al. (2012), Esbensen et al. (2013) [GREAT study #3]	3820 Sixth and seventh grade students. ½ male and mostly ethnic minority	GREAT life skills gang prevention	*Antisocial*: No. *Gang*: Yes, positive
Garcia (2002)	26 High school reservation youth. All male and mostly Pima-Maricopa Indian	Values-based career intervention	*Antisocial*: Not assessed. *Gang*: No
Godley and Velasquez (1998)	1318 Elementary school students. ½ male and mostly ethnic minority	Logan Square school and community-based substance use and gang prevention	*Antisocial*: Not assessed. *Gang*: Yes, positive

(continued)

Table 12.1 (continued)

Study	Sample	Intervention	Intervention Effects
Gold and Mattick (1974)	515 Gang youth in high crime neighborhood. All male and predominantly Black	Chicago Youth Development Project's Boys Club	*Antisocial*: No (but no significance tests reported). *Gang*: Not assessed
Goldstein and Glick (1994)	55 Gang members from "youth care agencies." Age, gender, and ethnicity not reported	Aggression Replacement Training (ART)	*Antisocial*: Yes, positive. *Gang*: Not assessed
Harrell et al. (1999)	668 At-risk youth from "distressed" neighborhoods. Mostly male and Black	Children At Risk (CAR) delinquency and drug prevention program	*Antisocial*: Yes, positive. *Gang*: No
Huey Jr et al. (2014) [and McDaniel (2011)]	27 Adolescent gang offenders from probation camps. Mostly male and Latino	Behavioral Employment Program (BEP)	*Antisocial*: Yes, positive. *Gang*: No
Josi and Sechrest (1999)	230 Young CYA adults, primarily gang involved. Mostly male and minority	Lifeskills'95 parole reentry program	*Antisocial*: Yes, positive. *Gang*: Yes, positive
Miller (1962)	377 Gang-involved youth and young adults. Mostly white and male	Midcity Project "total community" intervention	*Antisocial*: No. *Gang*: Not assessed
Peters (1996), Mobile, AL	374 Nonviolent adjudicated teens. Mostly African American, all male	Environmental Youth Corps (EYC) military-style boot camp intervention	*Antisocial*: No. *Gang*: Not assessed
Reckless and Dinitz (1972)	1094 Seventh grade males rated as "possible" or "likely" to become delinquent and not finish school. Mostly White and involved in "gang fights"	Enhanced classroom curriculum with role-model supplement	*Antisocial*: No (but no significance tests reported). *Gang*: No (but no significance tests reported)
Rodriguez (1997)	36 Fifth grade "gang leaders." Mostly male and "Mexican"	Feeder-Stream Program focused on decision-making	*Antisocial*: Not assessed. *Gang*: Yes, positive
Schlossman and Sedlak (1983)	Juvenile parolees, mostly Polish. Sample size, age, and gender not reported	Chicago Area Project (CAP) intensive support intervention	*Antisocial*: Yes, positive (but no significance tests reported). *Gang*: Not assessed

(continued)

Table 12.1 (continued)

Study	Sample	Intervention	Intervention Effects
Spergel et al. (2003), Chicago, Little Village	493 Violent gang-involved adolescents and young adults. Mostly male and Latino	Comprehensive Community-Wide Approach to Gang Prevention, Intervention, and Suppression Program (i.e., Comprehensive Gang Program Model)	*Antisocial:* Yes, positive. *Gang:* Not assessed
Spergel et al. (2005a), Bloomington-Normal	180 Probation/school-referred adolescents and young adults. Mostly male, African American, and gang-involved	Comprehensive Gang Program Model	*Antisocial:* No. *Gang:* Yes, positive
Spergel et al. (2005b), Mesa	354 School and court-referred adolescents and young adults. Mostly male, Latino, and gang-involved	Comprehensive Gang Program Model	*Antisocial:* Yes, positive. *Gang:* No
Spergel et al. (2005c), Riverside	369 Adolescents, mostly gang members and affiliates. Mostly male and Mexican-American	Comprehensive Gang Program Model	*Antisocial:* Yes, positive as well as *negative*. *Gang:* No
Spergel et al. (2005d), San Antonio	230 Mostly adolescent, gang members. Mostly male and Mexican-American	Comprehensive Gang Program Model	*Antisocial:* No. *Gang:* No
Spergel et al. (2005e), Tucson	Mostly adolescent, gang members. Mostly male and Mexican-American	Comprehensive Gang Program Model	*Antisocial:* No. *Gang:* No.
Thompson and Jason (1988)	117 Eighth graders at risk for gang involvement. Mostly male, but ethnicity unclear	Broader Urban Involvement and Leadership Development (BUILD) anti-gang workshops	*Antisocial:* Not assessed. *Gang:* No
Totten and Dunn (2011)	128 Young adults, all current or past gang members or affiliates. Mostly male and Canadian aboriginal	Regina Anti-Gang Services (RAGS) intervention	*Antisocial:* Yes, positive. *Gang:* Yes, positive
Tremblay et al. (1996)	166 7-year olds showing disruptive behavior in school. All male and White French Canadian	Montreal Prevention Intervention	*Antisocial:* Yes, positive. *Gang:* Yes, positive

(continued)

Table 12.1 (continued)

Study	Sample	Intervention	Intervention Effects
Valdez et al. (2013)	200 Adolescents, all gang-affiliated and alcohol/drug users. Mostly male, all Mexican-American	Brief Strategic Family Therapy (BSFT)	*Antisocial:* Yes, positive. *Gang:* No
Wiebush et al. (2005), Denver	150 Incarcerated juvenile offenders. All male, mostly ethnic minorities	Intensive Aftercare Program (IAP)	*Antisocial:* Yes, but *negative.* *Gang:* Not assessed
Wiebush et al. (2005), Las Vegas	247 Incarcerated juvenile offenders, mostly gang members. All male, mostly ethnic minorities	IAP	*Antisocial:* Yes, but *negative.* *Gang:* Not assessed
Wiebush et al. (2005), Norfolk	118 Incarcerated juvenile offenders. All male, mostly African-American	Intensive Parole Program (IPP)	*Antisocial:* Yes, but *negative.* *Gang:* Not assessed
Williams et al. (2012)	122 Adolescents, all "pre-gang" or gang-involved. All female, mostly Latina	Movimiento Ascendencia intervention program	*Antisocial:* Yes, positive. *Gang:* Not assessed
Willman and Snortum (1982)	200 Adolescents and young adults, all gang members and chronic offenders. All male, mostly Hispanic	Police employment intervention	*Antisocial:* No. *Gang:* Not assessed
Wodarski et al. (1979)	60 Sixth and eighth grade students with social/academic problems. Mostly male and White	Preparation through Responsive Educational Program (PREP)	*Antisocial:* Yes, positive. *Gang:* Yes, positive

sample studies (e.g., $n=20$ for Dole 2005) to have the same weight as large sample studies (e.g., $n=5935$ for Esbensen and Osgood 1999), which effectively gives "low precision" results undue influence in narrative reviews (Borenstein et al. 2009). Third, given the way we operationalized "positive effects" (i.e., any significant effects favoring the intervention, in the absence of negative outcomes), those studies assessing only a few outcomes were disadvantaged over those assessing many outcomes. In other words, studies that included many outcome variables had more opportunities to show positive results than those with only a few. Fourth, vote counting approaches reveal nothing about the *magnitude* of intervention effects, and thus little can be said as yet about the clinical or social significance of gang-focused interventions.

To address these limitations, we next present results from our meta-analytic synthesis of the literature, with effect sizes derived from 26 studies. Random effects analysis showed that overall effects for antisocial behavior were small and nonsignificant, $d=.07$, $p=.20$. Effect sizes for antisocial behavior ranged from

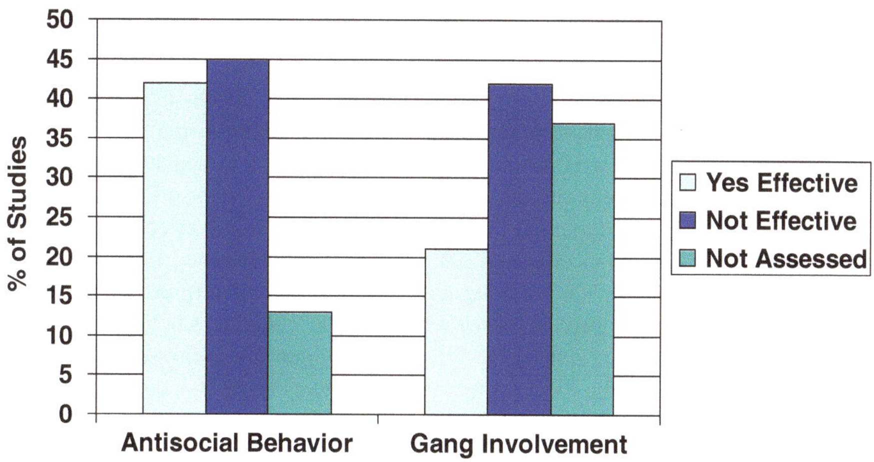

Fig. 12.1 Percentage of trials showing positive or null effects for antisocial behavior and/or gang involvement

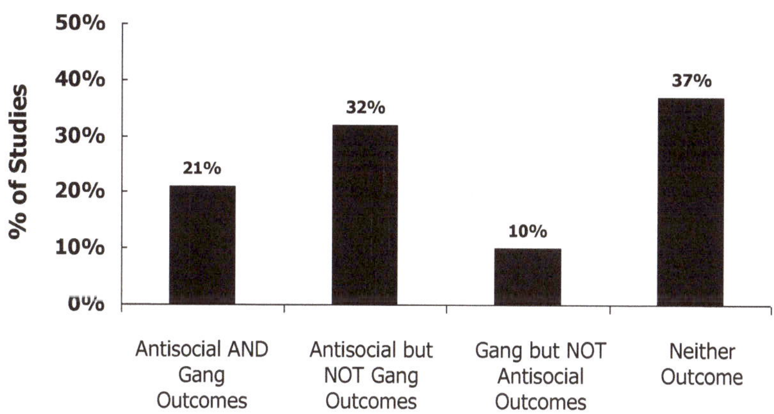

Fig. 12.2 Percentage of trials (out of 19) showing positive effects for antisocial behavior and/or gang outcomes

−.33 to 1.09 across studies, and subsequent analyses showed significant heterogeneity across studies, $Q(16)=29.67$, $p=.02$, $I^2=46.08\,\%$. Analyses for gang involvement showed statistically significant effects of small magnitude, $d=.29$, $p=.03$. Moreover, there was substantial heterogeneity among studies (ES range=−.29 to 1.95), $Q(15)=96.11$, $p=.00$, $I^2=84.39\,\%$, suggesting that additional factors could significantly moderate the effects of intervention on gang involvement. This possibility will be addressed in future studies.

12.5 Challenges and Limitations

The evidence thus far presents a mixed picture of the effects of gang-focused interventions on antisocial behavior and gang involvement. On the one hand, the majority of studies showed some efficacy in preventing/remediating antisocial behavior, gang involvement, or both (Table 12.1, Fig. 12.2). On the other hand, effect size coefficients indicated that these interventions had no overall effect on antisocial behavior, and only a small effect on gang involvement. However, methodological limitations in the current literature argue for caution when interpreting these findings. We briefly identify three of these methodological challenges below.

Gang involvement and antisocial behavior are often not assessed in the same study. Consistent with the "facilitation" perspective (Thornberry et al. 2003), an implicit assumption in the literature is that gang involvement is a causal contributor to problem behavior; thus interventions that reduce gang involvement should lead to decreases in antisocial behavior. However, because only half of the 38 studies assessed both antisocial behavior and gang involvement as intervention outcomes (Fig. 12.2), a test of this mediating process was not possible in many studies.

The omission of gang-related data is perhaps the most significant challenge in this literature. Many studies assessed gang involvement at baseline to identify those with gang ties, but did not conduct follow-up evaluations to determine how intervention actually affected gang affiliation (e.g., Di Placido et al. 2006; Wiebush et al. 2005). Curiously, a handful of interventions that were clearly identified as gang prevention or remediation programs nonetheless failed to examine gang outcomes (e.g., Williams et al. 2012; Willman and Snortum 1982). For example, Willman and Snortum (1982) evaluated an employment program for 200 predominantly Hispanic gang members, with experimental youth compared to a matched control group. Although the authors theorized that their employment intervention might work by reducing gang cohesiveness, they were unable to test this hypothesis because gang outcomes were not assessed at posttreatment. Indeed, none of the studies included in this review evaluated whether changes in gang involvement were functionally linked to reductions in antisocial behavior.

There is little uniformity in the assessment of gang involvement. Beyond the question of *whether* gang involvement is assessed are concerns about the lack of consistency across studies or investigators in *how* gang involvement is measured. In the selected studies, gang involvement was derived from one of three sources: (1) archived gang membership databases operated by law enforcement, schools, or other agencies, (2) police-defined gang arrests, or (3) participant self-report. By far, the most common approach was self-report, which characterized 88 % of studies that included gang outcomes. Yet, even among self-report studies, there was enormous diversity in gang assessment, with measures ranging from standardized gang involvement scales, to idiosyncratic gang items (e.g., "are you currently a member of a gang?" "are you now in a gang?"), to unspecified gang items. Indeed, measurement variation was so great that in no instance did we find overlap across investigators in how gang involvement was measured.

This lack of measurement consistency is a concern primarily because comparing across studies is difficult given that meanings of gang involvement can vary dramatically depending on methodology (Esbensen et al. 2001). Indeed, in one of the few studies to use multiple measures, Huey Jr et al. (2014) showed differential outcomes depending on the measure utilized. Based on results from a small pilot trial, they found that gang youth randomized to the Behavioral Employment Program (BEP) showed marginally significant reductions in gang membership (based on the Gang Membership Inventory) compared to controls, but no treatment effects were found for two other indices of gang involvement (Huey Jr et al. 2014).

Effect size data is often missing. A final concern is that many studies did not provide sufficient data for effect size estimation. In most meta-analyses, effect size statistics are estimated using post-intervention proportions (e.g., % arrested; % who are gang members) or means and standard deviations (e.g., average "gang behavior" rating; average self-report of delinquent behavior). Unfortunately, only 82 % of the studies in this review included data necessary to determine effect size; moreover, 45 % of these studies were missing effect size data for some variables but not for others. Given that the majority of studies (55 %) were missing effect size data for at least some key variables, the preliminary findings reported here should be interpreted with caution. For papers published or completed within the past 10 years, we are currently contacting authors to request data necessary for complete effect size estimation.

12.6 Model Gang Intervention Evaluations

Despite the challenges noted above, we did identify several research programs that should serve as models for how to conduct gang intervention evaluation. Below we briefly summarize findings from three of these programs. Although the design features of these studies were quite good, notably the intervention effects across each program were mixed.

GREAT. The Gang Resistance Education and Training (GREAT) program stands out from other gang intervention programs for several reasons. First, it was tested in three evaluations of increasing rigor by Esbensen and colleagues (Esbensen and Osgood 1999; Esbensen et al. 2001, 2012, 2013). Second, GREAT was substantially adapted in successive trials to respond to unfavorable findings from earlier studies (e.g., no treatment effects for gang membership), as well as critiques concerning the theoretical underpinnings of the original program (e.g., GREAT was modeled after DARE, a failed drug prevention program; Esbensen et al. 2013). Third, gang involvement and antisocial behavior were measured identically for each study, allowing for comparison of outcome effects across trials.

The original GREAT consisted of 9 weekly lessons taught to seventh grade students by uniformed law enforcement officials. The lessons contained didactic components (e.g., learning about crime and its effects on victims) and skills-focused instruction (e.g., role play of conflict resolution strategies) designed to equip students with the skills to resist peer pressure to join a gang. The first evaluation by Esbensen and Osgood (1999) was quasi-experimental and cross-sectional, and examined posttreatment outcomes for almost 6000 students in 42 schools over 11 cities. This evaluation yielded positive treatment effects for 16 of 33 outcomes, including drug use and minor offenses; notably, there were no significant effects for gang membership.[1]

The second evaluation of GREAT (Esbensen et al. 2001) was also quasi-experimental, but improved upon the first by using a longitudinal design. The sample included over 3500 sixth and seventh grade students in 22 schools located in six cities across the United States, and outcomes were assessed repeatedly over 4 years. Comparisons between the treatment group and control group yielded positive treatment effects for five of 32 outcomes. An analysis of program effects over the posttreatment period yielded positive trends for program participants compared to controls for four of 32 outcomes, including person-related self-reported delinquency and property-related self-reported delinquency. However, no significant program effects were observed for gang membership.

Given the program limitations revealed in these evaluations, GREAT was revised and modeled after two well-regarded and effective school-based prevention programs (Life Skills Training and the Seattle Social Development Model). Moreover, the curriculum was updated to reflect a renewed focus on risk factors that research had demonstrated to be important for gang affiliation. Evaluation of the revised GREAT program (Esbensen et al. 2013) utilized a randomized controlled trial (classrooms were randomized to GREAT or control) with a sample of almost 4000 youth in 31 schools across seven US cities. At 1-year follow-up, 12 of 33 outcomes showed significant treatment effects, including association with delinquent peers and gang membership. At 4-year follow-up, 10 of 33 outcomes showed significant treatment effects, including gang membership.

Although significant intervention effects were found in each of the GREAT evaluations, effect sizes were consistently small in magnitude. Thus, the effectiveness of GREAT as a clinically meaningful approach to preventing gang involvement and antisocial behavior is debatable. However, because the replications and design improvements across trials are unusual in the gang intervention literature, this series of studies deserves special attention as a model for gang intervention design and evaluation.

The Spergel Comprehensive Model. Spergel's Comprehensive Community-wide Gang Program Model is perhaps the most cited example of effective, community-based gang intervention in the United States. Controlled evaluations were conducted at six sites across the United States between 1992 and 2000, with outcomes focused primarily on gang and antisocial behavior (Spergel et al. 2003, Spergel et al. 2005a, b, c, d, e, 2006). At each site, the program partnered with local organizations and law enforcement to implement violence and delinquency intervention strategies through intensive contacts with gang youth.

---

[1]This null effect on gang membership is based on Esbensen and Osgood's (1999) "full" sample analysis. When the authors restricted analysis to schools with more balanced samples, GREAT was significantly more effective at reducing self-report of "ever" being in a gang (Esbensen and Osgood 1999).

The program used five main strategies, focusing primarily on suppression, and to a lesser extent, social intervention (outreach and crisis intervention), social opportunities provision, community mobilization, and organizational change and development. The overarching model was guided by social disorganization theory, and the program relied heavily on support from local government and law enforcement (including police, parole, probation, and district attorneys) and youth outreach teams, which included influential former gang members.

The Comprehensive Model was implemented in six US cities (Chicago, Mesa, Riverside, Bloomington/Normal, San Antonio, and Tucson), which represented a range of small, medium, and large cities, with gang problems of different severities. Across sites, program and comparison samples were matched as closely as possible by arrest records, demographics, gender, and gang involvement.

The original program was implemented in a community in Chicago (Little Village), and became the prototype for the five demonstration projects that followed. Nearly all participating youth ($n = 195$) were Mexican and Mexican-American, and all identified as gang members at project initiation. By the end of the 4.5-year evaluation period, program youth at the Chicago site showed significantly greater reductions in violent arrests and drug arrests than two matched comparison samples (Spergel et al. 2003). There were no significant intervention effects for total arrests or property arrests, and gang membership outcomes were not assessed.

However, Table 12.1 shows that program effects across the five replication sites were mixed. One site (Mesa) showed positive program effects on recidivism (based on arrest rates) compared to control groups, three sites (Bloomington, San Antonio, Tucson) reported no significant program effects, and one site (Riverside) reported a mix of positive and negative effects (i.e., the program was effective at reducing serious violence arrests, but program youth were more likely than controls to be re-arrested for drug offenses). Thus, when considering the overall pattern of results, the best conclusion is that the Comprehensive Model is a promising approach with inconsistent effects.

Despite these modest outcomes, there are several features of this approach that deserve further mention. First, of the 28 programs summarized here, the Comprehensive Model is the only approach that attempts to integrate prevention, rehabilitation, and suppression activities to address the multiple factors that contribute to gang violence. Given the complexities of gang membership and violence in the United States, comprehensive approaches such as this may have more promise for addressing the gang problem across a wide variety of community settings. Second, because program implementation data were collected across all intervention sites, the investigators were able to assess the potential role of intervention fidelity with regard to program outcomes. One important discovery was that implementation failure appeared to be partly responsible for poor program effects at the unsuccessful sites (Spergel et al. 2006). Finally, although the cross-agency partnerships fostered by investigators were not sustained in the long-term, this program shows that it is possible to get competing social agencies, community groups, and law enforcement to collaborate in service of gang prevention and intervention efforts (Spergel et al. 2006).

BSFT. Despite evidence linking family-level risk to gang initiation and violence, only one controlled study has evaluated the effects of family-focused intervention on gang-related outcomes. Valdez et al. (2013) tested the efficacy of adapted Brief Strategic Family Therapy (BSFT) for gang-affiliated Mexican American youth and their families. BSFT is a 12–16 session, family-based treatment that focuses on identifying and changing maladaptive family interaction patterns, particularly those related to youth problem behaviors. Moreover, 3 hours of "gang diversion training" was incorporated into BSFT by raising the consciousness of parents to gang life and orienting parents to gang-diversion strategies.

Valdez et al. (2013) randomly assigned 200 gang-affiliated (i.e., self, friend, or family members in a gang), drug/alcohol using adolescents to adapted BSFT or control (i.e., referred to behavioral health or substance abuse services). At the 6-month follow-up, they found that adapted BSFT led to significantly greater reductions in parent-reported conduct problems than control. Also, marginal treatment effects were found for parent-rated hyperactivity and impulsivity, with BSFT showing stronger effects. Although gang-related adaptations were made to the core intervention, BSFT had no effect on gang affiliation.

This study has at least two key advantages over most gang intervention evaluations. First, Valdez et al. (2013) adopted and modified a well-validated intervention for reducing conduct problems (Szapocznik et al. 2012), and thus were able to avoid the costs, inefficiencies, and uncertainties of developing a gang intervention from scratch. Second, the study had several methodological strengths, including random assignment of youth/families to treatment conditions, fidelity monitoring to ensure provider adherence to the treatment model, use of a reliable gang affiliation outcome measure, and intent-to-treat analyses to address biases due to participant attrition. Thus, there is greater confidence that treatment effects were attributable to the intervention itself rather than to extraneous factors.

12.7 Discussion

Overall, this brief review offers a mixed view of the efficacy of interventions for preventing gang membership, reducing gang involvement, or addressing problem behavior in gang-involved individuals. Our "vote counting" approach suggested that antisocial behavior might be somewhat more amenable to intervention efforts than gang involvement (i.e., 42 % of studies found positive effects for antisocial behavior whereas 21 % found positive effects for gang involvement); however, our meta-analysis shows that these interventions may have modest effects on gang involvement, while having minimal impact on antisocial behavior. Challenges to synthesizing this literature include inconsistency in defining gang membership across studies and insufficient data available in many studies to calculate effect sizes. Future analyses will investigate potential moderators of intervention effects, such as ethnicity and intervention type.

References

[*References marked with an asterisk indicate studies included in the meta-analysis.]

*Agopian, M. W. (1990). The impact of intensive supervision probation on gang drug offenders. *Criminal Justice Policy Review, 4*(3), 214–222.

*Arbreton, A. J. A., & McClanahan, W. (2002). *Targeted outreach: Boys and Girls Clubs of America's approach to gang prevention and intervention*. Philadelphia: Public/Private Ventures.

Borenstein, M., Hedges, L. V., Higgins, J. P. T., & Rothstein, H. R. (2009). *Introduction to meta-analysis*. West Sussex, England: Wiley.

*Braga, A. A., Piehl, A. M., & Hureau, D. (2009). Controlling violent offenders released to the community: An evaluation of the Boston Reentry Initiative. *Journal of Research in Crime and Delinquency, 46*(4), 411–436.

*Cohen, M. I., Williams, K., Bekelman, A. M., & Crosse, S. (1995). Evaluation of the National Youth Gang Drug Prevention Program. In M. W. Klein & C. L. Maxson (Eds.), *Modern gang reader*. Los Angeles, CA: Roxbury.

*Di Placido, C., Simon, T. L., Witte, T. D., Gu, D., & Wong, S. C. P. (2006). Treatment of gang members can reduce recidivism and institutional misconduct. *Law & Human Behavior, 30*(1), 93–114.

*Dole, K. (2005). *The effect of the Balance Program on aggression in the classroom*. Unpublished doctoral dissertation. San Francisco, CA: University of San Francisco.

Esbensen, F. -A. (2000). *Preventing adolescent gang involvement*. Bulletin. Washington, DC: US Department of Justice, Office of Juvenile Justice and Delinquency Prevention.

*Esbensen, F.-A., & Osgood, D. W. (1999). Gang Resistance Education and Training (GREAT): Results from the national evaluation. *Journal of Research in Crime and Delinquency, 36*(2), 194–225.

Esbensen, F.-A., Osgood, D. W., Peterson, D., Taylor, T. J., & Carson, D. C. (2013). Short- and long-term outcome results from a multisite evaluation of the G.R.E.A.T. program. *Criminology & Public Policy, 12*(3), 375–411.

*Esbensen, F.-A., Osgood, D. W., Taylor, T. J., Peterson, D., & Freng, A. (2001). How great is G.R.E.A.T.? Results from a longitudinal quasi-experimental design. *Criminology and Public Policy, 29*(1), 87–118.

Esbensen, F.-A., Peterson, D., Taylor, T. J., & Osgood, D. W. (2012). Results from a multi-site evaluation of the G.R.E.A.T. program. *Justice Quarterly, 29*(1), 125–151.

Esbensen, F.-A., Winfree, L. T., Jr., He, N., & Taylor, T. J. (2001). Youth gangs and definitional issues: When is a gang a gang, and why does it matter? *Crime & Delinquency, 47*(1), 105–130.

*Garcia, J. L. (2002). *A values-based career intervention for at-risk Native American boys*. Unpublished doctoral dissertation. Arizona State University.

Godley, M., & Velasquez, R. (1998). Effectiveness of the Logan Square Prevention Project: Interim results. *Drugs and Society, 12*(1–2), 87–103.

*Gold, M., & Mattick, H. W. (1974). *Experiment in the streets: The Chicago Youth Development Project*. Ann Arbor, MI: Institute for Social Research.

*Goldstein, A. P., & Glick, B. (1994). Aggression replacement training: Curriculum and evaluation. *Simulation & Gaming, 25*(1), 9–26.

*Harrell, A., Cavanagh, S., & Sridharan, S. (1999). *Evaluation of the children at risk program: Results 1 year after the end of the program*. NIJ Research in Brief, NCJ 178914.

Hedges, L. V., & Olkin, I. (1985). *Statistical methods for meta-analysis*. Orlando, FL: Academic Press.

Higgins, J. P. T., Thompson, S. G., Deeks, J. J., & Altman, D. G. (2003). Measuring inconsistency in meta-analyses. *British Medical Journal, 327*(7414), 557–560.

Howell, J. C. (2007). Menacing or mimicking? Realities of youth gangs. *The Juvenile and Family Court Journal, 58*(2), 9–20.

Howell, J. C. (2010). *Gang prevention: An overview of research and programs*. Washington, DC: U.S. Dept. of Justice, Office of Justice Programs, Office of Juvenile Justice and Delinquency Prevention.

*Huey, S. J., Jr., Smith, C. A., McDaniel, D. D. (2014). *The Behavioral Employment Program for juvenile gang offenders: A pilot randomized trial*. Unpublished manuscript.

*Josi, D. A., & Sechrest, D. K. (1999). A pragmatic approach to parole aftercare: Evaluation of a community reintegration program for high-risk youth offenders. *Justice Quarterly, 16*(1), 51–80.

Klein, M. W., & Maxson, C. L. (2006). *Street gang patterns and policies*. New York: Oxford University Press.

Klein, M. W., Weerman, F. M., & Thornberry, T. P. (2006). Street gang violence in Europe. *European Journal of Criminology, 3*(4), 413–437.

Lipsey, M. W., & Wilson, D. B. (2001). *Practical meta-analysis*. Thousand Oaks, CA: Sage.

McDaniel, D. D. (2011). *Reducing gang involvement through employment: A pilot intervention*. Unpublished doctoral dissertation. Los Angeles, CA: University of Southern California.

*Miller, W. B. (1962). The impact of a "total-community" delinquency control project. *Social Problems, 10*(2), 168–191.

*Peters, M. (1996). *Evaluation of the impact of boot camps for juvenile offenders: Mobile interim report*. Washington, DC: U.S. Department of Justice, Office of Juvenile Justice and Delinquency Prevention.

*Reckless, W., & Dinitz, S. (1972). *The prevention of juvenile delinquency: An experiment*. Columbus: Ohio State University Press.

Rodriguez, D. M. (1997). *An evaluation of "the Feeder Stream Program": A crime prevention program*. Unpublished doctoral dissertation. Fresno: California State University.

Schlossman, S., & Sedlak, M. (1983). The Chicago area Project revisited. *Crime & Delinquency, 29*(3), 398–462.

Spergel, I. A., Wa, K. W., Grossman, S. F., Jacob, A., Choi, S. E., & Sosa, R. V., et al. (2003). *Evaluation of the Gang Violence Reduction Project in Little Village: Final report summary*. Chicago, IL: University of Chicago, School of Social Service Administration.

Spergel, I. A., Wa, K. M., & Sosa, R. V. (2005a). *Evaluation of the Bloomington-Normal comprehensive gang program*. Report submitted to the Office of Juvenile Justice and Delinquency Prevention. Washington, DC: Unpublished report. Accessible at the National Criminal Justice Reference Service.

Spergel, I. A., Wa, K. M., & Sosa, R. V. (2005b). *Evaluation of the mesa gang intervention program (MGIP)*. Washington, DC: Report submitted to the Office of Juvenile Justice and Delinquency Prevention. Accessible at the National Criminal Justice Reference Service.

*Spergel, I. A., Wa, K. M., & Sosa, R. V. (2005c). *Evaluation of the Riverside Comprehensive Community-Wide Approach to Gang Prevention, Intervention and Suppression*. Report submitted to the Office of Juvenile Justice and Delinquency Prevention. Washington, DC: Unpublished report. Accessible at the National Criminal Justice Reference Service.

Spergel, I. A., Wa, K. M., & Sosa, R. V. (2005d). *Evaluation of the San Antonio comprehensive community-wide approach to gang prevention, intervention and suppression*. Report submitted to the Office of Juvenile Justice and Delinquency Prevention. Washington, DC: Unpublished report. Accessible at the National Criminal Justice Reference Service.

*Spergel, I. A., Wa, K. M., & Sosa, R. V. (2005e). *Evaluation of the Tucson comprehensive community-wide approach to gang prevention, intervention and suppression*. Report submitted to the Office of Juvenile Justice and Delinquency Prevention. Washington, DC: Unpublished report. Accessible at the National Criminal Justice Reference Service.

Spergel, I. A., Wa, K. M., & Sosa, R. V. (2006). The comprehensive, community-wide, gang program model: Success and failure. In J. F. Short & L. A. Hughes (Eds.), *Studying youth gangs* (pp. 203–224). Lanham, MD: AltaMira Press.

Szapocznik, J., Schwartz, S. J., Muir, J. A., & Brown, C. H. (2012). Brief strategic family therapy: An intervention to reduce adolescent risk behavior. *Couple and Family Psychology: Research and Practice, 1*(2), 134–145.

*Thompson, D. W., & Jason, L. A. (1988). Street gangs and preventive interventions. *Criminal Justice and Behavior, 15*(3), 323–333.

Thornberry, T. P., Krohn, M. D., Lizotte, A. J., Smith, C. A., & Tobin, K. (2003). *Gangs and delinquency in developmental perspective*. New York: Cambridge University Press.

Totten, M., & Dunn, S. (2011). *Final evaluation report for the North Central Community Association Regina Anti-Gang Services Project*. Gatineau, QC.

*Tremblay, R. E., Masse, L., Pagani, L., & Vitaro, F. (1996). From childhood physical aggression to adolescent maladjustment: The Montreal Prevention Experiment. In R. D. Peters & R. J. McMahon (Eds.), *Preventing childhood disorders, substance abuse, and delinquency* (pp. 268–298). Thousand Oaks, CA: Sage.

*Valdez, A., Cepeda, A., Parrish, D., Horowitz, R., & Kaplan, C. (2013). An adapted brief strategic family therapy for gang-affiliated Mexican-American adolescents. *Research on Social Work Practice, 23*(4), 383–396.

Wiebush, R. G., Wagner, D., McNulty, B., Wang, Y., & Le, T. N. (2005). *Implementation and outcome evaluation of the intensive aftercare program: Final report*. National Council on Crime and Delinquency (95-JN-FX-0023).

Williams, K., Cohen, M. I., & Curry, D. (2012). *Evaluation of youth gang drug intervention/prevention programs for female adolescents*. Report submitted to the U.S. Department of Justice. Washington, DC: Unpublished report.

*Willman, M. T., & Snortum, J. R. (1982). A police program for employment of youth gang members. *International Journal of Offender Therapy and Comparative Criminology, 26*(3), 207–214.

Wodarski, J. S., Filipczak, J., McCombs, D., Koustenis, G., & Rusilko, S. (1979). Follow-up on behavioral interventions with troublesome adolescents. *Journal of Behavior Therapy and Experimental Psychiatry, 10*(3), 181–188.

Wong, J., Gravel, J., Bouchard, M., Morselli, C., & Descormiers, K. (2012). *Effectiveness of street gang control strategies: A systematic review and meta-analysis of evaluation studies*. Ottawa, ON: Law Enforcement and Policy Branch, Public Safety, Canada.

Chapter 13
The Real Deal: On Positive, Street-Oriented Role Models in Response to Dutch Gangs and Youth at Risk

Jan Dirk de Jong

13.1 A Response to Gangs with Role Models

The present-day gang problem in the Netherlands appears to be contradictory because youth crime is down while social tensions pertaining to problematic youth groups are high. This has provided opportunities for new developments in approaching the problem, such as the use of positive, street-oriented role models with a local background.[1] In recent years we have seen a continuing decline of Dutch youth crime according to statistics (Kalidien et al. 2011; Smit et al. 2012; Van der Laan et al. 2014). The explanations for this steady decline leave much room for debate because the effects of changes in the way the National Police and the Ministry of Security and Justice register youth crime are still unclear (Bervoets et al. 2013; WODC/Bureau in press). In contrast with the statistical decline, there is growing concern about problematic youth groups and gangs that remain a problem, mainly among certain ethnic minorities in disadvantaged neighborhoods (De Jong 2012a; Drogt 2014; Roks 2015). This concern pertains to the belief that youth crime in the Netherlands is getting "tougher" in the sense that the decreasing population of young offenders are committing more serious and violent crimes at an increasingly younger age (De Groot et al. 2007; Weijers and Eliaerts 2008; Ferwerda et al. 2013).

[1] By street-oriented we mean that the person acting as a role model has grown up in a social environment that the Dutch urban youth identify as "the streets," and is familiar with the code of conduct and behavioral expectations that pertain to Dutch "street culture" (De Jong 2007, 2010). At present this cultural orientation has also shifted from the local street corners to several social media (Roks 2012; Van den Broek 2013).

J.D. de Jong (✉)
Faculty of Social Work and Applied Psychology, University of Applied Sciences Leiden, Leiden, The Netherlands
e-mail: jong.de.jd@hsleiden.nl

C.L. Maxson, F.-A. Esbensen (eds.), *Gang Transitions and Transformations in an International Context*, DOI 10.1007/978-3-319-29602-9_13

These troublesome developments have made dealing with problematic youth groups and gangs one of the government's top policy priorities. In 2009, the Ministry of Security and Justice established a special program to reduce youth crime, called the Action Program for Youth at Risk in Youth Groups (Actieprogramma Risicojeugd en Jeugdgroepen). This program responds to gangs with repressive measures such as swift and consistent punishment for offenses in order to reduce crime (which includes changes in adolescent criminal law that came into force in 2014). But the comprehensive "problematic youth group approach" that is at the center of this program also puts emphasis on prevention. Investing in early intervention creates important opportunities to keep minors from embarking on the wrong path (Van der Put et al. 2013). Furthermore, offering support and care after young offenders have served their sentence helps prevent them from re-offending (Van Wingerden et al. 2010).

The first evaluation of the new gang program is promising (Van Burik et al. 2013). These results are mostly illustrated by a statistical decrease in the amount of gangs, which are counted yearly by using the Shortlist Method (Ferwerda and van Ham 2014; Beke et al. 2000).[2] On the other hand, policymakers and practitioners share a general conception that the program needs further development. In some disadvantaged neighborhoods the problem of youth gangs seems to remain unchanged. The gang members are still getting "tougher" (Van Ham et al. 2014) and the recidivism rate is remarkably high (Wartna et al. 2013). This current situation has paved the way to explore new ways of influencing (aspiring and former) gang members by using positive, street-oriented role models with a local background.

This recent development in the Netherlands and how it has led to the first exploration of responding to gangs with these role models will be explained in this chapter. Then, an ethnographic experiment with role models will be described in more detail. The experiment is being conducted in Rogue District, a disadvantaged neighborhood in a Dutch city where youth gangs and gang members continue to be a serious problem. The preliminary findings of this qualitative research show promise in the way we deal with Dutch youth gangs and suggest comparative research questions that can inform evidence-based knowledge about the use of such role models.

13.2 A New Development in the Netherlands

The idea of handling a gang problem by using positive, street-oriented role models with a local background as a "softer" approach is certainly not new in international gang research (Klein 1995). The way that role models have been used in different programs varies greatly from Scared Straight programs (Finckenauer et al. 1999) to local outreach workers (Decker et al. 2008), personal mentors (Langhout et al. 2004), and Big Brothers or Big Sisters (Grossman and Tierney 1998). Reports on the efforts to use ex-criminals or ex-gang members to help youth at risk desist from

[2] The number of criminal youth gangs in the Netherlands is said to have fallen from 89 in 2010 to 17 in 2013 (Government of the Netherlands 2015).

participating in crime or gang membership are inconclusive about their influence (Petrosino et al. 2000; Klenowski et al. 2010; Lilienfeld et al. 2010). Some argue that research tends to show more negative outcomes than positive, in particular because these programs can have harmful effects such as deviancy training (Dishion et al. 1996). However, a few well-known programs that use ex-gang members are still running and seem to be successful, such as Homeboy Industries (see http://www.homeboyindustries.org/fatherg/) and Homies Unidos (see http://homiesunidos.org/), both located in Los Angeles, and Cure Violence (see http://cureviolence.org/partners/illinois-partners/) in Chicago (originally called Cease Fire).

Even though using role models with a local, street-oriented background (such as ex-gang members) is not new, it appears to be a novelty in the Netherlands (Rovers et al. 2013). In addition to its innovative appearance, there does not seem to be an aura of negative experiences or research results that surround the notion of using a local role model with "straatkrediet" or street credit (Van Gemert 2015). The reason the idea comes across as new and promising presumably lies in the fact that for many years the prevention of youth crime and gang membership in the Netherlands has been largely left to professional youth work organizations and social services. Most of these practitioners have roots outside the community they are serving (Hazekamp and Sluiter 2012). At present these professionals also need to be highly educated in order to qualify. Differences in the geographic, socioeconomic and ethnic backgrounds of such practitioners can make it difficult for them to gain local trust (Hoijtink 2006). Without that trust they fall short in bridging the gaps between conventional civil society, an organizational culture that cares greatly about accountability, and the "street culture" of disadvantaged neighborhoods (Wright and Decker 1997; Fleisher 1998; Anderson 1999). Also a lack of community mobilization in these neighborhoods creates additional obstacles in coordinating and targeting services to meet the needs of Dutch gang members (Klooster 2013; Vugts 2014).

13.2.1 The Idea of Using Local Role Models in the Netherlands

In the wake of this situation and its shortcomings, some relevant new developments are taking place in the Netherlands. The Dutch government is encouraging citizens to get more involved and actively participate in maintaining the welfare state (Hurenkamp et al. 2012), including the issues of crime, safety, and social services (Van den Brink et al. 2012; Sieckelink et al. 2013). Important questions still have to be answered on how community members can contribute to the collective resilience of disadvantaged neighborhoods (Verwer and Walberg 2012). Meanwhile an unknown number of citizens with informal authority among the local youth—some of them ex-gang members—are already actively dealing with their gang problems (often voluntarily). These people organize activities, help gang members with problems and exert their influence or informal authority to steer them away from crime and gang activity. Usually these volunteers or entrepreneurs are hardly noticed or taken seriously by policy makers that operate on a higher level in the organizational structure of approaching the gang problem. If by exception the activities of these non-professionals are brought to light and receive some attention, in the end their efforts are generally overshadowed by regular youth work organizations, social services, or established non-governmental organizations (NGOs) (DeTolk and Hazekamp 2014; Van Gemert 2015).

While doing fieldwork for gang research in disadvantaged neighborhoods in cities such as Amsterdam, The Hague, Zoetermeer, and Leiden, more and more of these local key figures with influence and informal authority among gang members started to present themselves (De Jong 2012b, 2013a, 2014a, b). At the beginning these findings seemed to be no more than a by-product, because looking at these key figures or their activities was never a main goal in these research projects. An important reason for this omission was that their local and informal forms of prevention or intervention were usually not incorporated in official responses to gangs by the municipal government or the police, who commissioned the research.

Another interesting fact that came to light in all of these research sites was that some "passionate" frontline professionals (in the form of district police officers, youth counselors, or probation officers) did have close and personal relationships with these important community members. These professionals made good use of the social network, influence, and authority of these locals. However, they kept these relationships largely to themselves in order to ensure the trust and confidentiality that was needed to work with them. What is interesting about these discoveries is that at each site "what works" did not seem to be the main concern in finding a better response to a gang problem. Well-known methods for approaching gang problems were already processed in municipal programs (De Groot et al. 2007; Versteegh et al. 2010), and more customized "evidence-based" responses that are available in the Netherlands were provided by the Dutch government in a database used by many practitioners and policy makers (see http://www.wegwijzerjeugdenveiligheid.nl/instrumenten/database-aanpakken-jeugdgroepen/). It turned out that "who works" (in terms of personal professional skills combined with unique individual traits and local social network) determined to a significant extent whether "what works" in theory actually did or did not work in practice.

In the Netherlands some research has been done on why and how these professional "passionados" (Eysink Smeets et al. 2013) seem to be able to make that difference, where their colleagues fall short using the same methods or protocols (Van Acker 2012; Werdmölder 2012; Moors and Bervoets 2013; Bervoets 2015). But the person who was most important and successful in making a difference in the lives of gang members did not always turn out to be the professional. In those cases the local key figure with influence and informal authority appeared to be the decisive factor, acting as a positive "role model" in the eyes of the gang members. He or she was the one who reached the "unreachable" gang youth, involved them in positive and pro-social activities, helped them with difficult personal problems (finding work, housing, and professional help), and got them to stop certain delinquent activities (at least for a while and with more success than the professionals). These findings aroused interest to start identifying these local, street-oriented role models and study their activities more closely in a research project. The practical goal was to look at ways to embed these new possibilities more structurally as an established component in a comprehensive approach to local gang problems.

13.2.2 A First Dutch Research Project with Street-Oriented Role Models

Some preliminary empirical findings and tentative ideas on the concept of positive, street-oriented role models immediately caught on as they were presented in early reports and lectures. Also the concept got some media attention through newspaper articles and radio shows. This exposure inspired the municipality of Amsterdam to commission the first official research project on finding and using role models in a response to gangs. In the context of dealing with delinquent youth and gang members who require an Intensive Forensic Approach (IFA), the municipal government and local youth care institution Spirit wanted to explore the possibilities of "role models" (Bontes 2013; De Jong 2013b). Shortly after this research project got started, the Ministry of Security and Justice took notice and made these efforts a part of their special Action Program for Youth at Risk in Youth Groups (I. Opstelten, Secretary of Security and Justice, personal communication, May 6th 2014; see also Government of the Netherlands 2014).

The fieldwork for this exploratory research took place in seven disadvantaged neighborhoods with gang problems. These locations provided "behind the scenes" access for the researcher because of the reputation he had built in the earlier gang research projects.[3] In each of these seven neighborhoods local, street-oriented role models were identified by comparing information provided by professionals, non-professionals (e.g., neighbors), and youth (also gang youth). Once the role models were identified, data on their activities and influence was gathered by semi-structured interviews with these role models about their personal history, what they do, how they do it, and why. Data was also gathered by participant observation when the role models were interacting with local youth (during the day and in the evenings). Time spent in the field and the weekly frequency of observations varied per neighborhood (from 1 or 2 months to over a year, and from once or twice a week to almost 5 days a week in some periods, especially in Amsterdam).

During the fieldwork more structured interviews were held with gang youth, who were identified as gang members on lists provided by local law enforcement. Their involvement in troublesome youth groups was also confirmed by information of the locals. In some neighborhoods this meant three respondents, in others over fourteen. In total I interviewed 47 gang youth who were all boys. Their ages ranged from 12 to 24 years old and all except one had a migrant background (38 of them Moroccan). They were asked about their own life, growing up in the neighborhood, youth crime and

[3] Two of these neighborhoods were located in Amsterdam, three in The Hague, one in Leiden, and one in Zoetermeer.

gangs, and about the activities of the local role models. Furthermore, I interviewed relevant non-gang community members (also youth) on what should be done about the local gang problems, and many professionals such as shopkeepers, sports instructors of martial arts schools, teachers, youth workers, youth counselors, social services, social workers of the housing association, contributors working for NGOs on prevention projects, municipal officials, police officers, probation officers, and attendance officers. On average I interviewed about five non-gang community members and twelve local professionals per neighborhood about the activities of the role models.

A first analysis of this qualitative data produced some preliminary insights into how a positive role model with a local, street-oriented background can serve as an attractive example of a pro-social role in the community that a young person can hope to fulfill. Also, the findings provided examples of where we can look for potential role models of this nature in localized social networks. It produced insights into the kind of help and support they offer. And the findings gave some idea of how we can determine whether these key figures are suitable to be an effective role model for local gang youth (characteristics, skills, and singular qualities). All of this illustrated a possible added value such role models could have in an approach to gang problems as a counterforce to the seductions of gang life (De Jong 2013c).

The promising results from these exploratory research efforts supported additional research to test the effectiveness of these local role models. A next step was organizing regular "thinktanks" for the government as well as group sessions in which professionals (policy makers and practitioners) and youth from disadvantaged neighborhoods could reflect on research outcomes and share their experiences concerning the use of "role models." The results of these group sessions were compared with the findings of the earlier fieldwork to further develop understanding of what a positive, street-oriented role model is, what he or she means to gang members, and what he or she does in terms of prevention (De Jong 2014c). The preliminary results were presented at a convention on "Using role models in dealing with problematic youth groups: why and how?" organized by the Dutch Centre for Crime Prevention and Safety (CCV) and the Ministry of Security and Justice (see http://www.wegwijzerjeugdenveiligheid.nl/nieuws/details/article/geslaagde-bijeenkomst-over-positieve-rolmodellen/). In workshops several role models and the "passionate" professionals that collaborated with them, shared their experiences with other (potential) role models, practitioners, and policy makers.[4]

13.2.3 *Showing Anger with Love*

The most striking finding that has come out of the data so far and that appears to be a constant at all the research sites is important to describe at this stage as it refers to the core of the concept of positive, street-oriented role models. It pertains to what 41 of the 47 interviewed gang members say they need most and seem to be missing in conventional or established preventive measures in the Dutch gang approach.

[4]The article is planned to be published in a special edition on "Positive Criminology" in the *Dutch Journal on Culture and Crime* (2016, in press).

These troubled youth state that getting help with finding suitable work, housing and dealing with all kinds of personal problems are indeed of central concern when desisting from criminal activities and gang involvement. But they also clearly express that what is generally lacking in their lives is being seen or "recognized" as a "real" somebody in their social environment; that is, having a sense of belonging and acceptance, experiencing a sense of usefulness or social worth, and feeling that they mean something to somebody. Some of the gang members are of the opinion that a youth gang at least fulfills some of these needs (even if only temporarily). All of them seem to agree that these are needs that are not met by regular youth work or youth care, with the exception of a few "passionate" practitioners (whose inspiring actions are not seen as representative for their professional organizations).

On the contrary, the gang youth claim they perceive the positive, street-oriented role models that are active in their social environment to be more genuine and sincere in their efforts to help. These role models try to correct their behavior by talking to them on the streets about misbehavior, criminal conduct, and gang involvement. They suggest other options based on their own life experiences (as people who grew up in the neighborhood) and try to help them solve problems (sometimes by personally escorting these youth to authorities or to organizations they need to visit in order to solve some of those problems). The methods of correcting bad behavior that these role models use can seem unconventional, or even harsh and aggressive in some instances (in the eyes of an outsider). The role models that get angry with youth argue they have invested their own time and energy. They can take breaking a promise or showing up late without notice (or not at all) very personally, especially when the youth also is "showing attitude" (stoer doen). This means that emotions can run high, and verbal or physical threats are sometimes part of the interactions that have been witnessed. But when asked about these conflicts afterwards, some of these youth interpret this conduct as "caring for real." One kid labeled it as "anger with love" (not much different from a concerned parent or older sibling).

Whether these more extreme interactions are crossing a line is an important question that still remains to be answered. What is important at this stage is that the responsive connection between suitable role models with informal authority and gang members that is found in these data indicates that they are perceived as "the real deal," where professionals may not be. This perception of true commitment, understanding, and involvement appears to be the main added value of the local, street-oriented role model that might potentially fill an important gap in the preventive measures in our Dutch approach to the gang problem.

13.3 A Role Model Experiment in Rogue District

For the time being it is still unclear what these findings will mean in terms of new possibilities and potential changes in our comprehensive approach to Dutch youth gangs. We are in the final stage of identifying types of role models, describing what they do that others don't (or won't), and finding ways of implementing their activities in the existing approaches to gang problems. An exciting opportunity arose out of all the exposure of the preliminary findings. In a city in the Western part of The Netherlands, a disadvantaged neighborhood called Rogue District[5] has had a persistent gang problem for many years (with more than a hundred young offenders). To respond to this problem the municipal government has made a renewed effort to develop and implement an updated approach. In association with the police, the public prosecution service, probation, social services, youth care, and youth work, they have focused on the "Top X"[6] repeat offenders of serious and violent crimes. Despite these efforts the evaluation of this approach has shown disappointing results, especially in reaching the more "hard core" problematic youth and gang members through preventive measures. It has been decided that further development of the approach will devote greater attention to involving parents, schools, and the neighborhood. In line with these decisions some government officials felt the need to explore the possibilities of finding and using local "role models" and "key figures" to get better results.

The original intent of these officials was just to explore new opportunities. They asked me as a researcher to do 3 months of fieldwork to find out if I could find positive role models with informal authority among the gang youth in Rogue District, and whether these role models would be willing and able to participate. Apart from these main questions, they wanted to learn in more detail what particular contribution such role models could make in offering perspective to youth at risk, and reducing delinquent behavior and recidivism. This also meant looking at how these role models could be connected to the formal partner organizations, and how their activities could be integrated in the existing plan of these professionals to deal with the gang problem.

13.3.1 Finding Local Role Models in Rogue District

Rogue District has had a bad reputation for many years. It used to be known for "white" criminals and youth gangs that were mostly connected to a few notorious Dutch families living in trailer parks. Now the young gang members are more predominately of Moroccan descent. They are the children of working class migrants whose families settled here around the 1980s. Many of the original migrants in this part of the city are descendants from the Eastern part of the Rif Mountains in the North of Morocco, between the cities of Al Houceima and Nador. The years of interweaving social network has led to a very close-knit community that is said to be almost inaccessible to outsiders. At the start of the research this image was

[5] The name "Rogue District" is made up for reasons of anonymity.

[6] Many Dutch cities that have gang problems have adopted a Top X-model based on the Top 600 approach that has been used in Amsterdam. In order to make the city safer this approach focuses on dealing with the Top X offenders of high-impact crimes, such as home invasions, street robberies, and stick-ups. In Amsterdam this list consists of 600 offenders, in other cities it varies from a Top 25 to a Top 100.

presented by the municipal government as an important reason for the inability of the established institutions to make much progress in dealing with their "Moroccan" gang problem.

In order to do the necessary fieldwork, two conditions had to be met. One was obtaining the cooperation of Said Bensellam, a well-known role model of Moroccan descent with promising local contacts who also worked in this Dutch city as a bouncer (Bensellam 2010; Van Gemert 2015). Another condition was that none of the established institutions or other interested parties would be made fully aware of what we were doing (looking for informal key figures who have a positive influence on gang members) while doing our fieldwork. This way I hoped to get more reliable information in a relatively short period of time and also good access to the living rooms or street corners where I wanted to gather our "backstage" data.

During the fieldwork I quickly found (potential) role models in a small gym that was frequented by many gang members and also their non-gang friends from the same neighborhood. In the gym they seemed to find some sense of purpose and belonging outside the gang and the street life, and in a more constructive way. I also witnessed the workings of the informal authority in the gym and on the streets by watching these potential role models (most of them martial arts champions). Furthermore, I discovered a handful of local professionals—such as a district police officer and a youth counselor—who were perceived by the gang members as "their people" and as adults who were sincerely concerned about their well-being.

After the fieldwork was concluded I reported the findings to city hall in December 2014, causing some unrest among the established youth work and youth care organizations (De Jong 2015a). Finding a few local, street-oriented role models in Rogue District and theorizing about what their contribution might be in a response to the gang problem, however, was not a satisfactory result. Although our recommendations on how to implement these findings in the existing approach were well received by the municipal officials and the police, it was clear that it would take a lot of time for them to act on them. An important reason for this delay was the fact that the budget for preventive measures for youth crime and gang membership was already set and spent for the next couple of years.

I did not want to wait that long to develop the next phase and had already raised expectations among the local population during our fieldwork. I therefore asked permission from the municipal government to develop an experimental role model project. Said Bensellam and I collaborated with the "passionate" professionals and the people connected to the gym in Rogue District. Together we devised a plan to have potential role models and youth (including former gang members) exercise their informal authority by monitoring the streets of their neighborhood at the upcoming New Year celebration. Those who participated wanted to do something for their community, but they were also motivated by the party they could have at the gym. There they could take in the youth that would normally be roaming the streets. The money that was needed for the party was collected through a gift from a NGO "Business and Society" that tries to find suitable jobs for unemployed youth from this area.

This first attempt to do something positive with the (potential) role models was successful and had a noticeable impact on the neighborhood that night in terms of less damage to (public) property or other forms of trouble (violence, crime). Furthermore, the mayor of the city came by personally to show his appreciation and the initiative also got a lot of local media attention. The question now was how I could shape these efforts into a more durable experiment.

13.3.2 Goals and Conditions of the Experiment

What the "passionate" professionals and our informal collaborators wanted to accomplish was made clear from the beginning. The professionals expressed they were frustrated by the lack of progress in the professional gang approach. Based on their own experiences working with informal key figures in this area they also expected results involving them more structurally. The key figures and potential "role models" mostly wanted to better their personal situations (in terms of income, working conditions, housing or otherwise), to receive more recognition for their efforts in helping out the community, and to have some positive influence on the new generation (including their own brothers and sisters). From the researcher's viewpoint, the long-term goal was to learn if the active parts in the existing role model projects also turn out to be the deciding factors in an experimental project of our own design. Answering that question would help to confirm, reject, or adjust the assumptions being made based on the preliminary insights of the first research project on using local, street-oriented role models.

In order to accomplish these goals the researcher, together with a few professionals and key figures, formed an informal working group of ten people: Team Rogue District. In the next 6 months (January–June 2015) we were going to find out who among the young adults and youth have the potential and motivation to become suitable local role models. We also needed to learn what kind of projects and initiatives they would find appealing to stimulate a better outlook on life for youth and reduce crime, recidivism, and gang involvement. Last but not least, we had to find possibilities and resources to realize these "grassroots" projects and initiatives. Meanwhile, qualitative data was being gathered by the researcher while organizing and participating in these activities, and also by interviewing stakeholders, key figures, (potential) role models, and the youth involved.

While the team had started to meet on a regular basis and some activities were quickly organized (such as a big debate between fifty youth, municipal officials, and police officers at the gym), the conditions of the experiment started to change in an unforeseen way. The established youth work and youth care organizations were now fully aware of this citizens' initiative that was developing in Rogue District. Instead of trying to collaborate and offer help (resources or expertise) in order to get better results, they started to take countermeasures. They clearly perceived the initiative as a threat to their current dealings with the municipal government and future assignments. These countermeasures existed of spreading rumors, trying to call to account certain municipal officials or putting pressure on other professionals who are involved, and mimicking activities under the name of "Rogue District Role Modelzzz."

Apart from the counteractions of outside parties that felt threatened, certain interests of the supporting partners of the project also influenced conditions. Even though Team Rogue District does not operate under the supervision of the municipal government and the role model project gets no official funding, it needs their support and collaboration in order to succeed and have some lasting effects. The police are also an important partner. But both parties turned out to have more complex interests than just reducing youth crime and preventing gang membership. The municipal government wanted to use the informal authority and influence of the role models among the gang members to connect (potential) success to the established institutions they were already funding for the next years. That way they could legitimize their current spending program and maintain current relationships with important institutions. At the same time, the police had plans for developing an "ambassadors" project within their own organization. This project would benefit greatly from using the new developments and contacts in Rogue District. These underlying interests had a negative effect on the conditions of our vulnerable experiment, because there was no foundation in terms of a stable organization with facilities and structured activities. The collaboration with locals was based on a few fresh and fragile positive developments in a disadvantaged neighborhood characterized by negative relationships with formal organizations, in particular the municipal government and the police. The pressure put upon the experiment to deliver a number of "role models" that could fit neatly into the existing approach to the gang problem was an unwelcome development. It could damage the perception of the intentions of Team Rogue District and the "street credibility" of the locals who got involved.

On top of all this we were soon confronted with internal problems. Within Team Rogue District two persons had too much of a personal agenda in terms of self-interest. Because of their unreliability or uncooperative behavior they turned out to be unfit to serve the common interest of the project: making a difference in the lives of the youth in their neighborhood they identify with and feel connected to. Fortunately, two potential role models could quickly take their place as core members of the team. Besides this development we were plagued by a lack of trust, sense of responsibility, organizational experience, and steering capacity among the non-professional community members. The (potential) role models and local youth made it difficult at times to keep faith as people turned out to be very unreliable when it comes to commitments.

These changing conditions greatly limited the possibilities of conducting our experiment as we seemed to be losing too much control. The way out of this was to also register all of these developments as important data and to be as open about these setbacks as we could possibly be (showing understanding for all the parties concerned and without pointing fingers or making enemies). We started out searching for ways to motivate the local, street-oriented role models, seeing what they could accomplish, and how their efforts could affect the lives of gang members in a positive way. But now the whole process of social change in organization of crime prevention in Rogue District had become just as relevant in order to assess what key components and deciding factors in a role model project might be.

13.3.3 Preliminary Findings in Rogue District

The 6 months the role model experiment has been running within these precarious conditions have brought forth some interesting preliminary findings (De Jong and Bensellam 2015). First, the unmet needs of the gang youth have become clear. Even though they have access to a (brand new) youth center and there are social services scattered over the neighborhood, gang members do not use these facilities and are hardly reached by youth or social workers. When asked about what is lacking in the current welfare system and why they feel at home in the gym, they express the need for a connection with recognizable people who show real commitment, understanding, and involvement (also by being strict and seeing through their "street talk" or "horseplay"). The youth gave examples of a few professionals who possess those qualities and break protocol by getting truly involved (even mad and verbally aggressive). Also they described the local, non-professional role models, with street names such as "Street Soldier" and "Wolf Man," that they listen to for that same reason. Similar to what was found in the earlier research, these youth perceive the emotional and sometimes harsh responses of such "passionate" professionals and the "role models" to be a sign of responsivity and true engagement.

The next thing that came out of the experiment was the capacity of the role models to work together with the "passionate" professionals to mobilize the local youth using their extensive local social network and informal authority. When things fell into place and everybody stuck to their commitments it appeared a lot can be achieved in a short amount of time. Events they organized with Ramadan—the traditional month when Muslims fast during the day—had a huge turnout (over 150 youth) and cost very little. In the evenings and nights that are traditionally risky times during this month (as a lot of youth hit the streets late at night after dinner and full of energy), they were able to reach the more hard core gang members and involve them in free activities in the gym. A selection of role models and local youth were able to engage a few police officers in an official exercise at a training center at the Police Academy. After physical training to break the ice they practiced making stops and arrests (where the youth took on the role of the police and got to play the part of a "bad cop" based on their own experiences). This exercise led to hefty but honest discussions on "professional treatment" and other problematic issues that had been bothering youth and police.

These and other activities showed the potential of the role model project in spite of all the inside and outside forces that kept influencing conditions in a negative way. As soon as a promising connection was made between local youth and some professionals, for example, with the police training, interested parties tried to capitalize on this with their own agenda. This pressure and involvement of outsiders threatened to break the very thin line that was beginning to bridge the gap between the community and the official institutions. On the other hand, jealous or suspicious individuals inside the community initiated rumors or patronized those who made the effort to help out. And the outside stakeholders who were afraid to lose their future share of the prevention-business were still trying to create obstacles. Nonetheless, the way role models exerted their influence, combined with the fact that some "unreachable" gang members were now being reached, was perceived as a positive change in the situation in Rogue District. To what extent these first efforts have already had some tangible effect on providing more appealing social opportunities for gang members or reducing youth crime and gang membership in a more durable way, is hard to say. Recent measurements of developments in crime and the feelings of safety of residents point in the right direction, but with the chaotic situation surrounding the experiment it is impossible to clearly demonstrate a connection. In the same period other initiatives have started up as well and some well-known gang members were arrested and locked up.

In the months to come we shall see how the role model project develops further and how the internal and external forces will keep changing conditions. What is clear so far is that the preliminary findings concerning the needs of the gang members in this experiment are consistent with the earlier findings in the existing role model projects. Like the others, these youth express a need for help with many aspects of their lives, but on top of this they clarify their unmet needs to be seen, to belong, to feel significant, and to have someone who cares about them. From these first findings we can conclude that it makes sense to put far more emphasis on "who works" in addition to what works in helping gang members desist and build a life in conventional Dutch society that appeals to them as valuable and meaningful. This includes gaining more knowledge on how "passionate" professionals make a difference (sometimes despite the counteractions of their respective organizations instead of support) and how to effectively use the non-professional "role models." Without the empathic and responsive connection with a person who is perceived as "the real deal," there seems to be little hope for effective and durable correction of delinquent behavior, at least in those Dutch disadvantaged neighborhoods where the gang problem appears to be persistent.

Apart from some encouraging first results concerning the possible added value of using positive, street-oriented role models in a local response to gangs, there were also a few discouraging discoveries. The unexpected countermeasures of some professional organizations responsible for crime prevention in Rogue District were disappointing, but not surprising. Also the political pressures that came out of underlying interests of our partners created obstacles. But the most disheartening development seemed to be the locals (some of them "negative" role models) who tried to undermine what the potential role models were trying to build up by spreading gossip and patronizing ringleaders. This brings us to the question whether what we have learned so far researching the use of role models in the Netherlands shows enough promise to go on experimenting.

13.4 Does the Use of Street-Oriented Role Models Show Promise?

Based on some of the best practices that have been studied in the ongoing research on existing role-model projects (De Jong and Bensellam 2015) and on the first findings of the role model experiment in Rogue District (De Jong 2015b), we can conclude that the potential of an added value of using role models in a Dutch gang response appears promising. The research shows that the activities of local, street-oriented role models help to fulfill important needs of the gang youth in terms of receiving recognition, having a sense of belonging, and feeling significant and connected to caring adults (with whom they identify and who have status in their social environment). The data portray that these needs are not always sufficiently met in the way we now organize our professional preventive measures in the Netherlands. Solving these shortcomings by using local, street-oriented role models as additional help seems possible. Addressing these needs is important because the challenges facing many gang youth in today's disadvantaged neighborhoods are even greater than those confronting former Dutch generations.

Like their predecessors this generation of gang youth is aware they generally come from a poor background and lack social opportunity. But on top of this, these Dutch kids perceive themselves as (being treated as) second-class citizens because they are labeled as an ethnic minority (especially concerning youth with a Moroccan and Muslim background). In addition, many of them also experience being seen as even more divergent from "normal" because of extra labels that they receive early on in their school careers such as Oppositional Defiant Disorder (ODD), Conduct Disorder (CD), and Mild Intellectual Disability (MID). These feelings of deprivation, discrimination, and being "different" enhance the urges these kids have to find others who will see them for who they are, accept them as someone who is a "normal" part of a social group and to whom they matter as unique individuals within that social group (Teeuwen 2012; Kaal 2013). At the same time all these factors result in their very limited perception of the possible (peer) groups in which they can fulfill these generic human needs as a young person growing up. This limitation increases greatly the peer pressure they experience in the one group—the gang—that will take them in and help them satisfy these needs, if only for a short while (De Jong and van Gemert 2010).

If the goal is to structurally implement such role model projects in a comprehensive approach to Dutch street gangs, there is still a lot to be learned. Above all we need more knowledge on how to determine what a suitable street-oriented role model is (does this differ per research area, per gang, or per individual?), how to find them in local social networks (where to start looking and how to confirm what we think we have found?), what personal qualities they need to possess (how to measure those?), and what concrete activities or programs they will devise (are these always custom-made for the neighborhood or could a more general scheme be useful?).

Subsequently, we need to address the problems concerning the implementation of the additional activities of non-professional role models in an existing gang approach made up of collaborating, professional organizations. There are logistic and organizational issues that need to be addressed, with special attention for dealing with the amount of control and influence outside parties need to have that might endanger the position, flexibility, and credibility of the role models in the community. Also there is the essential issue of measuring results. In theory we expect a successful role model project to contribute to a response to gangs by being a productive counter-force for gang involvement and providing more appealing social opportunities for youth at risk. We also expect them to provide additional leverage for professional organizations by exerting influence, using informal authority and transporting trust in their favor (even contributing to public safety in recurring situations of public disorder, like in the example of the New Year celebration in Rogue District). But connecting the possible "outcome" of role model projects to measured results in crime or gang involvement might be tricky. Particularly when professional partner organizations have an interest to claim victories for themselves as they often are better equipped to show accountability by working with standardized methods and present their "output" in impressive, official reports.

Therefore, an important underlying question is how to move the professional organizations and the non-professional role models into a working model of cooperation rather than competition. This might turn out to be one of the toughest questions to answer, as the potential success of a role-model project in dealing with the persistent gang problems in Dutch disadvantaged neighborhoods, should diminish the need for the certain services and institutions. And a reality we need to face in the Netherlands is that dealing with youth crime and gang problems is also a just commercial business to some of these organizations (Decker and Curry 2002).

The answers to all of these questions cannot be given based on the first exploratory research on a few projects in different Dutch cities and the experiment in Rogue District. This research has shed some light on a new phenomenon in the Netherlands and how this might be of additional importance in our response to gang problems. What is needed now is comparative research on different projects and experiments based on more standardized questions, concepts, categories, and methods. We also need international comparative research on street-oriented role model projects, or other local prevention projects that focus on combining community mobilization, the influence and informal authority of key figures and creating social opportunities with organizational change in a response to gang related crime (Decker and Curry 2003). Which of those projects have been successful and can we determine how the active parts in the projects in other countries compare to our Dutch findings?

Only by starting to build this body of knowledge can we work towards some sort of evidence-based claim that positive, street-oriented role models can make an important contribution to a response to Dutch gangs. Hopefully, such a claim can also help overcome the underlying counterforces that make it so difficult and sometimes frustrating to develop durable role model projects and work towards more long-term results in responding to persistent gang problems.

References

Anderson, E. (1999). *Code of the street. Decency, violence and the moral life of the inner city.* New York: W.W. Norton.

Beke, B., Van Wijk, A., & Ferwerda, H. (2000). *Jeugdcriminaliteit in groepsverband ontrafeld. Tussen rondhangen en bendevorming*. Amsterdam, The Netherlands: SWP.

Bensellam, S. (2010). *Kleine jongen. Het verhaal van mijn leven*. Amsterdam, The Netherlands: Van Gennep.

Bervoets, E. (2015). De straat op: frontlijnwerkers bij jeugdoverlast. Het vermeende gat tussen politie- en jongerenwerk bij overlastbestrijding. *Cahiers Politiestudies, 34*, 69–81.

Bervoets, E., Ferwerda, H., Bremmers, B., Keijzer, D., & Appelman, T. (2013). *Daling jeugdige verdachten in Amsterdam. Op zoek naar mogelijke verklaringen*. Arnhem: Lokale Zaken/Bureau Beke.

Bontes, M. (2013). *Deelproject Mentoraten binnen de Intensieve Forensische Aanpak (IFA)*. Amsterdam, The Netherlands: Spirit.

De Groot, I., Steketee, M., Boutellier, H., Braam, H., & Tierolf, B. (2007). *Greep op jeugdcriminaliteit. 'Evidence based' methodiek voor aanpak en preventie*. Utrecht: Verwey-Jonker Instituut.

De Jong, J. D. A. (2007). *Kapot moeilijk. Een etnografisch onderzoek naar opvallend delinquent groepsgedrag van 'Marokkaanse' jongens*. Amsterdam, The Netherlands: Aksant.

De Jong, J. D. A. (2010). We houden het lekker 'straat'. In P. Deelman (Ed.), *Over straatcultuur en groepsdynamiek* (pp. 13–28). Dordrecht, The Netherlands: Stichting Maatschappij, Veiligheid en Politie.

De Jong, J. D. A. (2012a). Typically Moroccan? A group dynamic explanation of nuisance and criminal behavior. In F.-A. Esbensen & C. L. Maxson (Eds.), *Youth gangs in international perspective. Results from the Eurogang Program of Research* (pp. 225–236). New York: Springer.

De Jong, J. D. A. (2012b). *Verbinden wat voor handen is. Haalbaarheid van een Jeugd Preventie Team (JPT) in Amsterdam Oost: de Indische buurt en Transvaal*. Amsterdam, The Netherlands: Gemeente Amsterdam, Stadsdeel Oost/Stichting Connect Initiatieven.

De Jong, J. D. A. (2013a). *De Prinsjes van de Kingstreet. Naar een probleemgerichte aanpak van overlast en jeugdcriminaliteit in de Koningstraat: Hoefkade*. Amsterdam/Den Haag: Rebond/Politie Haaglanden, Analyse en Research.

De Jong, J. D. A. (2013b). *Rolmodellen en het risico op recidive. De inzet van een mentor als positief rolmodel ter vermindering van criminaliteit en recidive van jonge Amsterdamse veelplegers*. Amsterdam: Rebond/Gemeente Amsterdam, Directie Openbare Orde en Veiligheid.

De Jong, J. D. A. (2013c). Gekopieerd gezag of originele autoriteit. Respect onder 'Marokkaanse' straatjongens en gezag op straat. In S. Sieckelinck, S. van Buuren & H. El Madkouri (Eds.), *Onbevoegd gezag. Hoe burgers zelf de gezagscrisis aanpakken* (pp. 242–251). Utrecht/Den Haag: FORUM/Boom Lemma.

De Jong, J. D. A. (2014a). *Stedelijke problemen, sterke schouders. Naar een probleemgerichte aanpak van problematische (jeugd)groepen in Buytenwegh: Wegstapelplein*. Amsterdam/Den Haag/Zoetermeer: Rebond/Politie Haaglanden, Analyse en Research/Gemeente Zoetermeer, Directie Openbare Orde en Veiligheid.

De Jong, J. D. A. (2014b). *Jong geleerd, fout gedaan. Naar een probleemgerichte aanpak van problematische jeugdgroep 'JUP': Bureau Leiden-Zuid*. Amsterdam/Leiden: Rebond/Gemeente Leiden, Team Openbare Orde en Veiligheid/Nationale Politie, Eenheid Hollands-Midden/Openbaar Ministerie.

De Jong, J. D. A. (2014c). *Denktank III: Rolmodellen en problematische jeugdgroepen*. Amsterdam, The Netherlands: Rebond Onderzoek en Advies.

De Jong, J. D. A. (2015a). Rolmodellen laten risicojeugd hun levenskunst zien. *Secondant, Platform en Magazine voor Maatschappelijke Veiligheid*. Retrieved 30 March, 2015, from http://www.ccv-secondant.nl/platform/article/rolmodellen-laten-risicojeugd-hun-levenskunst-zien/

De Jong, J. D. A. (2015b). *Burgerinitiatief Rolmodellen Rogue District: Verslag verloop van januari tot augustus 2015*. Amsterdam, The Netherlands: Rebond.

De Jong, J. D. A., & Bensellam, S. (2015). *Rolmodellen voor risicojeugd. De sleutel tot Rogue District?* Amsterdam, The Netherlands: Rebond.

De Jong, J. D. A., & van Gemert, F. H. M. (2010). *Een studie naar het concept groepsdruk*. Amsterdam/ Den Haag: Vrije Universiteit/Wetenschappelijk Onderzoeks- en Documentatiecentrum (WODC).

Decker, S. H., Bynum, T. S., McDevitt, J., Farrell, A., & Varano, S. (2008). *Street outreach workers: best practices and lessons learned: innovative practices from the Charles E. Shannon Jr. Community Safety Initiative Series*. Institute on Race and Justice Publications. Paper 15. Retrieved June 14, 2015, from http://docs.rwu.edu/sjs_fp/15/

Decker, S. H., & Curry, G. D. (2002). "I'm down for my organization": The rationality of responses to delinquency, youth crime and gangs. In A. R. Piquero & S. G. Tibbitts (Eds.), *Rational choice and criminal behavior* (pp. 197–218). New York: Routledge.

Decker, S. H., & Curry, G. D. (2003). Suppression without prevention, prevention without suppression: Gang intervention in St. Louis. In S. H. Decker (Ed.), *Policing gangs and youth violence* (pp. 191–213). Belmont, CA: Wadsworth/Thompson Learning.

DeTolk, A., & Hazekamp, J. L. (2014). *Self made. Ondernemend jongerenwerk met toekomst*. Amsterdam, The Netherlands: SWP.

Dishion, T. J., Spracklen, K. M., Andrews, D. W., & Patterson, G. R. (1996). Deviancy training in male adolescent friendships. *Behavior Therapy, 27*(3), 373–390.

Drogt, M. (2014). *Rollin' met mannen die de straat kennen*. Amsterdam, The Netherlands: BOXPress-Education.

Eysink Smeets, M., Bervoets, E., Bik, J., & Schram, K. (2013). *"Je voelt je heel onveilig en heel alleen..." Burgers over de impact van 'ogenschijnlijk onaantastbaren'. En over wat daaraan zou moeten gebeuren*. Amsterdam, The Netherlands: Landelijke Expertisegroep Veiligheidspercepties i.s.m. Lokale Zaken.

Ferwerda, H., Beke, B., & Bervoets, E. (2013). *Jeugdgroepen van toen. Een casusonderzoek naar leden van drie criminele jeugdgroepen uit het einde van de vorige eeuw*. Arhem: Bureau Beke (uitgegeven in de reeks Politiekunde van het Programma Politie en Wetenschap).

Ferwerda, H., & van Ham, T. (2014). *Problematische jeugdgroepen in Nederland. Omvang en aard in het najaar van 2013*. Arhem: Bureau Beke.

Finckenauer, J. O., Gavin, P. W., Hovland, A., & Storvoll, E. (1999). *Scared Straight. The panacea phenomenon revisited*. Prospect Heights, IL: Waveland Press.

Fleisher, M. S. (1998). *Dead end kids. Gang girls and the boys they know*. Madison: University of Wisconsin Press.

Government of the Netherlands. (2014). Aanpak problematische jeugdgroepen loont: Daling zet door. http://www.rijksoverheid.nl/nieuws/2014/05/06/aanpak-problematische-jeugdgroepen-loont-daling-zet-door.html

Government of the Netherlands. (2015). Reducing Youth Crime. http://www.government.nl/issues/youth-crime/reducing-youth-crime

Grossman, J., & Tierney, J. (1998). Does mentoring work? An impact study of the Big Brothers Big Sisters program. *Evaluation Review, 22*(3), 403–426.

Hazekamp, J. L., & Sluiter, J. (2012). *Klein handboek netwerk jonge ondernemers in het jongerenwerk. Schakel tussen jongereninitiatieven en maatschappelijke organisaties*. Amsterdam, The Netherlands: Stichting Connect Initiatieven/Netwerk Amsterdamse Helden.

Hoijtink, M. (2006). Teruggeworpen op jezelf in welzijnswerk. In E. Tonkens, J. Uitermark, & M. Ham (Eds.), *Handboek Moraliseren. Burgerschap en ongedeelde moraal* (pp. 55–67). Amsterdam, The Netherlands: Van Gennep.

Hurenkamp, M., Tonkens, E., & Duyvendak, J. W. (2012). *Crafting citizenship: Negotiating tensions in modern society*. Basingstoke & New York: Palgrave MacMillan.

Kaal, H. (2013). *Ongewoon moeilijk, Jeugdige delinquenten met een LVB als (voortdurende) bron van zorg*. Den Haag: Boom Lemma.

Kalidien, S. N., de Heer-de Lange, N. E., & van Rosmalen, M. M. (Eds.). (2011). *Criminaliteit en rechtshandhaving 2010. Ontwikkelingen en samenhangen*. Meppel/Den Haag: Boom Juridische uitgevers/Wetenschappelijk Onderzoek- en Documentatiecentrum (WODC), Ministerie van Veiligheid en Justitie/Centraal Bureau voor de Statistiek (CBS)/Raad voor de Rechtspraak.

Klein, M. W. (1995). *The American street gang. Its nature, prevalence and control*. New York: Oxford University Press.

Klenowski, P. M., Bell, K. J., & Dodson, K. D. (2010). An empirical evaluation of juvenile awareness programs in the United States. Can juveniles be "Scared Straight"? *Journal of Offender Rehabilitation, 49*(4), 254–272.

Klooster, E. (2013). *Hangplek Holland. Waarom de opvang van straatjongeren steeds mislukt*. Amsterdam, The Netherlands: Meulenhoff.

Langhout, R., Rhodes, J., & Osborne, L. (2004). An exploratory study of youth mentoring in an urban context: adolescents' perceptions of relationship styles. *Journal of Youth and Adolescence, 33*(4), 293–306.

Lilienfeld, S. O., Lynn, S. J., Ruscio, J., & Beyerstein, B. L. (2010). *50 great myths of popular psychology. Shattering widespread misconceptions about human behavior*. Malden, MA: Wiley-Blackwell.

Moors, H., & Bervoets, E. (Eds.). (2013). *Frontlijnwerkers in de veiligheidszorg. Gevalstudies, patronen, analyse*. Den Haag: Boom Lemma.

Petrosino, A., Turpin-Petrosino, C., & Finckenauer, J. O. (2000). Well-meaning programs can have harmful effects! Lessons from experiments in Scared Straight and other like programs. *Crime and Delinquency, 46*(3), 354–379.

Roks, R. A. (2012). @Malinowski heb je ping? *Kwalon, 17*(3), 34–42.

Roks, R. A. (2015). *In de h200d. Een eigentijdse etnografie over de inbedding van criminaliteit en identiteit*. Rotterdam, The Netherlands: Erasmus Universiteit Rotterdam.

Rovers, B., Bervoets, E., & Keijzer, D. (2013). *De rol van (ex-)deliquenten in politiewerk. Een verkenning van mogelijkheden en praktijken's*. Hertogenbosch/Rotterdam: BTVO/Lokale zaken.

Sieckelink, S., van Buuren, S., & El Madkouri, H. (Eds.). (2013). *Onbevoegd gezag. Hoe burgers zelf de gezagscrisis aanpakken*. Den Haag/Utrecht: Boom Lemma/Forum.

Smit, P., de Waard, J., & Berghuis, B. (2012). Criminaliteit blijft dalen. Toename veiligheid mede door burgers en bedrijfsleven. *Secondant, Tijdschrift van het Centrum voor Criminaliteitspreventie en Veiligheid, 26*(2), 34–37.

Teeuwen, M. (2012). *Verraderlijk gewoon. Licht verstandelijk gehandicapte jongeren, hun wereld en hun plaats in het strafrecht*. Amsterdam, The Netherlands: SWP.

Van Acker, J. (2012). *De gerespecteerde leerkracht: Professioneel omgaan met probleemgedrag*. Nijmegen/Antwerpen: Ministrando.

Van Burik, A. E., Hoogeveen, C., de Jong, B. J., Vogelvang, B., Addink, A., & van der Steege, M. (2013). *Evaluatie aanpak criminele jeugdgroepen*. Woerden/Den Haag: Van Montfoort/Bureau Alpha/ Nederlands Jeugdinstituut (NJI)/ Wetenschappelijk Onderzoeks- en Documentatiecentrum (WODC).

Van den Brink, G., van Hulst, M., de Graaf, L., & van der Pennen, T. (2012). *Best persons en hun betekenis voor de Nederlandse achterstandswijk*. Den Haag: Boom Lemma.

Van den Broek, J. B. A. (2013). *Van de straathoek naar Facebook. Een onderzoek naar het gebruik van social media door jongeren binnen de straatcultuur*. Rotterdam, The Netherlands: Erasmus University Rotterdam, Criminology Department (Masterthesis).

Van der Laan, A., Goudriaan, H., & Weijters, G. (2014). *Monitor jeugdcriminaliteit. Ontwikkelingen in de aantallen verdachten en strafrechtelijke daders 1997–2012*. Cahier 2014-7. Den Haag: Wetenschappelijk Onderzoeks- en Documentatiecentrum/Ministerie van Veiligheid en Justitie.

Van der Put, C., Assink, M., Bindels, A., Stams, G. J., & de Vries, S. (2013). *Effectief vroegtijdig ingrijpen. Een verkennend onderzoek naar effectief vroegtijdig ingrijpen ter voorkoming van ernstig delinquent gedrag*. Amsterdam/Den Haag: Universiteit van Amsterdam, Faculteit Pedagogische Wetenschappen/WODC.

Van Gemert, F. H. M. (2015). *Straatkrediet. Biografie van Said Bensellam*. Meppel: Just Publishers.

Van Ham, T., Bremmers, B., & Ferwerda, H. (2014). *Wisseling van de wacht. Een verkennend onderzoek naar de opkomst van een nieuw type veelpleger*. Arhem: Bureau Beke.

Van Wingerden, S., Alberda, D., Moerings, M., Wartna, B., & van Wilsem, J. (2010). *Recidive en nazorg. Onderzoek onder oud-bewoners van Exodus, DOOR, Moria & Ontmoeting*. Den Haag: Boom Lemma.

Versteegh, P., van der Plas, T., & Nieuwstraten, H. (2010). *The best of three worlds. Effectiever politiewerk door een probleemgerichte aanpak van hot crimes, hot spots, hot shots en hot groups*. Apeldoorn: Politieacademie, Lectoraat Intelligence.

Verwer, R., & Walberg, A. (2012). *Een kwestie van vertrouwen. Werking en versterking van collectieve weerbaarheid in achterstandsbuurten*. Amsterdam, The Netherlands: Pallas.

Vugts, P. (2014). *Doorgeschoten. De nieuwe generatie onstuitbare criminelen*. Amsterdam, The Netherlands: Uitgeverij De Kring.

Wartna, B. J. S., Alberda, D. L., & Verweij, S. (2013). *Wat werkt in Nederland en wat niet? Een meta-analyse van Nederlands recidiveonderzoek naar de effecten van strafrechtelijke interventies*. Den Haag: Boom Lemma.

Weijers, I., & Eliaerts, C. (2008). *Jeugdcriminologie. Achtergronden van de jeugdcriminaliteit*. Den Haag: Boom Lemma.

Werdmölder, H. (2012). *De werkmeester. Het belang van de verbindende schakel bij het stoppen van crimineel gedrag*. Den Haag: Boom Lemma.

WODC/Bureau Beke (forthcoming in 2015/2016). *Daling jeugdcriminaliteit en registratie-effecten*. Den Haag/Arnhem: Wetenschappelijk Onderzoeks- en Documentatiecentrum (WODC)/Bureau Beke.

Wright, R. T., & Decker, S. H. (1997). *Armed robbers in action. Stickup and street culture*. Boston, MA: Northeastern University Press.

Chapter 14
Collaboration as Usual? The Swedish Approach to Prevention and Intervention with Troublesome Youth Groups

Torbjörn Forkby and Russell Turner

14.1 Introduction

If you were living in a Swedish city in the late nineteenth century it is likely that you would have come into contact with "gang boys" in one way or another. This could have been through direct contact with them, seeing groups of young people standing on street corners, or indirectly by reading about them in the newspaper. Even back then, like now, the phenomenon of gangs was often at the top of the social problem agenda. The issue of how to respond to these social disturbances[1] was seen as a major challenge for socially engaged people of the time as well as for the authorities. The problem was largely discussed as a moral deficit among the working class, and thus was to be countered by better socialization in schools and a more general respect for Christian values (Lundström and Sallnäs 2003). An official report from 1907 from the Department of Education and Religious Affairs, summarizing inspections from public schools, made a connection between Christian values, schools, and "gang boys."

> The indifference to Christian education and a Christian way of living among the adults, the indulgent and weak upbringing in the homes, the education of Christianity in schools that in many cases is watered down and fails to imprint in memory even the most basic religious beliefs […] are some of the reasons for the great crowds of gang boys appearing in many places. (Ecklesiastikdepartementet 1907; our translation)

[1] We refer to gangs here within the wider notion of social disturbances. This is because current political and operational discussions about gangs in Sweden also occur within the broader notion of tackling social disturbances.

T. Forkby (✉) • R. Turner
Department of Social Work, University of Gothenburg, Gothenburg, Sweden
e-mail: torbjorn.forkby@socwork.gu.se

C.L. Maxson, F.-A. Esbensen (eds.), *Gang Transitions and Transformations in an International Context*, DOI 10.1007/978-3-319-29602-9_14

Back then, also like now, the conditions or causes of these social disturbances and moral degeneration were also largely seen as residing in the confluence of urbanization, poor living conditions and housing, poverty, and young people without occupation. The latter can in part have been due to a lack of job opportunities, but also from legislation from 1881 designed to prevent child labor. This legislation can have left large groups of young people without occupation—at least after school—to seek new "leisure" opportunities. In fact, the "boy gang" problem was perceived as so bound up with societal conditions and responsibilities that the appointed commission from 1898 proposing the first child welfare legislation was popularly called "the boy gang committee." Teachers, who were considered an authority on child rearing, discussed these "gang boys" in their union journal as follows:

> Every era has its catchwords. So does ours. And one of our most used catchwords is "gang boys." As far as it is possible for one to remember, there has been a lot of troublemakers and violent people (…) when a disturbance has occurred over by Kungsholmen,[2] it has been declared that "The Kungsholmen Gang" has been there again. If some rowdy 20-year-old youngsters at Liljeholmen have pulled knives or thrown bottles at each others' heads, this is credited to the Liljeholmen Gang account. (Svensk lärartidning[3] 1898; our translation)

With the above prologue, we would like to raise the issue of culture and cultural history for understanding gang transformations and in particular for analyzing responses to gang prevention and intervention strategies. In a suggestion for concepts for comparative culture analyses, the French anthropologist Claude Lévi-Strauss proposed a division between cold and hot cultures (Lévi-Strauss 1966). With this temperature metaphor he defined cold cultures as societies characterized by high stability—not or very slowly changing—where members behave in accordance with fixed roles with fairly fixed mind-sets about their understanding of the world and their place in it and where they act according to traditional behavior patterns. Hot cultures, on the other hand, were defined as those societies with a high rate of turnover, where time is perceived as linear not circular; development and change are taken-for-granted notions seen as necessary to strive for, possible to achieve and to which one has a moral obligation to contribute. In these cultures where change is normative, more freedom but also more pressure is put on individuals and groups to develop their own futures (see Bauman 1991).

Somewhat mirroring this broad (and perhaps reductionist, Lee Klein 1995) attempt to analyze cultures, the Chicago school of sociology started during the 1930s to explore the link between environmental conditions and behavior, thereby focusing on socialization, identity formation, and navigation strategies in fast changing and growing cities (Chaskin 2010). When it comes to understanding crime and delinquent behavior, social disorganization theory was developed from studies on crime rates in different areas in relation to population stability and change, migration in relation to cities' spatial organization (Shaw and McKay 1942), and also specifically on mapping of gangs (Thrasher 1927). In fast changing (hot) areas the connection to former social norms, control, and bonds is partially lost and especially young people are left to make

[2] Names of places refer to districts in Stockholm.

[3] Swedish Teachers Journal.

their own way. This has been found to increase feelings of insecurity and the level of youth crime and delinquency, including the establishment of gangs. More recent social disorganization scholars also highlight that patterns of interaction in the local community, informal social control, social cohesion and resources and economic deprivation seem to be factors that influence crime rates (Pratt and Cullen 2005; Sampson et al. 2002).

Borrowing the temperature metaphor from Lévi-Strauss, Sweden at the turn of the nineteenth century could—in terms of the rapid urbanization, migration, and industrialization processes—probably be defined as a relatively hot society when compared to those indigenous cultures anthropologists used to study. Compared to other countries, Sweden at the turn of the twentieth century could be characterized not by continuous change but by stability, in terms of the fairly long democratic tradition, the established welfare sector, and absence of war (at least since the campaign against Norway in 1814). Hence, Sweden's culture and specifically its social welfare history can be seen against these stable social and political conditions.

Current responses to troublesome youth groups are broadly speaking also formed under these cool conditions. Nevertheless, in terms of a within-country analysis of Sweden there are different degrees of warmth, reaching from mildly warm to very hot areas. Sweden could thus be described in terms of the Icelandic geography—sporadic very hot places with geysers steaming, roaring, and bursting out, but in general surrounded by lots and lots of cold and seemingly unchanging conditions.

The hot places are a number of relatively poor districts, often concentrated in the suburbs of the bigger cities where a large share of the inhabitants are migrants from different parts of the world—and where the composition of inhabitants fluctuates depending on where wars, conflicts, or human disasters of other kinds are taking place. Given its population, Sweden receives a high number of immigrants. For example, in 2014 it took in the most asylum-seekers of all European countries, largely due to the war in Syria (Eurostat 2015). This provides Sweden with a new immigrant population that is young in terms of its emerging cultural history in the new "home" country. This presents new challenges of integration and developing a sense of belonging, alongside the existing issues of poor housing and economically deprived neighborhoods.

On the other hand, we have the colder zones in Sweden, characterized by a fairly well-organized society, doubly controlled and supported by the "Great society" as determined by the Swedish social democratic (universalistic) welfare model (and its long-standing history and cultural pride of place). In this model, the state and public institutions traditionally have been responsible for administering and delivering different services to meet the rights and need of the individual (Esping-Andersen 1990). In some ways, this leans towards a social collectivist culture, where it is ultimately the state's responsibility to safeguard but also enable the individual. A potential upshot of this is that the causes of (and solutions to) individual actions are understood first and foremost as a problem of collective (and state) responsibility, as opposed to a more individualistic account.

In this chapter we want to frame our discussions of Sweden's approach to troublesome youth groups against the backdrop of this idea of cultural social welfare discourse and different cultural "climate zones": will there be tensions and built-up pressure, the breaking of thunder or perhaps just a blending of temperature leading to a somewhat warmer climate but still retaining a mildness that has been familiar for quite some time? More specifically, the aim of the chapter is to describe and discuss the responses, strategies, and measures used to deal with gangs in Sweden from around the turn of the twentieth century: what responses have been developed and how can we understand why this particular way of doing things was chosen? Were there hot-headed decisions in response to crises, or cool calculations that collaboration was the answer?

It is only in fairly recent history that gangs have (re)emerged as a social problem that has been acknowledged in research, practice, and the media in Sweden. Rostami et al. (2012) conducted (possibly the first) mapping of gangs—according to the Eurogang definition (Klein et al. 2001)—in Sweden. They concluded that street gangs do exist, contrary to assertions to the contrary from other Swedish criminologists. Examples of gang research can also be found in neighboring Nordic countries, for example, Pedersen and Lindstad (2011) on Danish street gangs. One explanation for the absence of gang discourse in Sweden, at least in terms of research, may be that the concept of criminal networks instead of gangs was for a number of years the dominant term and gang terminology such as continuity, structures, leaders, and control of membership was less in use. Statistical network analyses using crime statistics showed a complex map of individuals tied together in different ways and in constellations that varied over time (Sarnecki and Pettersson 2001). Another possible reason for the lack of attention to street gangs can be found in the focus in Sweden on outlaw biker communities such as the Hells Angels and the Bandidos. We thus introduce our discussion in this chapter with an account of how street gangs or troublesome youth groups became perceived as a social problem (or disturbance) in recent years in Sweden. We then go on to outline and discuss the societal responses.

Since these processes are clearly a product of recent history, Sweden can be viewed as a case study of interest to other countries, particularly in terms of the shape that discourses of prevention and intervention can take and the consequences of these discourses for actual gang prevention and intervention practice. The questions that will be discussed are: What strategies or practices were undertaken? What kind of logic did these strategies and practices follow and how new or traditional were the responses? From a theoretical viewpoint the issue of Swedish gang prevention and intervention strategies captures how a society reacts to understand, intervene, and control a social threat that appears as new. "Case Sweden" is also interesting from the social cognitive perspective of understanding how a society's framing of the gang problem—and the responses it subsequently develops—can find strength in but also be blinded by its cultural history. As many occupied in gang research have pointed out—"gang" is a floating concept; it is barely separable from ideas in the popular media industry, news reports, or politics (Klein 2001). How do the appointed social authorities and practitioners then understand the issue of gangs and in what kind of interventions do they invest time and energy? The latter is of particular interest when the conceptualization of the "problem" with which the Swedish authorities have to deal is in turn so permeated with visions of gangs from American culture that it is hard for them to see their own situation. There is the potential not to see the "elephant on the street" by saying "We don't have American elephants here."[4]

14.2 The Present Gang Issue in Sweden

To set some further cultural context about Sweden, let us begin by illustrating some points about the general development of crime in Sweden. As in many other countries (both the USA and in the EU in general), Sweden's crime statistics show a positive development; there has been a decrease during recent years (the period referred to here is 1986–2012) regarding theft, youth crime, attitudes towards delinquency and criminal behavior, and feelings of risk and insecurity (Lindgren 2013). In contrast, reports of violence needing medical attention and sexual assaults have increased during the same period and lethal violence has stayed at approximately the same level. Gothenburg, Sweden, had 1.7 cases of murder per 100,000 inhabitants on average during the first years of the twenty-first century (EU cities vary from 1 per 100,000 in Vienna, Austria and Bucharest, Romania to 6–8 in Vilnius, Lithuania and Tallinn, Estonia, compared with New York at 5.1 homicides per 100,000 inhabitants (Lindgren 2013)). Of the 103 shootings in Gothenburg during the years 2008–2015,[5] 75 % occurred in what we mention as hot places, i.e., socially disadvantaged communities in suburban areas as described above.

It would have been better to use "gang situation" rather than "issue" as the subheading to this section. However, this would have implied more hard facts and better data about names and numbers of gangs, members, gang-related crimes, territoriality, and so on. We do not have this in Sweden and we do not have any tradition of surveys on this subject and we therefore cannot give any exact figures or historical trends regarding street gangs—but we still have a gang issue (at least if one applies the Eurogang definition of a street gang, Klein et al. 2001). And there are strategies in place for preventing youth from joining gangs, interventions directed to gang-related violence and support programs for exit-processes. From time to time there has been quite intense media coverage of gangs ranging from the mapping of groupings and individuals, homicides and violence, to articles and reports on societal responses. In some ways, the media coverage works as a possible upside to the current lack of facts and figures. Since the gang issue is current history we may be better off analyzing how gangs are represented in the media and other public discourses and how this is connected to societal responses (Spector and

[4] We are of course well aware that there is no such thing as American elephants. The point being that the USA by and large also does not have a proliferation of the kind of street gangs most well represented in the mainstream American movie industry, an observation reflected in the title of the first Eurogang volume, "The Eurogang Paradox" (Klein et al. 2001).

[5] Only up until February 28th 2015.

Kitsuse 1977). In other words, it is possible to pinpoint more precisely how the gang issue was constructed as a social problem, and how it was put on the interventionist agenda in Sweden. This process occurs in the interplay between social actors such as gang members, media, and public officials, and their respective interpretations and various dramatic incidents (Fairclough 1995).

For this discussion we have chosen to focus mainly on Gothenburg, the second largest city in Sweden with around 500,000 inhabitants. Our choice here is both convenience, since we have more data on gang prevention and intervention responses in this city,[6] and because the gang situation in Gothenburg has to some extent functioned as a focal point for how national strategies and responses have been formed.[7] At the time of writing, a police-led gang suppression campaign—which has been in operation in the city for about a year, with support from the national police in terms of extra personnel to complement local police—is about to end. Results from this campaign included seizure of over 250 weapons (of which 60 were automatic rifles) and narcotics (233 kg marijuana, 131 kg amphetamine, and 21.5 kg cocaine). There were 50 shootings in Gothenburg during 2014; a substantial number of these are thought to be related to what has been referred to as territorial gangs. This is an increase since 2011 when there were 24 shootings and 2012 with 30 shootings. Once again, there is a lack of solid information about whether the shootings are gang-related or not. At the time of writing there were 14 murders related to gangs committed between 2011 and March 2015 in Gothenburg, of which two have ongoing prosecutions against likely suspects.

The territorial aspect to these gangs is thought to be primarily linked to friendship groupings developed between children from the same neighborhoods and schools (Björk 2006; Forkby and Liljeholm Hansson 2011). Prominent among police and media explanations for these events are disagreement/conflicts over the drug trade and inter-group revenge for various "disrespectful" behaviors or talk (Liljeholm Hansson 2014). While it has been hard for the police to investigate many of these shootings and thereby reach a clear picture of causes and processes, the shootings nevertheless have been concentrated in relatively deprived neighborhoods with higher rates of low-income households, employment, and new immigrants than in other parts of the city. We can return here to the notion of cultural hot-spots erupting in particular suburbs of Gothenburg that have a faster pace of change. In these suburbs, there is a concentration of people newly arrived in Sweden and who often have been forced to leave behind a life in the home country. Thus there can be greater pressure for such people both in (re)building a new life combined with doing this in a new and perhaps strange culture where the "rules" of behavior can appear to be in flux.

---

[6] We draw on three empirical studies: (1) a 5-year long research project evaluating Young & Safe in Gothenburg (Forkby 2008); (2) a study of involvement in, the character of and exit from street gangs in Gothenburg (Forkby and Liljeholm Hansson 2011); and (3) an evaluation of the SSPF model in Gothenburg (Turner et al. 2015). "Young & Safe" and "SSPF" are explained later in the chapter. All three studies were conducted at the Research and Development Unit, The Gothenburg Regional Association of Local Authorities (FoU i Väst/GR).

[7] This is despite the fact that lethal violence, for example, in 2014, was worse in both Stockholm and Malmö (Sweden's two other large cities) than in Gothenburg (Swedish Crime Prevention Council 2015).

The start of the current gang situation is 4th July 2001, and the setting is one of the largest public beaches in Gothenburg: Näset. In the afternoon a disagreement took place between two, at that time relatively unknown, groups who shot at each other on the beach in front of children and families. Prior to this event, gangs were mainly understood as the biker communities Hells Angels and Bandidos, or alternatively sometimes as a prison phenomenon. When these biker gangs were perceived as a threat, this was mainly to each other. The conflict between the gangs at the public beach escalated between these, but also between other, rival groups. Shootings occurred in other public places, through restaurant windows and even car bombs detonated in inner city areas. Now gangs became clearly perceived as a threat to ordinary people, public order, and even to the brand of Gothenburg in that capital investors, tourism, and other enterprises would be deterred. During this period, a number of different groups/gangs, which were aspiring to gain more influence and status, increased their share of the media and political attention (Forkby and Larsen 2005; Forkby 2008).

When dealing with and discussing the "gang issue" in Sweden today, there is a broad array of definitions ranging from delinquent youth groups, territorial groups, hang-arounds or "wannabe" gangs, and prospects to outlaw biker gangs. The biker gangs and other criminal networks were involved in "heavy-end" organized crime. The street or youth gang issue tends with a few exceptions to be located in the three bigger cities, where Gothenburg has had the most focus in recent years. The increased attention on gang activity is evident in (and possibly amplified by) the media. A search of a database of Swedish newspapers (www.Retriver.se, retrieved 23 January 2015) using the search string "gang-criminality" shows a marked increase in articles starting from 2001. While there were just four articles that contained this word[8] in 2000, 18 articles were published in 2001, 96 articles in 2008, and in 2014 we found 293 articles (so far the greatest number was reported in 2012 with 490 articles—see Fig. 14.1 for a bar graph of the number of articles per year). During the first 6 months of 2015, 296 articles were published, which means that 2015 will have one of the highest numbers of newspaper articles on gangs to date.

Of course everyone does not see gangs as social evils. On the contrary, according to an ethnographic study of gang involvement (Forkby and Liljeholm Hansson 2011), a range of alternative discourses about gangs competes with the dominating media discourse. For some young people, gangs functioned as a magnet with a special attraction for those with weak bonds to society, feelings of not belonging or exclusion and/or whom were low-achievers in school. In the gang they became *someone*, achieved a sense of respect that compensated for the discomfort and low self-esteem arising from different experiences of marginalization or underachievement. These findings concerning the "insider experience" of being in a gang resonate with other international research about the attractions of being in a gang, such as a sense of a belonging and connectedness with others, self-esteem (in terms of status) and a sense of direction about the future, specifically in terms of access to money and (illegitimate) employment (Harris et al. 2012). In this sense, the gang issue in Sweden can be seen as having many commonalties with other countries. The difference perhaps is how the problem and its solution were framed.

---

[8] In Swedish, gang criminality is just one word: gängkriminalitet.

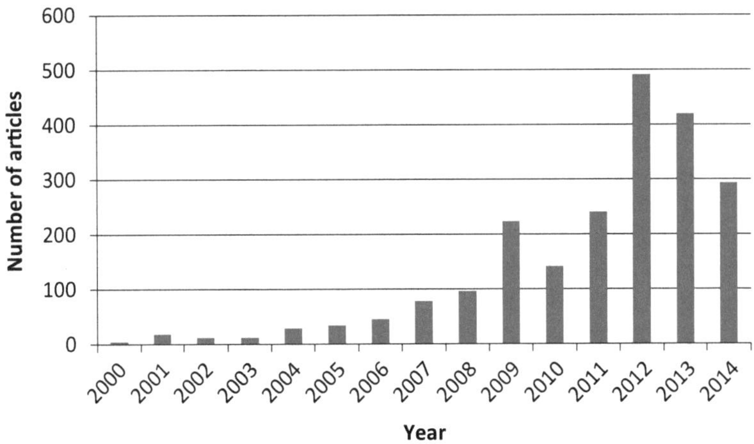

Fig. 14.1 Articles published in Swedish newspapers during 2000–2014 containing the word "gang criminality"

14.3 The Formation of the Current Swedish Approach

The policy of today draws on a history in Sweden of prevention strategies that share a common feature concerning how to respond to social disturbances and related problems. Broadly speaking, this approach can be summed up as follows: do what you think is required from your local situation, but do it in collaboration. This policy of joint, but locally decided action and cooperation is so embedded that it has almost been the goal in itself, and not (just) the means to address the social problem. For example, looking at relations between social services and the police since at least the 1940s, better collaboration has been the most prominent and constant call from policy makers (Edvall Malm 2012). As we will see there is *still* the same call for collaboration concerning what prevention workers should be doing.

Before we go further let us clarify the focus of our discussion. In our analysis we focus on key strategies or aspects of prevention or intervention *viewed as important*, not on the various, specific things different stakeholders actually do (or are supposed to do) in relation to gangs and troublesome youth groups. Moreover, there are supplementary internal strategies, especially from the police, regarding gang suppression, which are not explored in this discussion. There are also other potential collaboration strategies than those discussed below. However, from being involved in research in this area for several years as well as following other research and policy developments, we regard the choice of developments in Gothenburg as justifiable and exemplary entry points to understand the Swedish approach, and its possible advantages and shortcomings.

Now let us focus on the present gang prevention strategy, and the case of Gothenburg. Alongside the growing media coverage of—for Gothenburg—these wholly new and spectacular "gang-related" events, local politicians also became interested in (or pressured into) developing a response to the "gang problem." The mayor at the time—Göran Johansson—called in the heads of a number of city departments as well as local and regional representatives of national organizations, such as the police, to develop a plan. A key piece of information from the police was that in approximately three out of four cases the youth involved in these new gangs lived in just four of Gothenburg's (then) 21 city districts (Johansson 2004); these districts were those which also had the most negative socioeconomic indicators. These top-level discussions resulted in a central steering group tasked with addressing this new "gang boy" problem. At this point, it could be argued that this new social threat was poorly understood, other than that it involved groups of young people from particular city districts committing crime. Despite this lack of knowledge about these youth groups, we already see a tendency to look to multi-agency collaboration for answers (see Crawford 1998). A particular strength in this approach is that responsibility for developing strategies and solutions is shared and that knowledge, at least in theory, can be pooled (Huxham 2000). The central steering group, comprising its broad-ranging multi-agency partners, was tasked and ready to act. A potential weakness in a collaborative solution-finding approach at a top-level though is that the development of strategies relies on a style of consensus-based decision-making where parties are reluctant to propose novel approaches. The danger here is that collaboration within a central steering group becomes a mutual approval of familiar or existing patterns of working, resulting in a continuation of the status quo (we return to this point later in the chapter).

A key issue in Swedish public administration concerns the amount of power at different administrative levels. Some organizations, such as the police, operate as a national organization with power devolved to regional levels. Other key players, such as schools, social services, and youth workers, are steered autonomously at city district level.[9] Developing a citywide response in Gothenburg involving the police (regional/national level), the mayor's office (city-level), and, for example, schools and social services (city-district level) thus involved competing stakes of power and interest where everyone is responsible but it is much harder for someone to take the lead. Consequently, the central steering group was to some extent compelled to devolve decision-making and solution-finding activities to the city districts. Their solution to this was to hold a number of developmental workshops in the four city districts most affected by this new gang phenomenon. Was this a collaborative "passing the buck" or a genuine attempt to resolve the dilemma of collaboration across different administrative levels of power? Again, there is strength in collaborative working—this time at more of a grass-roots level—but the risk remains that "new" proposals for interventions will be grounded in implicit cultural practices and "business-as-usual," in contrast to looking externally for new and effective practices

[9] City districts in Sweden's larger cities are primarily autonomous in terms of delivery of school, social, and youth leisure services, with the rule of law being the key steering principle for national governance.

and methods. In other words, the focus moves from a question of problem analysis and effective interventions to one of what internal organization needs to be undertaken and which collaborative structures need to be established. The emphasis on structure rather than content may have also been driven more by the urge to be seen as a legitimate actor in the field than a desire to challenge collectively accepted thoughts and ideas (Powell and DiMaggio 1991). Zooming out to a large cultural level, this initial way to respond can be viewed as being in line with Swedish social welfare history; that it is the state—and in turn the municipalities, city districts, and so on—that provides structures to safeguard citizens' rights and needs. What the structures are then "filled with" is another issue.

14.4 Responses Begin to Take Shape

The developmental workshops in the city districts resulted in the suggestion to develop the Young & Safe project, which was established in 2004. This would initially be an over-arching, city-level organization working to *support* the four city districts with the gang issue. Note that the city districts ultimately retained the mandate to decide what they actually would implement. With the establishment of Young & Safe, the discourse takes a clearer form: the key problem to address is now framed in terms of working "to prevent the recruitment of youth to gangs." Thus a central goal of Young & Safe would be preventative and diversionary; to stop or prevent young people being recruited to gangs (see Forkby 2008). One could argue at this point that this framing of the problem presupposed existing gang members who were actively "recruiting." Moreover, the preventative focus misses or ignores the tougher issue of dealing with the existing gang members. Young & Safe initially comprised a number of homegrown responses such as having social workers stationed with the police to expedite contacts with social services and supply the police with better knowledge about a young person's situation, in cases of youth arrest (Forkby 2007). Other responses included network interventions toward youth's risk and needs (Forkby 2006), and a redirection of resources to the youth issue (Forkby 2008). A common thread to these and other responses developed within Young & Safe was the focus on developing operational *structures* rather than developing the content of interventions and responses. The question remains one of "How shall we collectively organize ourselves?" and less one of "What shall we concretely do differently?"

A key tool in Young & Safe was the development of a collaboration model where representatives from schools, social services, the police, and youth leisure services (what is called "youth work" in some countries) would regularly meet to identify young people[10] at risk of joining gangs. The model was dubbed the SSPF collaboration—Schools, Social Services, Police, and general open access youth work (youth leisure services)—and was initially established in 2006 (Forkby 2008). Inspiration

[10] Twelve to eighteen year olds.

came from a similar model that had existed in Denmark for some time—the SSP model (without the participation of youth leisure services). It is interesting to note that the Danish SSP approach was considered a promising model to borrow from despite a lack of evaluation.[11] Again, we see in the development of SSPF the over-arching theme of looking to collaboration and the sharing of responsibility as the solution; this solution brings a focus on organizational structures rather than actual methods. One slightly more critical way to understand why the SSP model was chosen was that it was a model which most closely resembled an implicit Swedish way of doing things; a preference for a collective taking of responsibility through multi-agency structures. Older collaboration structures could in many cases quite easily be redressed into slightly modified new clothes to become seemingly fresh responses to the new gang problem. In looking to methods from other countries—and in particular methods with at least some research support—the issue of a cultural translation of the method to the "home country" is often raised: will the method work *here*? One way to address some of these concerns and to try and find methods that would seem a better fit for the "home country"—for example, in terms of welfare and legal structures—is to look to neighboring countries. This is perhaps more relevant in Europe where most countries have clear neighbors with greater cultural similarities. However, in only looking to what is culturally similar, there is the chance that implicit cultural values about how to understand and respond to a particular societal problem gain a greater influence in decision-making than perhaps what would otherwise be explicitly intended.

The Gothenburg SSPF model however represented a bolder step towards addressing prevention of gang involvement. Multi-agency working groups would now aim to work with youth at the individual and group level. Through a fixed meeting structure—for example, weekly or bi-monthly—multi-agency meetings would use pooled knowledge to identify at-risk youth or groups of youth, develop joint plans of action, and deliver these plans in collaboration. City districts would have a local SSPF-coordinator responsible for local operations. The working groups would also be governed by steering groups, tasked with resolving resource and other organizational issues, so that the working group could focus on the at risk youth. Each city district would autonomously run its own SSPF, but with central process support from Young & Safe. Potential issues of city districts deviating from or not implementing the model could *in theory* be resolved via Young & Safe's city-level central steering group.

The steering group was however later disbanded along with a reorganization of and re-formulation of the role for Young & Safe. It went from a freestanding position, answering to the Mayor's office (and thus the top political level in Gothenburg), to integration into a unit in a new department in the city's administration: the Department of Social Resources. Left for Young & Safe was the process facilitator role, operating on the city districts' request or invitation, which placed the steering mandate solely in the hands of the city districts. This turn-around could be seen as an attempt to strengthen the crime prevention work in Gothenburg since Young & Safe was incorporated into a department along with other units with other kinds of crime prevention

[11] There are, for example, a number of policy and practice documents concerning SSP in Denmark, but no formal outcome evaluations.

assignments. The move, however, deconstructed Young & Safe's position as bearer of the primary response to the gang issue and thereby weakened its capacity and authority. One explanation for this change is that Young & Safe was perceived by some people as organizationally challenging—in other words, not "in line" with other established or even new and important players with a stake in the gang issue (Forkby and Larsen 2005). Furthermore, the formation of the Department of Social Resources made Young & Safe somewhat obsolete as a strategic coordinating actor, and the steering role was taken over by a group of top-officials from this new department and the police. Whatever the reasons for this restructuring, the consequence for the SSPF model was that no role or department at the central level was assigned with a governing directive of SSPF, such as ensuring methods brought together comprehensive knowledge about interventions with grass-roots know-how.

With the introduction of SSPF, we see the familiar themes of collaboration, collective responsibility, and the focus on structures, rather than methods. The difference this time was that there was now more structure to help focus on individuals or groups of individuals. We also see a model that promotes consensus or experience-based decision-making when it comes to methods or interventions. The formation and content of action plans—and what actually gets delivered—are by and large left to joint discussion at the local-level and reliant on *existing* practices. To some extent, this consensus-driven approach is necessary to resolve the issue of a central city-level structure being managed by autonomous city districts but comprising partners such as the police who are managed within regional and national structures. An important mechanism in the SSPF model perhaps is not so much what gets delivered but that existing interventions could be delivered faster and in a more coordinated fashion. A collaborative, consensus-driven agenda, however, potentially misses a chance to rethink methods and try and test new forms of intervention or alternatively to use tried and tested methods from the international literature, in other words, evidence-based interventions. In particular, the SSPF approach can be criticized because the key issue of how to define youth "at risk" was largely left to each working group and the identification of risk and needs relied on the presumed expertise of participants in the working group. In short, no standard way of working with risk factors and thus interventions related to these was proposed.

The SSPF model attracted the attention of other city districts in Gothenburg; the model was viewed as desirable, interesting, and potentially effective for youth-at-risk. The attraction could possibly be explained by the fact that the model expanded upon preexisting models of collaboration used in the districts, together with the fact that Young & Safe had become a city-wide concept. Another factor was that additional districts were also now confronted with gang issues, which in turn could be related to the new focus on gangs and a growing use of gang discourse within, for example, the city's administration. At an organizational and structural level, there was also a reorganization within the police, which made previous geographical (city-district level) divisions dysfunctional, as well a political policy to keep the city together: "a problem in one district, is also a problem for the city as a whole" (and the adoption of similar techniques by the other city districts would display joint responsibility).

At this stage of expansion, there was no information about the actual effectiveness of the model. But the model was deemed reasonable—familiar and challenging—enough *potentially* to achieve good results, and a sense of commitment to and engagement in implementing the model followed. Consequently the model was rolled out to all ten[12] Gothenburg city districts. As not all districts experienced the same level of troublesome youth groups, the original objective of preventing youth joining gangs was now widened to include youth at risk of crime more generally. The intention was still to focus on individuals or groups of individuals, though each city district was at liberty to implement the model to suit local needs. There could be an advantage in allowing multi-agency prevention models to be flexible enough that they can be adjusted locally. The dilemma is, however, when local autonomy means that a multi-agency model can be adjusted so much that it becomes unrecognizable, and in turn makes collaboration *more* difficult. For example, if partners in SSPF come to meetings with very different views about the aims and purpose of the meeting, this potentially increases frustration between agencies and decreases faith and trust in the other agencies, which could make multi-agency collaboration in the future more difficult. Such multi-agency problems have previously been noted in the gang evaluation literature, for example, by Decker and Curry (2003). In their evaluation of the SafeFutures program, they noted variable implementation of the program and concluded that changing the behavior of at-risk youth may be easier than changing the behavior of the system that responds to such youth (Decker and Curry 2003). A worse outcome of a proliferation of models deviating from the key purpose of SSPF is that it could fail on two highly valued aspects in the Swedish social model: safeguarding the needs of the individual and providing an equal service to young people regardless of where they live.

14.5 Developments at the National Level

Thus far the focus in this discussion has been on Gothenburg, with some of our analyses linking to wider Swedish social welfare history and culture. Although we see Gothenburg as being an exemplary case in point, it is important to note that there were also developments at the national level, both in terms of prevention but also in promoting desistance. In 2008, the government established a commission to look at solutions to these joint problems. In terms of gang prevention, the commission's report (SOU 2010:15) looked at international research on risk factors for joining gangs, but regarding responses, e.g., prevention and intervention methods, the focus was primarily on existing Swedish collaboration structures such as SSPF or on the existing frameworks by which social services need to abide legally. Admittedly, research on models and methods for gang prevention could be said to be in its infancy, but the lack of attention to the international literature on

[12]After an administrative reorganization, the number of city districts changed from 21 to 10.

interventions is remarkable. We argue that implicit cultural values about how things should be done may have played a role. The preference for collaboration and collective structures seemed to be present also at the national level.

A central suggestion arising out of the commission's report was to establish Social Intervention Groups (SIGs) at the local, municipal level. These groups would comprise regular meetings between representatives from schools, social services, and the police to co-ordinate plans of action at the individual level. In other words, the SSPF model was more or less proposed as the national strategy for Sweden's gang prevention,[13] even though SIGs would work with an extended age-range (15–25 year olds). Suggestions for actual methods or content of interventions in SIGs remained at a structural and organizational level, that is, suggestions were left open as to who will do the work, with which partners, and what work. Again, history seems to repeat itself; it is not that these proposals should be critiqued for their content, rather for what is absent: suggestions for actual interventions or methods based on sound evaluation research, where available, were missing. The mandate for what actually gets delivered is instead handed to local decision-making and local practice. Where national proposals focus on which collaborative structures are needed—and not on what interventions for individuals or groups should be delivered—there is the risk that the collaborative structures are seen as the desired end-result and not the process to achieve results.

The evaluation of the pilot phase of SIGs (in 12 sites across Sweden) included description of implementation problems such as variable operational aims and objectives between pilot sites (Wollter et al. 2012). The evaluators stated that being unable to implement (or agree upon) basic definitional issues resulted in a number of pilot areas either working with youth other than those in SIGs' supposed target group or working with very few youth at all. They also reported feedback from pilot areas from professionals who thought it would be a better idea to wait until the youth were older and had themselves tired of gang life; in other words, a "do-nothing" intervention! Criticism aside, we make this point to exemplify how national proposals devoid of content for interventions do little to ensure that actual interventions are delivered for the youth who most need them (see Pressman and Wildavsky 1983).

In conclusion, the national proposals concerning SIGs brought a clearer focus on the issue of troublesome youth groups and gangs with a will to look outside of Sweden for ideas for how to *understand* the issue. We also, however, maintain that there was a sociocultural blind spot when it came to response strategies, such as developing prevention and interventions. Implicit values and ideas about "the way things are done" were perhaps guiding decisions more than necessary. The pitfall of letting implicit culture determine what gets done is that an internal—or an in-group—discourse about "best practice" goes unexamined and unchallenged, and a discourse of "best evidence" is side-lined. On

[13] Youth leisure services were not included this time. We speculate that this may in part be based on implicit cultural values of which agencies are viewed as having responsibility but also power (tools, knowledge, and legal mandate) to address the youth gang problem.

the one hand, important cultural values of collaboration, consensus, and collective responsibility are maintained. On the other hand, the response strategies which are developed may fall into an *appearance* of action when it is really business-as-usual.

14.6 Implications of the Swedish Approach: SSPF in Action

During 2014 and 2015 one of the authors of this paper was involved in an implementation evaluation of SSPF in Gothenburg (see Turner et al. 2015). Part of this work assessed whether SSPF was "evaluation ready." Epstein and Klerman (2012) argue that before a program can be evaluated it should among other things have a clear, testable program theory and be well implemented in terms of inputs, throughputs, and program fidelity in terms of A first implication of the Swedish approach to gang prevention is that tension arises between consensus-based decision-making and program fidelity in terms of intervention content and not just organizational/collaborative structures. With an open-policy on which actual interventions are delivered—such as in SSPF and SIGS—the professionals involved can play to their strengths, delivering interventions they are best placed to deliver. On the other hand, an open-policy can result in a proliferation of methods and intervention content, which have varying degrees of support from the intervention literature. At best, dedicated and experienced staff are free to devise collaborative methods that can very quickly adapt to new challenges with gangs and troublesome youth groups. This is particularly relevant in Gothenburg's "hot" zones where the nature of the youth gang problem seems to be constantly changing. Here, rapid and local responses are key. At worst, the Swedish model allows for multi-agency meetings solely to focus on internal organizational issues and youth do not make it onto the agenda at all.

In our evaluation of SSPF in Gothenburg, we explored how the over-arching structure of SSPF had been implemented in ten city districts and one neighboring municipality. Despite the SSPF model being designed to promote action with either individuals or groups of youth, only four city districts used the model in this way. In these four districts we saw a clear focus on the early identification of at-risk youth, the formation of joint action plans, and interventions delivered in tandem. This synergy—of acting together and acting early—is the key mechanism in SSPF. We also saw another central aspect of the model in action, that is, local-level professionals offering their specialist competence in collaboration. For example, each group of professionals from the four partners in SSPF would discuss what interventions they could deliver and how these could be combined, such as police and social services making home visits together to discuss their concerns with parents and the young person in question. An important aspect of multi-agency collaboration in Sweden is that the young person (or their parents, if the youth is under 16) must give consent to agencies sharing information. Obtaining consent can be a delicate matter and here we also saw examples of joint discussions identifying a professional (such as a sports instructor) who was best placed to approach the individual or their parents.

In the four districts that fully implemented the SSPF model, practice was, however, variable regarding interventions for gangs or groups deemed at risk of becoming gangs. Only one of the four districts showed a concrete way of responding to the gang as a group phenomenon, as opposed to selecting individuals in the group for intervention. This group approach involved a mapping of the group members' risk and protective factors, their group behavior such as where they hung out, and an effort to determine the links between members. Various interventions from the police and social services were then coordinated. Although the group itself was not called in together, efforts were made to call parents in to joint meetings with personnel from the school, social services, and the police. This approach bears some similarity to the Pulling Levers model[14] (see Kennedy 2011; Braga and Weisburd 2012; and Chap. 16 in this volume), though operating at a lower level of risk of harm (for example, peer robbery was the most serious crime in the sample). This approach to gangs in SSPF could also be seen as being heavier on the carrot and softer on the stick in comparison to Pulling Levers. This is in part appropriate to the risk level but also perhaps reflective of a Swedish way of doing things; for example, in Sweden youth under 16 cannot be prosecuted by the courts but in extreme circumstances can be taken into secure care by social services, though this is very much a last resort. Given that SSPF originally came about as a response to the idea of recruitment to gangs, the model can be criticized in that all but one city district had no clear way of approaching the gang as a group phenomenon. Of course, this is not to detract from the potential of individual-level interventions being effective at preventing young people from getting involved in gangs. The main point is that the local development of measures in the city districts could be seen as missing the issue of gangs as a group. Effective interventions for young people in or at risk of joining gangs require work on a number of fronts: universal measures, selective individual interventions but also measures targeted at the gang as group phenomenon.

The other city districts, however, had implemented a version of the model that was further from the intention to work at the individual or group level. Four city districts had a model which was "problem-oriented" in that multi-agency meetings would identify youth or groups of youth in need of intervention, but had not yet succeeded in implementing individual- or group-level work. The remaining three districts had instead an "internal orientation" where discussions focused instead on *how* the work should be organized, such as on which youth to focus and which partners would lead the effort to identify youth. Across these seven districts, each district coordinator was aware that the focus of SSPF was supposed to be on individual/group-level working. In trying to understand why implementation—and thus fidelity to the model—was so varied we identified a number of key factors related to the open-policy on interventions and methods as well as the local-level consensus-based approach to decision-making concerning interventions.

[14] In short, the Pulling Levers model is a "carrot and stick" approach with among other things increased police surveillance of the person and/or group's activities and a threat of maximum possible prosecution with removal of assets. This is combined with positive offers from a range of community services, such as employment, educational, and social services. Often, the entire gang is "called in" together along with their families or other close relations and offered an ultimatum. For a full description, see Kennedy (2011).

14.7 Teasing Out Fidelity Problems

Coordinators' clarity about how collaboration at the individual level would operate was key. Given that SSPF only provides an over-arching organizational structure, it makes sense that a "knowledge gap" about methods needs to be filled by the coordinator's own experience and knowledge. To some extent, a good measure of will and determination to do individual/group-level work was needed alongside personal experience and knowledge of how to work with at-risk youth (though it could be argued that a coordinator's will and determination arises from the confidence that comes with knowledge and experience). Such determination and knowledge were particularly beneficial when other local partners needed convincing or motivating into action. In particular, those coordinators that succeeded with getting individual/group-level work in operation all had strong backgrounds in individual-level youth social work. Such backgrounds though were not a requirement of the model and in some cases it was local-level decision-making (plus a dose of happenstance) that meant that the person with the right competencies ended up in the coordinator role.

Another key factor for successful implementation concerned methods or systems to jointly conduct individual-level work. The four city districts which had implemented interventions with individuals and to some extent with groups all had homegrown forms and templates for joint action plans. The city districts with these homegrown templates drew on their own professional knowledge and it can be speculated that it was a combination of knowledge, experience, and will to work in this way which led to the joint plans being formed. What we saw in other city districts was information about the youth "problem"—either generally or specifically in terms of individuals—being embroiled in local-level discussions about who was to do the work, how it was to be done, the barriers to undertaking individual-level work, and so on. In short, consensus-based local-level power for determining intervention content—a key feature of a Swedish model to gang prevention—*can* result in high-quality work adaptable to fast-changing, "hot" conditions where staff with the right competencies and experience happen to be in place. At risk of belaboring the point, the risk with this approach is that the model quickly de-rails without the right people to steer it.

14.8 Exploring Implications of the Swedish Approach (Contd.)

A second implication of a Swedish approach is a related dilemma of preserving professional role boundaries. In terms of local-level public administration in Sweden, there is a tendency towards preserving the roles and power of local-level organization of schools, social, and youth leisure services. To some extent, the SSPF model is both a solution and a threat to this autonomy. How individuals respond and act within the SSPF forum can range from a welcoming of the solution to resistance. Admittedly, this dilemma is observed in the implementation of many programs. SSPF and SIGs provide an opportunity to cross traditional boundaries and form new groupings of professionals in an "issue-focused," rather than an organizationally focused, response. The problem is, however, that the collaborative and collective feature of SSPF and perhaps of a Swedish approach more generally runs right to the top; there is no clear leadership for the model when things go awry. In a consensus-driven model, even at the steering group level, there is risk for collective drift into, for example, diffusion of purpose, vague aims and disorganized or uncoordinated action.

In our evaluation of SSPF in Gothenburg we found that the coordinators in the city districts felt the need for a central steering function to stipulate more clearly how the model should be implemented. As city districts are by and large autonomous municipalities, the only kind of central control was via process leaders who could provide support *on invitation* from city districts. This method of support relies on city districts identifying they have a need for support and then asking for it. To some degree the process leaders became skilled at inviting themselves, but it became a thin line to tread. As mentioned, the original citywide steering group that initiated SSPF was disbanded, thus removing any over-arching responsibility or means to steer the actual work. In this way, it was largely left to individuals' own imperative to challenge existing and implicit ideas about professional role boundaries between organizations (and our evaluation showed that this was only successful in just under half of the city districts).

At the grass roots level in Sweden, professional discretion and organizational autonomy sets limitations on importing and implementing new methods from other actors. The amount of attention that can be given to a new innovation must be balanced between perceived core obligations and existing peripheral ones. For example, national legislation, regulations, and governing bodies, for some actors, play a very important role. Within a collective, consensus-based model—especially concerning national proposals—local services such as schools have a vested interest in managing all sorts of existing priorities, such as legislative issues, national recommendations, and responding to the social issues of the day. In short, running an organization is very much about being perceived as a legitimate and professional actor: defensible decisions must be made and priorities (and what should be excluded) must be managed to gain organizational resources and professional capacity (Scott and Meyer 1994). Giving attention to a new actor, such as SSPF, is a risky business since it takes time, effort, and can be distracting from what is seen as the core work of the organization. And to import a new method, often with uncertain results in the specific context in question, is also viewed with caution. The organization has to relearn and invest in all sorts of resources, not to mention potentially exposing existing practices to criticism—if the new method is a better method, the traditional way of doing things must have been wrong to some extent.

The upshot of this can be argued to be unfavorable conditions for looking externally to best evidence and investing time and energy to develop and implement such interventions. The reliance on existing knowledge and on the experience of local-level personnel, at least in the current Swedish model, can produce a stalemate in terms of developing specific content for interventions. On the other hand, Swedish social workers have at least 3.5 years of university training, which should provide a good grounding for applying evidence-based methods. The dilemma in an open-model such as

SSPF becomes also one of professional pride and autonomy. Again, in our evaluation of SSPF, interventions (in those four city districts that were delivering interventions) were based on a general risk and protective factors approach, which in turn could be viewed as a sound approach. On the other hand, specific knowledge on dealing with troublesome youth groups—for example, Pulling Levers or the OJJDP's "Best practices to addressing community gang problems" (Holder Jr et al. 2010)—had not been considered.

A third and final reflection on the Swedish model is the culturally implicit idea that the problem and its solution is structural—in terms of social conditions—and collective, in terms of that it is society's role and responsibility to react; the role of the individual has less explanatory power. There are a number of consequences of this. Firstly, the emphasis on structural conditions means that, for example, in the media and in political discourse, there are calls for better youth leisure services, more jobs for young people, and so on. Whilst these are important factors *for a much-wider range of youth than just gang-members*, such structural factors are only part of the equation. Discussions of individual and group-level factors—at least in Swedish political and organizational discourse, not necessarily so in public opinion—are secondary to a focus on structural issues. This filters down, possibly through implicit cultural values, so that individualistic and especially group interventions within SSPF are also rare. In terms of individual interventions, we are thinking of one-to-one cognitive-behavioral programs for violence and/or criminal thinking as part of a wider package. This is not to relegate the importance of standard social work, such as finding decent housing, obtaining legitimate employment, and repairing or renewing positive social relationships. However, in some, or indeed many, cases individual- or group-level factors may be more urgent to address than familial or socioeconomic risk factors. For example, Klein and Maxson (2006) identify individual and peer risk factors as being the most consistent risk factors in the research literature for joining a gang.

To target gangs as a group phenomenon does not necessarily mean working with the members together, even though this can be the case for outreach work and the like, or even for gang "call ins" as used in the Pulling Levers model. There are generally held to be clear risks associated with working with groups of at-risk youth. These risks can arise from group processes where the members strengthen each other's anti-social behavior and attitudes, what Dodge et al. (2006) have labeled deviancy training. Working with the group or gang, however, means understanding how individuals are linked together, what the possible influence on the individual from the group is, what attitudes are presented toward individuals as group members and the awareness of the power that the group can put on individuals wanting to get out, or to make them willing to re-enter (see Pyrooz et al. 2010). These forces are not to be understood as forces exclusively coming from the group to the individual, but as a mutual attraction in which the individual finds identity, roles, and social bonds and the group can be strengthened from gaining another member (Forkby 2008; Harris et al. 2012; Pedersen and Lindstad 2011).

Secondly, the prominence of the collective responsibility of society—and by this we mean the state and its local level authorities—places too much emphasis on the statutory agencies, thus missing other important players. Here we are thinking of local community groups, housing organizations, voluntary and charitable organizations, and sports or other interest organizations. Such players could provide a valuable addition to the input of the statutory agencies.

14.9 Conclusion

In this chapter, we use Gothenburg and "Case Sweden" as an example to explore how a culture responds to a seemingly new problem of troublesome youth groups and how cultural values both about the nature of the problem and its solution impact how interventions are formed and delivered. Despite Sweden being a culturally "cold" zone in Lévi-Strauss (1966) terms, it nevertheless has its share of "hot spots," in part due to rapidly changing demographics concentrated in specific and often already socioeconomically deprived areas, often city suburbs. In some ways, parts of Sweden's cities are currently undergoing a social transformation that other cities such as London, New York, and Los Angeles saw earlier in their histories. With these social transformations in progress, we witness the (re)appearance of youth gangs and other troublesome youth groups, often framed within a broader notion of social disturbance. We can also track how responses are formed to these "hot spots" in a cold climate leaning on implicit cultural values. Traditional approaches of collective organization and consensus-based design of interventions seem to hold sway. In some ways, this preserves the implicit Swedish ideal of the state taking responsibility for the individual in need, but in other ways maintains a methodological status quo in the face of a new and potentially intractable problem. A focus on organizational structures ensures that all statutory agencies are at the table and responsibility is shared; a focus primarily on structure though is potentially at the cost of devising effective intervention content.

Clearly a benefit of a Swedish approach to fast-changing youth problems is that local multi-agency work has the possibility to react swiftly to new issues. Particularly where arising problems are yet to be understood or have no clear cut response, a local solution needs to be found and found quickly. A Swedish approach—with an open-policy structure and locally decided content—could be seen as a way to meet these "hot" problems with as cool a head as possible. The rejoinder is, however: what is put in place when things cool down and the local youth problem is better understood? When does it become time to focus on developing knowledge about intervention content or even move to a single-agency style delivery? The danger is that culturally implicit approaches developed in response to "hot" problems become the normal way of working and development and improvement of methods—intervention content—can be hampered. For example, even though the range of needs presented by youth at risk of gang involvement may always have multi-systemic aspects, once these needs in the local population are better understood and more predictable, a single agency may be better placed to deliver specific interventions for these needs. By way of conclusion, we speculate that the role for multi-agency, local-level, consensus-based interventions—what we think characterizes a Swedish model—may provide a valuable function in responding to such "hot" problems in cold climates. This needs to be followed, however, by the development of specific content for interventions and application of clear models for troublesome youth groups, designed with recourse to existing best practice research.

And then again, the problem of how to deal with gangs can be understood in relation to Matland's (1995) analyses of different implementation problems: is there conflict or consensus in how to understand the phenomenon, and what degree of conflicts or joint understandings are there about what to do? In "Case Sweden" the demand for collaboration could be seen as either a way to overcome conflicts or to ride on the wave of an established status quo. In either case, the lack of more specific directives for what should be done and achieved by this collaboration-as-usual can be a reflection of the simple fact that gangs provide a "wicked" problem to which good solutions are very hard to find. In these cases governance through network and partnerships could fulfill the demand for action when not really knowing what to do.

References

Bauman, Z. (1991). *Modernity and ambivalence*. Oxford, England: Polity Press.

Björk, M. (2006). *Ordningsmakten i stadens periferi. En studie av polisiära gänginsatser i Göteborg 2004–2005*. Eslöv: Symposion.

Braga, A., & Weisburd, D. (2012). The effects of "pulling levers" focused deterrence strategies on crime. *Campbell Systematic Reviews*, 2012:6. Oslo: The Campbell Collaboration.

Chaskin, J. R. (2010). The Chicago school: A context for youth intervention research and development. In J. R. Chaskin (Ed.), *Youth gangs and community intervention* (pp. 3–23). New York: Columbia University Press.

Crawford, A. (1998). *Crime prevention and community safety: Politics, policies and practices*. Harlow, England: Longman.

Decker, S. H., & Curry, G. D. (2003). Suppression without prevention, prevention without suppression: Gang intervention in St. Louis'. In S. H. Decker (Ed.), *Policing gangs and youth violence* (pp. 191–213). Belmont, CA: Wadsworth.

Dodge, K. A., Dishion, T. J., & Lansford, J. E. (2006). *Deviant peer influences in programs for youth: Problems and solutions*. New York: Guilford Press.

Ecklesiastikdepartementet. (1907). *Berättelse om Folkskolorna för år 1904*, afarbetad i Kungliga Ecklesiastikdepartementet. Stockholm: Centraltryckeriet.

Edvall Malm, D. (2012). *Det socio-polisiära handlingsnätet: Om kopplingar mellan polis och socialtjänst kring ungdomars kriminalitet och missbruk*. Umeå: Institutionen för socialt arbete, Umeå universitet.

Epstein, D., & Klerman, J. A. (2012). When is a program ready for rigorous impact evaluation? The role of a falsifiable logic model. *Evaluation Review, 36*(5), 375–401.

Esping-Andersen, G. (1990). *The three worlds of welfare capitalism*. Cambridge, England: Polity Press.

Eurostat. (2015). Asylum statistics. Retrieved April 23, 2015, from http://ec.europa.eu/eurostat/statistics-explained/index.php/Asylum_statistics

Fairclough, N. (1995). *Media discourse*. London, England: Edward Arnold.

Forkby, T. (2006). *Socialt nätverksarbete: Alliansbildning, makt och retorik*. Göteborg: FoU i Väst/GR.

Forkby, T. (2007). *Socialt arbete i polisens värld. Samverkans villkor och organisering*. Göteborg: FoU i Väst/GR.

Forkby, T. (2008). *Gängrelaterat ungdomsarbete. En utvärdering av Ung och Trygg i Göteborg*. Rapport 1:2008. Göteborg: FoU i Väst/GR.

Forkby, T., & Larsen, T. (2005). *Katalysatormodellen i brottspreventiv samverkan. Utvärdering av Ung och Trygg i Göteborgs första fas*. Rapport 9:2005. Göteborg: FoU i Väst/GR.
Forkby, T., & Liljeholm Hansson, S. (2011). *Kampen för att bli Någon. Bilder av förorten och riskabla utvecklingsvägar i Göteborg*. FoU-rapport 1:2011. Göteborg: FoU i Väst/GR.
Harris, D., Turner, R., Atkinson-Shepherd, S., & Garrett, I. (2012). Understanding the psychology of gang violence: Implications for designing effective violence interventions. *Ministry of Justice Research Series*, 2/11. London, England: Ministry of Justice.
Holder, E. H., Jr., Robinson, L. O., & och Slowikowski, J. (2010). *Best practice to address community gang problems. OJJDP's comprehensive gang model, second edition*. Washington, DC: U.S. Department of Justice Office of Justice Programs.
Huxham, C. (2000). The challenge of collaborative governance. *Public Management, 2*(3), 335–357.
Johansson, J. (2004). "Rekrytering till kriminella gäng", cited in T. Forkby & T. Larsen (2005), *Katalysatormodellen i brottspreventiv samverkan. Utvärdering av Ung och Trygg i Göteborgs första fas*. Rapport 9:2005. Göteborg: FoU i Väst/GR.
Kennedy, D. M. (2011). *Don't shoot: One man, a street fellowship, and the end of violence in inner-city America*. New York: Bloomsbury.
Klein, M. W. (2001). Resolving the Eurogang paradox. In M. W. Klein, H.-J. Kerner, C. L. Maxson, & E. G. M. Weitekamp (Eds.), *The Eurogang paradox: Street gangs and youth groups in the U.S. and Europe*. Dordrecht: Kluwer Academic.
Klein, M. W., Kerner, H.-J., Maxson, C. L., & Weitekamp, E. G. M. (Eds.). (2001). *The eurogang paradox: Street gangs and Youth groups in the U.S. and Europe*. Dordrecht: Kluwer Academic.
Klein, M. W., & Maxson, C. L. (2006). *Street gang patterns and policies*. New York: Oxford University Press.
Lee Klein, K. (1995). In search of narrative mastery: Postmodernism and the people without history. *History and Theory, 34*(4), 275–298.
Lévi-Strauss, C. (1966). *The savage mind*. Chicago: University of Chicago Press.
Liljeholm Hansson, S. (2014). Berättelser om ungdomsgäng i förorten. Genus. Makt, Moral. Göteborg: Göteborgs universitet, Institutionen för socialt arbete.
Lindgren, S.-Å. (2013). *Brottsutvecklingen i Västra Götaland och Göteborg, 1986–2011/12. En sammanvägning av register-och intervjuuppgifter*. Göteborg: Chalmers och Göteborgs Universitet.
Lundström, T., & Sallnäs, M. (2003). Klass, kön och etnicitet i den sociala barnavården. *Socialvetenskaplig tidskrift, 10*(2–3), 193–213.
Matland, R. E. (1995). Synthesizing the implementation literature: The ambiguity conflict model of policy implementation. *Journal of the Public Administration Research and Theory, 5*(2), 145–174.
Pedersen, M. L., & Lindstad, J. M. (2011). *Første led i fødekaeden? En undersøgelse af børn og unge i kriminelle grupper*. Copenhagen: Justitsministeriets Forskningskontor.
Powell, W., & DiMaggio, P. J. (Eds.). (1991). *The new institutionalism in organizational analysis*. Chicago: Chicago University Press.
Pratt, T. C., & Cullen, F. T. (2005). Assessing macro-level predictors and theories of crime: A meta-analysis. In M. Tonry (Ed.), *Crime and justice: A review of research* (Vol. 32, pp. 373–450). Chicago: University of Chicago Press.
Pressman, J., & Wildavsky, A. (1983). *Implementation. How great expectations in Washington are dashed in Oakland*. Berkeley: University of California Press.
Pyrooz, D. C., Decker, S. H., & Webb, V. J. (2010). The ties that bind: Desistance from gangs. *Crime & Delinquency, 60*(4), 491–516.
Rostami, A., Leinfelt, F., & Holgersson, S. (2012). An exploratory analysis of Swedish street gangs applying the Maxson and Klein Typology to a Swedish gang dataset. *Journal of Contemporary Criminal Justice, 28*(4), 426–445.
Sampson, R. J., Morenoff, J. D., & Gannon-Rowley, T. (2002). Assessing "neighborhood effects": Social processes and new directions in research. *Annual Review of Sociology, 28*, 443–478.
Sarnecki, J., & Pettersson, T. (2001). *Criminal networks in Stockholm*. Stockholm: Department of Criminology.
Scott, W. R., & Meyer, J. W. (1994). *Institutional environments and organizations*. London: Sage.

Shaw, C. R., & McKay, H. D. (1942). *Juvenile delinquency and urban areas: A study of rates of delinquents in relation to differential characteristics of local communities in American cities*. Chicago: University of Chicago Press.

SOU (2010:15). *Kriminella grupperingar—motverka rekrytering och underlätta avhopp*. Statens Offentliga Utredningar 2010:15. Stockholm: Regeringskansliet.

Spector, M., & Kitsuse, J. I. (1977). *Constructing social problems*. Menlo Park, CA: Cummings.

Swedish Crime Prevention Council. (2015). Retrieved July 2, 2015, from www.bra.se

Thrasher, F. M. (1927). *The gang: A study of 1,313 gangs in Chicago*. Chicago: Chicago University Press.

Turner, R., Nilsson, Å., & Jidetoft, N. (2015). SSPF—Ett fokus på ungdomar i riskzon. FoU-rapport 2: 2015. Gothenburg, Sweden: FoU I Väst/GR.

Wollter, F., Kassman, A., & Oscarsson, L. (2012). *Utvärdering av sociala insatsgrupper: Individinriktad samverkan kring unga i riskzonen*. Stockholm: Ersta Sköndal Högskola.

Chapter 15
Policing Gangs and Organized Crime: Reflections on Conceptual Confusion and Its Consequences from Two Swedish Case Studies

Amir Rostami

15.1 Introduction

The question of gangs and organized crime in Sweden has become increasingly confusing, as law enforcement, media, and policy makers tend to apply the label "organized crime" to all forms of criminal organizing. It does not matter if the organization in question is a highly organized criminal enterprise such as a biker-gang, an institutionalized organization such as a mafia, or a loosely structured group such as a street gang. The label "organized crime" is used without any consideration of the ecological and organizational differences between forms of criminal organizing. This confusion becomes all the greater when new labels such as "elite-gangs," "mafia-gangs," "ethnic-gangs," "ghetto-gangs," "youth-mafia," and "mobile serious organized crime" are used to describe what are simply criminal collaborations.

Gangs in Sweden can be traced back to the early 1990s, when international outlaw motorcycle club gangs (OMCG) became part of the Swedish criminal scene, and today Sweden has over 3000 members in gangs with identifiable symbols and signs. Despite this development, the debate about gangs and organized crime has ranged from denial of its existence to colorful depictions of an emerging threat to Swedish democracy by organized criminal entities (Rostami et al. 2012). Therefore, as in many other European countries, there is strong political will to introduce legal definitions of organized crime and gangs, and to implement deterrence approaches and harsher criminal policy as a response to the growing gang problem. All this occurs despite reports of negative experiences from countries that have chosen this path (e.g., Klein and Maxson 2006; Klein 2007; Ayling 2011).

A. Rostami (✉)
Department of Sociology, Stockholm University, Stockholm, Sweden
e-mail: amir.rostami@sociology.su.se

C.L. Maxson, F.-A. Esbensen (eds.), *Gang Transitions and Transformations in an International Context*, DOI 10.1007/978-3-319-29602-9_15

Definitions of organized crime used by European countries and governmental agencies are mostly based on the policy definitions provided by the European Union (EU)[1] and the United Nations Office on Drugs and Crime (UNTOC).[2] The definition provided by UNTOC and EU were the European Union introduced a legislative measure containing a policy definition of criminal organization in 1998. The United Nations Convention against Transnational Organized Crime, adopted by General Assembly resolution 55/25 of 15 November 2000, and the Council of the European Union framework decision on the Fight against Organized Crime[3] in 2008 was another attempt to harmonize national and international legislative instruments in defining organized crime and combat its various forms (Calderoni 2010). Unfortunately, these definitions have not clarified what is unique about organized crime but instead have created confusion (Paoli and Beken 2015). For example, Levi and Lord (2011) have criticized these policy definitions because they cover everything from Italian mafia cartels to three burglars who run a window cleaning company. Still the Swedish and European law enforcement and government agencies insist on using these definitions in their planned gang suppression operations and crime prevention strategies (e.g., Polismyndigheten 2015).

At the same time, problem- and intelligence-oriented approaches have become a core component of the efforts of Swedish law enforcement to tackle such social

[1] The Council of Europe asked member States to apply the following criteria when defining crime or criminal groups as "organized crime." See European Union (doc 6204/2/97 Enfopol 35 Rev 2). The definition is as following: *Mandatory criteria*: (1) Collaboration of three or more people. (2) For a prolonged or indefinite period of time. (3) Suspected or convicted of committing serious criminal offences. (4) With the objective of pursuing profit and/or power; Optional criteria: (5) Having a specific task or role for each participant. (6) Using some form of internal discipline and control. (7) Using violence or other means suitable for intimidation. (8) Exerting influence on politics, the media, public administration, law enforcement, the administration of justice or the economy by corruption or any other means. (9) Using commercial or business-like structures. (10) Engaged in money laundering. (11) Operating on an international level. In addition to the minimum characteristics (the "mandatory criteria" 1–4), at least two of the "optional criteria" need to be applicable to qualify a criminal group or crime as organized crime.

[2] According to The United Nations Convention on Transnational Organized Crime (UNTOC) Article 2: (a) "Organized criminal group" shall mean a structured group of three or more persons, existing for a period of time and acting in concert with the aim of committing one or more crimes or offences established in accordance with this Convention, in order to obtain, directly or indirectly, a financial or other material benefit; (b) "Serious crime" shall mean conduct constituting an offence punishable by maximum deprivation of liberty of at least 4 years or a more serious penalty; (c) "Structured group" shall mean a group that is not randomly formed for the immediate commission of an offence and that does not need to have formally defined roles for its members, continuity of its membership, or a developed structure.

[3] Council framework decision 2008/841/JHA of 24 October 2008 on the fight against organized crime article 1: (1) "criminal organisation" means a structured association, established over a period of time, of more than two persons acting in concert with a view to committing offences which are punishable by deprivation of liberty or a detention order of a maximum of at least 4 years or a more serious penalty, to obtain, directly or indirectly, a financial or other material benefit; (2) "structured association" means an association that is not randomly formed for the immediate commission of an offence, nor does it need to have formally defined roles for its members, continuity of its membership, or a developed structure.

problems. In order to apply a problem-solving approach, it is crucial to phrase and describe the problem correctly. The first stage of problem solving is actually to identify if there is a problem to be solved. Inadequate definitions can have a negative effect on crime prevention strategies and police operations because inadequate definitions can result in inadequate understanding of the "problem" and consequently result in inadequate strategies and choice of methods in operations targeting the "problem." A useful definition of the phenomenon should aim to define distinct elements, such as the level of relations, organizational elements and dimensions of the collective identity and recourses of organized criminal collaborations. The question is whether it is possible to address all these dimensions in a single unifying definition of organized crime. If all forms of criminal collaboration meet the criteria for organized crime, then what does it even mean to have a definition?

Gangs and other forms of organized crime groups are evolved and shaped by their particular social, economic, and political contexts. Inadequate definitions create difficulties in framing these problems and do not take into consideration the importance of differentiation between various gangs and other forms of criminal organizing in terms of social response and policing (e.g., Matsuda et al. 2012). This creates ambiguity and confusion rather than clarity, which should be the fundamental aim of a definition (e.g., Finckenauer 2005; Hagan 2006).

Inadequate policy or legal definitions of organized crime and gangs can unintentionally create a shortcut for law enforcement and government representatives to label individuals as gang members and racketeers for incarcerating them for as long as possible instead of tackling the deeply rooted social problems that lead to gang involvement.

In this chapter, I consider the consequences of conceptual confusion on policing gangs and organized crime in Sweden. I bring together the results of two case studies, and argue that policy makers and practitioners need to understand conceptual differences and similarities between different forms of criminal organizing instead of making up new labels without defined meaning. Rather, it is important to identify the type and level of organizing before planning a response, since gangs and other forms of organized criminal collaboration exist on a continuum and vary in time and space.

15.2 The Consequence of Working Without Proper Problem Definition

Intelligence analyses and assessments have become vital components of problem-solving approaches in policing, especially in the fight against gangs and organized crime (Leinfelt and Rostami 2012; Rostami and Mondani 2015). These assessments have also served as guidelines in policymaking, with potential implications for law-making and criminal policy. In this context, the field of social network analysis has received increasing attention for the study of criminal networks and in criminal intelligence analysis (Masys 2014). Most of these assessments and analyses consist of crime network data from official co-offending data. Official co-offending data suffers from various selection biases (Rostami and Mondani 2015). For example, crimes that never were discovered are not covered by the data; in addition, certain populations are at higher risk of detection and thus are registered more often (Gelman et al. 2007).

Rostami and Mondani (2015) analyzed the intelligence assessments of the Swedish police to investigate whether different data sources influence the results of network analysis. The authors examined one specific Swedish street gang using three different datasets: intelligence, surveillance, and co-offending data. The datasets came from a planned operation by the Swedish police gang task force in response to a specific street gang, with the goal of incarcerating strategically positioned gang members and ultimately suppressing the gang. The gang was targeted by law enforcement in Sweden for more than 4 years. As a consequence, the authorities put considerable effort and resources into collecting intelligence. The police intelligence assessment (based on intelligence gathering) consisted of a mapping of social relations among gang members. In major operations targeting specific crime groups and networks, the police surveillance, investigation and intelligence branches work in close collaboration to collect intelligence in order to eradicate the targeted gang. In this particular case, the gang task force never defined the gang in the planned operation, apart from the fact that individuals were defined as gang members because they wore symbols and other signs of gang affiliation. The ecological and organizational dimensions of the gang were never specified, and no further understanding of its evolving context was put into the assessment.

In the study under discussion, Rostami and Mondani built networks from different data sources, and compared them by computing graph distance, centrality, and clustering measures. The main finding of this study clearly indicates that different data sources on the same gang have a fundamental impact on the results. Different datasets for the same phenomenon produce fundamentally different pictures. The same individuals have different ranking in their importance, depending on the dataset and measure. Consequently, it becomes difficult to decide whom to target in a planned operation based on these sets of data. The authors concluded that the network based on intelligence analysis was substantially different from those based on surveillance and co-offending networks. This was interpreted as an indication that the view presented by police intelligence assessments can greatly distort the actual facts, and that they suffer from various biases. The authors also concluded that the intelligence assessment based on limited network data should be viewed critically and strengthened by the simultaneous use of other data sources.

One reason why this intelligence assessment was so limited was that the targeted phenomenon was never defined. The assessment focused on a single frame of analysis, such as social relations, without considering other important factors. The ecological and organizational dimensions of the targeted gang were not taken into account, nor was there an assessment of which policies and measures were the most appropriate. The only goal was to incarcerate strategically positioned gang members without considering whether this would have the intended preventive effect or not. Without initially defining the targeted problem and choosing an appropriate strategy for gang control, law enforcement officials were unable to specify the organizational dimensions and understand its evolving context. The gang was defined as a gang only because the gang members described themselves as gang members. There was for example no assessment of type of gang, level of organizational growth, duration, and crime pattern or gang identity. Instead, an assumption was made that certain structural dimensions of the gang in question were real, with the consequence that the operational methods employed increased the identity and cohesiveness of the gang (Rostami and Leinfelt 2012a). This is problematic, since gang cohesiveness is central to the nature and control of street gangs, because stronger gang cohesiveness can result in more gangs and more gang crime (Klein 1995).

Overall, in understanding and preventing gangs and other forms of criminal organizations, law enforcement officers and other practitioners need to undertake a deep analysis of its social, economic, and political causes. Instead of single-level analysis and faulty problem definitions, officials need to thoroughly analyze its causes, the organizational dynamics, and the effects of biases on the analysis results. Doing so will facilitate tailoring responses to these phenomena, for example, using the basic Scanning and Analysis of the SARA model of approaching crime problems.

In our case, the main response from law enforcement was "stop and search" gang members and affiliates without further analysis of its consequences. Since the gang was evolving, this choice of tactical response contributed to strengthening the gang cohesiveness and by law enforcement's own assessment the gang became more resistant to gang control efforts (Leinfelt and Rostami 2012; Rostami and Mondani 2015).

15.3 The Consequence of Working with Broad Definitions

In response to gang developments since the 1990s, the Stockholm County Police has implemented a number of initiatives against gang and organized crime in Stockholm. One of the biggest initiatives is project NOVA, a joint effort launched by the county police chief in September 2003 to "combat serious organized crime." NOVA uses the definition of organized crime promulgated by the EU,[4] and classifies all forms of crime-oriented groups such as street gangs, outlaw motorcycle club gangs, crime networks, and others as organized crime. There is no reference to the type of groups that should not be included; rather it is up to the management of the Stockholm County Police and NOVA to choose the crime groups that they consider suitable. In 2008, the project name was changed from NOVA to Action Group NOVA (i.e., task force) (Rostami et al. 2014).

[4] See footnote 2.

NOVA's operational approach has been to employ two teams of six police officers. Its main task was, and is to this day, to identify, arrest, and prosecute persons deemed to be most problematic with respect to gangs and organized crime. The intention of the Swedish police in founding NOVA was to prevent gangs and other forms of "organized crime" from emerging in Stockholm and to do so through suppression and aggressive pursuit of those on the NOVA watch-list. When the Stockholm County Police first presented the project, they described the purpose of the task force as:

> A confrontational approach that can be described as almost zero-tolerance. The goal is to prosecute, disrupt, and bring identified networks and individuals out of balance. The methodology should be seen as a complement to conventional reconnaissance and other traditional operations. (Rostami et al. 2014, p. 6)

Rostami et al. (2014) studied the effectiveness of the NOVA initiative by comparing official statements with prosecution statistics and internal documents related to the joint effort. One of the findings of this study was that, while police officials labeled the anti-gang task force as a success in the media, analyses of prosecution statistics and internal police documents demonstrated a less-than-ideal picture of this operation. While the official message by the police was that NOVA was a successful and effective blow to organized crime in Stockholm, the NOVA personnel expressed their frustration about not making any evident progress towards reaching their goals. For example, one NOVA manager stated, "We are, unfortunately, just whipping around on the surface when it comes to serious organized crime" (Rostami et al. 2014, p. 13).

In 2009, NOVA had the responsibility of targeting 24 crime groups operating in Stockholm County with only two teams of police officers. The 24 groups targeted in 2009 included traditional street gangs, outlaw motorcycle gangs, mafia-type organizations, and more loosely connected youths committing robberies and thefts. The study found that while NOVA officers consistently worked on cases, few groups were targeted by police investigations and operations on a consistent basis. Four of the 24 crime groups (17 %) were never subjected to any activity[5] at all during the year. Eleven crime groups (46 %) were subject to 1–5 activities. Only two crime groups, the outlaw motorcycle club Bandidos MC and the so-called Syriac Mafia (Södertälje nätverket), were targeted between 15 and 20 times during the entire year of 2009, although a closer inspection of these figures suggests that 81 % of the activities against the Syriac Mafia were conducted during 1 week and thus did not represent a sustained effort across the year. In total, no substantial effect regarding decline of crime or membership could be found during the examined period.

One of the conclusions of the study was that despite the failure of NOVA as an anti-gang initiative, the Stockholm County Police utilized the media to disseminate information to the public in hope of accomplishing particular organizational goals and heightening the legitimacy of the police in the public eye. The police leadership stated on the police website:

> It has shown very good results, says N (county police chief). NOVA has caused the reduction in a variety of crimes, as their perpetrators have been arrested and convicted for their

[5] Activity meaning for example stop and search, search of premises, house search, arrests, and fines.

[previous] crimes. NOVA has severely disrupted serious and organized crime. (Rostami et al. 2014, p. 8)

The authors further concluded that instead of framing the problem and targeting the group in their evolving context by problem solving and a flexible approach, NOVA operations were characterized by a lack of definitional boundaries between different groups (Rostami et al. 2014). Basically, no distinction was made between these 24 different groups. Mafia-type organizations, outlaw motorcycle club gangs, street gangs, and loosely connected crime networks were targeted with the same strategy and methods leading to failure in reducing and controlling the targeted groups.

In sum, a broad definition can have consequences just as negative as not using any definition at all because a broad definition can result in targeting various forms of crime groups as gangs. By officially labeling and targeting various forms of crime groups as gangs, the authorities run the risk of "constructing" gangs by giving crime groups a brand, status, media attention, and consequently public fear, alienation and a gang identity. A broad definition can also create barriers for resource optimization because it is basically difficult to assess and prioritize which "problem" should be addressed. Without proper conceptualization of the problem, law enforcement efforts are doomed to be misguided and ineffective.

15.4 The Need to Clearly Conceptualize and Better Understand the Emergence of Criminal Organization

The most fundamental roles of law enforcement in a modern democratic society are to keep peace and order, to enforce law, to protect persons and property, and to investigate crimes. Basically, policing involves a set of activities aimed at preserving the security of social order (Wright 2002; Reiner 2000). Law enforcement also has special duties such as countering terrorism, gangs, and other forms of criminal organization (Levi 2007, 2008; Wright 2002). To fulfill its main duties and responsibilities, law enforcement has developed policies and models to prioritize and focus their activities.

The standard model of policing consists of a traditional reactive response to crime, random patrolling, crime investigation once an offence has been detected, and response to specific requests from individuals or groups that require immediate response. There is a reliance on suppressive force and the legal system as the primary means of trying to control and reduce crime (Cordner and Sheehan 1999; Weisburd and Eck 2004). However, during the last four decades, several paradigms in police strategies have been developed to deal with the limitations of the standard policing model. For example, Community-Oriented Policing (COP), Problem-Oriented Policing (POP), Intelligence-Led Policing (ILP), and CompStat have moved policing to adopt a more proactive and preventive model in response to crime (Tilley 2008; Newburn 2005). The essence of proactive police strategies involves police on their own initiative, systematically collecting and assessing information about crime as well as strategies for its reduction and prevention (Crank 1998). One core element of intelligence-led policing and other proactive strategies is based on some type of crime or intelligence analysis of information regarding a specific problem. Essentially, it is about collecting information or receiving information from an intelligence source on the subject the police is targeting. Intelligence is then assessed and serves as a guide to police management and operations with the goal of detecting, reducing, or disrupting criminal activity, or solving a problem (Ratcliffe 2008; Tilley 2008). Together, crime intelligence and assessments have a tactical and strategic role in policing and constitute a basis for planned operations. Even threat assessments by law enforcement agencies around the world, such as Europol, FBI and the Swedish police, which serve as a guide to policy makers, are to a larger extent based on some sort of intelligence analysis.

As a result, the modern model of policing has moved in the direction of problem solving as a central strategy (Newburn 2005). As such, the management of the Swedish police and all planned operations in the organization are based on the Polisens Underrättelsemodell (PUM), a model based on the National Intelligence Model (NIM), which in turn derives from ideas drawn from intelligence-led policing (e.g., Gottschalk 2010; Tilley 2008; Rikspolisstyrelsen 2011). As such, the problem and intelligence assessment of gangs and organized crime have gradually become a core component in crime investigations and tactical and strategic intelligence assessments, which in turn form the basis for operational and strategic decision making by policy makers and practitioners.

At the same time, law enforcement organizations are presented with a particular challenge when it comes to policing gangs and organized crime. To increase the legitimacy of the police in society, law enforcement makes use of the media to disseminate constructed information (Chermak 1995). The failure of law enforcement agencies to adequately control gangs and organized crime can erode the reputation of the police and lead to police cynicism (Kirk and Papachristos 2011). The police and other government officials may feel pressure to portray their efforts to combat gangs and organized crime in a way that maintains and enhances their reputation concerning their ability to respond to and control crime, and to carry out the policy objectives set by government in an efficient manner. In this regard, the use of broad definitions can be desirable because the police can choose how and which part of the efforts should be presented to gain the public's confidence (Rostami et al. 2014).

This conceptual confusion creates problems since there is substantial consensus among researchers and practitioners about the need to identify the type of problem in question before implementing societal policies (Goldstein 1990). Different types of problems require different types of policies and measures (Klein and Maxson 2006; Rostami and Leinfelt 2012b). Failure to accurately identify the problem may result in efforts that are misguided and at best ineffective and at worst counterproductive. This confusion becomes problematic because decisions and actions taken at different levels will not have the intended effect. Since the need to control organized crime is and has been used to justify and explain a wide range of legislative measures in the European Union, with significant impacts on civil rights, inadequate assessments can give rise to serious long-term consequences (Symeonidou-Kastanidou 2007).

Conceptual confusion also makes it difficult to assess community intervention efforts and other governmental policies when the target is ill defined. For example, it is an open question whether law enforcement agencies are successful in targeting organized crime when they incarcerate members of youth groups. Do stop-and-search policies aimed at peripheral members of a subgroup of Hells Angels MC strike a powerful blow at this international outlaw motorcycle club? If we cannot determine the true nature of organized crime and gangs, how can we hope to understand and study the efficiency of society's efforts at prevention or intervention? If a problem is not well defined, how can that problem be analyzed and appropriate measures and solutions be implemented?

From the results of our two recently published studies, I conclude that a broad definition can have consequences just as negative as not using any definition at all. After all, without a broad understanding of the ecological and organizational differences between forms of criminal organizing there is a risk that society's efforts will be misguided and ineffective. Without stipulating what is being targeted, policies, laws, and other actions will be based on inaccurate assessments, which in turn may have negative policy implications.

A project has recently been initiated with funding from Riksbankens Jubileumsfond (the Swedish Foundation for Humanities and Social Sciences) with the purpose of contributing to an understanding of the emergence of criminal organizing, such as gangs and organized crime.[6] The project intends to elaborate a model that can explain the degree of organization as an endogenous process in which past criminal behavior and criminal collaborations are the main focus. The project aims to propose crime prevention strategies and polices at an early stage, before the (criminal) organizations (re-)organize themselves and become maximally resilient. We hope that the project results in studies on criminal organizing and provides better advice to policy makers and practitioners in their efforts to prevent crime.

References

Ayling, J. (2011). Criminalizing organizations: Towards deliberative lawmaking. *Law & Policy, 33*(2), 149–178.

Calderoni, F. (2010). *Organized crime legislation in the European Union: Harmonization and approximation of criminal law, national legislations and the EU framework decision on the fight against organized crime*. Berlin, Germany: Springer.

[6]Institute for Future Studies (2015). http://www.iffs.se/projekt/kriminella-natverk-och-kriminell-organisering/

Chermak, S. M. (1995). *Victims in the news: Crime and the American news media*. Boulder, CO: Westview Press.
Cordner, G. W., & Sheehan, R. (1999). *Police administration*. Cincinnati, OH: Anderson.
Crank, J. P. (1998). *Understanding police culture*. Cincinnati, OH: Anderson.
Finckenauer, J. O. (2005). Problems of definition: What is organized crime? *Trends in Organized Crime, 8*(3), 63–83.
Gelman, A., Jeffrey, F., & Alex, K. (2007). An analysis of the New York City Police Department's "Stop-and-Frisk" policy in the context of claims of racial bias. *Journal of the American Statistical Association, 102*(479), 813–823.
Goldstein, H. (1990). *Problem-oriented policing*. Philadelphia: Temple University Press.
Gottschalk, P. (2010). *Policing organized crime: Intelligence strategy implementation* (Advances in police theory and practice series). Boca Raton, FL: Taylor & Francis.
Hagan, F. E. (2006). "Organized crime" and "organized crime": Indeterminate problems of definition. *Trends in Organized Crime, 9*(4), 127–137.
Kirk, D. S., & Papachristos, A. V. (2011). Cultural mechanisms and the persistence of neighborhood violence. *American Journal of Sociology, 166*(4), 1190–1233.
Klein, M. W. (1995). *The American street gang: Its nature, prevalence, and control*. New York: Oxford University Press.
Klein, M. W. (2007). *Chasing after street gangs: A forty-year journey*. Upper Saddle River, NJ: Pearson Prentice Hall.
Klein, M. W., & Maxson, C. L. (2006). *Street gang patterns and policies*. New York: Oxford University Press.
Leinfelt, F., & Rostami, A. (2012). *The Stockholm gang model: PANTHER*. Stockholm: Erlander.
Levi, M. (2007). Organized crime and terrorism. In M. Maguire, R. Morgan, & R. Reiner (Eds.), *The Oxford handbook of criminology* (pp. 771–809). Oxford, England: Oxford University Press.
Levi, M. (2008). Policing fraud and organised crime. In T. Newburn (Ed.), *Handbook of policing* (pp. 522–552). Cullompton, England: Willan.
Levi, M., & Lord, N. (2011). Links between corruption and organised crime, and research Gaps. In D. Thelesklaf & P. G. Pereira (Eds.), *Non-state actors in asset recovery* (pp. 39–61). Bern: Peter Lang.
Masys, A. J. (2014). *Networks and network analysis for defence and security*. Berlin: Springer.
Matsuda, K. N., Esbensen, F.-A., & Carson, D. C. (2012). Putting the "Gang" in "Eurogang": Characteristics of delinquent youth groups by different definitional approaches. In F.-A. Esbensen & C. L. Maxson (Eds.), *Youth gangs in international perspective: Results from the Eurogang program of research*. New York: Springer.
Newburn, T. (2005). *Policing: Key readings*. Cullompton, England: Willan.
Paoli, L., & Beken, T. V. (2015). Organized crime: A contested concept. In L. Paoli (Ed.), *The Oxford handbook of organized crime*. New York: Oxford University Press.
Polismyndigheten. (2015). *Polisens rapport om organiserad brottslighet 2015*. Stockholm: Polismyndigheten.
Ratcliffe, J. (2008). *Intelligence-led policing*. Cullompton, England: Willan.
Reiner, R. (2000). *The politics of the police*. New York: Oxford University Press.
Rikspolisstyrelsen. (2011). *Polisen-en presentation*. Stockholm: Rikspolisstyrelsen.
Rostami, A., & Leinfelt, F. (2012a). Bridging science and pragmatism. In F. Leinfelt & A. Rostami (Eds.), *The Stockholm gang model—PANTHER*. Erlander: Stockholm.
Rostami, A., & Leinfelt, F. (2012b). The Stockholm Gang Intervention and Prevention Project (SGIP): Introducing a holistic approach to gang enforcement. In F.-A. Esbensen & C. L. Maxson (Eds.), *Youth gangs in international perspective: Results from the Eurogang program of research*. New York: Springer.
Rostami, A., Leinfelt, F., & Holgersson, S. (2012). An exploratory analysis of Swedish street gangs: Applying the Maxson and Klein Typology to a Swedish gang dataset. *Journal of Contemporary Criminal Justice, 28*(4), 426–445.

Rostami, A., Melde, C., & Holgersson, S. (2014). The myth of success: The emergence and maintenance of a specialized gang unit in Stockholm, Sweden. *International Journal of Comparative and Applied Criminal Justice, 39*(3), 199–217.
Rostami, A., & Mondani, M. (2015). The complexity of crime network data: A case study of its consequences for crime control and the study of networks. *PLOS ONE, 10*(3), e0119309.
Symeonidou-Kastanidou, E. (2007). Towards a new definition of organised crime in the European Union. *European Journal of Crime, Criminal Law and Criminal Justice, 15*(1), 83–103.
Tilley, N. (2008). Modern approaches to policing: Community, problem-oriented and intelligence-led. In T. Newburn (Ed.), *Handbook of policing* (pp. 373–403). Cullompton, England: Willan.
Weisburd, D., & Eck, J. E. (2004). What can police do to reduce crime, disorder and fear? *The Annals of the American Academy of Political and Social Science, 593*(1), 42–65.
Wright, A. (2002). *Policing: An introduction to concepts and practice*. Cullompton, England: Willan.

Chapter 16
Pulling Levers on Gang Violence in London and St. Paul

James A. Densley and David Squier Jones

16.1 Introduction

Offenders and victims of homicide and gun violence are disproportionately members of small, readily identifiable, street groups (Decker and Pyrooz 2010), many of which satisfy the Eurogang definitional criteria (Klein and Maxson 2006). All gangs are groups, but not all groups are gangs. Gangs may be "qualitatively different" groups (Klein and Maxson 2006, pp. 11–12), but the group processes and honor code of the street underlying the cyclical, reciprocal, and retaliatory nature of violence perpetrated in furtherance of all street groups "warrant special attention" (Papachristos 2009, 2012, p. 49; Anderson 1999; Decker et al. 2013). Such is the logic behind Group Violence Intervention (GVI), a well-documented gang violence reduction strategy, consistent with problem-oriented policing models (Goldstein 1990), that began life as "Operation Ceasefire" in Boston in the 1990s (Braga et al. 2001) and now is codified by the National Network for Safe Communities (2013).

In the neo-classical criminology tradition (Cornish and Clarke 1986), GVI is a focused deterrence or "coerced abstinence" strategy comprising various tactics (Kleiman 2009, p. 40). GVI begins with a problem analysis, such as a systematic review of all violent incidents and an audit or mapping of all violent groups in any given jurisdiction (see Papachristos 2012). Once the key players are identified, coordinated law enforcement action against the most violent group follows in an effort to demonstrate to other groups that violence will not be tolerated (National Network for Safe Communities 2013). Next, community moral voices and social

J.A. Densley (✉)
School of Law Enforcement and Criminal Justice, Metropolitan State University,
St. Paul, MN, USA
e-mail: james.densley@metrostate.edu

D.S. Jones
School of Criminology and Criminal Justice, Northeastern University,
Boston, MA, USA

C.L. Maxson, F.-A. Esbensen (eds.), *Gang Transitions and Transformations in an International Context*, DOI 10.1007/978-3-319-29602-9_16

service providers partner with law enforcement to engage directly with violent group members (and through them, their associates) in a "call-in," or face-to-face meeting, at a venue of civic importance (Kennedy 2011).

The call-in is perhaps the most famous GVI tactic, to the extent it is commonly misrepresented as the entire strategy (for a discussion, see Kennedy 2011). At each call-in, group members receive three direct, mutually reinforcing messages. First, police and prosecutors communicate that future violence in furtherance of the group will be met with swift, severe, and certain consequences, in part because the entire group will be held accountable for violence perpetrated by any one member. In other words, if one group member violates the terms of the ceasefire, law enforcement will *pull* every civil and criminal *lever* available (e.g., outstanding warrants, probation and parole violations, open cases) to dismantle the entire group (Braga and Weisburd 2012a, b; Kennedy 1997). Second, community representatives articulate why violence is morally reprehensible and henceforth unacceptable. In doing so, they clarify and reinforce the community's standards, aspirations, frustrations, and expectations, but also reintegrate group members back into the community on the condition of nonviolence. The strong presence of police and community working together, moreover, "heighten[s] the perceived risk of apprehension" and sanction (Braga and Weisburd 2012b, p. 349). Third, social service providers inform group members that genuine help is available for those who want it, thus facilitating an honorable exit from street life via counseling, employment, education, and training (National Network for Safe Communities 2013).

GVI has been criticized for exaggerated claims of violence cessation, a lack of durability, and failure to address root causes of violence (Fagan 2002; Rosenfeld et al. 2005). However, from the original "Boston Miracle" (Papachristos et al. 2007, p. 226) to initiatives in Minneapolis (Kennedy and Braga 1998), Indianapolis (McGarrell et al. 2006), Chicago (Papachristos et al. 2007), Stockton (Braga 2008), Cincinnati (Engel et al. 2013; Tillyer et al. 2012), and even Glasgow (Deuchar 2013), there is "strong empirical evidence" for GVI's effectiveness (Braga and Weisburd 2012b, p. 25). This chapter contributes to this evidence base by exploring GVI variations in Saint Paul, Minnesota (USA), and London, England (UK). True to Eurogang traditions (Klein 2006), this study is based on comparisons. The central question is whether or not Saint Paul and London implemented GVI-like focused deterrence with reasonable fidelity to its core principles. To this end, findings are organized around these principles: (1) problem analysis; (2) demonstration enforcement action; (3) community moral voices and social services; (4) the call-in; and (5) maintenance and ensuring program integrity (National Network for Safe Communities 2013). The chapter concludes with discussion of the two case studies and implications for future gang and group violence intervention efforts.

16.2 Policing Gangs in Saint Paul

The City of Saint Paul is Minnesota's capital and its second largest city with a population of approximately 290,770 (U.S. Census Bureau 2012). Saint Paul's resident population is 55.9 % non-Hispanic White, 15.7 % Black, 15 % Asian, 9.6 % Hispanic/

Latino, with 3.8 % being of other or mixed races. Within Saint Paul, 22.8 % of residents live below the poverty level. The Saint Paul Police Department (SPPD) is a full-service medium-city police department with approximately 600 peace officers and 200 non-sworn employees (Criminal Justice Information Services 2013).

Like most major cities in the United States, Saint Paul has a problem with violent street groups that affiliate along racial or ethnic lines. Some of these gangs may officially associate with or unofficially identify with large Chicago- and Los Angeles-based gang franchises (Howell 2012). Increasingly, however, traditional gangs are splintering off into smaller "cliques" and crews running a few blocks (Williams 2015). Saint Paul has approximately 30 gangs that adhere to the consensus Eurogang definition, according to police sources (see Bumgarner et al. 2016). The actual number of gangs and gang members in Saint Paul is unknown because there has never been a community-wide gang assessment in the city. Minnesota once had an interagency gang unit, the Metro Gang Strike Force, and a gang database, GangNet, but both famously collapsed in 2009 following officer-involved improprieties (Aba-Onu et al. 2010; Ellison 2011; Huff and Barrows 2015). Since then, SPPD has maintained a stand-alone gang unit but has lost the will and mechanism to tag incidents as being "gang related" within their Records Management System (RMS).

16.3 Policing Gangs in London

London is the capital and most populous city of England and the United Kingdom and a leading financial and cultural center. According to 2011 Census estimates, 60 % of London's eight million inhabitants are White, 20 % are of Asian and mixed-Asian descent, 15 % are of Black and mixed-Black descent, 5 % are Mixed race, and 1 % are Arab. Approximately 35 % of Greater London's population was born outside the UK and 28 % of its population lives in poverty. London Boroughs are 32 subdivisions of Greater London for local services, each with their own Borough Councils. London's Metropolitan Police Service (MPS), the territorial police force responsible for law enforcement in Greater London, comprising approximately 30,000 sworn police officers and 18,000 non-sworn employees, is divided into Borough Operational Command Units that are directly aligned with each of the 32 Boroughs (Mayor's Office for Policing and Crime 2015).

Like Saint Paul, London has gangs, but only in recent years were they formally acknowledged (for a discussion, see Densley 2013). According to unpublished MPS intelligence, there are 186 recognized gangs in London, comprising approximately 3600 gang members; however, the MPS definition is broader than the consensus Eurogang definition, including, for example, organized criminal networks. Fifty-eight gangs are considered particularly active, accounting for two-thirds of offenses where a named gang has been identified as being involved (Greater London Authority 2015). MPS data show 1306 "gang nominals" (i.e., individuals police suspect of gang involvement based on arrest and conviction data, corroborated and uncorroborated intelligence, and social media or CCTV content) currently subject to judicial restrictions such as civil gang injunctions, electronic tagging, or supervision on probation (Greater London Authority 2015).

16.4 Method

This exploratory study compares and contrasts GVI-like initiatives in Saint Paul and London. The data are derived from qualitative interviews with a purposive sample of 13 key stakeholders from both cities (seven in Saint Paul and six in London), including representatives from law enforcement, the community, and social service providers. One limitation of the data is interviewees provided only a retroactive account of the two interventions. The sampling technique also inherently introduces subjective forms of bias. Data therefore are triangulated with media reports, published statistics, and, in the case of London, the first author's earlier ethnographic fieldwork in the gang industry (see Densley 2013). David M. Kennedy, Director of the Center for Crime Prevention and Control at John Jay College of Criminal Justice and the National Network for Safe Communities, was also interviewed twice via telephone for his perspective on the two interventions. Kennedy has worked with stakeholders in both St. Paul and London to evaluate GVI efforts discussed herein.

The interviews were semi-structured and conversational in nature, averaging 90 min in duration (range: 30 min to 3 h), and undertaken in a neutral setting of the interviewees' choosing. Interviews were designed to explore GVI processes in Saint Paul and London, including problem profiles, tactics used, and perceived strengths and challenges. All interviewees gave informed consent, but to maintain confidentiality, they are identifiable only by city code and interview sequence number (STP for Saint Paul or LON for London). Interviews were not recorded, but rather, the authors took extensive written notes throughout, which we independently coded then compared using NVivo qualitative data software to reach a high degree of inter-coder reliability. Findings are examined below vis-à-vis the objective principles of GVI and the practical experience of GVI in other jurisdictions (see National Network for Safe Communities 2013).

16.5 Findings

16.5.1 Problem Analysis

16.5.1.1 St. Paul

In early 2011, SPPD's Gang Unit noticed an escalation in retaliatory violence between local factions of two rival Latino gangs—18th Street and Sureños 13. Intelligence from social media and a confidential informant also indicated the 18th

Street Gang was poised to initiate a large number of girls into their ranks through a process that included sexual assault (Gottfred 2011). Immediate intervention was needed. Utilizing gang intelligence and criminal records, officers decided to target the active members of the gang. In the past, SPPD had served warrants on the gang's so-called "frequent flyers" (STP 3) that resulted in arrests, but traditional enforcement had failed to reduce violence long term because gang members were rarely caught with anything that would warrant lengthy detention and the juvenile status of offenders all but precluded correctional incapacitation. In this context, and inspired by a talk they had attended on the Boston Gun Project 1 year earlier (STP 2), the Gang Unit desired to serve a different kind of warrant; one that would include a search, but in lieu of automatic arrest, an invite to dinner at a local community center for conversation about the need to stop the violence now before it was too late.

Initially, the Gang Unit's unorthodox plan to search but not arrest gang members drew criticism from SPPD administrators. The approach was perceived as "soft on crime" and out of sync with the instant gratification of traditional enforcement strategies (see Gervais 2011). As one interviewee noted, the "touchy feely approach is tough for some cops to digest" (STP 3). In recognizing that enforcement had thus far failed, however, the administration eventually approved the program. By identifying the most violent group and the most violent individuals within the group, moreover, they had conformed to GVI principles.

16.5.1.2 London

In response to an uptick in teenage homicide in 2007 and 2008 (see Hallsworth and Young 2008), delegations of senior police officers and seasoned social service providers took the 8000 mile round-trip journey from London, England, to Cincinnati, Ohio, and High Point, North Carolina, to observe GVI and its sister program, Drug Market Intervention (see Kennedy and Wong 2012), in action. Many returned to London sold on the benefits of GVI, but sketchy on the details, and keen to rewrite the strategy to conform with the "paradoxical" (Klein 2001) false narrative that London gangs and American gangs were fundamentally different (i.e., London gangs were fluid and armed with knives and American gangs were structured and armed with guns). In so doing, practitioners discounted important *similarities* between violent groups, such as "pluralistic ignorance" in respect to group norms (e.g., supposedly not caring about going to prison or being violently victimized) (Kennedy 2011; Matza 1964), to emphasize trivial *differences* between them, such as their size and ethnic composition. The rush to "be first" or "take credit" for London's GVI incarnation, moreover, placed interested parties in conflict with each other. What followed was a "myopic" focus on the "call-in showpiece" at the expense of other aspects of the GVI strategy and "wasted time" reconciling differences in organizational structures, professional values, and accountability and reporting mechanisms across key stakeholders (LON 3). The result was isolated, individualized, GVI efforts that never truly "got off the ground" (LON 4).

To compound the problem, group violence in London transcended Borough boundaries (Densley 2013; Pitts 2008), but GVI was funded and administered on a per Borough basis. The Mayor's Office for Policing and Crime (MOPAC), for example, sets the direction and budget for the MPS on behalf of the Mayor, which is operationalized at the Borough level. Likewise, gang nominals in London are placed on Borough-specific gangs matrices that are not uniform across Boroughs. Some Boroughs include juvenile gang nominals, for example, while others do not. As a result, GVI at times engaged the "wrong people" and neglected the complex *group* dynamics motivating and sustaining *group* violence (LON 3). Indeed, in some Boroughs, practitioners worked only with select (or, LON 1 said, "accessible and amenable") people, which prompted change on an individual level, but not on a group level where it was most needed.

16.5.2 Demonstration Enforcement Action

16.5.2.1 Saint Paul

Unlike many other Minnesota police agencies, SPPD had never engaged in a "warrant sweep strategy" (STP 2) of serving multiple suspects in multiple jurisdictions in the same day prior to 2011. This was a large-scale logistical undertaking and officers wanted to proceed with caution because it was something different to present to the courts. The supporting affidavit included standard language explaining what the searches would be for, and who the individuals were in the search with their legal names and street names. The affidavit provided a history and problem profile of the 18th Street Gang, both its origins in Los Angeles and its incarnation in Saint Paul, where there was a schism and now two different sects. A Judge known for his support of the Latino community reviewed the affidavit and "approved and issued the warrant authorizing the searches of the homes" and the call-in in lieu of immediate arrest (STP 2).

A multi-agency team of local and federal law enforcement served the warrants, executed the searches, and informed the gang members that if they attended the scheduled "notification" 48 h later, they would avoid arrest (STP 1). Police provided suspects and their families with a letter signed by the Gang Unit Commander outlining the structure and purpose of the call-in and SPPD's intention to provide childcare and food as incentives for full participation. Parents were also told translators and members of the Mexican Consulate (see below) would be present and available to answer questions. Officers had parents fill out a form with their commitment to attend, specifying the size of their party and childcare needs. The home visits, in turn, enabled law enforcement to subtly verify home addresses and ascertain levels of parental support and risk at home. Some parents were surprised to learn about their child's involvement in gangs and most were appreciative of the personal and proactive approach taken. Search warrants, a tool so often confrontational, thus became a mechanism for collaboration.

16.5.2.2 London

The MPS launched the new Trident Gang Crime Command—an expansion of Operation Trident, which focused exclusively on shootings in the black community—in February 2012 with a series of coordinated police raids that resulted in 515 "gang-related" arrests and the recovery of small quantities of guns, knives, and drugs. However, none of this was in the name of focused deterrence. Instead, it was business as usual—general deterrence through demonstrated enforcement action, not unlike the infamous Operation Hammer suppression effort in Los Angeles (see Klein and Maxson 2006). Of the 515 people arrested in London, only 254 were charged, which implies there was insufficient evidence against 233 of them and more rigorous problem analysis was needed (Metropolitan Police Service 2012). The absence of any "focused" demonstration enforcement action was tied to the fact that, in further deviation from GVI principles, GVI in London has been less about violence reduction and more about "redemption" or "personal transformation" (D. Kennedy, personal communication, February 17, 2015). Indeed, consistent with individualized risk and protective factor approaches to crime reduction (Higginson et al. 2014), social service providers in some instances tried pulling people out of gangs with promises of employment, education, and training, "without any police input whatsoever" (LON 1).

16.5.3 Community Moral Voices and Social Services

16.5.3.1 Saint Paul

The 18th Street Gang primarily comprised youth from undocumented Latino families that either avoided police contact for fear of deportation or lacked the cognitive academic language proficiency (in some cases, basic interpersonal communicative skills) in English necessary to participate in community conversations. Many gang members often served as "cultural liaisons" between their parents and the outside world, enjoying a degree of impunity, which made engagement difficult (STP 3). In an effort to boost community and parental cooperation in GVI, therefore, the SPPD consciously sought out community moral voices, eventually finding them at the local Mexican Consulate. The Mexican Consul herself attended the call-in and addressed all attendees in Spanish. She assuaged community concerns by defining GVI not as an immigration enforcement mechanism, but rather a violence reduction effort (although she stressed immigration enforcement could occur if group violence continued). Her office also offered expedited services to families such as Mexican passport application and renewal, all of which played a significant role in "getting community buy in" (STP 6).

Another key partner was the Neighborhood House's Gang Reduction and Intervention Program (GRIP), a social service initiative that steers young people away from gangs and crime toward a brighter future. The Neighborhood House is a landmark social service agency where people can meet over Latin American cuisine to learn about Latino culture and celebrate friendship and personal responsibility. GRIP includes weekly meetings with speakers and field trips, free gang-tattoo removal (plastic surgeons and nurses donate their time to perform the laser treatments), tutoring, boxing lessons, social support systems and volunteer work in the community, and the program's director put his own moral voice behind the SPPD. Other community activists offered intervention services and attended the call-in to address the gang members directly.

16.5.3.2 London

GVI was part of the Government's response to the 2011 Summer Riots, which began after a controversial black death in police custody but were largely (wrongly, see Densley and Mason 2011) blamed on gangs. Given many young people cited resentment of police in general, and the tactical use of frequent "stop and search" in minority communities in particular, as precipitating factors in their riot participation (Lewis et al. 2011), the need for reconciliation between law enforcement and the community was paramount. Unfortunately, it never fully occurred. In their haste to apprehend those involved in the Summer 2011 disorders—an operation that resulted in nearly 5000 arrests and over 1000 custodial sentences—the MPS neglected to acknowledge the role of policing in past and present injustice and how it was a hurdle to the promotion of community trust. One interviewee (LON 2) accused the MPS of conducting stops without "reasonable suspicion" and making arrests without "probable cause."

If gangs are typically neighborhood-based (n.b., neighborhoods do not necessarily correlate with administrative Borough boundaries) and principally a reflection of the ethnic composition of those neighborhoods (Densley 2013), GVI can inherently result in disproportionate minority contact (see Kempf-Leonard 2007). Disproportionate minority contact is controversial at the best of times, but in the context of the 2011 riots, GVI felt like yet another malicious, deliberate, "attack on black youth" by a conspiratorial government, using the same precedent of "fast-track justice" (LON 4). The GVI focus on whole group accountability also evoked the Joint Enterprise doctrine in British law, which controversially allows the justice system to press charges against people for crimes that they did not commit if they knowingly assisted or encouraged the crime, and disproportionately affects black and minority ethnic communities (see House of Commons Justice Committee 2012). Taken together, community moral voices opted out of the conversation.

16.5.4 The Call-In

16.5.4.1 Saint Paul

The call-in was staged at a place of civic importance that appealed to the local Latino community—the Neighborhood House, a vibrant community hub that since 1897 has provided a safe space for immigrants, refugees, and low-income populations. Police posted flyers around the neighborhood to raise awareness and provided food and free childcare during the event to encourage families to attend. In addition to the Mexican Consulate, key members of the local Latino community, the county prosecutor, and agents from the FBI and ATF all attended the notification event. While no formal agreements were in place, the presence of federal agents "almost gave the illusion of federal involvement" (STP 1), which was beneficial from a deterrence standpoint.

About 70 people attended the call-in, including 17 of the 22 invited gang members, which surpassed all expectations. SPPD had prepared an exhibit showcasing the members' involvement in the gang, including photographs. The federal agents spoke first, proclaiming they were now aware and interested in this group's activities, and future violence may receive greater federal attention. Next, a Latino SPPD officer spoke to the group. Having grown up in the neighborhood, the officer told his life story, about how he achieved success and how violence contrasts with the moral obligations of the Latino community. Other officers then spoke to the group, and "laid out their case" (STP 2) against the gang members. The County Prosecutor spoke next and announced he had enough evidence to prosecute, but would prefer not to if gang members could change their behavior, consistent with the lever-pulling philosophy of GVI.

16.5.4.2 London

In January 2012, Enfield Borough police staged a high-profile call-in at Wood Green Crown Court; the setting was intended to reinforce the gravitas of gang crime. Consistent with GVI theory, the Court was a locale of civic importance, but critics argued it was "far from unthreatening" and "insensitive to the community's history with the criminal justice system" (LON 4). In contrast to the Neighborhood House in Saint Paul, for example, the court setting created an inherent status divide. Perhaps this is why people stayed away. Media coverage of the Enfield call in suggests gang members were "outnumbered by journalists" because only one-third of offenders invited (i.e., ten people) actually bothered to show up (Davey 2012). This attendance rate, however, was an improvement on a previous call-in in a different Borough, where, in a departure from the *group* principle of GVI, "serious gang nominals"[1] from *rival* gangs were intentionally invited to the same call-in, which subsequently "erupted into chaos and violence" and was abandoned after a service provider was stabbed (LON 2).

In the transcript from the 2012 Enfield call-in, one of the law enforcement representatives is quoted as saying, "We know where you live, who your families are, where you go to school. … If your parents are on benefits we might be coming to see if they are lawful" (Davey 2012). This language is consistent with Operation

[1] A phrase reserved for "reds" on the gangs matrix, the official police list that names individual gang members and classifies them from most to least violent, "from red to amber to green" (LON 1).

Ceasefire in Boston and other GVI efforts (see Kennedy 1998). However, the Enfield officer adds, "You may think you belong to a big gang, you may be 50 people, even 100, but we have 32,000 in our gang. It's called the Metropolitan police" (Davey 2012). This latter statement further alienated community moral voices because it reinforced the view of police as the "biggest gang"—a theme which emerged frequently during research into the 2011 London riots (see Lewis et al. 2011). According to one subject, the last thing the community wanted to hear was law enforcement celebrating its likeness to the violent group in question (LON 1).

Perhaps most surprising about the Enfield call-in was the absence of a deliverable social service message. Instead, the participants endured a long lecture about the realities of gang crime and the prospect of jail time and were told simply to "Go away and think about it" (Davey 2012). According to one interviewee who worked on this and other London Borough call-ins, however, the focus in other instances of GVI was too far over on the social service side, to the extent some gang members were told to "take the job or face the consequences" (LON 2). The implication is London struggled to maintain the "appropriate balance" between the "carrot and stick" (LON 1), despite the fact research suggests the *offer* of the carrot and the *threat* of the stick alone can be enough to change behavior (Kennedy 2011).

16.5.5 Maintenance and Ensuring Program Integrity

16.5.5.1 Saint Paul

SPPD Gang Unit officers checked in with the subjects and their parents 30 days after executing the original demonstration enforcement action of search warrants, and again 60 and 90 days later. They also had parents fill out progress reports and verify responses via interview. After 30 days, officers agree the call-in was still fresh in the minds of the gang members. Community moral voices continued to reinforce or "retail" (Kennedy et al. 2001) the message that violence would incur consequences and social service providers continued to monitor social networks for signs of impending action. This loss of anonymity disrupted the gang's activities: "People begin seeing ghosts," STP 1 observed. "They think every black SUV parked outside is a police undercover vehicle waiting for them to slip." At 60 and 90 days, however, interest began to wane and follow-up visits became more confrontational. Nevertheless, street violence declined sharply, not only for the 18th Street Gang, but also their rivals, the Sureños. Indeed, inspired by the perceived success of GVI, SPPD had prepared an affidavit to go after the Sureños, but never processed it because retaliatory violence ceased. This observed cessation supports the hypothesis that GVI in Saint Paul created a "spillover" of crime cessation beyond the directly affected group (Braga et al. 2013, p. 22).

Despite a lack of empirical gang-crime data related to the intervention, both murder and aggravated assault rates in Saint Paul declined significantly in 2011, the year GVI was conducted, which gang unit interviewees partially attributed to desistance in internecine violence between 18th Street and Sureños gang members.

The year 2011 was the only year in recent times where both homicides and aggravated assaults in Saint Paul were both well below the standard deviation. Of course, myriad variables could account for this decline—one limitation of ad hoc GVI is that program evaluation is not built in.

Of the 22 gang members targeted, six agreed to participate in GRIP, all of whom desisted from gangs and self-report their school attendance and performance improved following the intervention. It is not known whether the other gang members sought other community services, in part because some service providers were "territorial" over their work and did not readily share information with police (STP 5). SPPD interviewees complained they felt left "out of the loop" on what was going on, since they did not receive any qualitative updates beyond their own 30-60-90 day home visits. However, quantitative police data suggest only two of the 22 targeted gang members struggled with serious violence recidivism. One spent time in a residential juvenile facility and another moved to a different metropolitan area, where he was shot and killed (Burnes 2013). Three years later, all others were "off the radar" (STP 7).

Apparent success aside, this was a one-time initiative, which brings the maintenance principle of GVI into question. SPPD reticence toward nontraditional enforcement and turnover within the Gang Unit, which rarely is a permanent assignment, are possible explanations. So too is the concern that GVI cannot be implemented citywide because it is labor-intensive and Black or Hmong communities in Saint Paul also struggling with gang violence lack the collective efficacy of the Latino community, which research in other cities suggests is a common misconception (see Kennedy 2011). Further, political forces are minimizing Saint Paul's gang problem, rather than celebrating the fact the City "is on the cutting edge of combating it" (STP 2).

16.5.5.2 London

At the time of this writing, in Spring 2015, London is going back to the basics of GVI. MOPAC are providing £200,000 funding for "Operation Shield," which will be run in partnership with the MPS and three pilot Boroughs—Haringey, Westminster, and Lambeth—chosen for their well-established gang programs (Greater London Authority 2015). Shield will enable the MPS Trident team and local authorities to bring civil or criminal sanctions to "known gang members" if any supposed gang member carries out a serious crime. Penalties range from "recall to prison, gang injunctions banning them from parts of the capital or mixing with their associates, mandatory employment training courses or ejection from social housing. The offender who triggers action will be fast-tracked through the criminal justice system for swift sentencing" (Greater London Authority 2015). Shield will also incorporate social service providers and community moral voices. From the £200,000 funding, MOPAC have approved the support and advice of David Kennedy and the National Network for Safe Communities to a maximum value of £50,000.

16.6 Discussion and Conclusion

This chapter has presented a tale of two cities: one, Saint Paul, which reduced violence in a manner commensurate with GVI core principles despite only cursory understanding of the principles; and two, London, which consciously tried to implement GVI but for myriad reasons was unable to adhere to the essence of the strategy. "We should not be too critical of London," says David Kennedy; in fact many of the "mistakes" highlighted above were "perfectly predictable" and "exceedingly common" among cities trying to implement GVI for the first time and without explicit guidance and support from those who have done it before (personal communication, February 17, 2015). Perhaps this is what makes the Saint Paul case all the more remarkable—it was produced ad hoc and after only a 2-h introduction to GVI strategies during a conference presentation (STP 2). Whether or not the Saint Paul case constitutes a true GVI example is of course debatable. Kennedy points to the fact Saint Paul only ever called-in one group, for instance, as an example of circumventing a core focus on violence reciprocity (personal communication, February 17, 2015). Nevertheless, the case provides a number of useful takeaways for those interested in disrupting the "cycle of gang violence" (Decker et al. 2013, p. 384).

The architects of the Saint Paul intervention largely adhered to GVI principles. First, gang officers had significant knowledge about who the key offenders were. They had accordion files on different gang members and targeted the most prolific offenders for warrant service and call-in. Second, they collaborated with other agencies to serve warrants and secure attendance at the call-in. They used the County Prosecutor to ensure stronger prosecution against future violence. They mobilized community leaders and service providers such as GRIP to offer education, employment, and training to gang members to help them desist from violence and, eventually, the gang. They utilized the services of the Mexican Consulate to mitigate fears of deportation and unlock some of the failed narratives associated with disproportionate minority contact that had alienated police from the Latino community in the past. "Navigating the illegal population and turning it into an advantage… [by engaging] the Mexican government" (D. Kennedy, personal communication, April 8, 2014) was essential to garnering Latino community support in Saint Paul. They planned and conducted a call-in session with all the aforementioned parties, where the gang members were confronted, threatened, and offered services. And while the collaboration with the FBI and ATF were not as formalized as other lever-pulling programs, the mere presence of federal agents provided a credible impression that the federal government was taking an interest in their activities and that future repercussions could be far more serious. This call-in not only used the *carrot and stick* options of services or enforcement, but also gave the community a forum to express their intolerance of this group's violence (National Network for Safe Communities 2013).

Many other lever-pulling focused deterrence programs utilize working groups comprising many different stakeholders including academics (Kennedy 2011). These working groups can take months to implement a program and thousands of dollars in seed money. One novel aspect of the Saint Paul intervention was that it was created ad hoc by a few police officers because of an urgent need to intervene in an impending violence event. Despite the tight timeline and limited budget, this was "a well thought out… strategic… high quality… focused call-in" (D. Kennedy, personal communication, April 8, 2014). Utilizing community leaders and individuals who were familiar to and with the community showed genuine interest in the community and their group violence problem. SPPD's ability to create and successfully execute GVI in short order serves as an example of good problem-oriented policing that may provide guidance to other agencies that encounter an urgent situation which needs immediate action. Saint Paul could move faster than London because it was not hampered by competing funding priorities or community concerns of basic police incivility.

Moving forward, however, both cities need to formalize relationships with key stakeholders and form a collaborative work group for future programs. SPPD officers expressed concerns about the possible conflict of interest with some of the other organizations working with the gang members because they benefit from keeping clients and can be very territorial over what they are doing with that individual. Greater transparency could increase interagency accountability. Academic oversight, moreover, would help guide and evaluate police efforts, which, in turn, can establish sustainable evidence-based best practices that transcend one simple "operation." This starts with a full citywide assessment of current gangs and gang members codified into an electronic database that can be updated and utilized by future gang officers. These data can be used to implement problem-oriented best practices, build stronger criminal cases against offenders, and obtain future program funding through reprioritization of budgeting and potential grant awards.

References

Aba-Onu, U., Levy-Pounds, N., Salmen, J., & Tyner, A. (2010). Evaluation of gang databases in Minnesota and recommendations for change. *Information and Communications Technology Law, 19*(3), 223–254.

Anderson, E. (1999). *Code of the street*. New York: W.W. Norton.

Braga, A. (2008). Pulling levers focuses deterrence strategies and the prevention of gun homicide. *Journal of Criminal Justice, 36*(4), 332–343.

Braga, A., Apel, R., & Welsh, B. (2013). The spillover effect of focused deterrence on gang violence. *Evaluation Review, 37*(3), 314–342.

Braga, A., Kennedy, D., Waring, E., & Piehl, A. (2001). Problem-oriented policing, deterrence and youth violence: An evaluation of Boston's Operation Ceasefire. *Journal of Research in Crime and Delinquency, 38*(3), 195–225.

Braga, A., & Weisburd, D. (2012a). The effects of focused deterrence strategies on crime: A systematic review and meta-analysis of the empirical evidence. *Journal of Research in Crime and Delinquency, 49*(3), 323–358.
Braga, A., & Weisburd, D. (2012b). *The effects of "pulling levers" focused deterrence strategies on crime*. Oslo, Norway: The Campbell Collaboration.
Bumgarner, J., Hilal, S., & Densley, J. (2016). *Minnesota's criminal justice system*. Durham, NC: Carolina Academic Press.
Burnes, B. (2013, July 12). Independence police name fatal shooting victim. *Kansas City Star*. Retrieved August 14, 2015, from http://www.kansascity.com/2013/07/12/4342261/independence-police.html
Cornish, D., & Clarke, R. (1986). *The reasoning criminal: Rational choice perspectives on offending*. New York: Springer.
Criminal Justice Information Services. (2013). Minnesota full time law enforcement employees by city, 2012. Retrieved August 14, 2015, from http://www.fbi.gov/about-us/cjis/ucr/crime-in-the-u.s/2012/crime-in-the-u.s.-2012/tables/78tabledatadecpdf/table-78-state-cuts/table_78_full_time_law_enforcement_employees_minnesota_by_city_2012.xls
Davey, E. (2012, January 31). Gang members face stark choice at gruesome day in court. *BBC News*. Retrieved August 14, 2015, from http://www.bbc.co.uk/news/uk-england-london-16825265
Decker, S. H., Melde, C., & Pyrooz, D. C. (2013). What do we know about gangs and gang members and where do we go from here? *Justice Quarterly, 30*(3), 369–402.
Decker, S. H., & Pyrooz, D. C. (2010). Gang violence worldwide: Context, culture, and country. In Small Arms Survey (Ed.), *Small Arms Survey 2010: Gangs, groups, and guns* (pp. 128–155). Cambridge, England: Cambridge University Press.
Densley, J. (2013). *How gangs work: An ethnography of youth violence*. New York: Palgrave Macmillan.
Densley, J., & Mason, N. (2011). The London riots: A gang problem? *Policing Today, 17*(2), 14–15.
Deuchar, R. (2013). *Policing youth violence: Transatlantic connections*. London, England: IOE Press.
Ellison, M. (2011). *A failure of leadership: Lessons from the Metro Gang Strike Force*. Minneapolis, MN: Center for Integrative Leadership, University of Minnesota. Retrieved August 14, 2015, from http://www.leadership.umn.edu/research/documents/MetroGangintemplate.pdf
Engel, R., Tillyer, M., & Corsaro, N. (2013). Reducing gang violence using focused deterrence: Evaluating the Cincinnati Initiative to Reduce Violence (CIRV). *Justice Quarterly, 30*(3), 403–439.
Fagan, J. (2002). Policing guns and youth violence. *Future Child, 12*(2), 133–151.
Gervais, B. (2011, December 3). St Paul employs 'smarter, not softer' approach to gangs. St. Paul, MN: Pioneer Press. Retrieved August 14, 2015, from http://www.twincities.com/minnesota/ci_19459543
Goldstein, H. (1990). *Problem-oriented policing*. New York: McGraw-Hill.
Gottfred, M. (2011, April 27). St. Paul police try new tack to thwart gang initiation. St. Paul, MN: Pioneer Press. Retrieved August 14, 2015, from http://www.twincities.com/localnews/ci_17936659
Greater London Authority. (2015). 'One rule for all': Mayor launches tough new gang intervention programme. Retrieved August 14, 2015, from https://www.london.gov.uk/media/mayor-press-releases/2015/01/one-rule-for-all-mayor-launches-tough-new-gang-intervention
Hallsworth, S., & Young, T. (2008). Gang talk and gang talkers: A critique. *Crime Media Culture, 4*(2), 175–195.
Higginson, A., Benier, K., Shenderovich, Y., Bedford, L., Mazerolle, L., & Murray, J. (2014). *Predictors of youth gang membership in low- and middle-income countries: A systematic review*. Oslo, Norway: The Campbell Collaboration.
House of Commons Justice Committee. (2012). *Joint enterprise: Eleventh report of session 2010–12*. London, England: The Stationery Office Limited. Retrieved August 14, 2015, from http://www.publications.parliament.uk/pa/cm201012/cmselect/cmjust/1597/1597.pdf.
Howell, J. (2012). *Gangs in America's communities*. Thousand Oaks, CA: Sage.
Huff, C., & Barrows, J. (2015). Documenting gang activity: Intelligence databases. In S. H. Decker & D. C. Pyrooz (Eds.), *The handbook of gangs* (pp. 59–77). New York: Wiley.
Kempf-Leonard, K. (2007). Minority youths and juvenile justice: Disproportionate minority contact after nearly 20 years of reform efforts. *Youth Violence and Juvenile Justice, 5*(1), 71–87.

Kennedy, D. (1997). Pulling levers: Chronic offenders, high-crime settings, and a theory of prevention. *Valparaiso University Law Review, 31*(2), 449–484.

Kennedy, D. (1998). Pulling levers: Getting deterrence right. *National Institute of Justice Journal, 236*, 2–8.

Kennedy, D. (2011). *Don't shoot: One man, a street fellowship, and the end of violence in inner-city America*. New York: Bloomsbury.

Kennedy, D., & Braga, A. (1998). Homicide in Minneapolis: Research for problem solving. *Homicide Studies, 2*(3), 263–290.

Kennedy, D., Braga, A., & Piehl, A. (2001). Developing and implementing Operation Ceasefire. In U.S. Department of Justice Office of Justice Programs (Ed.), *Research report: Reducing gun violence: The Boston Gun Project's Operation Ceasefire*. Washington, DC: U.S. Department of Justice.

Kennedy, D., & Wong, S.-L. (2012). *The High Point drug market intervention strategy*. Washington, DC: U.S. Department of Justice, Office of Community Oriented Policing Services.

Kleiman, M. (2009). *When brute force fails*. Princeton, NJ: Princeton University Press.

Klein, M. (2001). Resolving the Eurogang paradox. In M. Klein, H. Kerner, C. Maxson, & E. Weitekamp (Eds.), *The Eurogang paradox: Street gangs and youth groups in the U.S. and Europe* (pp. 7–19). Dordrecht, The Netherlands: Springer.

Klein, M. (2006). The value of comparisons in street gang research. In J. F. Short & L. A. Hughes (Eds.), *Studying youth gangs* (pp. 129–143). Oxford, England: Altamira Press.

Klein, M., & Maxson, C. (2006). *Street gang patterns and policies*. New York: Oxford University Press.

Lewis, P., Newburn, T., Taylor, M., Mcgillivray, C., Greenhill, A., & Frayman, H., et al. (2011). Reading the riots: Investigating England's summer of disorder. Retrieved August 14, 2015, from http://eprints.lse.ac.uk/46297/1/Reading%20the%20riots(published).pdf

Matza, D. (1964). *Delinquency and drift*. New York: Wiley.

Mayor's Office for Policing and Crime. (2015). About the Met. Retrieved August 14, 2015, from http://content.met.police.uk/Site/About

McGarrell, E., Chermak, S., Wilson, J., & Corsaro, N. (2006). Reducing homicide through a "lever-pulling" strategy. *Justice Quarterly, 23*(2), 214–231.

Metropolitan Police Service. (2012, February 15). Met Police makes 515 gang-related arrests. Retrieved August 14, 2015, from http://content.met.police.uk/News/Met-Police-makes-515-gangrelated-arrests/1400006697452/1257246745756

National Network for Safe Communities. (2013). *Group violence intervention: An implementation guide*. Washington, DC: U.S. Department of Justice, Office of Community Oriented Policing Services. Retrieved August 14, 2015, from http://nnscommunities.org/uploads/GVI_Guide.pdf

Papachristos, A. (2009). Murder by structure: Dominance relations and the social structure of gang homicide. *American Journal of Sociology, 115*(1), 74–128.

Papachristos, A. (2012, July 5). What is a gang audit? *Huffington Post*. Retrieved August 14, 2015, from http://www.huffingtonpost.com/andrew-papachristos/what-is-a-gang-audit_b_1651386.html

Papachristos, A., Meares, T., & Fagan, J. (2007). Attention felons: Evaluating project safe neighborhoods in Chicago. *Journal of Empirical Legal Studies, 4*(2), 223–272.

Pitts, J. (2008). *Reluctant gangsters: The changing shape of youth crime*. Cullompton, England: Willan.

Rosenfeld, R., Fornango, R., & Baumer, E. (2005). Did Ceasefire, Compstat, and Exile reduce homicide? *Criminology and Public Policy, 4*(3), 419–450.

Tillyer, M., Engel, R., & Lovins, B. (2012). Beyond Boston: Applying theory to understand and address sustainability issues in focused deterrence initiatives for violence reduction. *Crime and Delinquency, 58*(6), 973–997.

U.S. Census Bureau. (2012). St. Paul (city) Minnesota. *State & County QuickFacts*. Retrieved August 14, 2015, from http://quickfacts.census.gov/qfd/states/27/2758000.html

Williams, B. (2015, April 22). "Clique" gangs vex prosecutors, youth workers. *MPR News*. Retrieved August 14, 2015, from http://www.mprnews.org/story/2015/04/22/gangs

Index

C.L. Maxson, F.-A. Esbensen (eds.), *Gang Transitions and Transformations in an International Context*, DOI 10.1007/978-3-319-29602-9

MIX
Papier aus verantwortungsvollen Quellen
Paper from responsible sources
FSC® C105338

If you have any concerns about our products,
you can contact us on
ProductSafety@springernature.com

In case Publisher is established outside the EU,
the EU authorized representative is:
Springer Nature Customer Service Center GmbH
Europaplatz 3, 69115 Heidelberg, Germany

Printed by Libri Plureos GmbH
in Hamburg, Germany